CLYMER
HONDA
450 & 500cc TWINS • 1965-1976

The world's finest publisher of mechanical how-to manuals

CLYMER
P.O. Box 12901, Overland Park, Kansas 66282-2901

Copyright ©1978 Penton Business Media, Inc.

FIRST EDITION First Printing August, 1971	**SEVENTH EDITION** *Revised by Mike Bishop*
SECOND EDITION *Revised to include 1972 models* First Printing June, 1972	First Printing August, 1978 Second Printing April, 1979 Third Printing March, 1980 Fourth Printing January, 1981
THIRD EDITION *Revised to include 1973 models* First Printing April, 1973	Fifth Printing October, 1982 Sixth Printing October, 1983 Seventh Printing February, 1985
FOURTH EDITION *Revised by Eric Jorgensen to include 1974 models* First Printing October, 1973	Eighth Printing October, 1986 Ninth Printing April, 1988 Tenth Printing December, 1989 Eleventh Printing January, 1992
FIFTH EDITION *Revised by Jim Combs to include 1975-1976 models* First Printing December, 1976	Twelfth Printing April, 1994 Thirteenth Printing July, 1997 Fourteenth Printing November, 2000 Fifteenth Printing February, 2004
SIXTH EDITION First Printing September, 1977	Sixteenth Printing October, 2008

Printed in U.S.A.

CLYMER and colophon are registered trademarks of Penton Business Media, Inc.

ISBN-10: 0-89287-685-9

ISBN-13: 978-0-89287-685-3

TOOLS AND EQUIPMENT: David Silver Spares at www.davidsilverspares.co.uk.

COVER: 1965 CB450KO "Black Bomber" owned and photographed by James Grooms. Special thanks to the Vintage Japanese Motorcycle Club at www.vjmc.org.

All rights reserved. Reproduction or use, without express permission, of editorial or pictorial content, in any manner, is prohibited. No patent liability is assumed with respect to the use of the information contained herein. While every precaution has been taken in the preparation of this book, the publisher assumes no responsibility for errors or omissions. Neither is any liability assumed for damages resulting from use of the information contained herein. Publication of the servicing information in this manual does not imply approval of the manufacturers of the products covered.

All instructions and diagrams have been checked for accuracy and ease of application; however, success and safety in working with tools depend to a great extent upon individual accuracy, skill and caution. For this reason, the publishers are not able to guarantee the result of any procedure contained herein. Nor can they assume responsibility for any damage to property or injury to persons occasioned from the procedures. Persons engaging in the procedure do so entirely at their own risk.

Chapter One
General Information

Chapter Two
Periodic Lubrication and Maintenance

Chapter Three
Troubleshooting

Chapter Four
Engine

Chapter Five
Clutch and Transmission

Chapter Six
Fuel and Exhaust Systems

Chapter Seven
Electrical System

Chapter Eight
Front Suspension and Steering

Chapter Nine
Rear Suspension

Chapter Ten
Brakes

Chapter Eleven
Frame

Appendix
Specifications

Index

Wiring Diagrams

CLYMER®

Publisher Shawn Etheridge

EDITORIAL
Editorial Director
James Grooms

Editor
Steven Thomas

Associate Editor
Rick Arens

Authors
Jay Bogart
Michael Morlan
George Parise
Mark Rolling
Ed Scott
Ron Wright

Technical Illustrators
Steve Amos
Errol McCarthy
Mitzi McCarthy
Bob Meyer

Group Production Manager
Dylan Goodwin

Production Manager
Greg Araujo

Senior Production Editor
Darin Watson

Production Editors
Holly McComas
Adriane Roberts
Taylor Wright

Production Designer
Jason Hale

MARKETING/SALES AND ADMINISTRATION
Sales Managers
Justin Henton
Matt Tusken

Marketing and Sales Representative
Erin Gribbin

Director, Operations–Books
Ron Rogers

Customer Service Manager
Terri Cannon

Customer Service Account Specialist
Courtney Hollars

Customer Service Representatives
Dinah Bunnell
Susan Ford
April LeBlond

Warehouse & Inventory Manager
Leah Hicks

Penton Media

P.O. Box 12901, Overland Park, KS 66282-2901 • 800-262-1954 • 913-967-1719

More information available at *clymer.com*

CONTENTS

QUICK REFERENCE DATA IX

CHAPTER ONE
GENERAL INFORMATION 1
   Manual organization   Parts replacement
   Service hints   Serial number location
   Safety first

CHAPTER TWO
TROUBLESHOOTING 5
   Operating requirements   Piston seizure
   Starting difficulties   Vibration
   Poor idling   High oil consumption
   Misfiring   Clutch slip or drag
   Flat spots   Transmission problems
   Lack of power   Poor handling
   Overheating   Brake system
   Backfiring   Lighting system
   Engine noises   Troubleshooting guide

CHAPTER THREE
PERIODIC LUBRICATION AND MAINTENANCE 10
   Routine checks   3,000 mile/6-month maintenance
   Periodic maintenance   6,000 mile/12-month maintenance
   500 mile/monthly maintenance   Engine tune-up
   1,500 mile/3-month maintenance

CHAPTER FOUR
ENGINE 27

- Removal
- Installation
- Cylinder head
- Cylinders
- Pistons, pins, and rings
- Camshafts
- Cam chain guides
- Valves and valve gear
- Oil filter
- Oil pump
- Crankcase side covers
- Crankcase
- Crankshaft

CHAPTER FIVE
CLUTCH AND TRANSMISSION 53

- Clutch
- Transmission (4-speed)
- Transmission (5-speed)
- Kickstarter

CHAPTER SIX
FUEL AND EXHAUST SYSTEMS 74

- Air cleaners
- Carburetors
- Throttle linkage
- Fuel tank
- Exhaust system

CHAPTER SEVEN
ELECTRICAL SYSTEM 89

- Charging system
- Battery
- Alternator
- Rectifier
- Regulator
- Ignition system
- Ignition coils
- Condensers
- Starter motor
- Starter clutch
- Starter solenoid
- Lighting system
- Horn
- Fuse
- Wiring harness
- Wiring diagrams

CHAPTER EIGHT
FRONT SUSPENSION AND STEERING 110

- Front wheel (drum brake)
- Front wheel (disc brake)
- Front forks (early, 2-spring)
- Front forks (early, 1-spring)
- Front forks (CB450 K3 and K4)
- Front forks (CB450 K5-K7)
- Front forks (CB500T)

CHAPTER NINE
REAR SUSPENSION 133

- Rear wheel
- Drive chain
- Sprocket
- Rear shocks
- Swinging arm

CHAPTER TEN
BRAKES **144**
    Front drum brake   Rear drum brake
    Front disc brake

CHAPTER ELEVEN
FRAME **154**
    Kickstand (sidestand)   Stripping the frame
    Centerstand   Painting the frame

APPENDIX
SPECIFICATIONS **157**

INDEX **160**

QUICK REFERENCE DATA

ENGINE TUNE-UP SPECIFICATIONS

Valve clearance	0.0012 in. (0.03mm) cold
Spark plug	
Type	NGK B-8ES, ND W24ES
Gap	0.028-0.032 in. (0.7-0.8mm)
Breaker point	
Gap	0.012-0.016 in. (0.3-0.4mm)
Dwell	90 ± 2.5° (2 cyl. scale)
Ignition timing	Static (see text)
Idle speed	1,000 rpm

ADJUSTMENTS*

Clutch lever free play	0.4-1.0 in. (10-25mm)
Rear brake pedal free play	0.8-1.2 in. (20-30mm)
Front brake lever free play	0.6-1.2 in. (15-30mm)
Throttle grip free play	10-15°

*See Chapter Two for adjustment procedures.

ELECTRICAL SYSTEM

Battery	12 volt, 12 Ah
Fuse	15A
Replacement lamps	
Headlight	12V, 35/50W
Tail/stoplight	SAE 1157 (12V, 3/32 cp)
Turn signals	SAE 1073 (12V, 32 cp)
Instrument lights	SAE 57 (12V, 2 cp)
Neutral indicator	SAE 57 (12V, 2 cp)
Turn signal indicator	SAE 57 (12V, 2 cp)
High beam indicator	SAE 57 (12V, 2 cp)

TIRES

	Front	Rear
Pressure		
Under 200 lb.	28 psi	28 psi
Over 200 lb.	28 psi	34 psi
Size	3.25 x 19	3.50 x 18

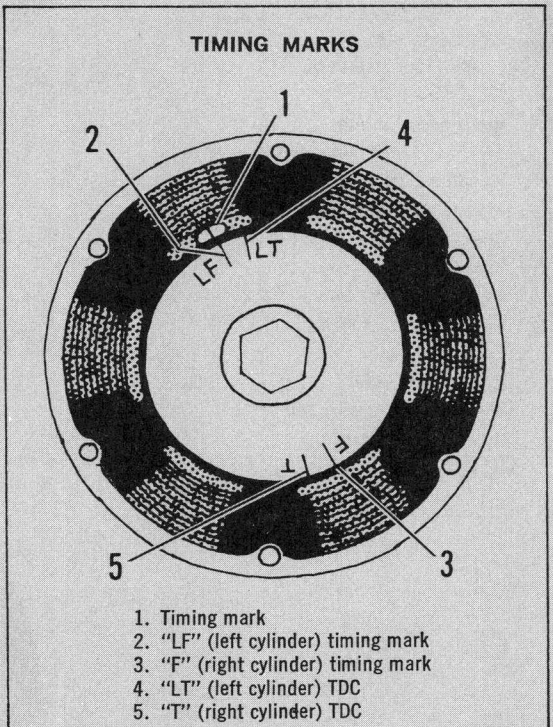

BREAKER POINTS

1. Base plate screws
2. Left cylinder points
3. Right cylinder points
4. Breaker point screws

TIMING MARKS

1. Timing mark
2. "LF" (left cylinder) timing mark
3. "F" (right cylinder) timing mark
4. "LT" (left cylinder) TDC
5. "T" (right cylinder) TDC

RECOMMENDED LUBRICANTS

	Temperature	Capacity	Type
Engine oil			
Multigrade	All	3.0 U.S. qt. (2.8 liters)	SAE 10W-40 or 20W-50, SE
Single grade	Above 59°		SAE 30, SE
	32-59°		SAE 20 or 20W, SE
	Below 32°		SAE10W, SE
Fork oil			
K1 and K2		9.0-10.00 oz. (285-295cc)*	SAE 10W-30
K3 and K4		7.0-7.30 oz. (220-230cc)*	SAE 10W-30
K5, K6, K7 (CB)		5.3-5.60 oz. (155-165cc)*	SAE 10W-30
K2, K3, K4 (CL)		9.0-10.0 oz. (285-295cc)*	Automatic transmission fluid
K5-K6 (CL)		5.30-5.60 oz. (155-165cc)*	Automatic transmission fluid
CB500T		6.2 6.5 oz. (185-191cc)**	Automatic transmission fluid
Swing arm bushing	All	—	Lithium grease
Drive chain	All	—	SAE 30 engine oil or special chain lubricant
Brake fluid	—	—	Marked "DOT-3" or "J 1703"

*Each fork leg dry after rebuild. Reduce amount by approximately .70 oz. (200cc) for refill.
**Refill after draining.

TIGHTENING TORQUES*

	Foot-pounds	Mkg
Front axle nut	54-61	7.5-8.5
Front brake torque bolt	13-20	1.8-2.8
Front fork bolt	47-58	6.5-8.0
Steering stem nut	65-87	9.0-12.0
Steering stem bolt	29-36	4.0-5.0
Handlebar bolt	18-25	2.5-3.5
Engine mounting bolt (10mm)	29-36	4.0-5.0
Engine mounting bolt (8mm)	13-20	1.8-2.8
Shock absorber nut	29-36	4.0-5.0
Shock absorber bolt	29-36	4.0-5.0
Swing arm bolt	51-65	7.0-9.0
Rear axle nut	58-87	8.0-12.0
Kickstarter bolt	13-20	1.8-2.8
Exhaust pipe clamp nut	6-9	0.8-1.2
Driven sprocket nut	29-36	4.0-5.0

*See page 13 for CB500T.

CHAPTER ONE

GENERAL INFORMATION

Introduced in 1965, the Honda 450 was the first Japanese bike to make any headway against the British twins and Harley Sportsters. The engine, ahead of its time in 1965, is still exotic and innovative enough to keep this workhorse in the Honda model line in an enlarged version. The CB500T, introduced in 1975, has a refined 498cc dual overhead cam engine that is a direct descendant of the original 450.

MANUAL ORGANIZATION

This book provides service information and procedures for all Honda 450 and 500 twins built from 1965 through 1976. Most dimensions and capacities are expressed in English units familiar to U.S. mechanics, as well as in metric units. Where conversion to inches could introduce errors in critical dimensions, only metric measure is specified. In any case, metric tools *are* required to work on the Honda.

This chapter provides general information specifications. **Figures 1 and 2** show the location of all identification tags.

Chapter Two provides methods and suggestions for finding and fixing troubles fast. Troubleshooting procedures discuss typical symptoms and logical methods to pinpoint the trouble. It also covers some test equipment useful for both preventive maintenance and troubleshooting.

Chapter Three explains all periodic lubrication and routine maintenance required to keep your bike in top running condition. Chapter Three also includes recommended engine tune-up procedures, eliminating the need to constantly consult chapters covering the various subassemblies.

Subsequent chapters describe specific systems such as the engine, transmission, and electrical system. Each chapter provides complete disassembly, repair, and assembly procedures in simple step-by-step form. If a repair is impractical for the home mechanic, it is so indicated. It is usually faster and less expensive to take such repairs to a dealer or competent repair shop. Specifications concerning a particular system are included at the end of the appropriate chapter.

Some of the procedures in this manual specify special tools. In all cases, the tool is illustrated either in actual use or alone. A well-equipped mechanic may find that he can substitute similar tools already on hand or that he can fabricate his own.

The terms NOTE, CAUTION, and WARNING have specific meanings in this manual. A NOTE provides additional information to make a step or procedure easier or clearer. Disregarding a NOTE could cause inconvenience, but would not cause damage or personal injury.

A CAUTION emphasizes areas where equipment damage could result. Disregarding a CAUTION could cause permanent mechanical damage; however, personal injury is unlikely.

A WARNING emphasizes areas where personal injury or even death could result from negligence. Mechanical damage may also occur. WARNINGS *are to be taken seriously*. In some cases, serious injury or death has been caused when mechanics disregarded similar warnings.

SERVICE HINTS

Most of the service procedures covered are straightforward and can be performed by anyone reasonably handy with tools. It is suggested, however, that you consider your own capabilities carefully before attempting any operation involving major disassembly of the engine.

Throughout this manual, keep in mind 2 conventions. "Front" refers to the front of the bike. The front of any component, such as the engine, is that end which faces toward the front of the bike. The left and right side refer to a person sitting on the bike, facing forward. For example, the shift lever is on the left side. These rules are simple, but even experienced mechanics occasionally become disoriented.

Disconnect battery ground cable before working near electrical connections and before disconnecting wires. Never run the engine with the battery disconnected; the alternator could be seriously damaged.

Protect finished surfaces from physical damage or corrosion. Keep gasoline and brake fluid off painted surfaces.

Frozen or very tight bolts and screws can often be loosened by soaking with penetrating oil, then sharply striking the bolt head a few times with a hammer and punch (or a screwdriver for screws). Avoid heat unless absolutely necessary since it may melt, warp, or remove the temper from many parts.

Avoid flames or sparks when working near a charging battery or flammable liquids such as brake fluid or gasoline.

During disassembly of parts, keep a few general cautions in mind. Force is rarely needed to get things apart. If parts are a tight fit, like a magneto on a crankshaft, there is usually a tool designed to separate them. Never use a screwdriver to pry apart components with machined surfaces such as crankcase halves and valve covers. You will mar the surfaces and cause leaks.

Make diagrams wherever similar-appearing parts are found. For instance, case cover screws are often not the same length. You may *think* you can remember where everything came from—but mistakes are costly. There is also the possibility that you may be sidetracked and not return to work for days, or even weeks; carefully laid out parts may become disturbed.

Tag all similar internal parts for location and mark all mating parts for position. Record number and thickness of any shims as they are removed. Small parts, such as bolts, can be identified by placing them in plastic sandwich bags and sealing and labeling bags with masking tape.

Wiring should be tagged with masking tape and marked as each wire is removed. Again, *do not rely on memory alone.*

Read each procedure completely while looking at the actual parts *before* beginning. Many procedures are complicated and errors can be disastrous. When you thoroughly understand what is to be done, follow the procedure step-by-step.

SAFETY FIRST

Professional motorcycle mechanics can work for years and never sustain a serious injury. If you observe a few rules of common sense and safety, you can enjoy many safe hours servicing your own machine. You could hurt yourself or damage the bike if you ignore these rules.

1. Never use gasoline as a cleaning solvent.
2. Never smoke or use a torch in the vicinity of flammable liquids, such as cleaning solvent in open containers.

GENERAL INFORMATION

3. Never smoke or use a torch in an area where batteries are being charged. Highly explosive hydrogen gas is formed during the charging process.

4. If welding or brazing is required on the machine, remove the fuel tank to a safe distance—at least 50 feet away. Welding gas tanks requires special safety procedures and must be performed by someone skilled in the process.

5. Use the proper sized wrenches to avoid damage to nuts and injury to yourself.

6. When loosening a tight or stuck nut, think about what would happen if the wrench should slip. Protect yourself accordingly.

7. Keep your work area clean and uncluttered.

8. Wear safety goggles during all operations involving drilling, grinding, or use of a cold chisel.

9. Never use worn tools.

10. Keep a fire extinguisher handy and be sure it is rated for gasoline and electrical fires.

PARTS REPLACEMENT

Honda makes frequent changes during a model year; some minor, some relatively major. When you order parts from the dealer or other parts distributor, *always order by engine and chassis number*. Write the numbers down and carry them with you. Compare the new parts to the old parts before purchasing them. If they are not alike, have the parts clerk expain the difference.

SERIAL NUMBER LOCATION

The frame and engine serial numbers are necessary for registration and parts ordering. The frame serial number is stamped on the steering head tube. See **Figure 1**. The engine serial number is stamped on the left side of the crankcase. See **Figure 2**. The first digit of each serial number identifies the model, e.g., 6000001 is a K6 and 7000001 is a K7 model.

CHAPTER ONE

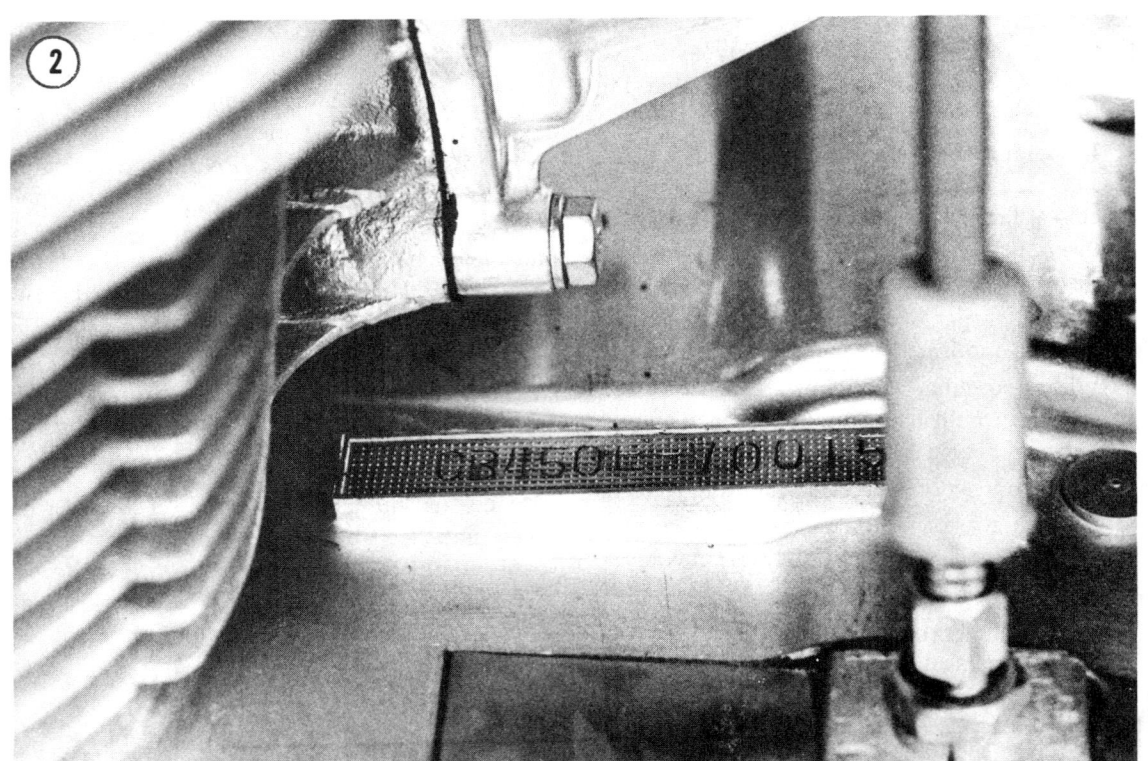

CHAPTER TWO

TROUBLESHOOTING

Diagnosing motorcycle ills is relatively simple if you use orderly procedures and keep a few basic principles in mind.

Never assume anything. Don't overlook the obvious. If you are riding along and the bike suddenly quits, check the easiest, most accessible problem spots first. Is there gasoline in the tank? Is the gas petcock in the ON or RESERVE position? Has a spark plug wire fallen off? Check the ignition switch. Sometimes the weight of keys on a key ring may turn the ignition off suddenly.

If nothing obvious turns up in a cursory check, look a little further. Learning to recognize and describe symptoms will make repairs easier for you or a mechanic at the shop. Describe problems accurately and fully. Saying that "it won't run" isn't the same as saying "it quit on the highway at high speed and wouldn't start," or that "it sat in my garage for three months and then wouldn't start."

Gather as many symptoms together as possible to aid in diagnosis. Note whether the engine lost power gradually or all at once, what color smoke (if any) came from the exhausts, and so on. Remember that the more complicated a machine is, the easier it is to troubleshoot because symptoms point to specific problems.

You don't need fancy equipment or complicated test gear to determine whether repairs can be attempted at home. A few simple checks could save a large repair bill and time lost while the bike sits in a dealer's service department. On the other hand, be realistic and don't attempt repairs beyond your abilities. Service departments tend to charge heavily for putting together a disassembled engine that may have been abused. Some places won't even take on such a job—so use common sense and don't get in over your head.

OPERATING REQUIREMENTS

An engine needs three basics to run properly: correct gas-air mixture, compression, and a spark at the right time. If one or more are missing, the engine won't run. The electrical system is the weakest link of the three. More problems result from electrical breakdowns than from any other source. Keep that in mind before you begin tampering with carburetor adjustments and the like.

If a bike has been sitting for any length of time and refuses to start, check the battery for a charged condition first and then look to the gasoline delivery system. This includes the tank, fuel petcocks, lines and the carburetor. Rust may have formed in the tank, obstructing fuel flow. Gasoline deposits may have gummed up carburetor jets and air passages. Gasoline tends to lose its potency after standing for long periods. Condensation may contaminate it with water. Drain old gas and try starting with a fresh tankful.

Compression, or the lack of it, usually enters the picture only in the case of older machines. Worn or broken pistons, rings, and cylinder bores could prevent starting. Generally, a gradual power loss and harder and harder starting will be readily apparent in this case.

STARTING DIFFICULTIES

Check gas flow first. Remove the gas cap and look into the tank. If gas is present, pull off a fuel line at the carburetor and see if gas flows freely. If none comes out, the fuel tap may be shut off, blocked by rust or foreign matter, or the fuel line may be stopped up or kinked. If the carburetor is getting usable fuel, turn to the electrical system next.

Check that the battery is charged by turning on the lights or by beeping the horn. Refer to your owner's manual for starting procedures with a dead battery. Have the battery recharged if necessary.

Pull off a spark plug cap, remove the spark plug and reconnect the cap. Lay the plug against the cylinder head so its base makes a good connection and turn the engine over with the kickstarter. A fat, blue spark should jump across the electrodes. If there is no spark, or a weak one, there is electrical system trouble. Check for a defective plug by replacing it with a known good one. Don't assume a plug is good just because it's new.

Once the plug has been cleared of guilt, but there's still no spark, start backtracking through the system. If the contact at the end of the spark plug wire can be exposed it can be held about 1/8 inch from the head while the engine is turned over to check for a spark. Remember to hold the wire only by its insulation to avoid a nasty shock. If the plug wires are dirty, greasy, or wet, wrap a rag around them so you won't get shocked. If you do feel a shock or see sparks along the wire, clean or replace the wire and/or its connections.

If there's no spark at the plug wire, look for loose connections at the coil and battery. If all seems in order here, check next for oily or dirty contact points. Clean points with electrical contact cleaner or a strip of paper. With the ignition switch turned on, open and close the points manually with a screwdriver.

No spark at the points with this test indicates a failure in the ignition system. Refer to the *Electrical System* chapter for checkout procedures for the entire system and individual components. Refer to *Periodic Maintenance* chapter to check and set ignition timing.

Note that spark plugs of the incorrect heat range (too cold) may cause hard starting. Set gaps to specifications. If you have just ridden through a puddle or washed the bike and it won't start, dry off plugs and plug wires. Water may have entered the carburetor and fouled the fuel under these conditions, but wet plugs and wires are the more likely problem.

If a healthy spark occurs at the right time, and there is adequate gas flow to the carburetor, check the carburetor itself at this time. Make sure all jets and air passages are clean, check float level and adjust if necessary. Shake the float to check for gasoline inside it and replace or repair as indicated. Check that the carburetors are mounted snugly and no air is leaking past the manifolds. Check for a clogged air filter.

Compression may be checked in the field by turning the kickstarter by hand and noting that an adequate resistance is felt, or by removing a spark plug and placing a finger over the plug hole and feeling for pressure. Use a compression gauge if possible. Compression should generally read 150 lbs. per square inch or more.

Valve adjustments should be checked next. Sticking, burned, or broken valves may hamper starting. As a last resort, check valve timing as described in Chapter Four.

POOR IDLING

Poor idling may be caused by incorrect carburetor adjustment, incorrect timing, ignition system defects, an intake manifold leak, or leakage between the carburetors at the balance tube. Check the gas cap vent for an obstruction.

MISFIRING

Misfirings can be caused by a weak spark or dirty plugs. Check for fuel contamination. Run

TROUBLESHOOTING

the machine at night or in a darkened garage to check for spark leaks along the plug wires and under the spark plug cap. If misfiring occurs only at certain throttle settings, refer to the carburetor service section for the specific carburetor circuits involved. Misfiring under heavy load as when climbing hills or accelerating is usually caused by bad spark plugs.

FLAT SPOTS

If the engine seems to die momentarily when the throttle is opened and then recovers, check for a dirty main jet in the carburetor, water in the fuel, or an excessively lean mixture.

LACK OF POWER

Poor condition of rings, pistons, or cylinders will cause a lack of power and speed. Check valve adjustment. Ignition timing should be checked along with automatic spark advance.

OVERHEATING

If the engine seems to run too hot all the time, be sure you are not idling it for long periods. Air cooled engines are not designed to operate at a standstill for any length of time. Heavy stop and go traffic is hard on a motorcycle engine. Spark plugs of the wrong heat range can burn pistons. An excessively lean gas mixture may cause overheating. Check ignition timing. Don't ride in too high a gear. Broken or worn rings and valves may permit compression gases to leak past them, heating heads and cylinders excessively. Check oil level and use the proper grade lubricants.

BACKFIRING

Check that the timing is not advanced too far. Check the automatic advance mechanism for broken or sticking parts. Check the fuel for contamination.

ENGINE NOISES

Experience is needed to diagnose accurately in this area. Noises are hard to differentiate and harder yet to describe. Deep knocking noises usually mean main bearing failure. A slapping noise generally comes from loose pistons. A light knocking noise during acceleration may be a bad connecting rod bearing. Pinging, which sounds like marbles being shaken in a tin can, is caused by ignition advanced too far or gasoline with too low an octane rating. Pinging should be corrected immediately or damage to pistons will result. Compression leaks at the head-cylinder joint will sound like a rapid on-and-off squeal.

PISTON SEIZURE

Piston seizure is caused by incorrect piston clearances when fitted, fitting rings with improper end gap, too thin an oil being used, incorrect spark plug heat range, or incorrect ignition timing. Overheating from any cause may result in seizure.

VIBRATION

Excessive vibration may be caused by loose motor mounts, worn engine or transmission bearings, loose wheels, worn swinging arm bushings, a generally poor running engine, broken or cracked frame, or one that has been damaged in a collision. See also *Poor Handling*.

HIGH OIL CONSUMPTION

High oil consumption and loss of compression often go hand in hand. Check condition of rings, pistons, cylinders, and valves. Worn valve stems or valve guides may be at fault. Use the correct grade of oil.

CLUTCH SLIP OR DRAG

Clutch slip may be due to worn plates, improper adjustment, or glazed plates. A dragging clutch could result from damaged or bent plates, improper adjustment, or even clutch spring pressure.

TRANSMISSION PROBLEMS

A grinding when shifting may be a result of worn synchronizers on the transmission gears or a sticking or non-disengaging clutch. Bent or broken teeth may cause hard shifting. A bent shifting rod or main shaft or layshaft could cause hard shifting. Popping out of gear could be due to worn dogs on the gears or misadjustment in the shifting mechanism.

POOR HANDLING

Poor handling may be caused by improper tire pressures, a damaged frame or swinging arm, worn shocks or front forks, weak fork springs, a bent or broken steering arm, misaligned wheels, loose or missing spokes, worn tires, bent handlebars, worn wheel bearings, or dragging brakes.

BRAKE SYSTEM

Sticking brakes may be caused by broken or weak return springs, improper cable or rod adjustment, or dry pivot and cam bushings. Grabbing brakes may be caused by greasy linings which must be replaced. Brake grab may also be due to out-of-round drums or linings which have broken loose from the shoes. Glazed linings or braks pads will cause loss of stopping power.

LIGHTING SYSTEM

Bulbs which continuously burn out may be caused by excessive vibration, loose connections that permit sudden current surges, poor battery connections, or installation of the wrong type bulb.

A dead battery, or one which discharges quickly, may be caused by a faulty generator or rectifier. Check for loose or corroded terminals. Shorted battery cells or broken terminals will keep a battery from charging. Low water level will decrease a battery's capacity. A battery left uncharged after installation will sulphate, rendering it useless.

A majority of light and horn or other electrical accessory problems are caused by loose or corroded ground connections. Check those first and then substitute known good units for easier troubleshooting.

TROUBLESHOOTING GUIDE

Table 1 is a "quick reference" guide that summarizes the troubleshooting process. Use it to outline possible problem areas, then refer to the specific chapter or section involved.

Table 1   TROUBLESHOOTING GUIDE

Item	Problem or Cause	Things to Check
Hard starting	Defective ignition system	Choke Breaker point condition Ignition timing Spark plug cables Ignition coil Condenser
	Defective fuel system	Choke Fuel cock Carburetor mounting Clogged fuel lines Clogged fuel tank cap vent Carburetor
	Engine	Piston, rings, cylinders Cylinder head
Loss of power	Poor compression	Piston rings and cylinders Head gaskets Leaking valves

(continued)

TROUBLESHOOTING

Table 1   TROUBLESHOOTING GUIDE (continued)

Item	Problem or Cause	Things to Check
Loss of power (cont.)	Overheated engine	Lubricating oil supply Clogged cooling fins Oil pump Ignition timing Slipping clutch Carbon in combustion chamber
	Improper mixture	Dirty air cleaner Choke lever position Restricted fuel flow Gas cap vent hole
	Miscellaneous	Dragging brakes Tight wheel bearings Defective chain Clogged exhaust system
Gearshifting difficulties	Clutch	Adjustment Springs Friction plates Steel plates Oil quantity
	Transmission	Oil quantity Oil grade Return spring or pin Change lever or spring Drum position plate Change drum Change forks
Steering	Hard steering	Tire pressures Steering stem head Steering head bearings
	Pulls to one side	Unbalanced shock absorbers Drive chain adjustment Front/rear wheel alignment Unbalanced tires Defective swing arm Defective steering head
	Shimmy	Drive chain adjustment Loose or missing spokes Deformed rims Worn wheel bearings Wheel balance
Brakes	Poor brakes	Worn linings Brake adjustment Oil or water on brake linings Loose linkage or cables
	Noisy brakes	Worn or scratched lining Scratched brake drums Dirt in brake housing Disc distortion
	Unadjustable brakes	Worn linings Worn drums Worn brake cams

CHAPTER THREE

PERIODIC LUBRICATION AND MAINTENANCE

A motorcycle, even in normal use, is subjected to tremendous heat, stress, and vibration. When neglected, any bike becomes unreliable and actually dangerous to ride. When properly maintained, the Honda 450 and 500T are among the most reliable bikes available and will give many miles and years of reliable, fast, and safe riding.

Service intervals are based on an average of 6,000 miles per year or 500 miles a month. If you ride more than this, follow the mileage schedule of maintenance. If you ride less than this, follow the time schedule. For example, engine oil must be changed every 1,500 miles or 3 months. If you ride less than 1,500 miles in 3 months, you still change the oil after 3 months.

This chapter describes all periodic maintenance required to keep your bike running properly. Routine checks are easily performed at each fuel stop. Other periodic maintenance appears in order of frequency. The engine tune-up, which must be performed every 3,000 miles or 6 months, is treated separately as the various procedures interact and must be done together. **Table 1** summarizes all periodic maintenance required in an easy-to-use form.

ROUTINE CHECKS

The following simple checks should be performed at each stop at a service station for gas.

Engine Oil Level

Remove dipstick and wipe it clean. Insert dipstick, but do not screw it in. Remove it and check level. It should be between the 2 marks on the dipstick. Top up as necessary with oil recommended in **Table 2**.

General Inspection

1. Quickly examine engine for signs of oil or fuel leakage.
2. Check tires for imbedded stones. Pry them out with the ignition key.
3. Make sure all lights work.

> NOTE: *At least check stoplight. It can burn out anytime. Motorists cannot stop as quickly as you and need all the warning you can give.*

PERIODIC MAINTENANCE

The following procedures are arranged according to frequency. Those listed first are done

PERIODIC LUBRICATION AND MAINTENANCE

every 500 miles or one month; those listed last, every 6,000 miles or 12 months.

Engine tune-up procedures, all of which must be done every 3,000 miles or 6 months, are properly called preventive maintenance. However, they should be done together, so they are treated together under *Engine Tune-up* in this chapter.

500-MILE/MONTHLY MAINTENANCE

Lights

Once a month, check all lights for proper functioning. Replace defective bulbs and fuses as they occur. Be sure to find the cause when replacing a defective fuse. Otherwise, the new fuse will probably burn out, too. Check headlight alignment and adjust if required.

Nuts, Bolts, and Other Fasteners

Constant vibration can loosen many fasteners on a motorcycle. Every 500 miles or monthly, check tightness of all fasteners on the following:

a. Engine mounts
b. Engine covers
c. Handlebars
d. Gearshift lever
e. Kickstarter
f. Exhaust pipe flange
g. Lighting equipment

Table 1   LUBRICATION AND MAINTENANCE SUMMARY

Interval	Item	Check Fluid Level	Replace	Lube	Inspect and/or Clean	Check and/or Adjust
Fuel stop	Engine oil	X				
	General				X	X
500 mile/ 1 month	Lights					X
	Fasteners					X
	Drive chain tension					X
	Tires					X
1,500 mile/ 3 months	Engine oil		X			
	Battery	X				
3,000 mile/ 6 months	Fuel strainer				X	
	Throttle cable				X	X
	Rear fork bushing			X	X	
	Wheels				X	
	Air filters				X	
	Cam chain					X
	Clutch					X
	Brakes (drum)					X
	Brake (disc)	X				X
	Engine tune-up					
	Valve clearance					X
	Spark plugs					X
	Breaker points					X
	Ignition timing					X
	Carburetor					X
6,000 mile/ 12 months	Front fork oil		X			
	Engine oil filter				X	
	Air filter		X			

Table 2 RECOMMENDED LUBRICANTS

	Temperature	Type
Engine oil	All	SAE 10W-40, SE
Multigrade	Above 59° F	SAE 20W-50, SE
Engine oil	Above 59° F	SAE 30, SE
Single grade	32-59° F	SAE 20 or 20W, SE
	Below 32° F	SAE 10W, SE
Fork oil*	All	SAE 10W-30 or Automatic Transmission fluid
Rear suspension bushing	All	Multi-purpose grease
Drive chain	All	SAE 30 engine oil

*See *Quick Reference Data* for capacities

Table 3 TIGHTENING TORQUES—CB40, CL450

	Foot-pounds	Mkg
Front axle nut	54-61	7.5-8.5
Front brake torque	13-20	1.8-2.8
Front fork bolt	47-58	6.5-8.0
Steering stem nut	65-87	9.0-12.0
Steering stem bolt	29-36	4.0-5.0
Handlebar bolt	18-25	2.5-3.5
Engine mounting bolt (10 mm)	29-36	4.0-5.0
Engine mounting bolt (8 mm)	13-30	1.8-2.8
Shock absorber nut	29-36	4.0-5.0
Shock absorber bolt	29-36	4.0-5.0
Swing arm bolt	51-65	7.0-9.0
Rear axle nut	58-87	8.0-12.0
Kickstarter bolt	13-20	1.8-2.8
Exhaust pipe clamp nut	6-9	0.8-1.2
Driven sprocket nut	29-36	4.0-5.0
Cylinder head	20-22	2.8-3.0

PERIODIC LUBRICATION AND MAINTENANCE

Table 4   TIGHTENING TORQUES — CB500T

Point	Ft.-Lb.	Mkg
Alternator rotor	22-25	3.0-3.5
Drive gear (oil filter rotor)	33-40	4.5-5.5
Spark plug	18-22	2.5-3.0
Cylinder head	20-22	2.8-3.0
Spoke	1.1-1.5	0.15-0.20
Rear fork pivot bolt	72-94	10.0-13.0
Rear axle shaft	60-72	8.0-10.0
Front fork bottom bridge	22-29	3.0-4.0
Steering stem nut	51-65	7.0-9.0
Front wheel axle shaft	40-47	5.5-6.5
5mm screw	2.5-3.6	0.35-0.50
6mm screw	5-8	0.70-1.10
5mm bolt, nut	3.3-4.3	0.45-0.60
6mm bolt, nut	6-9	0.80-1.20
8mm bolt, nut	13-18	1.8-2.5
10mm bolt, nut	22-29	3.0-4.0
12mm bolt, nut	36-43	5.0-6.0
6mm flange bolt	7-10	1.0-1.4
8mm flange bolt	17-22	2.4-3.0
10mm flange bolt	22-29	3.0-4.0

Tables 3 and 4 list torque values for most important hardware.

Drive Chain Tension

Every 500 miles or monthly, check drive chain condition and tension. Also, liberally apply clean engine oil or special chain lubricant. See **Figure 1**. To check chain tension:

1. Rest motorcycle on centerstand.
2. Shift transmission to NEUTRAL.
3. Check vertical play of chain as shown in **Figure 2**. Play should be about ¾ in.
4. Rotate rear wheel. Chain play should be the same at any position. If not, check for worn, kinked, or binding chain links.

Drive Chain Adjustment

If chain play is not about ¾ in., adjust tension as follows.

1. Rest motorcycle on centerstand.
2. Remove cotter pin from axle nut and loosen nut. See **Figure 3**.
3. Loosen locknuts on both adjusters. Turn adjusters equally in the same direction to increase or decrease tension. Make sure that the index mark on each side aligns at the same point on the graduated scales. See **Figure 3**.
4. Tighten the rear axle nut to 58-87 ft.-lb. (8-12 mkg) and install cotter pin.
5. Tighten adjuster locknuts.
6. Recheck chain tension.
7. Readjust brake pedal free play as described in Chapter Ten.

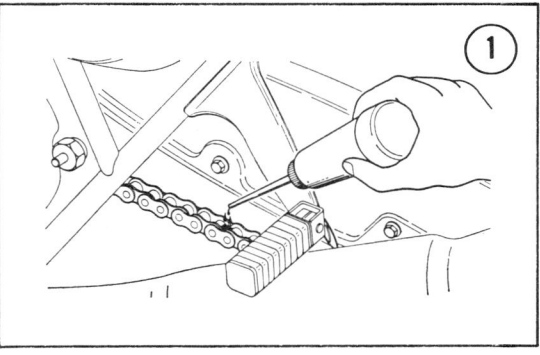

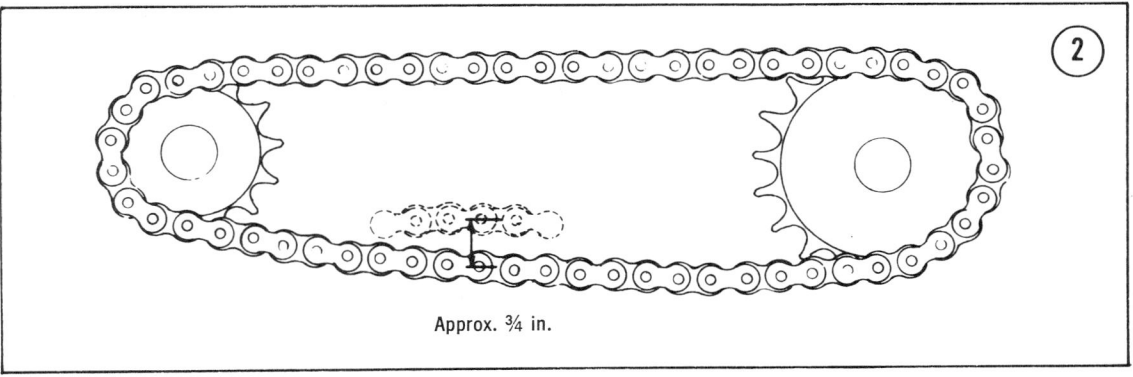

Approx. ¾ in.

Tire Inspection

Every 500 miles or monthly, check tire condition and air pressure. **Table 5** lists recommended pressures. Check tread for excessive wear, deep cuts, imbedded stones, and nails. If you find a nail in the tire, mark its location with a light crayon or chalk before pulling it out. This will help locate the hole in the inner tube.

1,500-MILE/3-MONTH MAINTENANCE

Engine Oil Change

Periodic oil changes will contribute more to engine longevity than any other single factor. Change the oil every 1,500 miles or 3 months; more often in dusty areas.

1. Warm the engine to its normal operating temperature.
2. Rest bike on centerstand.
3. Remove oil filler cap/dipstick.
4. Place container with at least 3-quart capacity under crankcase.

   NOTE: *Oil drains very quickly and splashes. Use a deep-sided container.*

5. Remove drain plug with 19mm wrench.

   WARNING
   Get your hand out of the way as soon as plug is ready to drop out. Hot oil drains very rapidly and could cause painful burns.

6. Let oil drain for at least 10 minutes.
7. Make sure O-ring in drain plug is in good condition, then install plug.
8. Pour waste oil into empty bleach bottle or similar sealable container and dispose of it properly.
9. Fill crankcase with about 3 U.S. qt. (2.5 Imp. qt. or 2.8 liters) of oil. See **Table 2** for recommended types.
10. Check oil level on dipstick with the bike level and on its centerstand.

Battery

Once every three months, check battery electrolyte level. Unlock and lift seat. Raise battery

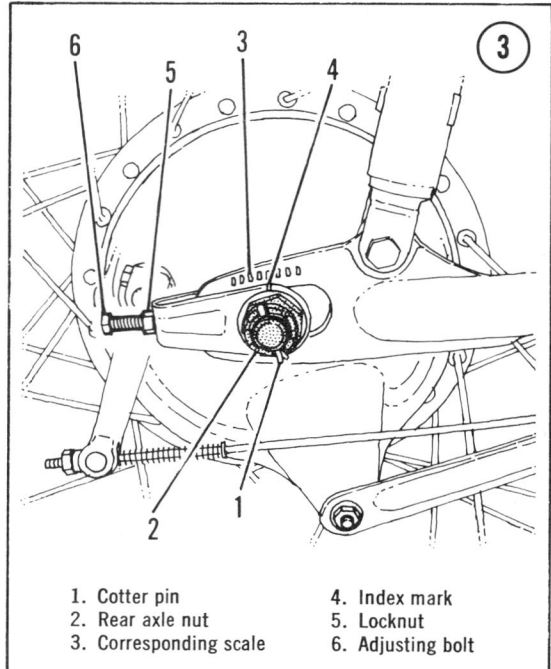

1. Cotter pin
2. Rear axle nut
3. Corresponding scale
4. Index mark
5. Locknut
6. Adjusting bolt

Table 5   TIRE PRESSURES

	Front	Rear
CB450, CL450		
Under 200 lb. load	28 psi	28 psi
Over 200 lb. load	28 psi	34 psi
CB500T		
Under 200 lb. load	28 psi	36 psi
Over 200 lb. load	28 psi	40 psi

PERIODIC LUBRICATION AND MAINTENANCE

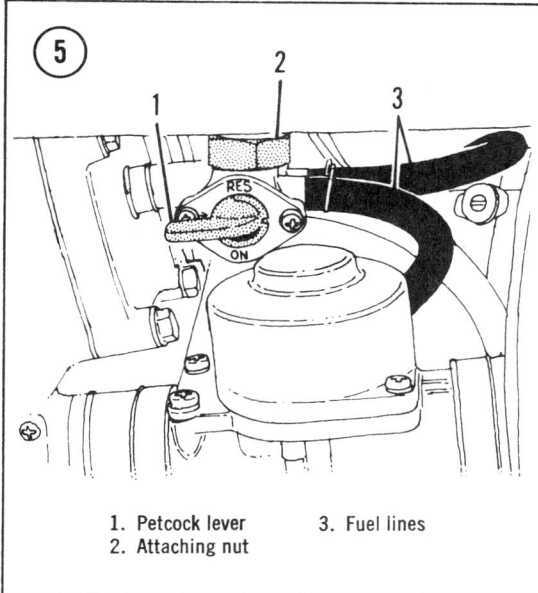

1. Petcock lever
2. Attaching nut
3. Fuel lines

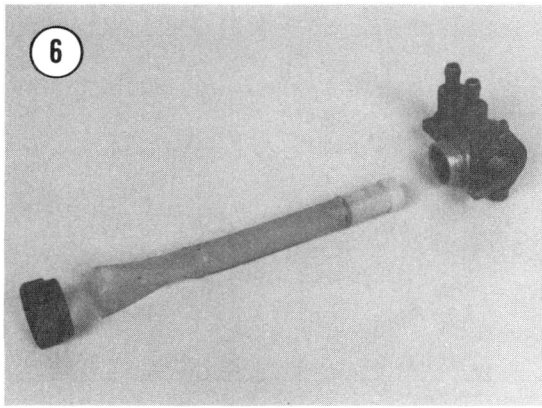

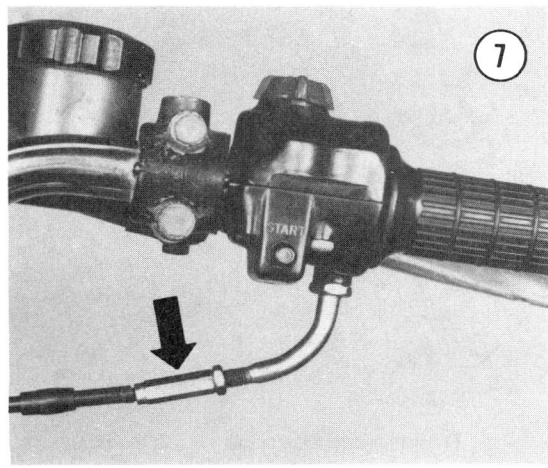

slightly to check the level on side of case. Maintain level between upper and lower lines. Top up as necessary with *distilled* water. Do not overfill.

3,000-MILE/6-MONTH MAINTENANCE

Fuel Strainer Cleaning

The fuel strainer should be cleaned every 3,000 miles or 6 months on CB/CL450 models. Unscrew strainer cap from fuel shut-off valve. See **Figure 4**. Pull out strainer. Wash strainer and cap in solvent. Remove all traces of foreign matter. Reinstall strainer in valve body. Screw on cap with O-ring in place. Turn fuel shut-off valve to ON and check for leaks.

On the CB500T, turn fuel cock lever to OFF, disconnect fuel tubes, and remove fuel tank. Drain fuel, using a well-ventilated area in which no open flames are present. Loosen fuel cock attaching nut (**Figure 5**) and remove fuel cock and filter from tank. Wash fuel filter (**Figure 6**) in solvent and reassemble, using a new gasket. Refill tank and check for leakage. Reinstall tank on bike.

Throttle Cable Inspection

Every 3,000 miles or 6 months, make sure throttle grip rotates smoothly from fully closed to fully open. Check with steering at both full right and full left. Check conditions of cable from grip to carburetors.

Make sure throttle grip free play is approximately 10-15° of grip rotation. If not, loosen adjuster locknut (**Figure 7**) and adjust.

Rear Fork Bushing

The rear swing arm bushing must be lubricated every 3,000 miles or 6 months with multipurpose grease. A fitting is provided on the frame. See **Figure 8** for CB450; **Figure 9** for CB500T.

Check condition of bushing by resting bike on centerstand and pushing hand against side of rear wheel. If there is any play, replace the bushing as described in Chapter Nine.

Wheels

Wheels must be trued to achieve proper handling and tire wear. Every 3,000 miles or 6 months, check for loose, bent, or broken spokes. Replace if necessary.

Air Filter Cleaning

Every 3,000 miles or 6 months, remove the air cleaner case and covers and loosen the connecting tube set screw. Remove the elements and clean them by tapping or blow them out with compressed air. Dry elements should be replaced if they become oil soaked.

When reassembling, be sure all joints, especially on the connecting tube, are airtight or unclean air may be sucked into the engine.

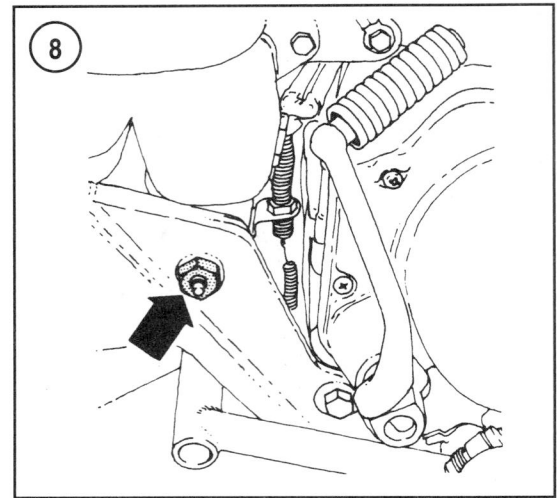

Cam Chain Adjustment

Adjust cam chain every 6 months or 3,000 miles.
1. Remove alternator cover.
2. Remove spark plugs.
3. Using a wrench on the alternator bolt, turn crankshaft counterclockwise until left piston is at top dead center as described in Steps 5 and 6, *Valve Clearance Adjustment*. On 4-speed models, continue turning a few degrees counterclockwise until the LT mark and index pointer align. On 5-speed models, continue to turn crankshaft 90° counterclockwise from TDC.
4. Loosen locknut (2), then bolt (1). Refer to **Figure 10**. A spring-loaded plunger automatically takes up chain slack.
5. Tighten bolt (1) and locknut (2).

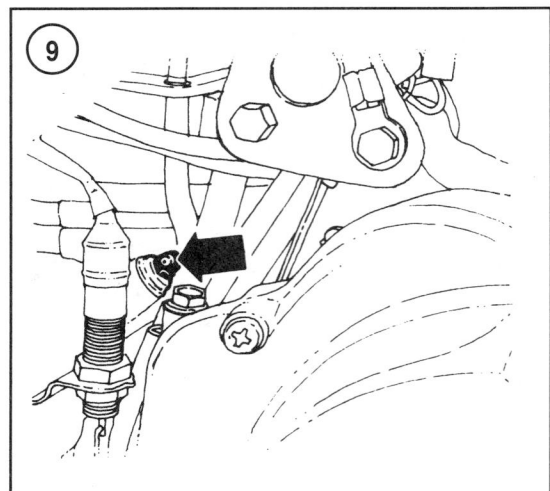

Clutch Adjustment

Every 3,000 miles or 6 months, check clutch lever free play. See **Figure 11**. Free play should be 0.4-1.0 in. (10-25mm). Adjust by loosening locknut at either end of cable and turning the adjusting nut.

If proper free play is still unattainable, adjust clutch with screwdriver on left crankcase cover. See **Figure 12**. Loosen the locking nut and turn adjusting screw to the left to increase free play and to the right to decrease it. Do not turn more than 90° past index mark in either direction. Lubrication groove must align. Tighten locking nut when proper adjustment has been made.

1. Tensioner adjusting bolt   2. Locknut

PERIODIC LUBRICATION AND MAINTENANCE

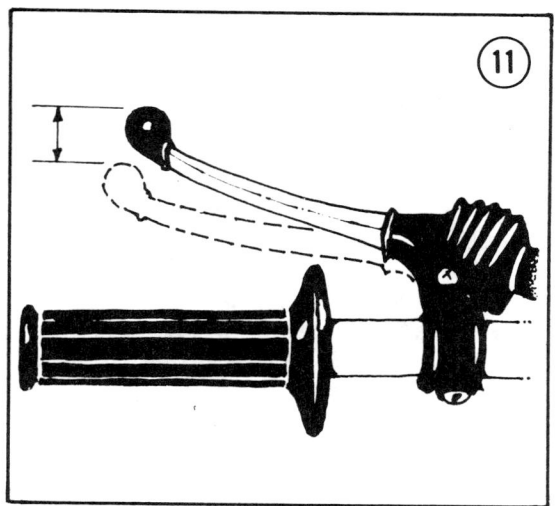

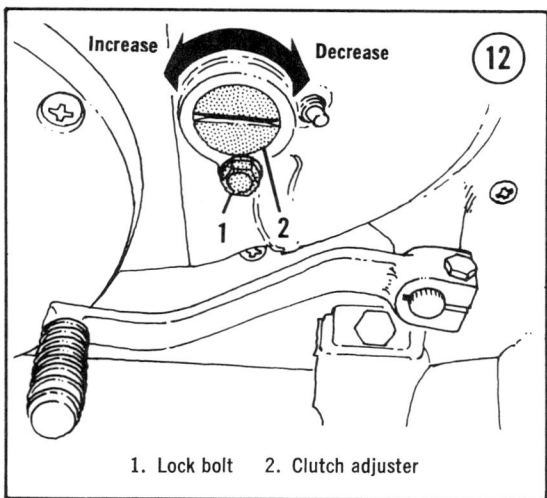

1. Lock bolt   2. Clutch adjuster

Front Brake Adjustment

With the drum-type brake, front brake lever free play should be 0.6-1.2 in. (15-30mm). Adjust by loosening the locknut on the cable end, either at the wheel or at the lever. Normally, the major adjustment is made at the wheel and fine adjustment at the lever adjuster. Refer to **Figure 13**.

Adjust lever play in early disc type front brake by loosening the locknut and turning the adjusting screw to obtain the proper lever play. See **Figure 14**. Late models have no adjustment.

Rear Brake Adjustment

Every 3,000 miles or 6 months, check pedal free play and adjust to 0.8-1.2 in. (20-30mm) if necessary. See **Figure 15**. Loosen the locknut. Turn the adjusting nut clockwise to decrease and counterclockwise to increase the free play. Refer to **Figure 16** for this procedure.

Disc Brake Fluid Level

Every 3,000 miles or 6 months, remove reservoir cap and fill to level mark. See **Figure 17**.

> **WARNING**
> *Use brake fluid clearly marked DOT 3 and/or SAE J1703 only. Others may vaporize and cause brake failure.*

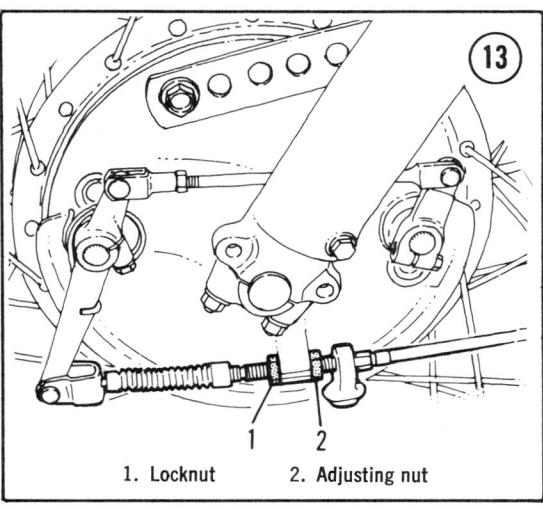

1. Locknut   2. Adjusting nut

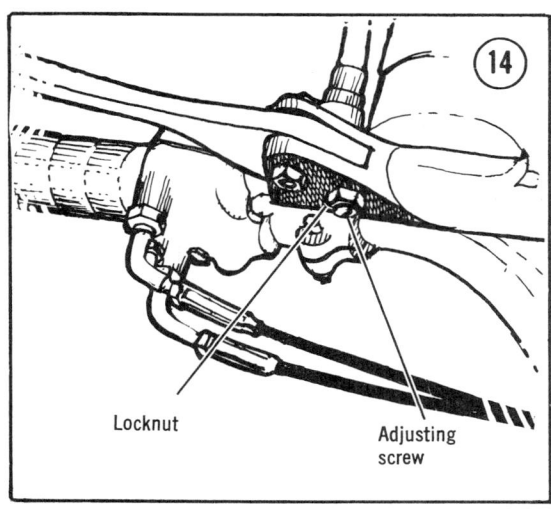

Locknut   Adjusting screw

Disc Brake Pad Inspection

Every 3,000 miles or 6 months, check brake pad thickness. Press inner housing of caliper toward disc. Measure clearance between face of inner caliper housing and brake disc. If less than 0.12 in. (3.0 mm), replace the pads as described in Chapter Ten.

6,000-MILE/12-MONTH MAINTENANCE

Front Fork Oil Change

Every 6,000 miles or 12 months, drain and replace front fork oil.
1. Unscrew drain plug (**Figure 18**) on each fork tube.
2. Pump fork up and down several times until oil has completely drained.
3. Install drain plug.
4. Remove both filler plugs (1, **Figure 19**).
5. Fill each fork leg with the quantity of ATF or 10W-30 oil listed in the *QRD* section at the front of the book.
6. Install filler plugs.

Oil Filter Cleaning

The centrifugal oil filter requires cleaning every 6,000 miles or 12 months; more often if the bike is ridden in dusty areas.
1. Remove oil filter cover (**Figure 20**) from the right crankcase cover.
2. Remove snap ring (or bolt on 4-speed models) securing oil filter cap.
3. Remove oil filter cap.
4. Refer to page 43 for rotor removal.
5. Clean cap in solvent.
6. Wipe rotor clean with solvent-saturated rag.
7. Install cap in rotor. Make sure that rib on cap fits in groove of rotor. See **Figure 21**.
8. Install snap ring.
9. Install oil filter cover. Align holes in cover with matching holes in crankcase. See **Figure 20**.

Air Filter Replacement

Every 6,000 miles or 12 months, remove air

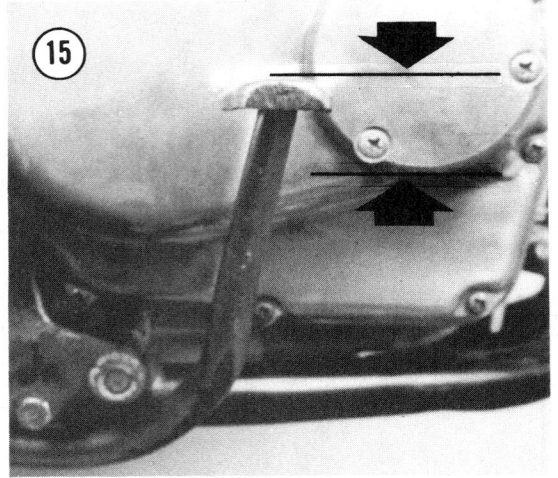

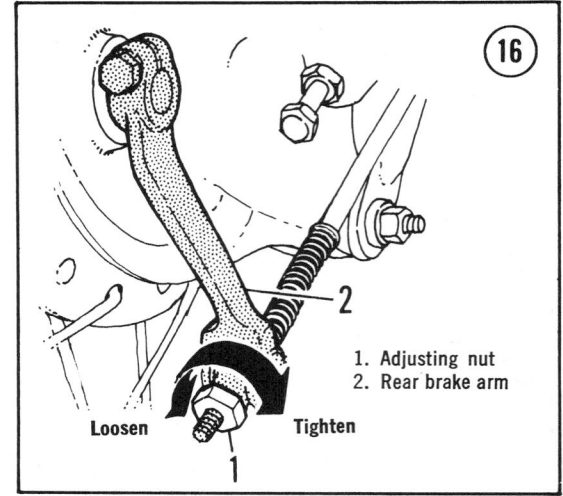

1. Adjusting nut
2. Rear brake arm

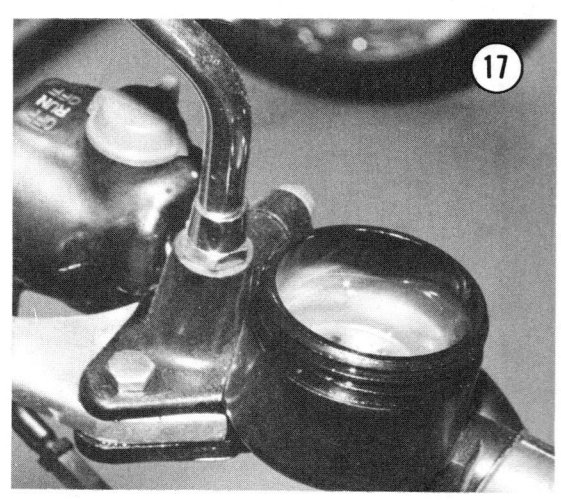

PERIODIC LUBRICATION AND MAINTENANCE

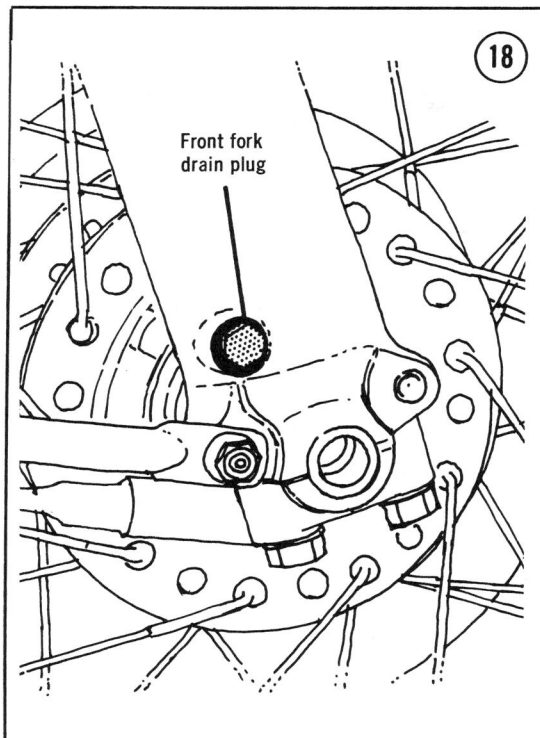

1. Top filler plugs
2. Handlebar bolts

filters as described previously under *Air Filter Cleaning*. Discard filters and install new ones.

ENGINE TUNE-UP

Engine tune-up consists of several accurate and careful adjustments to obtain maximum engine performance. Since different systems in an engine interact to affect overall performance, tune-up must be accomplished in the following order:

    a. Valve clearance adjustment.

    b. Ignition adjustment and timing.

    c. Carburetor adjustment.

Perform an engine tune-up every 3,000 miles

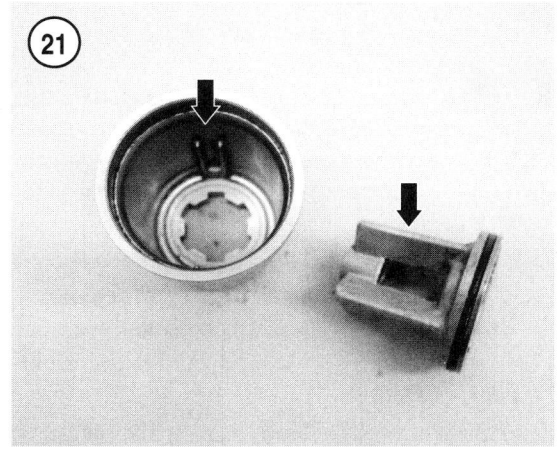

or 6 months. **Table 6** summarizes tune-up specifications.

Valve Adjustment

Four-stroke engines require periodic valve clearance adjustment. If valve clearance is too small, the valves may become burned, resulting in short life. Excessive clearance results in noise. In either case, engine power is reduced.

Valve clearance must be adjusted with the engine *cold*.

1. Remove fuel tank. See Chapter Six.
2. Remove all valve covers.

> NOTE: *Is may be easier to remove the carburetor caps first. Be sure to return each one to the carburetor from which it was removed.*

3. Remove breaker point cover (**Figure 22**) and alternator cover (**Figure 23**).
4. Remove both spark plugs.
5. Using a wrench on the center bolt, turn engine counterclockwise until LT mark on alternator rotor aligns with index pointer (**Figure 24**).
6. Examine marks on both camshafts. If *both* align with their respective indexes, rotate the engine 360 degrees counterclockwise until LT mark aligns again with its index pointer.
7. Insert a 0.0012 in. (0.03mm) feeler gauge between the exhaust valve cam and cam follower (**Figure 25**). A slight drag as the gauge is inserted indicates correct clearance.
8. If clearance is not correct, loosen cam follower locknut, then turn shaft with a screwdriver to adjust clearance. **Table 7** specifies the correct turning direction. Note that the shaft must be turned as shown in **Figure 26**. When clearance is correct, tighten the locknut and recheck clearance.
9. Repeat Steps 7 and 8 for the intake valve.
10. Rotate the engine 180 degrees counterclockwise until T mark aligns with its index.
11. Repeat Steps 7, 8, and 9 for the right cylinder.
12. Install covers, fuel tank, and spark plugs.

Table 6   ENGINE TUNE-UP

Spark plug	
Type	NGK B8ES or ND W24ES
Gap	0.028-0.032" (0.7-0.8mm)
Breaker point gap	0.012-0.016" (0.3-0.4mm)
Valve clearance	0.0012" (0.03mm) cold
Ignition timing	(See text)

Spark Plug Cleaning/Replacement

1. Grasp the spark plug leads as near to the plug as possible and pull them off the plugs.
2. Blow away any dirt which has accumulated in the spark plug wells.

> CAUTION
> *The dirt could fall into the cylinders when the plugs are removed, causing serious engine damage.*

3. Remove spark plugs with spark plug wrench.

> NOTE: *If plugs are difficult to remove, apply penetrating oil around base of plugs and let it soak in about 10-20 minutes.*

4. Inspect spark plugs carefully. Look for plugs with broken center porcelain, excessively eroded electrodes, and excessive carbon or oil fouling. Replace such plugs. If deposits are light, plugs may be cleaned in solvent with a wire brush or cleaned in a special spark plug sandblast cleaner.
5. Gap plugs to 0.028-0.032 in. (0.7-0.8mm) with a *wire* feeler gauge.
6. Install plugs with a *new* gasket. First, apply a *small* drop of oil to threads. Tighten plugs finger-tight, then tighten an additional ½ turn with a spark plug wrench. If you must reuse an old gasket, tighten only an additional ⅛ turn.

> NOTE: *Do not overtighten. This will only squash the gasket and destroy its sealing ability.*

Reading Spark Plugs

Much information about engine and spark plug performance can be determined by careful examination of the spark plugs. This information is only valid after performing the following steps.

PERIODIC LUBRICATION AND MAINTENANCE

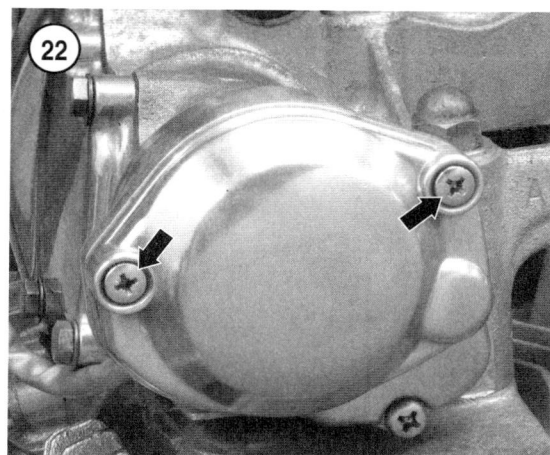

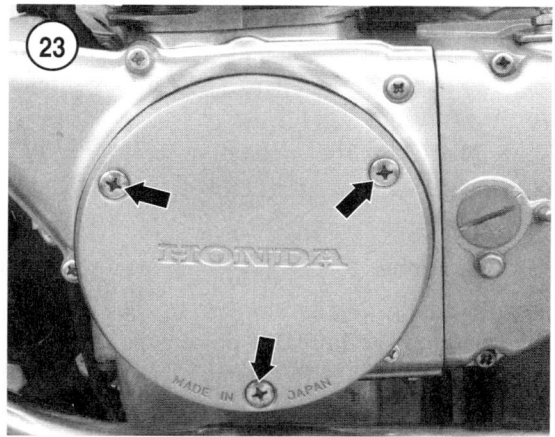

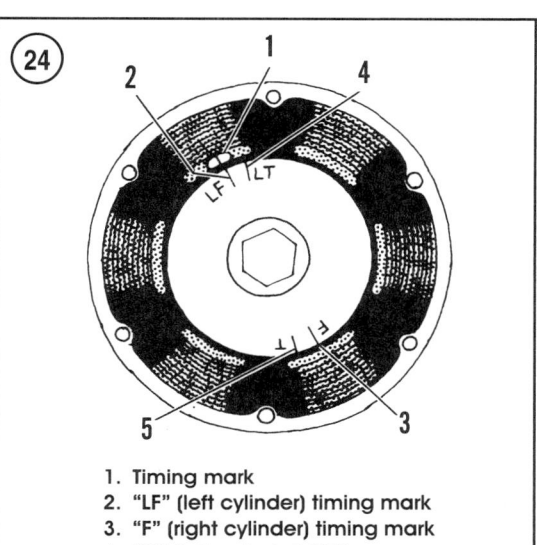

1. Timing mark
2. "LF" (left cylinder) timing mark
3. "F" (right cylinder) timing mark
4. "LT" (left cylinder) TDC
5. "T" (right cylinder) TDC

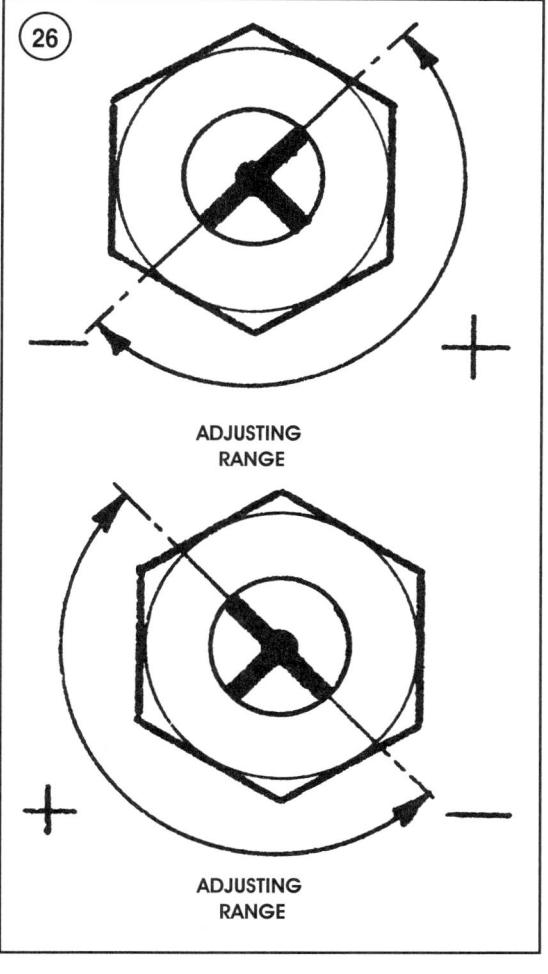

ADJUSTING RANGE

ADJUSTING RANGE

1. Ride bike a short distance at full throttle in any gear.
2. Turn off kill switch before closing throttle.
3. Pull in clutch and coast to a stop.
4. Remove spark plugs and examine them. Compare them to **Figure 27**.

Breaker Point Inspection and Cleaning

Through normal use, points gradually pit and burn. If this condition is not too serious, they can be dressed with a few strokes of a clean point file. Do not use emery cloth or sandpaper, as particles remain on the points and cause arcing and burning. If a few strokes of the file do not smooth points completely, replace them.

If points are still serviceable, after filing, remove all residue with lacquer thinner or special contact cleaner. Close the points on a piece of clean white paper, such as a business card. Continue to pull the card through the closed points until no particles or discoloration remain on the card. Finally, rotate the engine and observe the points as they open and close. If they do not meet squarely, replace them.

Adjust point gap and ignition timing as described below.

Breaker Point Replacement

If breaker points are badly damaged, replace them and adjust gap as described below.
1. Remove point cover.
2. Remove the 2 lock screws securing each point set.
3. Disconnect electrical wire from points and remove points.
4. Installation is the reverse of these steps.
5. Adjust point gap and ignition timing.

Breaker Point Adjustment

Breaker points must be examined every 3,000 miles. If in good condition, they can be cleaned and readjusted. If badly pitted, replace them and adjust new ones as described below.
1. Remove alternator cover.
2. Remove point cover.
3. Rotate crankshaft with a socket wrench or the kickstarter until one set of points opens fully.
4. Clean and inspect points as described earlier.
5. If points are in good condition, check gap with feeler gauge when points are fully open. Correct gap is 0.012-0.016 in. (0.30-0.40mm).
6. To adjust point gap, loosen breaker plate lock screws when breaker cam is at maximum lift (points fully open) and move the breaker plate to obtain correct gap. Tighten lock screws in this position.
7. Recheck gap after tightening screws.
8. Repeat Steps 3-7 for other set of points.
9. Set ignition timing.

Ignition Timing

Before adjusting ignition timing, be sure that the cam chain and breaker point gaps are properly adjusted. Refer to *Cam Chain Adjustment* and *Breaker Point Adjustment*.

A strobe-type timing light is necessary to obtain the best adjustment. To adjust timing with this unit, follow Steps 1 through 10. If no timing light is available, follow Steps 11 through 21.

1. Connect the timing light to the left cylinder, following its manufacturer's instructions.
2. Set the motorcycle on its centerstand, then remove the alternator cover.

NOTE: *Some oil may spray from the engine during this procedure.*

Table 7   VALVE CLEARANCE ADJUSTMENT

Cylinder	Valve	To reduce	To increase
Right	Intake	Counterclockwise	Clockwise
	Exhaust	Clockwise	Counterclockwise
Left	Intake	Clockwise	Counterclockwise
	Exhaust	Counterclockwise	Clockwise

PERIODIC LUBRICATION AND MAINTENANCE

⑳ SPARK PLUG CONDITION

NORMAL
- Identified by light tan or gray deposits on the firing tip.
- Can be cleaned.

GAP BRIDGED
- Identified by deposit buildup closing gap between electrodes.
- Caused by oil or carbon fouling. If deposits are not excessive, the plug can be cleaned.

OIL FOULED
- Identified by wet black deposits on the insulator shell bore and electrodes.
- Caused by excessive oil entering combustion chamber through worn rings and pistons, excessive clearance between valve guides and stems, or worn or loose bearings. Can be cleaned. If engine is not repaired, use a hotter plug.

CARBON FOULED
- Identified by black, dry fluffy carbon deposits on insulator tips, exposed shell surfaces and electrodes.
- Caused by too cold a plug, weak ignition, dirty air cleaner, too rich a fuel mixture, or excessive idling. Can be cleaned.

LEAD FOULED
- Identified by dark gray, black, yellow, or tan deposits or a fused glazed coating on the insulator tip.
- Caused by highly leaded gasoline. Can be cleaned.

WORN
- Identified by severely eroded or worn electrodes.
- Caused by normal wear. Should be replaced.

FUSED SPOT DEPOSIT
- Identified by melted or spotty deposits resembling bubbles or blisters.
- Caused by sudden acceleration. Can be cleaned.

OVERHEATING
- Identified by a white or light gray insulator with small black or gray brown spots and with bluish-burnt appearance of electrodes.
- Caused by engine overheating, wrong type of fuel, loose spark plugs, too hot a plug, or incorrect ignition timing. Replace the plug.

PREIGNITION
- Identified by melted electrodes and possibly blistered insulator. Metallic deposits on insulator indicate engine damage.
- Caused by wrong type of fuel, incorrect ignition timing or advance, too hot a plug, burned valves, or engine overheating. Replace the plug.

3. Start the engine, and let it idle at 1,100 rpm.

4. Direct the timing light at the alternator rotor. The LF mark should align with its index pointer (**Figure 28**). If not, refer to **Figure 29**. Loosen both screws (2) slightly, then move the entire base plate with a screwdriver inserted into pry slots (5). Clockwise rotation advances timing; counterclockwise rotation retards it. Tighten screws (2).

5. Stop the engine and again check left cylinder breaker point gap.

6. Connect the timing light to the right cylinder, then start the engine and again run it at 1,100 rpm.

7. Direct the timing light at the alternator rotor. The F mark should align with the index. If not, slightly loosen screws (3) for the right-hand breaker points, then vary the gap as necessary to adjust right cylinder timing. Be sure to tighten screws (3).

If a satisfactory adjustment cannot be obtained with point gap within specifications, loosen screws (2), then move the base plate until the F mark and points align. Tighten screws (2).

8. Stop the engine, then reconnect the timing light to the left cylinder. Adjust left cylinder timing by loosening screws (3) for the left-hand points, then moving the left breaker plate slightly.

> NOTE: *If a satisfactory adjustment cannot be obtained for both cylinders with point gap between 0.012-0.016 in. (0.30-0.40mm), replace the breaker points.*

9. Increase engine speed to 4,000 rpm. Direct the timing light at the alternator rotor. Check that the index pointer lies between the marks on the rotor (**Figure 30**).

10. Repeat Step 10 for the right cylinder.

> NOTE: *The following procedure is to be used only if a timing light is not available.*

11. Connect a 12-volt test lamp to the terminal on the left-hand breaker points and a good ground.

12. Remove both spark plugs.

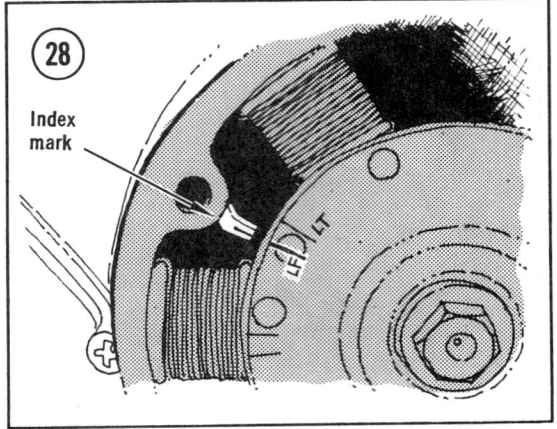

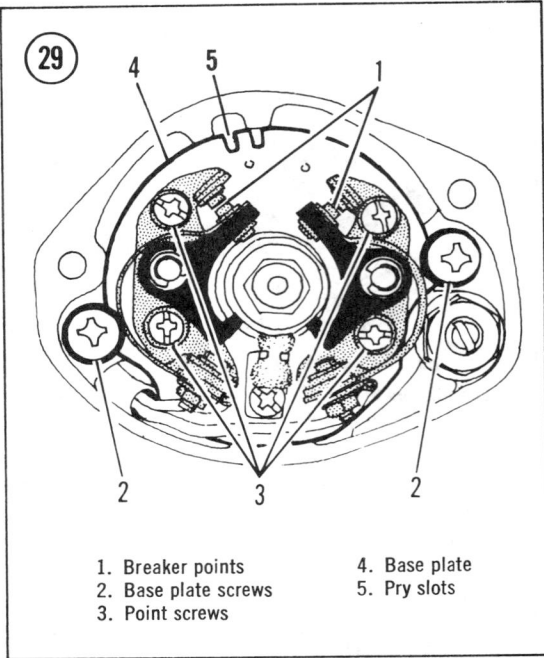

1. Breaker points
2. Base plate screws
3. Point screws
4. Base plate
5. Pry slots

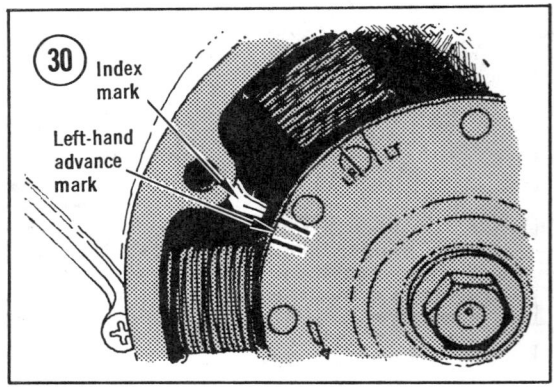

PERIODIC LUBRICATION AND MAINTENANCE

13. Turn ignition on.
14. Rotate the alternator *counterclockwise* until the LF mark aligns with the index pointer (**Figure 28**). If the light comes on just as the marks align, go on to Step 19. If not, continue with Steps 15 through 21.
15. Turn the rotor counterclockwise until the LF mark and index align. If you overshoot the mark, continue around until the marks align again.
16. Refer back to **Figure 28**. Loosen screws (2), then slowly turn the base plate with a screwdriver in pry slots (5) until the light just comes on. Tighten the screws (2).
17. Repeat Steps 15 through 17 required.
18. Rotate the alternator rotor 180 degrees counterclockwise until the F mark and index pointer align. If timing is correct, the light will come on just as the marks align. If so, no further adjustment is required. If not, continue with Steps 19 through 21.
19. Note whether the right cylinder is advanced or retarded. Timing is advanced if the light comes on before the marks align, and retarded it is comes on after.
20. If timing is advanced, reduce right cylinder point gap. Refer to *Breaker Point Adjustment*. Increase right cylinder point gap if timing is retarded. In either case, point gap must be within range of 0.012-0.016 in. (0.30-0.40mm).

21. If a satisfactory adjustment cannot be obtained, follow a procedure similar to that of foregoing Steps 8 and 9.

Ignition Advance Modification

On some bikes, idle speed does not always come back to the same value when the engine is accelerated. If carburetion and engine condition are reasonably good, the problem can usually be solved by bending the travel stops in the advance mechanism inward slightly, thus reducing the total advance by a few degrees. Be sure to bend each stop the same amount, so that both weights meet the stop at the same time.

After this modification, timing *must* be adjusted with a strobe-type timing light.

> NOTE: *Scribe a note to this effect inside the alternator cover.*

Carburetor Adjustment

1. Clean or replace air filter elements as described earlier.
2. Adjust one or both idle stop screws until exhaust pressure is the same on both sides and idle speed is 1,000 rpm. See **Figure 31**.

> NOTE: *To judge exhaust pressure, hold a thumb partially over each exhaust tip outlet. Note the exhaust force on each thumb; they should be equal.*

If idle speed does not decrease when screws are turned counterclockwise, loosen throttle cable locknut and turn adjuster about one turn to obtain some cable slack. See **Figure 32**.
3. Starting with either carburetor, adjust pilot screw slowly until maximum idle speed is obtained.
4. Adjust other carburetor in the same manner.
5. Recheck stop screw adjustment as described in Step 2.
6. Repeat Steps 2-5 as many times as necessary to achieve equal exhaust pressure at 1,000 rpm idle speed.
7. Make sure that both throttle valves move the same amount when the throttle is opened. If necessary, adjust cable adjuster at each carburetor. See **Figure 33**.

CHAPTER THREE

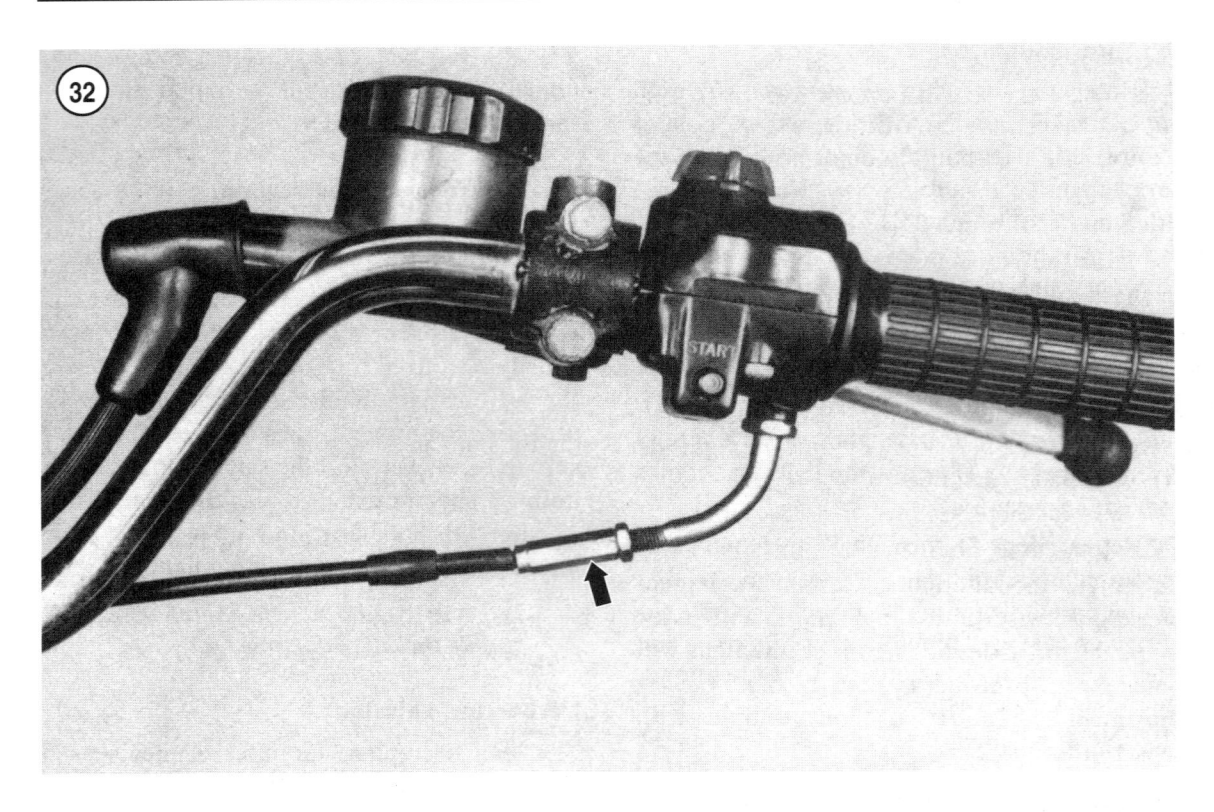

CHAPTER FOUR

ENGINE

The Honda CB500T engine is an enlarged version of the 450 engine. Apart from this factor, the engines are almost identical and the procedures given in this chapter apply to both engines. Part numbers are not necessarily interchangeable, however. Be sure to read *Parts Replacement* in Chapter One before ordering parts.

The 450/500 Honda engine is an air-cooled, 4-stroke vertical twin. A pair of overhead camshafts distinguish the design. Refer to **Figures 1 and 2** for sectional views showing details of engine construction.

Torsion bar valve springs cut down valve float or surging at high speeds, while an eccentric cam follower shaft does much to eliminate the need for frequent valve adjustment. Drive to the overhead camshafts is by a chain system using rollers to guide and quiet the moving chain.

The engine lubrication system is shown in **Figure 3**. Oil from the sump passes through a filter screen, the oil pump, and then into the lower crankcase. The crankshaft and transmission main shaft are lubricated along with the intake and exhaust camshafts. Oil thrown from the camshaft lubricates the cam chain guide rollers and the torsion bar valve springs. The countershaft and kickstarter pinion are lubricated by oil splashed from the sump.

Figure 4 illustrates the semi-hemispherical combustion chambers. This arrangement promotes better cooling and combustion efficiency. The head shape swirls and directs the gas/air mixture at the spark plug at the moment of firing, reducing the tendency of the engine to knock or ping with a lean mixture or poor grade of fuel.

ENGINE REMOVAL

1. Remove fuel tank. See Chapter Six.
2. Remove carburetors, mufflers, and exhaust pipes as described in Chapter Six.
3. Disconnect clutch cable from engine.
4. Remove gearshift lever and left foot peg.
5. Remove the front chain cover.
6. Remove the chain.
7. Unplug alternator and breaker point connectors. See **Figure 5**.
8. Disconnect spark plug wires.
9. Disconnect starter motor cable. See **Figure 6**.
10. Disconnect tachometer cable from engine. See **Figure 7**.
11. Loosen and remove 13 engine mounting bolts and lift the engine out from the left side. **Figure 8** shows the size and location of all bolts.

WARNING
The engine weighs about 140 lb. Plan on having a strong assistant on hand.

CHAPTER FOUR

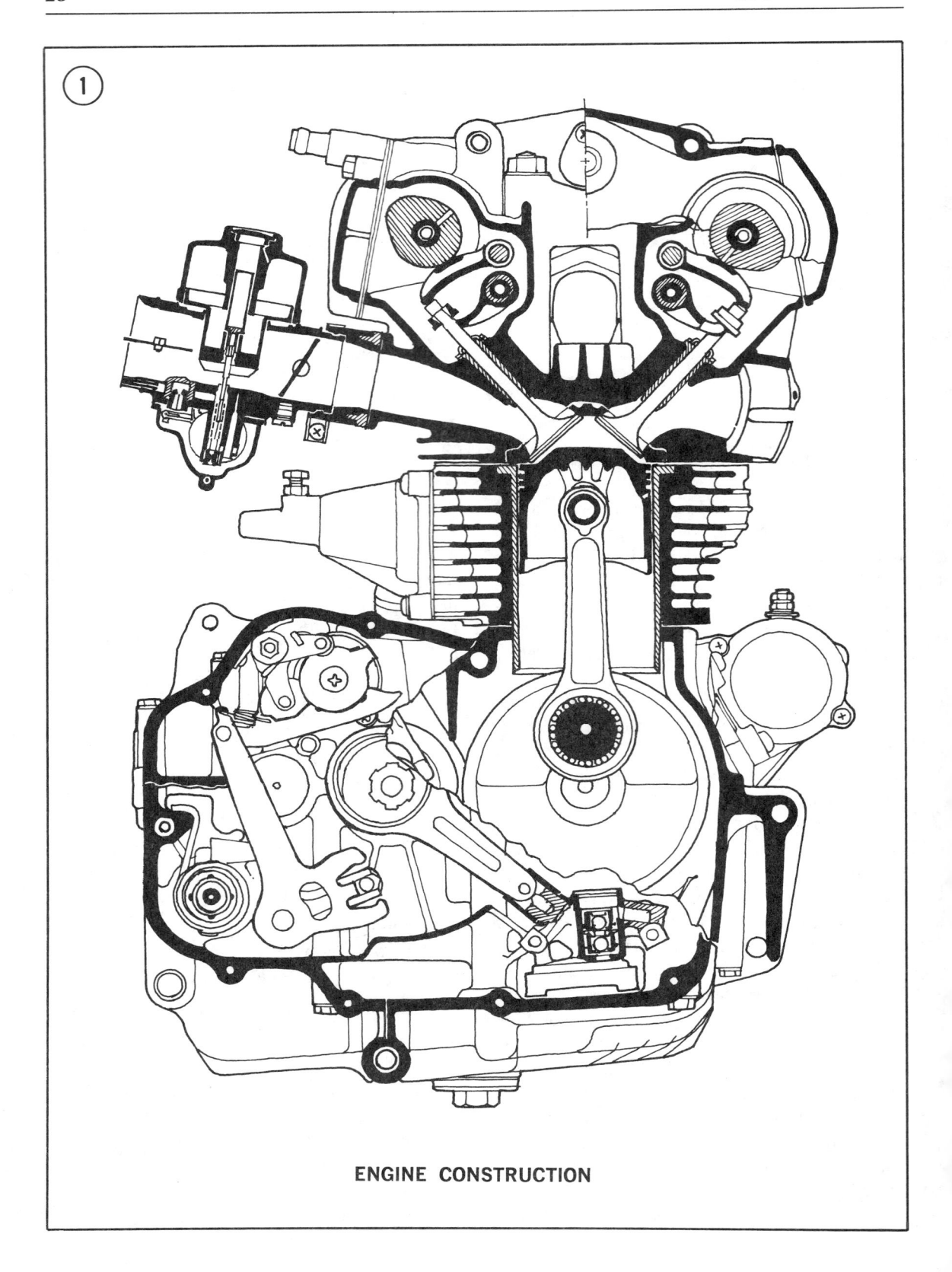

ENGINE CONSTRUCTION

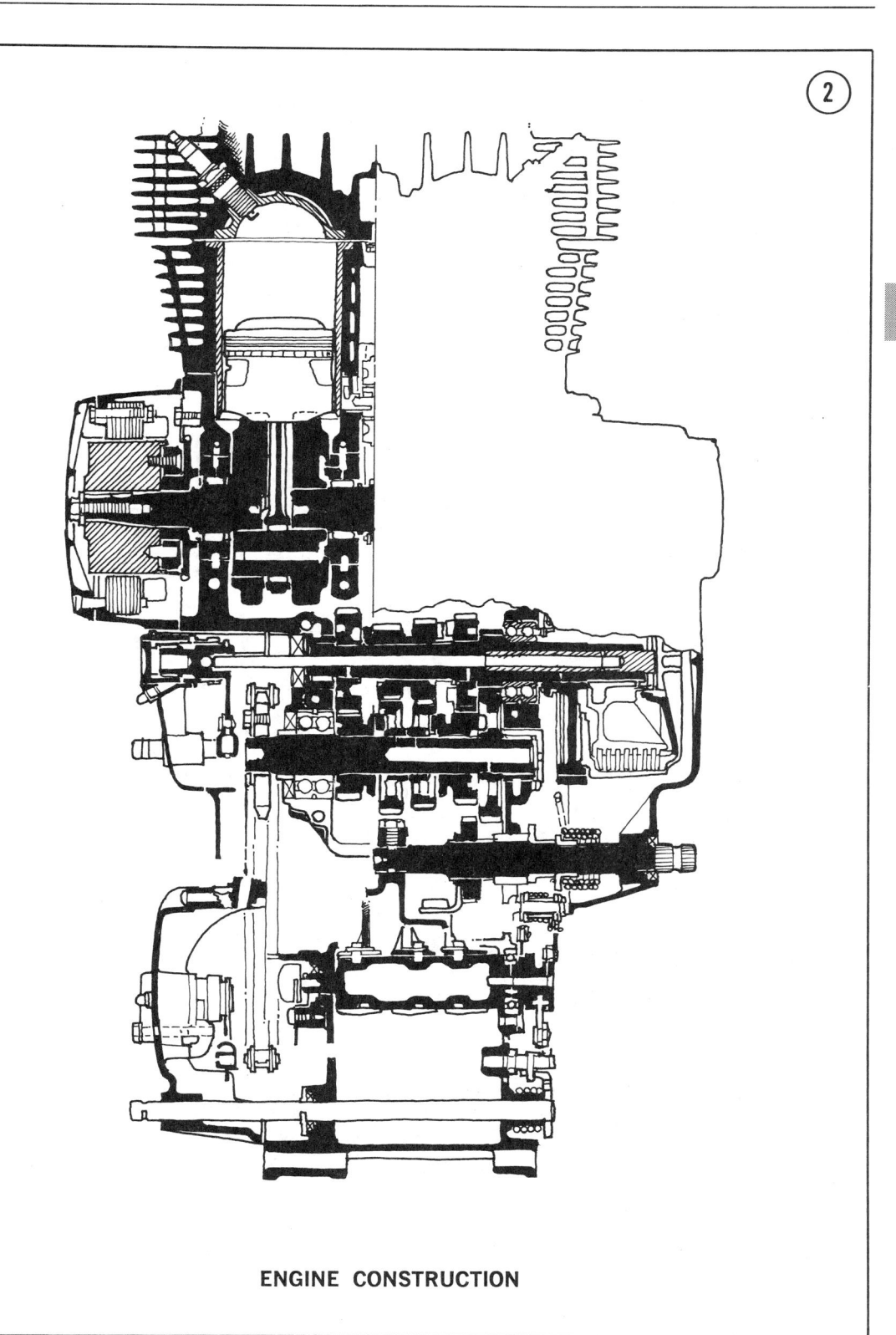

ENGINE

ENGINE CONSTRUCTION

CHAPTER FOUR

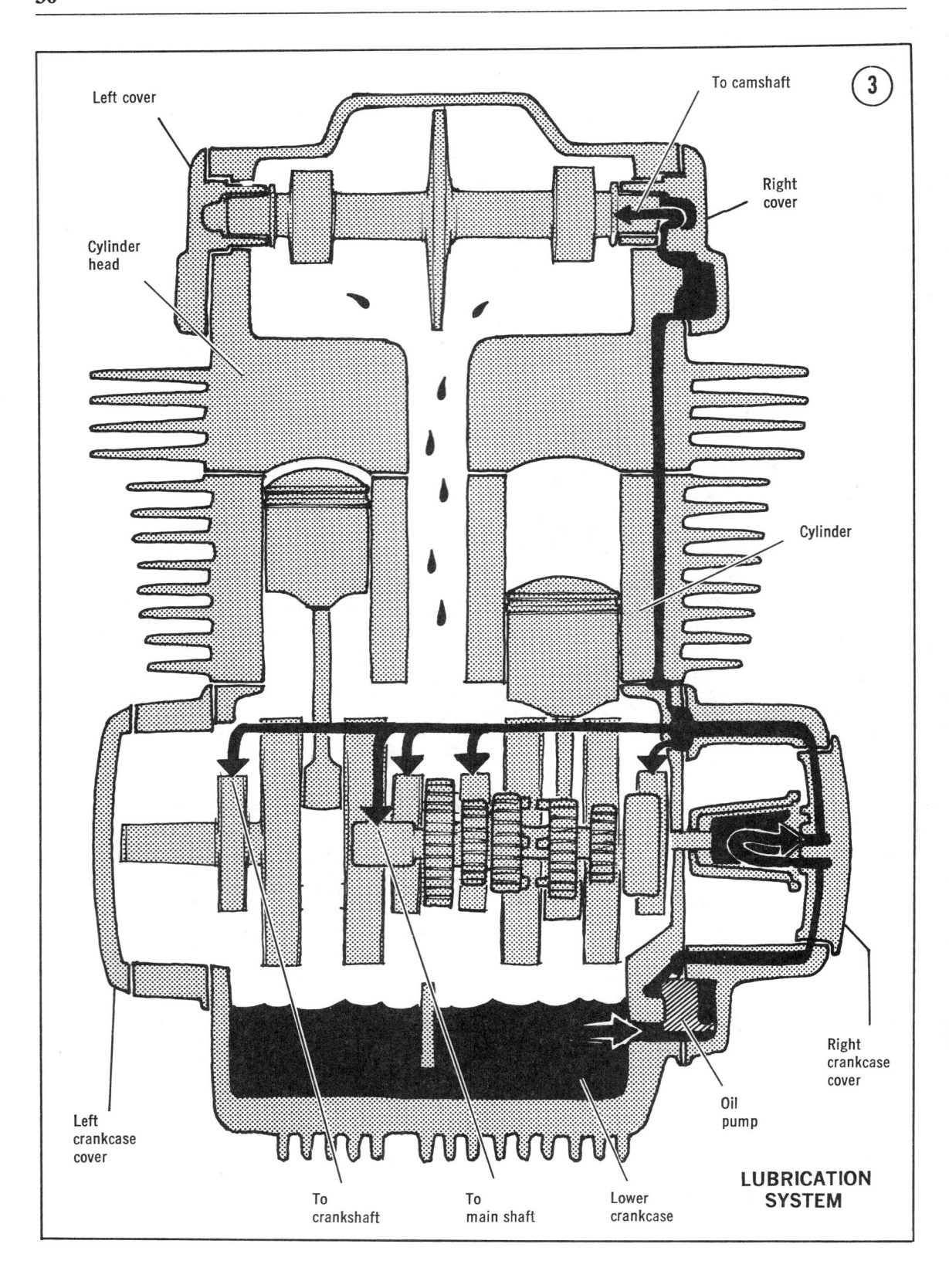

LUBRICATION SYSTEM

ENGINE

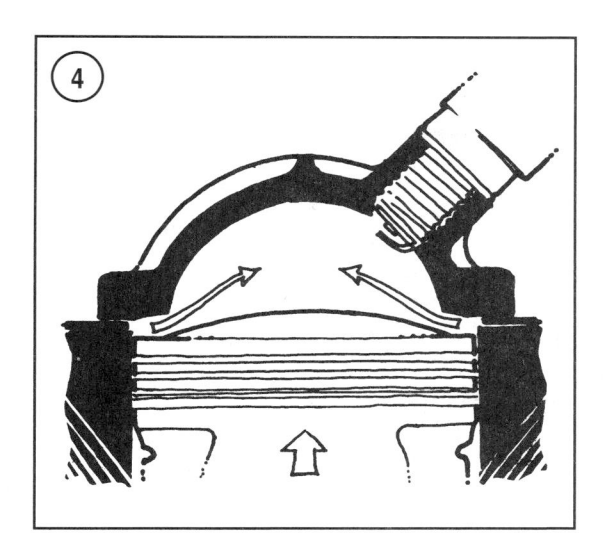

ENGINE INSTALLATION

1. Fit engine in frame and secure with mounting bolts. Install battery ground cable under mounting bolt shown in **Figure 9**. Terminal, bolt, and frame must be clean, bright metal at connection.

> NOTE: *Bolts go in from the right side with the nuts on the left side.*

2. Connect the tachometer cable and the starter motor cable.
3. Connect spark plug wires.
4. Plug in the alternator and breaker point connectors.

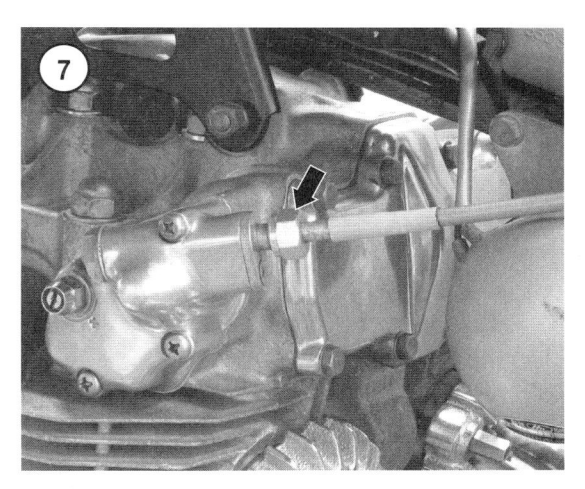

5. Install drive chain. Master link must be installed with the closed end pointing in the direction of normal travel. See **Figure 10**.

6. Install front chain cover. Make sure that the steel ball is located in the clutch shifter rod before installing. See **Figure 11**.

7. Install gearshift lever and left foot peg.

8. Connect clutch cable to engine.

9. Install carburetors, air cleaners, fuel tank, and exhaust system as described in Chapter Six.

10. Adjust clutch free play.

11. Perform engine tune-up as described in Chapter Three.

CYLINDER HEAD

Removal

1. Remove fuel tank, described in Chapter Six.
2. Remove intake and exhaust camshaft covers.
3. Remove spark plugs.
4. Rotate crankshaft until cam chain master link is accessible.
5. Disconnect cam chain with chain breaker (**Figure 12**).
6. Tie ends of chain with wire so the chain cannot drop into the crankcase. See **Figure 13**.
7. Remove 8 head nuts $1/4$ turn at a time, reversing the order shown in **Figure 14**.
8. Lift head off.

Installation

1. Make sure that guide pins are in place. See **Figure 15**.
2. Install new head gasket.
3. Install new stud seals over 2 right studs. See **Figure 15**.
4. Install cylinder head.
5. Place copper sealing washers on 2 right studs, and install cap nuts.
6. Place flat washers over remaining studs and install hex nuts.
7. Tighten nuts to 22 ft.-lb. (3 mkg) in the order shown in **Figure 14**.
8. Set valve timing as described later.

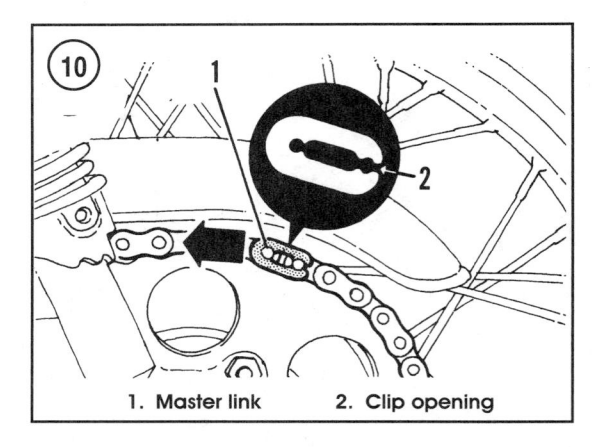

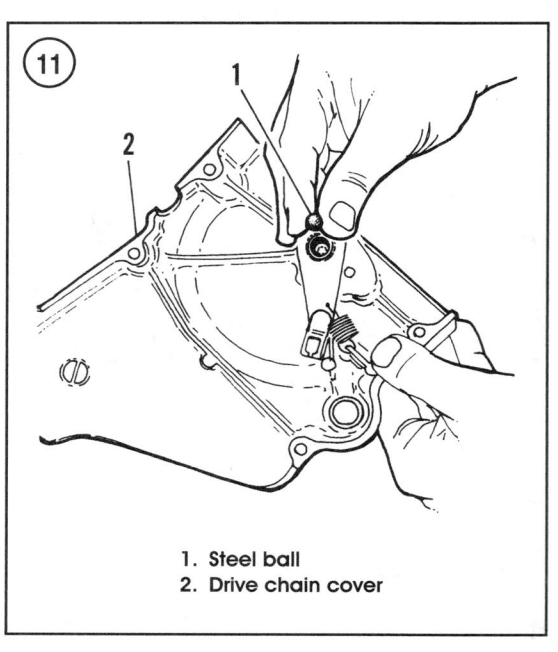

1. Master link
2. Clip opening

1. Steel ball
2. Drive chain cover

ENGINE

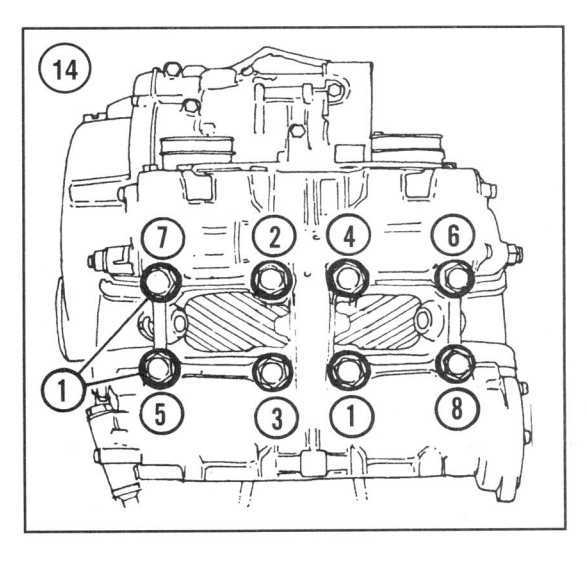

Tachometer Drive Seal

Oil leaks at the tachometer drive are easy to fix.
1. Remove the cable.
2. Turn a long, narrow wood screw along the shaft to pull out the old seal.
3. Coat the new seal with silicone lubricant.
4. Install new seal, using a deep socket or pipe of suitable diameter as a seal driver.

Valve Timing

Accurate valve timing is essential; if timing is incorrect, by even one tooth, the engine could be severely damaged.
1. Align the timing mark on each camshaft with the mark on the right bearing boss (**Figure 16**).

2. Align the LT mark on the generator rotor with the index mark on the stator to bring the left piston to TDC (**Figure 17**).

3. Install the chain on the camshaft sprockets. Insert a new master link, install the link plate (**Figure 18**), and peen the end of the pins to lock the plate in place. Vise Grips work well for this job; place a serration of the plier jaws directly on top of the pins and close the plier with pressure. The serration will expand the end of the pins.

4. Recheck the alignment of the timing marks.

CAUTION
Release the tensioner and check the alignment before installing the master link plate; if alignment changes, re-adjust the timing until it is accurate. If the timing is incorrect, the valves may contact the pistons.

CYLINDERS

Removal

1. Remove cylinder head as described earlier.
2. Lift off cylinders.

   NOTE: Do not let the chain fall into the crankcase.

Inspection

1. Measure bore with inside micrometer or cylinder gauge. Make measurements at 3 points (**Figure 19**) to check for taper. Compare results with **Table 1**.
2. Carefully clean the cylinder inside and out. Brush out all dirt from between the fins. Clean away any dirt on the cylinder sealing surfaces and remove the oil gasket on the crankcase end.

Installation

1. Install a new gasket on the crankcase end of the cylinder.
2. Install 2 guide pins in crankcase.
3. Install O-ring on cylinder skirt.
4. Rotate the crankshaft until pistons are out as far as possible.

CAUTION
While rotating the crankshaft, watch that piston skirts do not catch on the crankcase. This will crack the piston.

5. Apply a heavy coat of assembly lubricant to the piston.
6. Make sure that the ring gaps are evenly spaced 120° apart. See **Figure 20**. Compress the rings with ring compressors. Each compressor must be a 2-piece breakaway type so it can be removed.
7. Liberally oil the cylinder bore and slide the cylinder over the pistons. See **Figure 21**. Be careful not to break any cooling fins on the studs.
8. Install cylinder head as described previously.

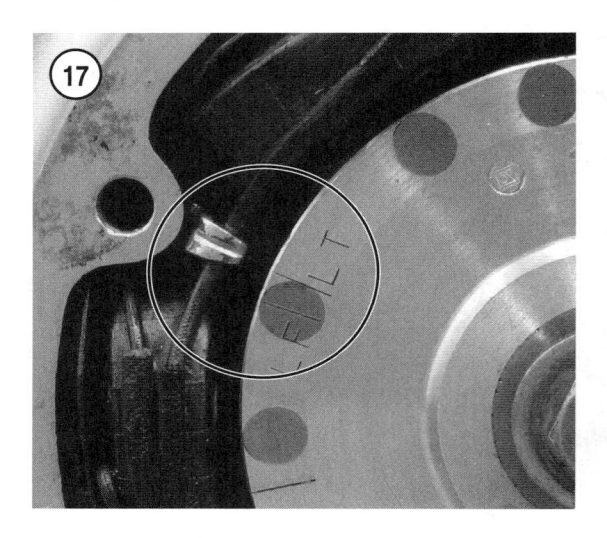

ENGINE

Table 1   CYLINDER BORE

Item	Standard value	Serviceable limit
Cylinder barrel	2.756-2.7564 in. (70.0-70.01mm)	Boring necessary when over 2.76 in. (70.11mm)
Cylinder out-of-round	Less than 0.0002 in. (0.005mm)	Boring necessary when over 0.002 in. (0.05mm)
Cylinder taper	Less than 0.002 in. (0.005mm)	Boring necessary when over 0.002 in. (0.05mm)

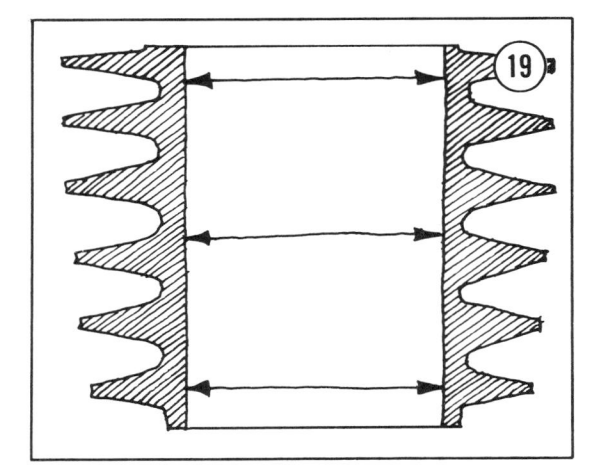

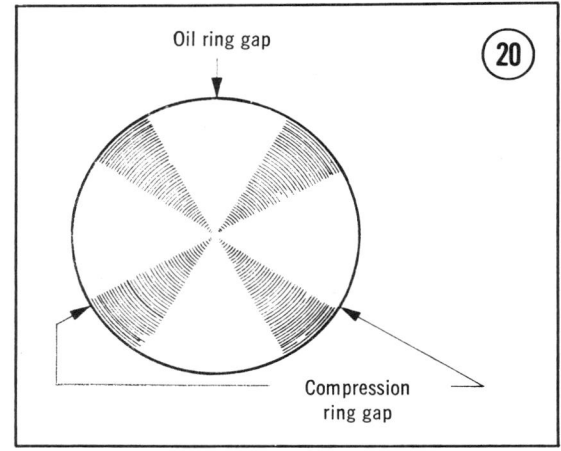

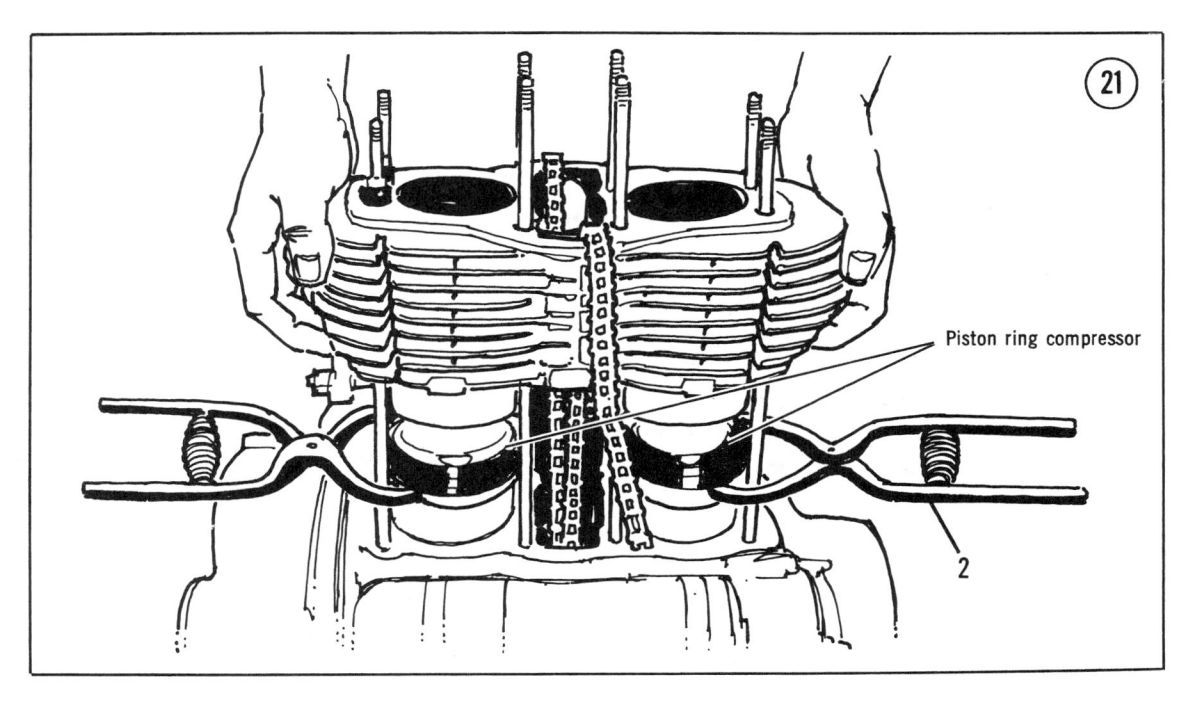

(19)

(20) Oil ring gap / Compression ring gap

(21) Piston ring compressor

PISTONS, PINS, AND RINGS

Removal

1. Remove the cylinder head and cylinders as described previously.

2. Mark the piston to make sure it is installed in the same place.

3. Rotate crankshaft until pistons are out as far as possible.

4. Before removing the piston pin, hold the connecting rod tightly and rock the piston as shown in **Figure 22**. Any rocking movement (do not confuse with sliding motion) indicates wear in the piston pin, rod bushing, piston pin bore, or more likely, a combination of all three. Mark the piston, pin, and rod for further examination.

5. Remove circlips at each end of piston pin.

6. Push piston pins out and remove pistons.

Inspection

1. Clean each piston thoroughly in solvent. Scrape carbon deposits from the top of the piston and ring grooves. Do not damage the piston.

2. Examine each ring groove for burrs, dented edges, and side wear. Pay particular attention to the top compression ring groove which usually wears more than the others.

3. Measure any parts marked in Step 4, *Piston Removal*, with a micrometer to determine which part or parts are worn. Any machinist can do this for you if you do not have micrometers.

Checking and Installing Piston Rings

1. Measure each ring for wear as shown in **Figure 23**. Insert each ring about 0.2 in. (5mm) into the bottom of the cylinder. To ensure that the ring is square in the cylinder, push it into position with the head of the piston. Gap on unworn rings should be 0.012-0.02 in. (0.30-0.50mm) for both compression rings, and 0.008-0.016 in. (0.20-0.40mm) for oil rings. The service limit for all rings is 0.031 in. (0.80mm). If the gap is smaller than specified, hold a small file in a vise, then file the ends of the ring.

2. Roll each ring around in its groove. See **Figure 24**. If any binding occurs, determine and correct the cause before proceeding.

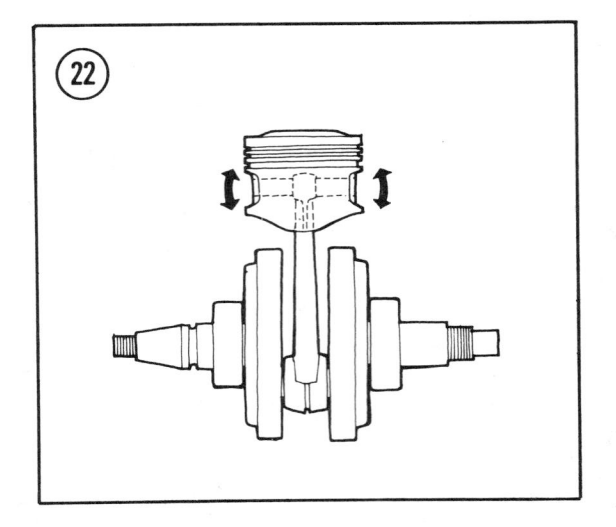

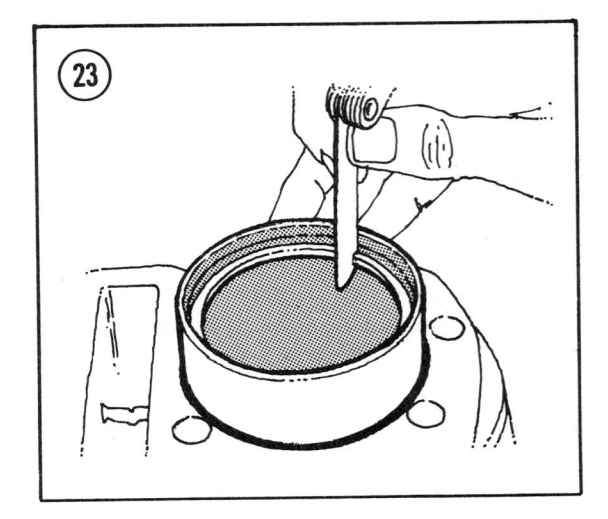

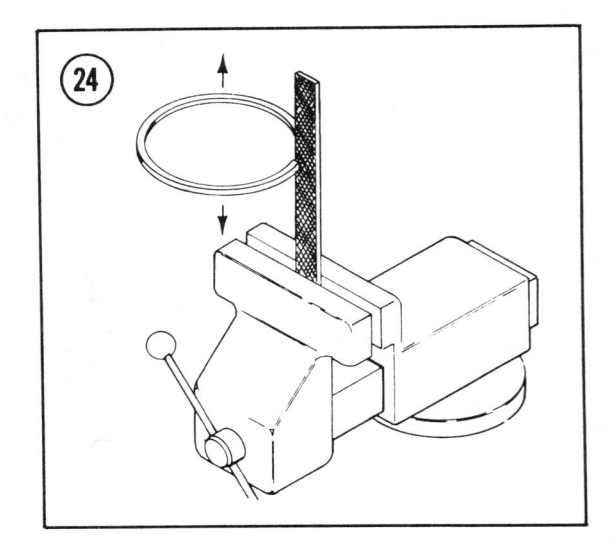

ENGINE

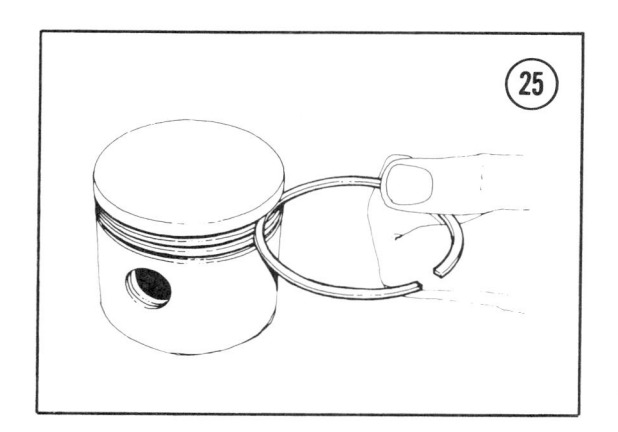

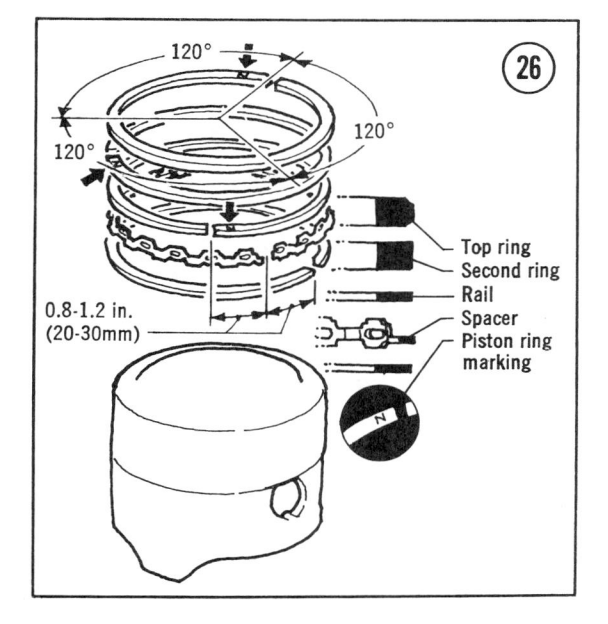

3. Measure ring side clearance in several places as shown in **Figure 25**. Standard clearance for top rings is 0.0016-0.0028 in. (0.040-0.070mm), and for second rings, 0.0008-0.0018 in. (0.020-0.045mm). The service limit for either ring is 0.006 in. (0.15mm).

4. Using a ring expander tool, carefully install the oil ring, then the second and top compression rings. Refer to **Figure 26** for details of ring installation.

Piston Installation

1. Install the rings on both pistons, following the procedures outlined above.

2. Rotate the crankshaft until connecting rods are out as far as possible.

3. Install a circlip in each piston in the piston pin hole nearest the inside of the engine.

4. Coat the connecting rod bushings, piston pins, and piston holes with assembly lubricant.

5. Place one piston over a connecting rod with the E pointing *toward the front* (exhaust) side of the engine. Insert the piston pin and push it in until it touches the circlip.

6. Insert the other circlip.

7. Repeat Steps 5 and 6 for the other piston.

8. Slide circlips around after installation so that their open ends are away from cut portion of the clip groove. See **Figure 27**.

CAMSHAFTS

Removal

1. Remove cylinder head as described earlier.

2. Remove locknuts from both sides of intake cam follower shaft.

3. Remove cylinder head side covers.

4. Remove intake camshaft.

5. Loosen locknut on right side of exhaust camshaft.

6. Remove tachometer gearbox.

7. Remove breaker point cover.

8. Remove locknut and breaker point assembly.

9. Remove spark advance unit and breaker point base.

10. Remove exhaust camshaft.

CHAPTER FOUR

Cam and Follower Inspection

1. Check the cam sprocket for wear or other damage.
2. Measure cam follower shaft journal diameter and cam follower bearing. See **Figure 28**. Compare with **Table 2**.
3. Measure cam lift as shown in **Figure 29**. Compare with **Table 2**.
4. Measure breaker point shaft runout as shown in **Figure 30**. Compare with **Table 2**.

Installation

1. Install intake cam follower on shaft. See **Figure 31** for proper alignment. Install in cylinder head.
2. Install intake camshaft in cylinder head. Oil pipe fitting must be on right side of head.
3. Install cylinder head side covers and make sure camshaft turns smoothly without binding.
4. Install locknuts and tighten temporarily.
5. Install exhaust cam follower on shaft, and install in cylinder head.
6. Install exhaust camshaft in cylinder head.
7. Assemble drive pinion and tachometer gearbox as shown in **Figures 32 and 33**.
8. Install the tachometer gearbox and secure

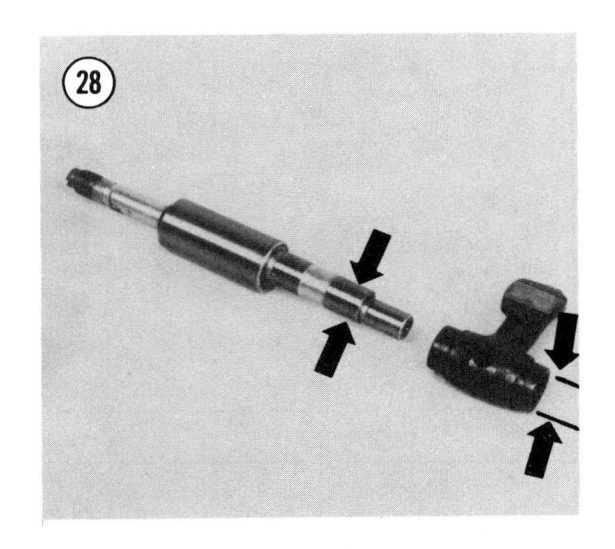

Table 2   CAM AND FOLLOWER

	Item	Standard value	Serviceable limit
1	Cam follower bearing diameter	0.4016-0.4023 in. (10.20-10.218mm)	Replace if over 0.4047 in. (10.28mm)
2	Cam follower shaft journal	0.3992-0.4009 in. (10.166-10.184mm)	Replace if under 0.3976 in. (10.10mm)
3	Camshaft journals, intake and exhaust	0.8648-0.8654 in. (21.967-21.980mm)	Replace if under 0.8622 in. (21.92mm)
4	Cam lift, intake and exhaust	0.1846-0.1853 in. (4.688-4.728mm)	Replace if under 0.1830 in. (4.65mm)
5	Breaker point shaft runout	0.0004 in. max. (0.01mm)	Replace if over 0.002 in. (0.05mm)

ENGINE

it. Make sure that the gears properly mesh with the camshaft.

9. Attach the breaker point base and check that the camshaft rotates smoothly without binding.

10. Install the spark advance unit and breaker point assembly. Tighten locknut temporarily.

11. Check camshaft end play to ensure that it is within 0.002-0.014 in. (0.05-0.35mm). Shims in 0.004 and 0.008 in. (0.1 and 0.2mm) are available for adjusting this clearance.

12. Adjust valve clearance as described in Chapter Three.

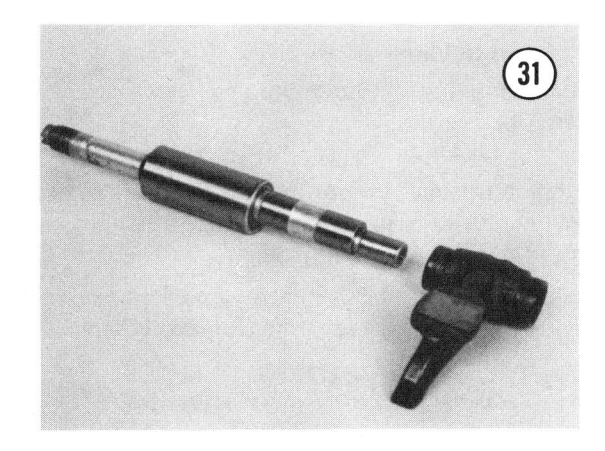

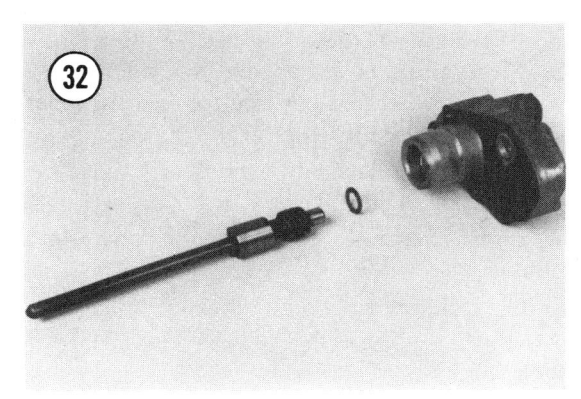

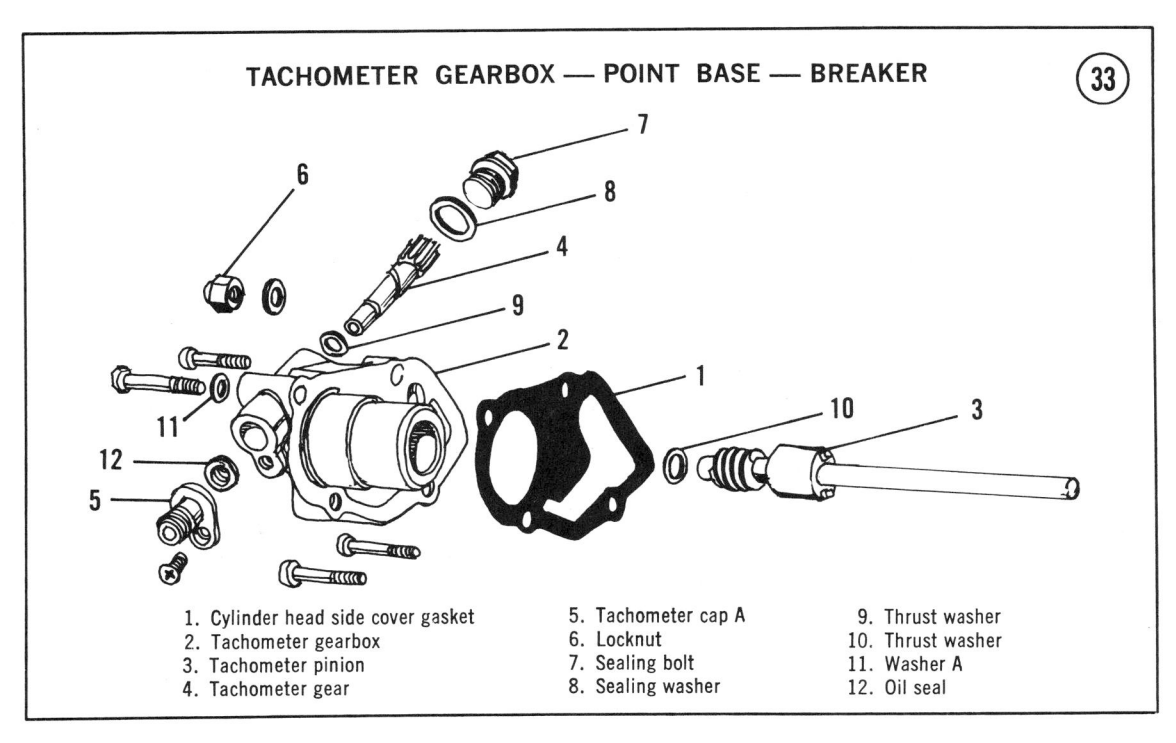

TACHOMETER GEARBOX — POINT BASE — BREAKER

1. Cylinder head side cover gasket
2. Tachometer gearbox
3. Tachometer pinion
4. Tachometer gear
5. Tachometer cap A
6. Locknut
7. Sealing bolt
8. Sealing washer
9. Thrust washer
10. Thrust washer
11. Washer A
12. Oil seal

CAM CHAIN GUIDES

Figure 34 shows the camshaft chain routing. A crankshaft sprocket drives the chain which in turn drives the 2 camshaft sprockets. A system of rollers guides the chain through the engine. An adjustable roller permits external adjustment of cam chain tension.

Chain Tensioner Removal/Installation

1. Leave adjusting bolt tight.
2. Remove 4 nuts securing tensioner to cylinder and remove tensioner.
3. Loosen locknut and remove adjusting bolt.
4. Remove roller, pushrod, and spring.
5. Clean all parts thoroughly in solvent.
6. Inspect roller and pushrod for wear or other damage. Replace if necessary.
7. Lubricate roller and pushrod with assembly lubricant or engine oil.
8. Insert pushrod, spring, and roller into housing.
9. Insert adjusting bolt and locknut.
10. Push tension roller inward and secure it with bolt.
11. Bolt tensioner to cylinder. Use a new gasket.
12. Adjust cam chain tension as described in Chapter Three.

Chain Roller Removal/Installation

Refer to **Figure 34** and **Figure 35** for this procedure.

To remove top roller (T, **Figure 34**), perform the following:

1. Remove cylinder head.
2. Remove intake camshaft.
3. Remove bolt securing roller pin.
4. Remove roller pin and roller.
5. Inspect O-ring. Replace if necessary.
6. Installation is the reverse of these steps.

To remove the side rollers (A, R, **Figure 34**), perform the following:

1. Remove cylinder head.
2. Remove bracket bolts and rollers from cylinder head.
3. Installation is the reverse of these steps. Lubricate liberally with assembly lubricant or engine oil.

To remove the bottom roller (B, **Figure 34**), perform the following:

1. Remove cylinder head and cylinder.
2. Remove guide roller pin and roller from crankcase.
3. Installation is the reverse of these steps.

VALVES AND VALVE GEAR

Torsion Bar Removal

Refer to **Figure 36**.

1. Remove cam follower and camshaft as described earlier.
2. Unscrew bolt securing torsion bar. Put tension on torsion bar arm in direction marked by arrow on end of torsion bar. Remove bolt.
3. Pull out torsion bar assembly.
4. Repeat Steps 1-3 for each valve. Keep valve parts for each valve separate from the others.

> **CAUTION**
> *Handle torsion bars extremely carefully. Even small nicks or scratches can cause failure.*

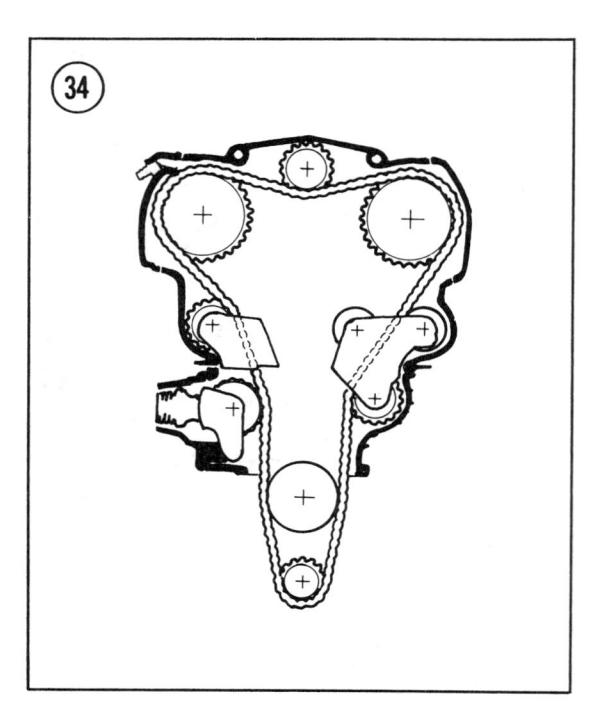

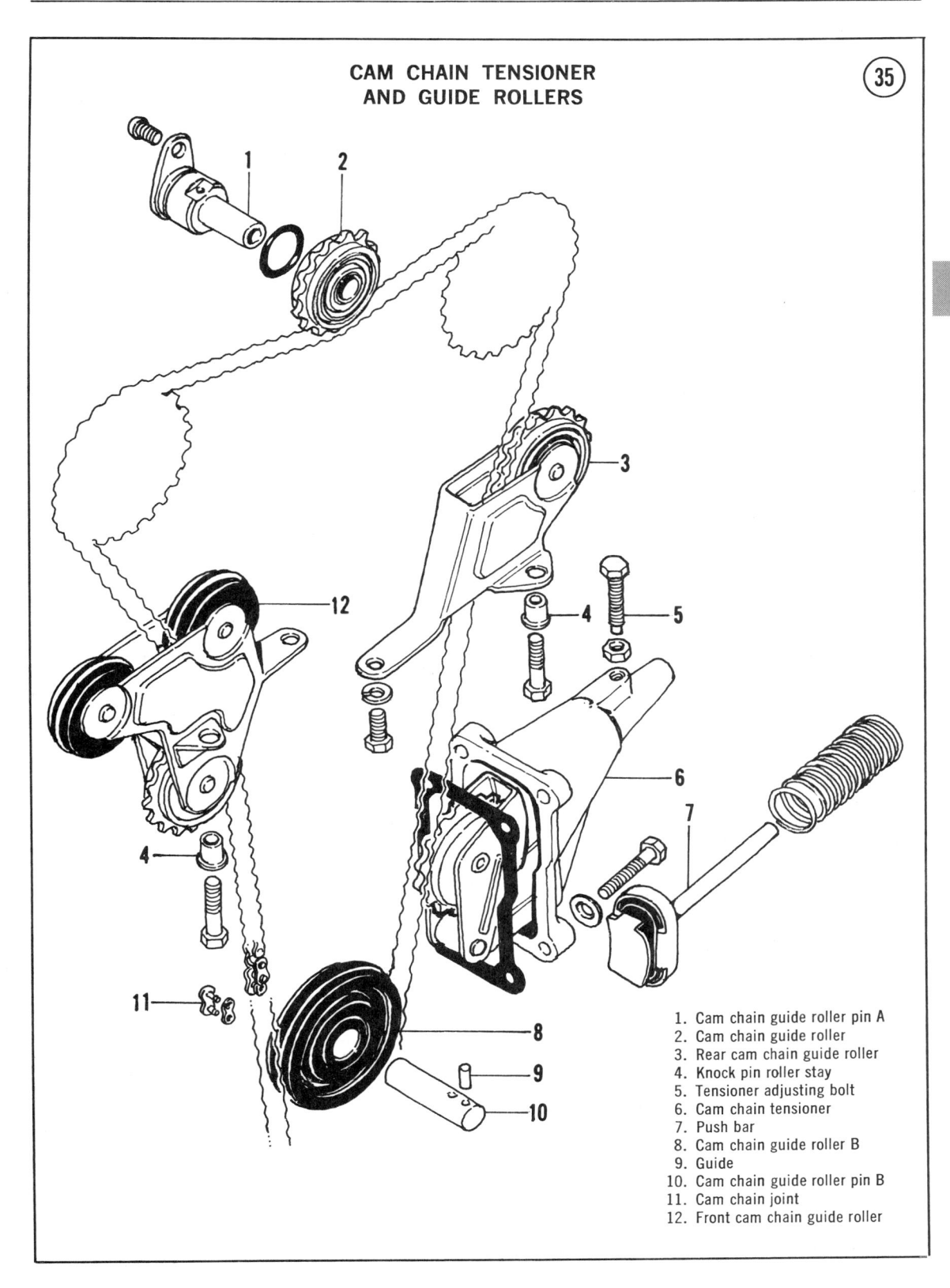

ENGINE

CAM CHAIN TENSIONER AND GUIDE ROLLERS

(35)

1. Cam chain guide roller pin A
2. Cam chain guide roller
3. Rear cam chain guide roller
4. Knock pin roller stay
5. Tensioner adjusting bolt
6. Cam chain tensioner
7. Push bar
8. Cam chain guide roller B
9. Guide
10. Cam chain guide roller pin B
11. Cam chain joint
12. Front cam chain guide roller

Torsion Bar Installation

1. Check torsion bars carefully for nicks, scratches, or signs of rust. Even minor damage can cause failure.
2. Insert outer arm and torsion bar into cylinder head. Fit outer arm onto torsion bar shaft. See **Figure 37**.

> Note: *Torsion bars are stamped either "A" or "B" (**Figure 38**) and are not interchangeable. See **Figure 39** for correct locations.*

3. Insert dowel pin for torsion bar holder.
4. Secure holder with bolt and tighten to 3.7-4.6 ft.-lb. (1.7-2.1 mkg).

Valve Removal/Installation

Refer to **Figure 40**.
1. Remove torsion bar assemblies as described earlier.
2. Remove valve retainer and cotter.
3. Remove 6 mm valve guide stop bolt.
4. Remove stop.
5. Remove valve guide seal cap.
6. Make sure there are no burrs on end of valve stem which could damage valve guide.
7. Remove valve.
8. Repeat Steps 2-7 for each valve. Keep valves in a holder so that they can be returned to the same location.
9. Inspect valves as described later.
10. Installation is the reverse of these steps. Return valves to same location.

> Note: *Early and late valves are different. When replacing valves in an engine with a high-lift cam, it is necessary to install early-type valves.*

Valve Inspection

1. Clean valves with a wire brush and solvent. Discard burned, warped, or cracked valves. Slightly damaged valves may be refaced.
2. Measure the valve stems for wear.
3. Remove all carbon and varnish from valve guides with a stiff spiral wire brush.
4. Insert the valves in the corresponding valve guides. Hold the valve just slightly off its seat

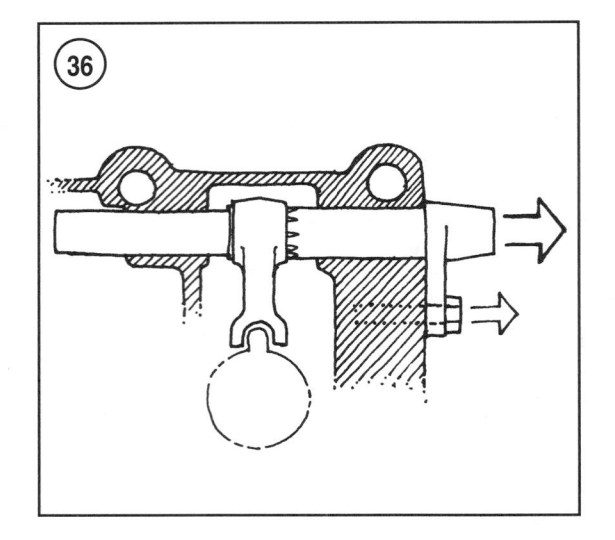

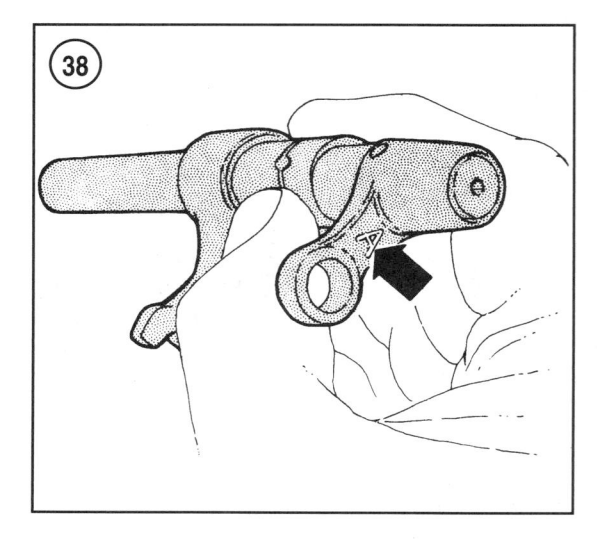

ENGINE

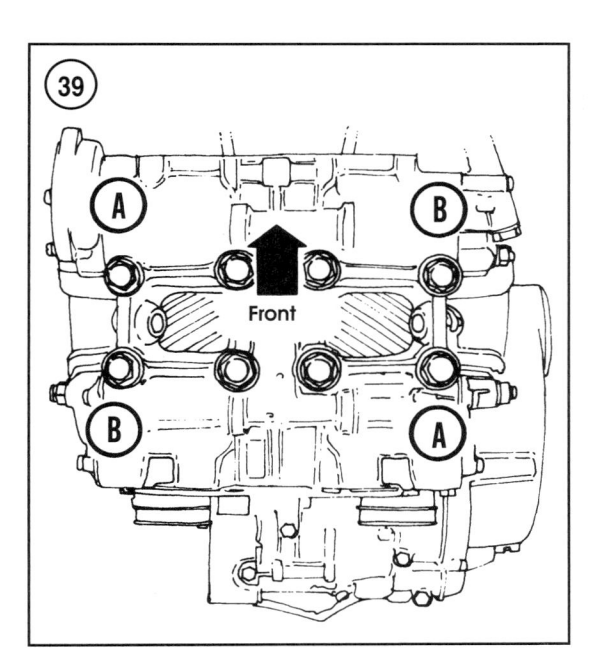

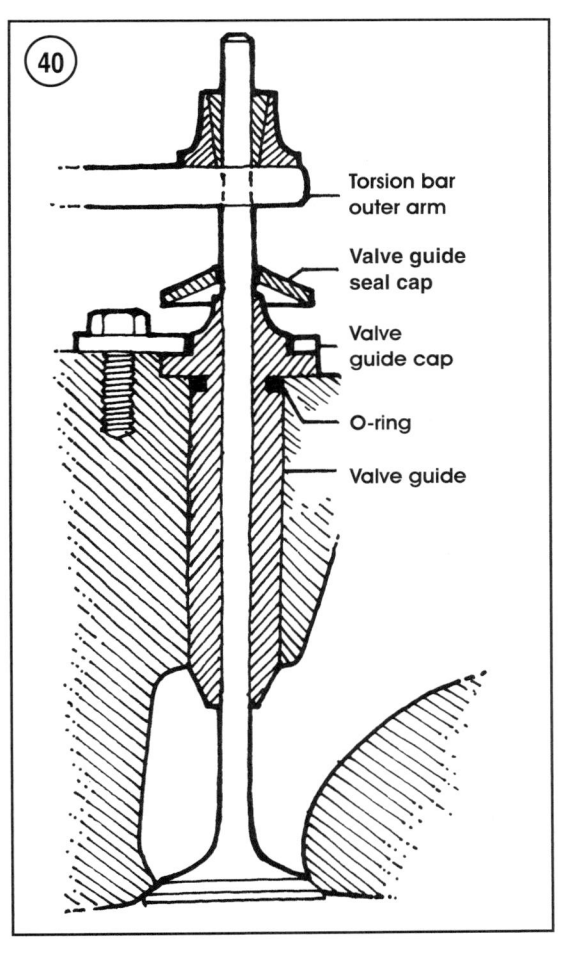

and rock it sideways. If it rocks more than slightly, the guide is worn and should be replaced. See *Valve Guide Replacement*.

5. Inspect valve seats. They must be reconditioned if worn or burned. This job should be performed by a dealer, machine shop, or small engine specialist.

Valve Guide Replacement

Valve guides should be replaced by your dealer or other experienced machine shop. Make sure they use slightly undersize guides and ream them to fit the valve stems. Also make sure they use a new O-ring under the guide flanges.

OIL FILTER

The oil filter is a centrifugal type which requires cleaning at least every 6,000 miles—more often in dusty areas.

1. Remove oil filter cover on right crankcase cover.
2. Remove snap ring (or bolt on 4-speed models) securing oil filter cap.
3. Screw 8 mm (6 mm bolt on CB500T) bolt into oil filter cap and pull cap out. See **Figure 41**.
4. Straighten tabs on lockwasher.
5. Remove locknut with a special T-handle wrench. See **Figure 42**.
6. Remove rotor.
7. Clean all parts thoroughly in solvent.
8. Check each part for wear or other damage.
9. Lubricate parts thoroughly in engine oil.

10. Installation is the reverse of these steps. Orient lockwasher as shown in **Figure 43**.

OIL PUMP

Removal/Installation

The oil pump and clutch outer hub must be removed as a unit. See *Clutch Removal/Installation* in Chapter Five.

Disassembly/Assembly

Figures 44 and 45 show exploded views of the early and late model oil pumps. After disassembly, clean all parts in solvent and inspect each for wear or damage. Lubricate all parts thoroughly during assembly.

CRANKCASE SIDE COVERS

Removal/Installation (Right Side)

1. Drain engine oil.
2. Remove kickstarter lever.
3. Remove right exhaust system on CB models.
4. Remove mounting screws and remove cover.
5. Remove oil fitler cover.
6. Clean all parts thoroughtly in solvent.
7. Check the mating surfaces for nicks and scratches that can cause leaks.
8. Installation is the reverse of these steps. be sure to match up puch marks on kickstarter lever and shaft. Tighten case screws uniformly.

Removal/Installation (Left Side)

There are 2 covers on the left side.
1. Remove the cover screws on the forward crankcase cover.
2. Disconnect alternator wires and remove cover with alternator stator.
3. Remove the stator from the cover. See Chapter Seven.

CAUTION
Do not clean cover in solvent with stator installed.

4. Remove gearshift lever.
5. Remove cover screws on aft cover.
6. Remove cover.

7. Clean both covers in solvent.
8. Check the mating surfaces for nicks and scratches that can cause oil leaks.
9. Installation is the reverse of these steps. Tighten case screws uniformly.

CRANKCASE

Disassembly/Assembly

Refer to **Figures 46, 47, and 48**.
1. Remove left crankcase cover.
2. Remove alternator, starter, and the starter drive gears.
3. Remove oil filter.
4. Remove clutch.
5. Remove gearshift spindle. Do not damage drum stop cam plate.
6. Remove 4 bolts from upper half and 11 bolts from lower half.
7. Separate upper and lower halves.
8. Inspect case halves as described later.
9. Assembly is the reverse of these steps. Make sure that sealing surfaces are completely clean and undamaged. Apply gasket cement to sealing surface of lower crankcase half. Do not get any cement on dowel pins or holes.

Inspection

1. Clean case halves thoroughly in solvent.
2. Check sealing surfaces for scratches, nicks, and other damage. If blemishes are very minor, dress them carefully with an oilstone.

CRANKSHAFT

Removal

1. Split crankcase halves as described earlier.
2. Remove center bearing bolts and remove crankshaft.

Inspection

Compare all measurements with **Table 3**.
1. Clean crankshaft in solvent.
2. Check crankshaft runout. See **Figure 49**.
3. Check main bearing clearance as shown in **Figure 50**.

ENGINE

⸮42

Table 3 CRANKSHAFT MEASUREMENT

	Item		Standard value	Serviceable limit
1	Crankshaft runout	A, B, C, and D	0.002 in. max. (0.05mm)	Replace if over 0.008 in. (0.2mm)
		E, F, and G	0.001 in. max. (0.02mm)	Replace if over 0.004 in. (0.1mm)
2	Main bearing radial clearance		0.0002-0.0005 in. (0.006-0.014mm)	Replace if over 0.001 in. (0.03mm)
3	Connecting rod small end		0.6699-0.676 in. (17.016-17.034mm)	Replace if over 0.6721 in. (17.07mm)
4	Connecting rod large end radial clearance		0-0.0003 in. (0-0.008mm)	Replace if over 0.0020 in. (0.05mm)
5	Connecting rod large end side clearance		0.0028-0.0130 in. (0.07-0.33mm)	Replace if over 0.0197 in. (0.5mm)
6	Connecting rod large end tilt		0.008-0.04 in. (0.2-1.0mm)	Replace if over 0.1181 in. (3.0mm)

46　　　　　　　　　　　　　　　　　　　　　　　　　　　　　　　　　　　　　CHAPTER FOUR

43

1. 16 mm locknut　　2. Oil filter rotor　　3. Tongued washer

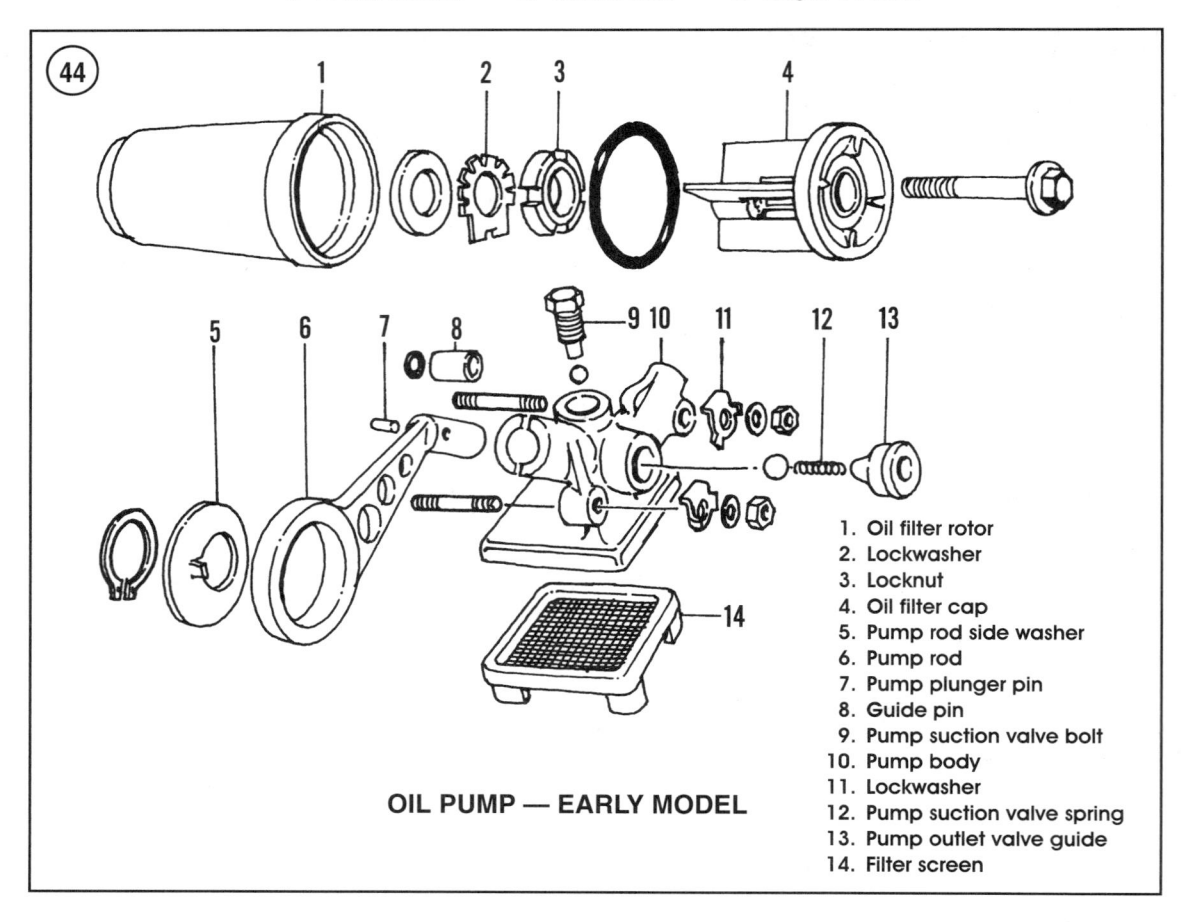

44

OIL PUMP — EARLY MODEL

1. Oil filter rotor
2. Lockwasher
3. Locknut
4. Oil filter cap
5. Pump rod side washer
6. Pump rod
7. Pump plunger pin
8. Guide pin
9. Pump suction valve bolt
10. Pump body
11. Lockwasher
12. Pump suction valve spring
13. Pump outlet valve guide
14. Filter screen

ENGINE

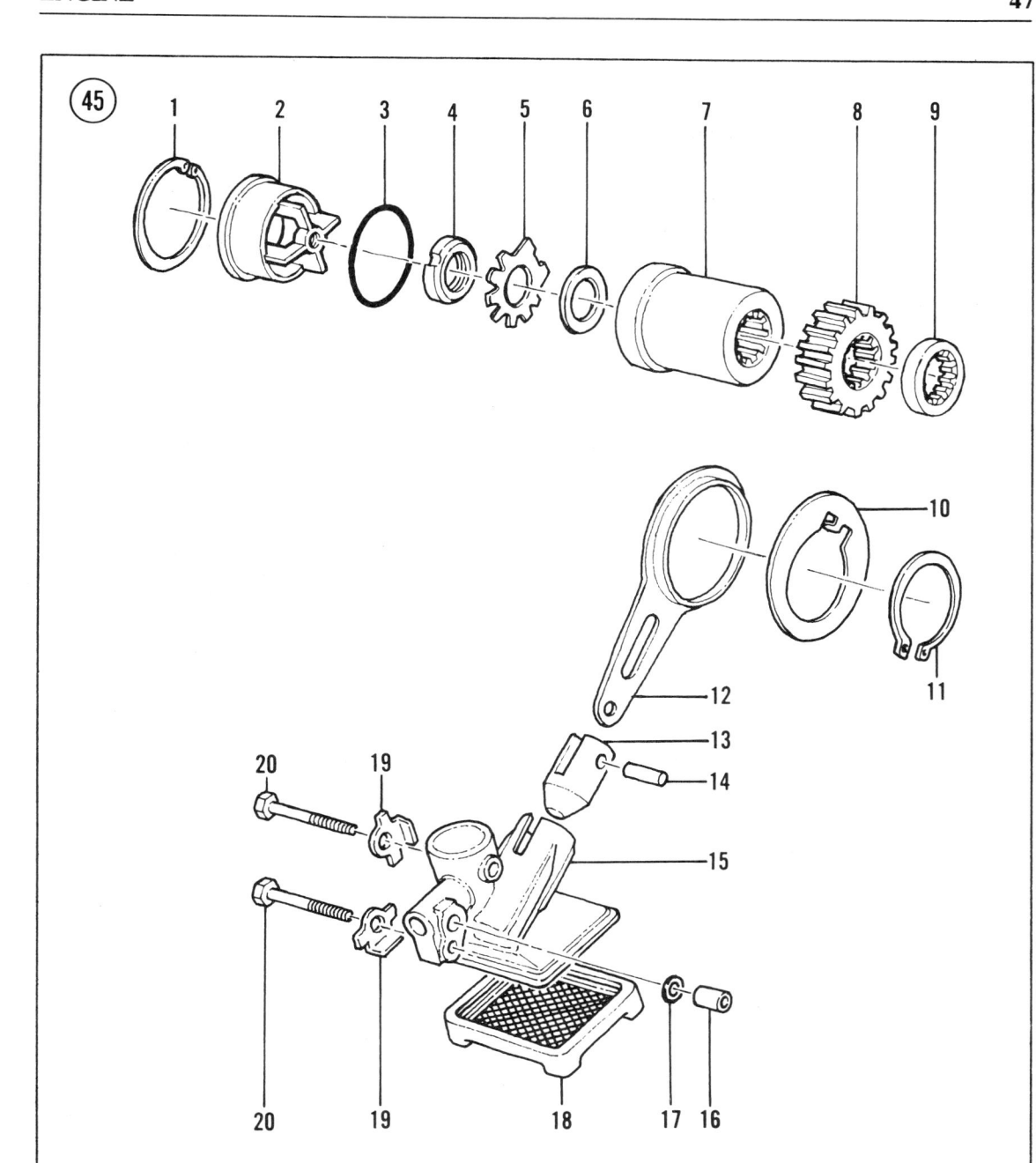

OIL PUMP — LATE MODEL

1. Internal circlip
2. Oil filter cap
3. O-ring
4. Locknut
5. Lockwasher
6. Filter rotor lockwasher
7. Filter rotor
8. Primary drive gear
9. Thrust washer A
10. Pump rod side washer
11. External circlip
12. Oil pump rod
13. Oil pump plunger
14. Plunger pin
15. Oil pump
16. Dowel pin A
17. O-ring
18. Oil filter screen
19. Lockwasher
20. Hex bolt

48　　　　　　　　　　　　　　　　　　　　　　　　　　　　　　　　CHAPTER FOUR

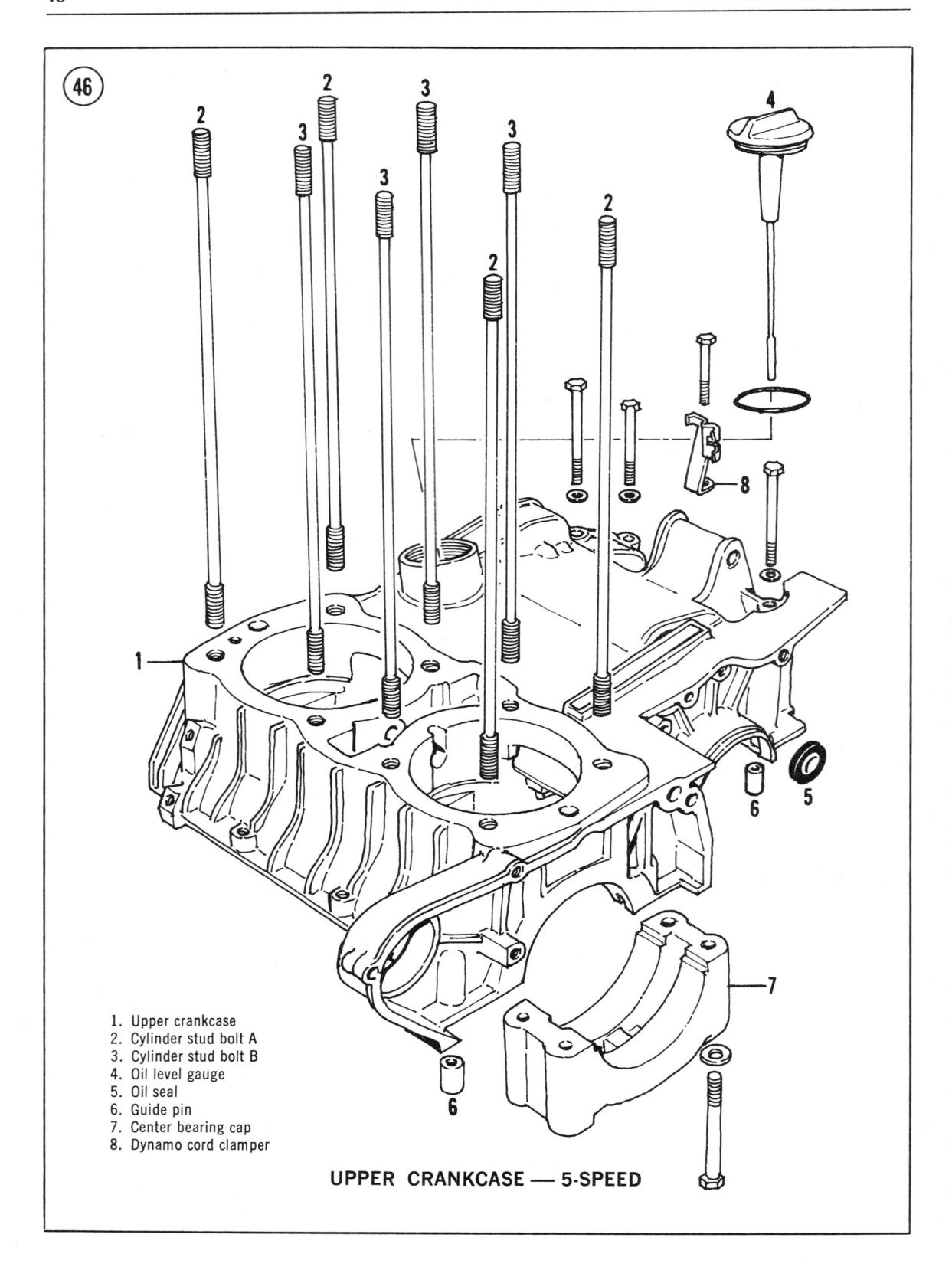

⑭

1. Upper crankcase
2. Cylinder stud bolt A
3. Cylinder stud bolt B
4. Oil level gauge
5. Oil seal
6. Guide pin
7. Center bearing cap
8. Dynamo cord clamper

UPPER CRANKCASE — 5-SPEED

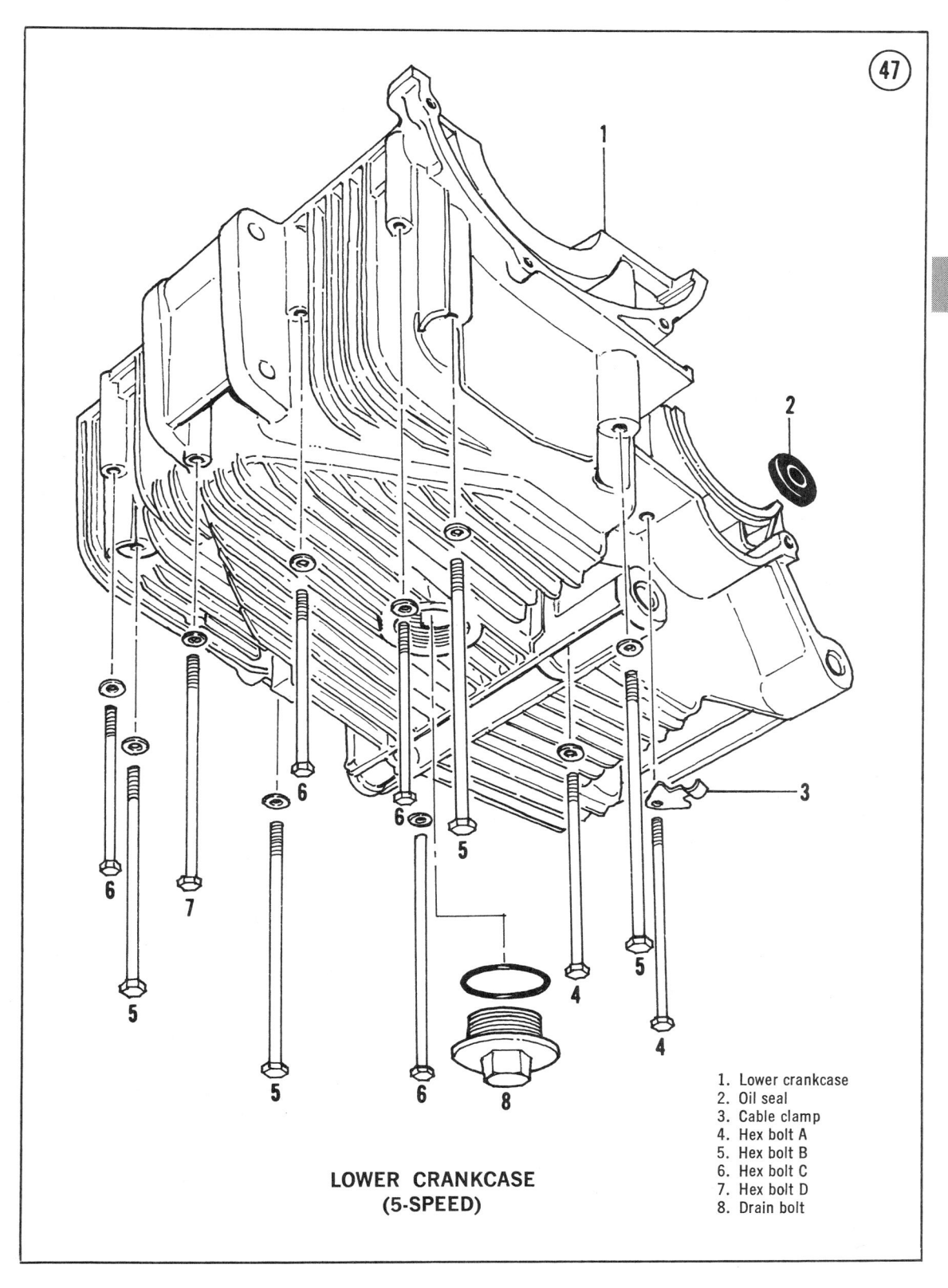

ENGINE

**LOWER CRANKCASE
(5-SPEED)**

1. Lower crankcase
2. Oil seal
3. Cable clamp
4. Hex bolt A
5. Hex bolt B
6. Hex bolt C
7. Hex bolt D
8. Drain bolt

50　　　　　　　　　　　　　　　　　　　　　　　　　　　　　　　CHAPTER FOUR

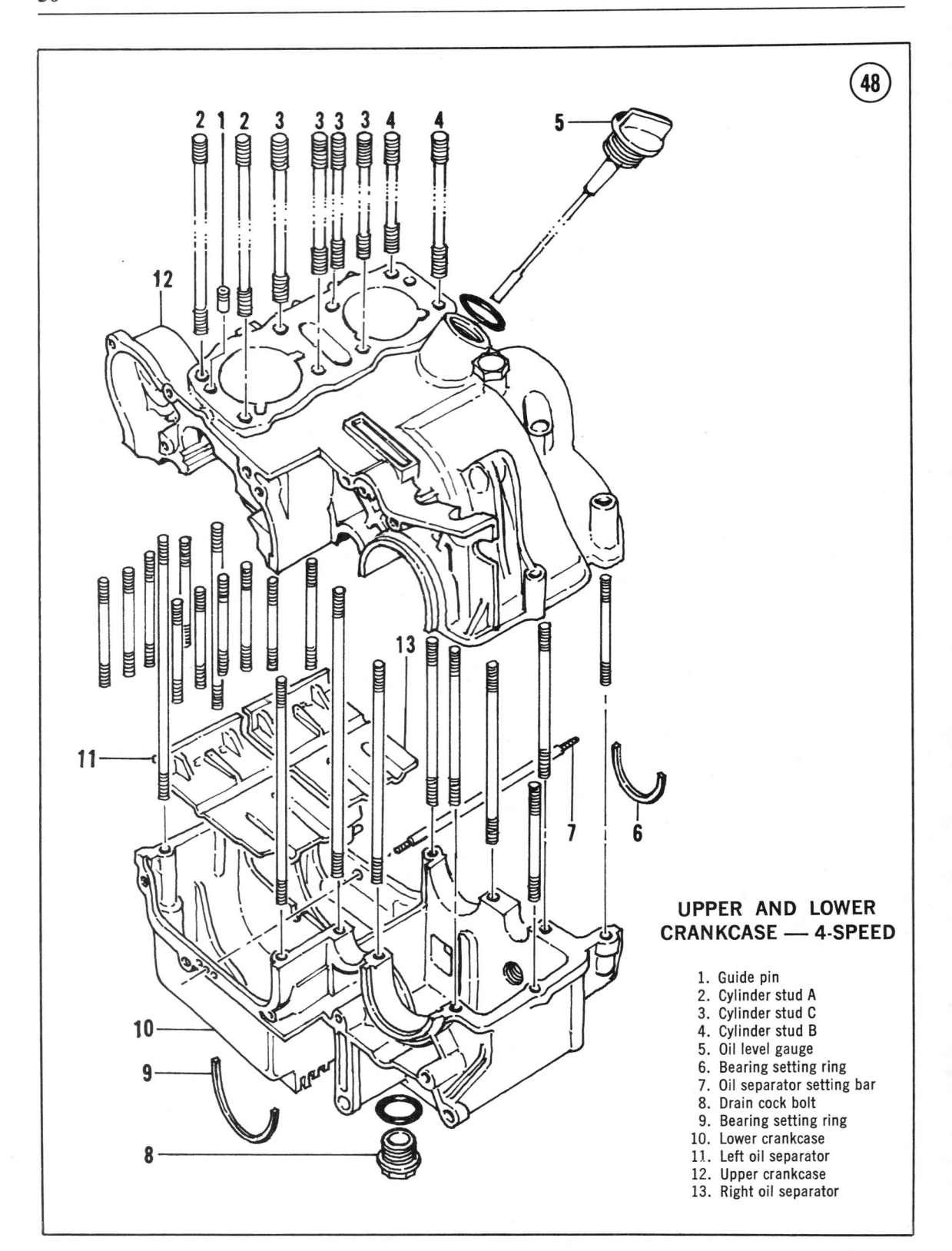

UPPER AND LOWER CRANKCASE — 4-SPEED

1. Guide pin
2. Cylinder stud A
3. Cylinder stud C
4. Cylinder stud B
5. Oil level gauge
6. Bearing setting ring
7. Oil separator setting bar
8. Drain cock bolt
9. Bearing setting ring
10. Lower crankcase
11. Left oil separator
12. Upper crankcase
13. Right oil separator

ENGINE 51

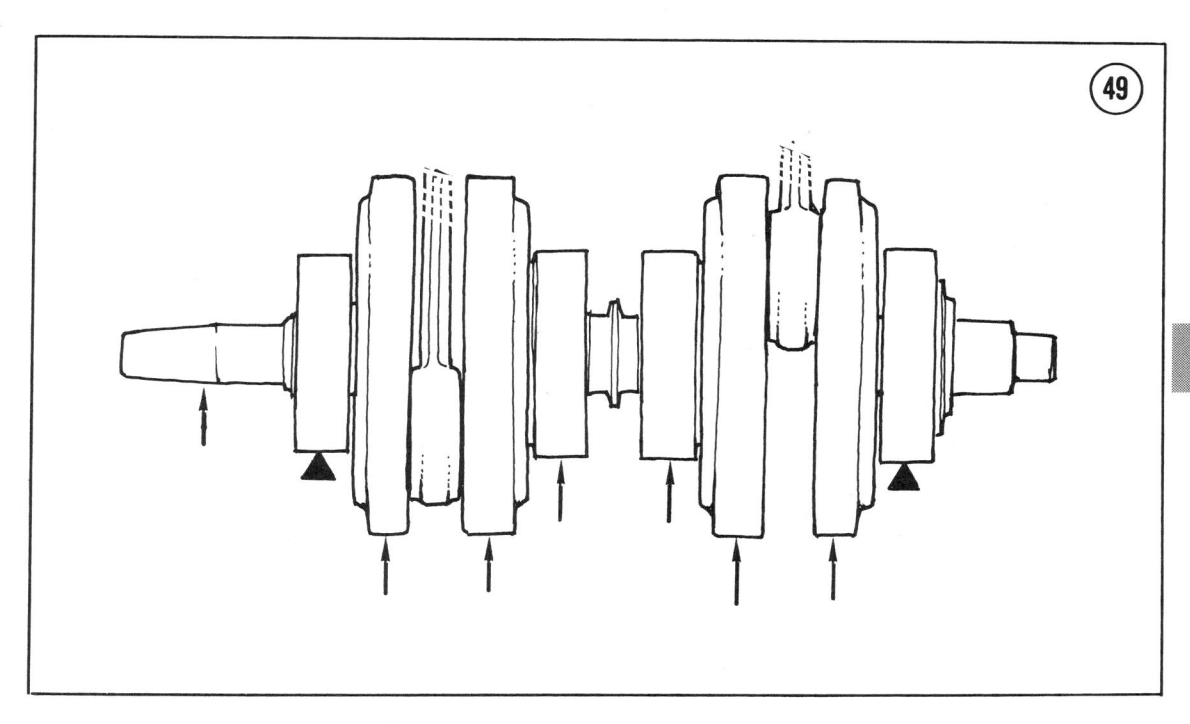

Figure 51

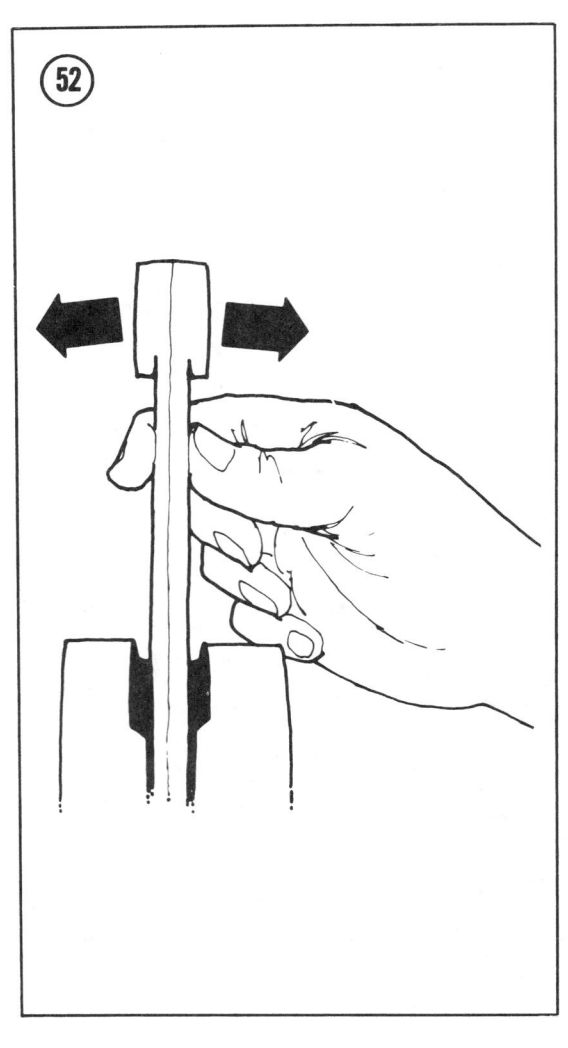

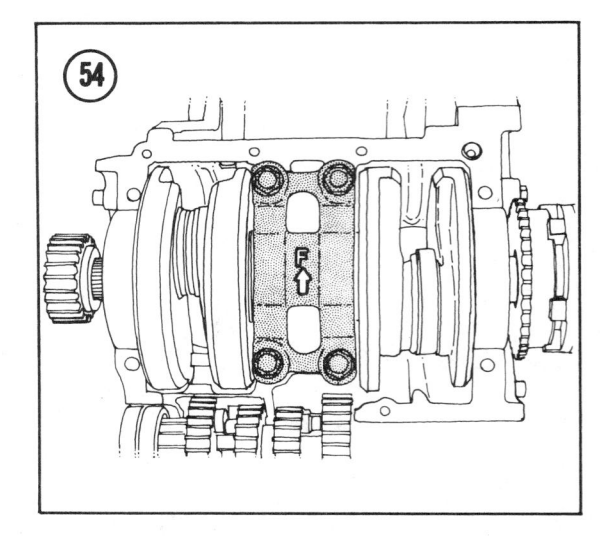

Figure 52

Figure 53

Figure 54

4. Check connecting rod clearance as shown in **Figure 51**.

5. Check connecting rod side clearance with a feeler gauge.

6. Check the connecting rod tilt. Refer to **Figure 52**.

Installation

1. Set crankshaft in place.

2. Install bearing caps. Note the location of dowel pins. Refer to **Figure 53**. Make certain the center bearing cap arrow points to the front of the engine (**Figure 54**).

3. Torque caps to 12-15 ft.-lb.

CHAPTER FIVE

CLUTCH AND TRANSMISSION

CLUTCH

Refer to **Figure 1** (450) **or 2** (500). When the clutch engages (lever released), the clutch springs force the clutch discs and plates together. This locks the clutch pressure plate to the center hub, permitting power transfer from the crankshaft to the transmission.

When the lever is pulled in, the clutch lifter thread rotates and moves inward. This pushes the thread against the pressure plate and releases the clutch.

Table 1 provides clutch specifications.

Removal/Installation

The clutch is mounted under the right crankcase cover. Refer either to **Figure 1 or 2**.

1. Remove the right crankcase cover.
2. Remove the oil filter as described in Chapter Four.
3. Remove bolts securing clutch pressure plate. Loosen diagonally opposite bolts, a turn at a time, until spring pressure is relieved to prevent warping the plate.
4. Remove pressure plate, friction discs, and clutch plates. See **Figure 3** (450) **or 4** (500).
5. Remove circlip and pull clutch center hub off. See **Figure 5** (450) **or 6** (500).
6. Straighten the lockwashers on the oil pump bolts and remove them. Remove clutch outer hub and oil pump as a unit. Refer to **Figure 7**.
7. Remove circlip securing oil pump rod and eccentric to clutch housing.
8. Remove pump rod and eccentric from clutch housing. Leave pump rod connected to pump.
9. Installation is the reverse of these steps.
10. Adjust clutch, described in Chapter Three.

Inspection

1. Clean clutch parts in a petroleum-based solvent such as kerosene.
2. Inspect gear teeth on housing for burrs, nicks, or other damage. Minor damage can be dressed up with an oilstone. Replace housing if damage is more extensive.
3. Measure free length of each clutch spring as shown in **Figure 8**. Compare with **Table 1**. Replace springs that are too short.
4. Measure thickness of each friction disc at several places around disc as shown in **Figure 9**. Compare with **Table 1**. Replace any that are too thin or worn unevenly.
5. Measure backlash (B) between friction discs and clutch outer housing with a feeler gauge. See **Figure 10**. Compare to **Table 1**. Replace discs if gap is incorrect.

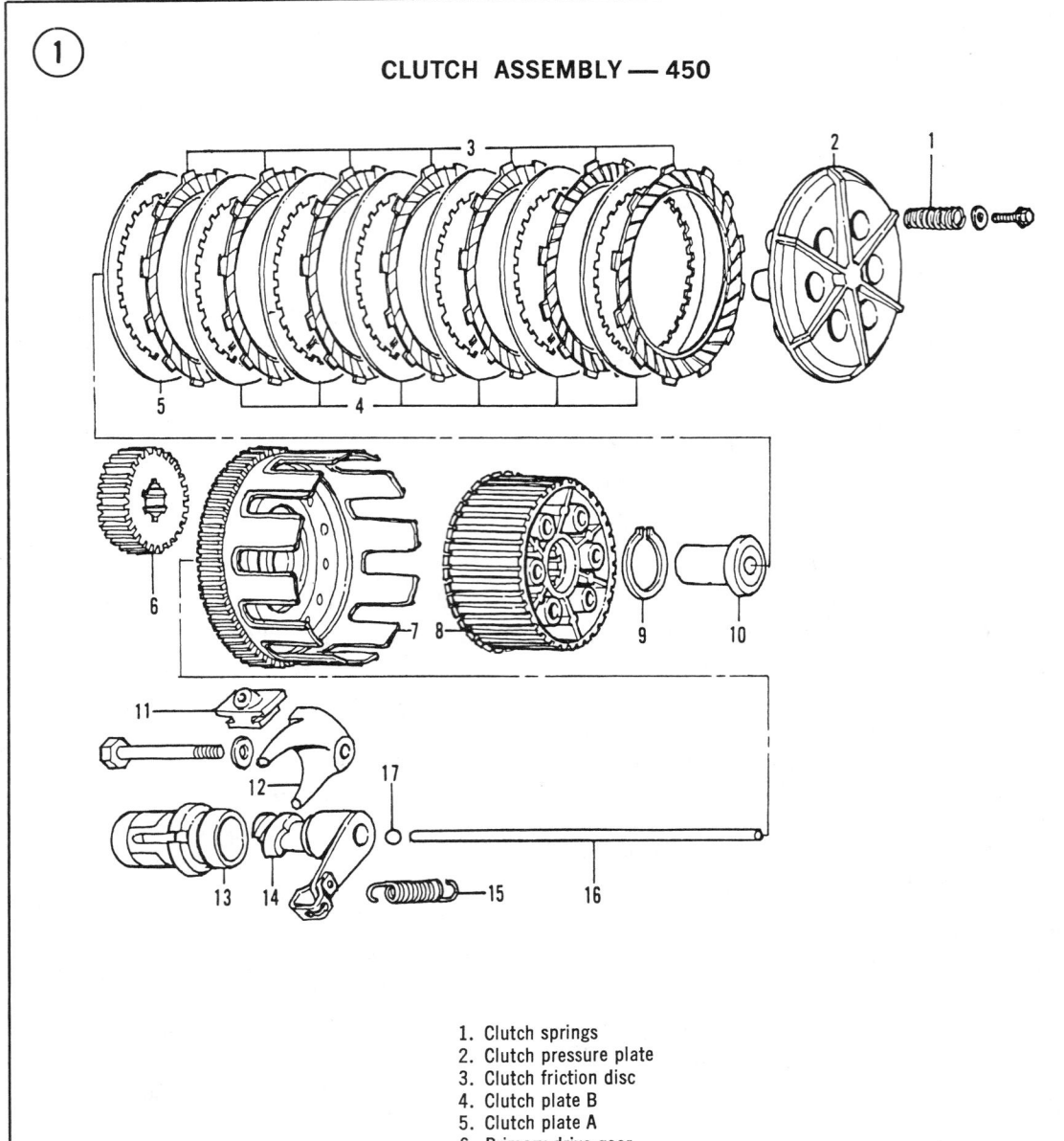

CHAPTER FIVE

① **CLUTCH ASSEMBLY — 450**

1. Clutch springs
2. Clutch pressure plate
3. Clutch friction disc
4. Clutch plate B
5. Clutch plate A
6. Primary drive gear
7. Clutch outer body
8. Clutch center
9. Circlip
10. Clutch throwout
11. Clutch cable seal
12. Clutch adjuster stop
13. Clutch adjuster
14. Clutch lifter
15. Clutch lever spring
16. Clutch lifter rod
17. Steel ball

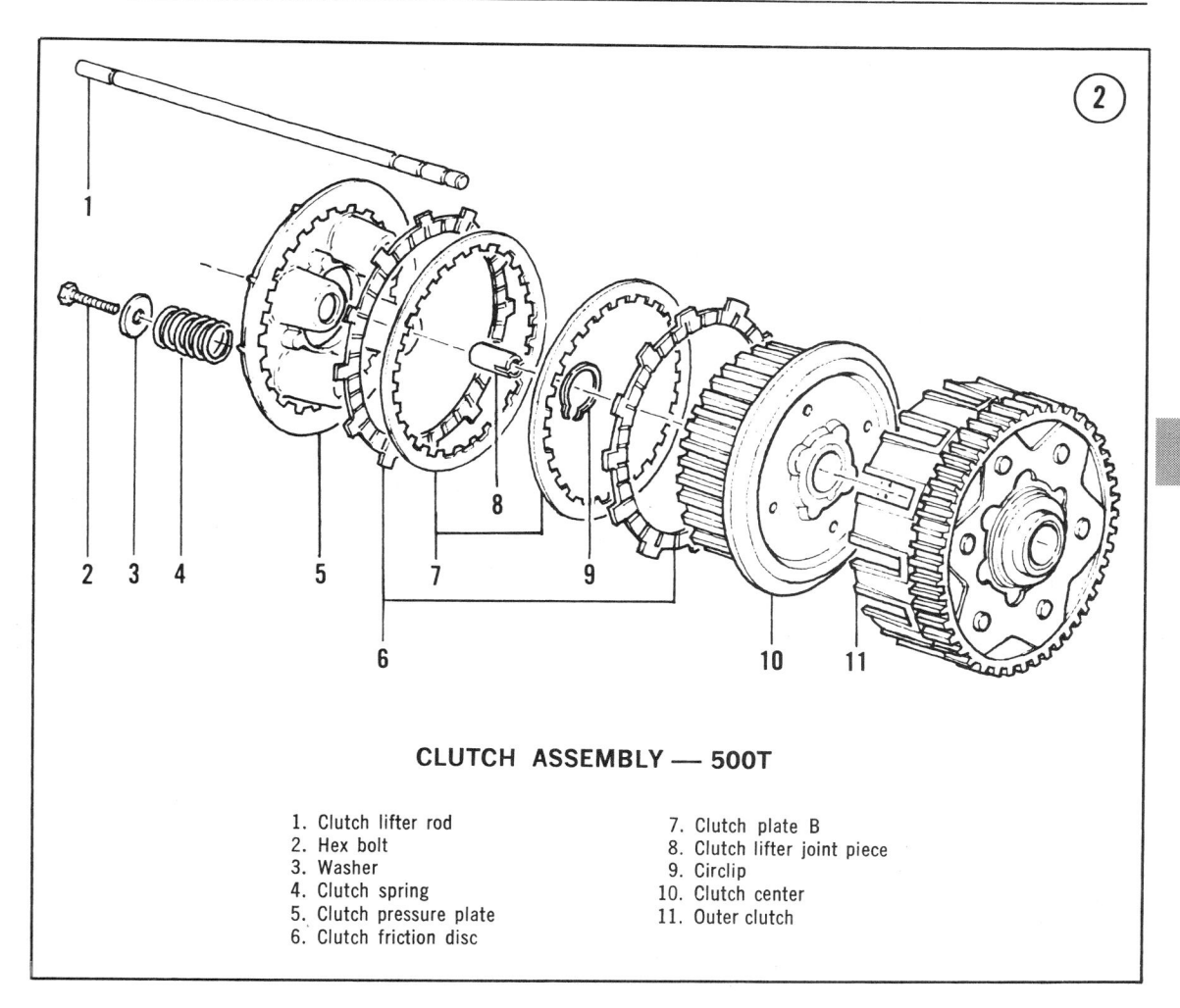

CLUTCH AND TRANSMISSION

55

CLUTCH ASSEMBLY — 500T

1. Clutch lifter rod
2. Hex bolt
3. Washer
4. Clutch spring
5. Clutch pressure plate
6. Clutch friction disc
7. Clutch plate B
8. Clutch lifter joint piece
9. Circlip
10. Clutch center
11. Outer clutch

CHAPTER FIVE

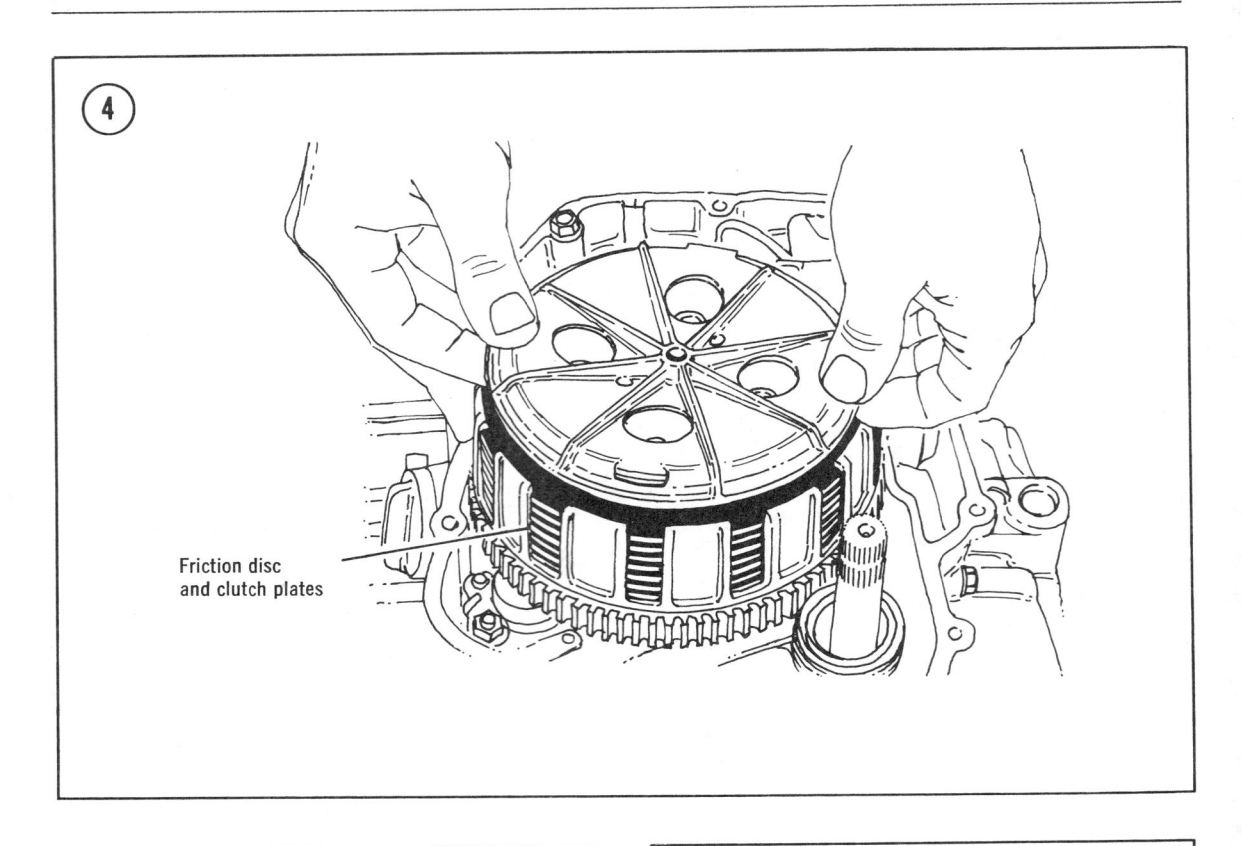

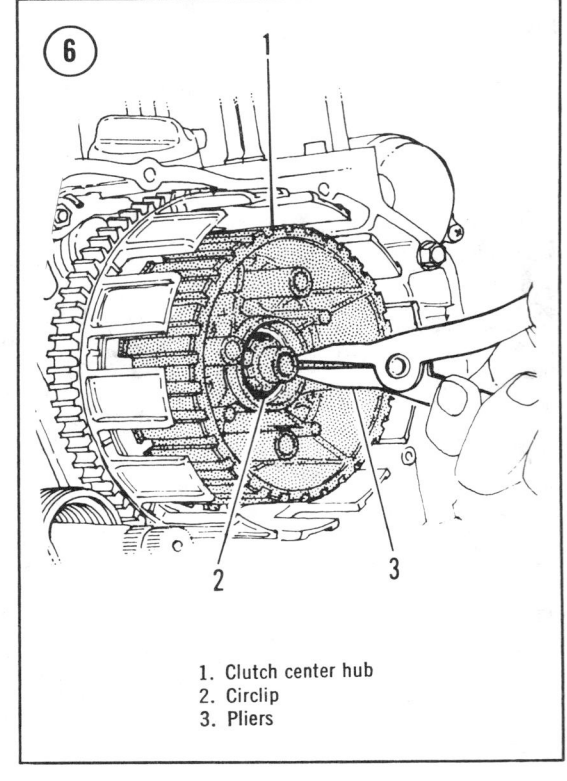

④

Friction disc
and clutch plates

⑤

⑥

1. Clutch center hub
2. Circlip
3. Pliers

CLUTCH AND TRANSMISSION

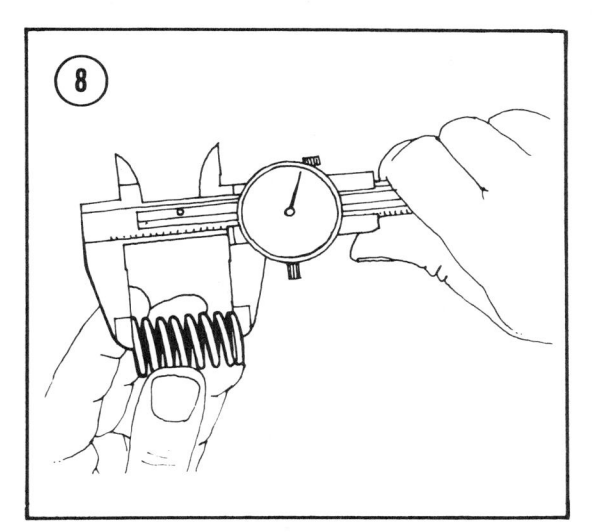

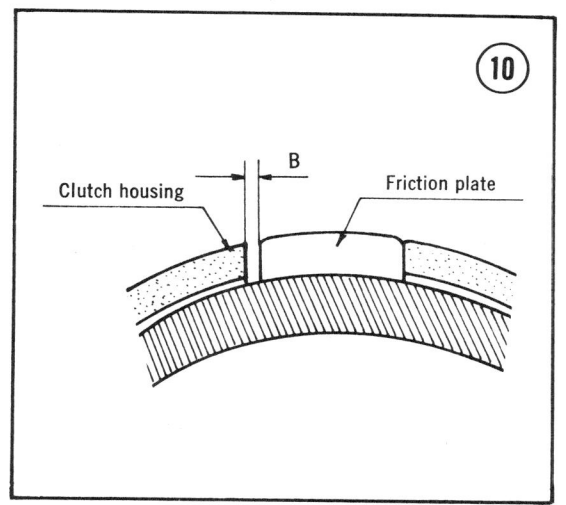

Table 1   CLUTCH SPECIFICATIONS

	New	**Wear Limit**
Friction disc thickness	0.135-0.141 in. (3.42-3.58mm)	0.122 in. (3.1mm)
Disc-to-housing backlash ①	0.012 in. (0.3mm)	0.032 in. (0.8mm)
Clutch plate distortion	0.006 in. (0.15mm)	0.014 in. (0.35mm)

Clutch spring
  Free length
  With load ①
	1.575 in. (40.1mm)
	1.047 in. (26.6mm) @
	71.6-77.2 pounds
	(31.6-34.7 kg)
		1.55 in. (39.4mm)

Clutch center hub-to-main shaft clearance ①	0.008-0.0024 in. (0.020-0.062mm)	0.0047 in. (0.12mm)

① Not specified for CB500T

6. Check all other parts for signs of wear or other damage. Replace suspect parts.

TRANSMISSION

The following description is for the 5-speed transmission. Except for the extra gear, the 4-speed transmission is similar. Main shaft gears are prefaced with the initial "M" and countershaft gears are prefaced with a "C".

Figure 11 shows the transmission in neutral. Fixed main shaft low gear (M1) meshes with free-rotating countershaft low gear (C1), free-rotating main shaft top gear (M5) meshes with sliding countershaft top gear (C5), sliding main shaft second and third gears (M2 and M3) mesh with the free-rotating countershaft second and third gears (C2 and C3), and the free-rotating main shaft fourth gear (M4) meshes with the splined countershaft fourth gear (C4). There is no power transfer from input to output.

Figure 12 shows the transmission in first gear. Power from the main shaft low gear (M1) is transmitted to the free-rotating countershaft low gear (C1). Splined countershaft fourth gear (C4) is engaged to the countershaft low gear through a dog to drive the countershaft and the drive sprocket mounted on the countershaft end.

Figure 13 shows second gear operation. The main shaft second gear (M2) transmits power to the free-rotating countershaft second gear (C2), which in turn transmits power to the countershaft top gear (C5) through a dog.

Figure 14 shows third gear operation. Power from the main shaft third gear (M3) is transmitted to free-rotating countershaft third gear (C3). Splined countershaft fourth gear (C4) is engaged to the countershaft third gear through a dog and drives the countershaft.

Figure 15 shows fourth gear operation. Free-rotating main shaft fourth gear (M4) is engaged to the main shaft second and third gears (M2 and M3) by a dog. Power then flows from the main shaft fourth gear (M4) to the countershaft fourth gear (C4) and to the countershaft.

Figure 16 shows fifth or top gear operation. Free-rotating fifth gear on the main shaft is engaged to the main shaft second and third gears (M2 and M3) by a dog and transmits power to

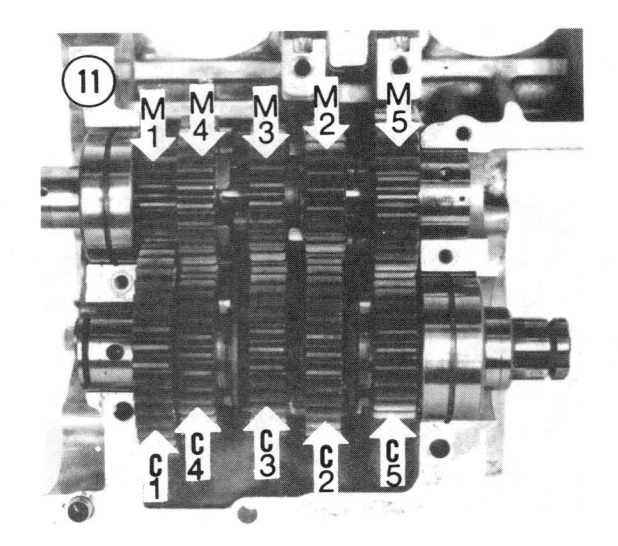

CLUTCH AND TRANSMISSION

the countershaft fifth gear (C5) and to the countershaft.

TRANSMISSION (4-SPEED)

Early CB450's have a 4-speed transmission.

Disassembly

Refer to **Figures 17 and 18**.

1. Remove engine as described in Chapter Four.
2. Remove left and right crankcase covers as described in Chapter Four.
3. Remove lower crankcase half as described in Chapter Four.
4. Lift each transmission shaft assembly from upper crankcase half.
5. Remove each bearing, gear, and thrust washer after first removing the associated circlip. Note carefully the order in which parts are disassembled. Also, note the orientation of each part as it is removed.

> NOTE: *Make notes on* **Figures 17 and 18** *to aid reassembly*.

6. Remove oil seals and bearings.
7. Disassemble gear shifter as described later.

Inspection

1. Clean all parts thoroughly in solvent.
2. Inspect each gear carefully for wear, broken teeth, pits, burrs, or roughness. Minor damage may be dressed with an oilstone. Gears with more extensive damage must be replaced.
3. Measure the countershaft and main shaft bushing outer diameters as shown in **Figure 19**. New parts measure 19.98-20.00mm for "M" and 19.96-20.00mm for "C". Replace if the measurement is less than 19.94mm.
4. Measure the backlash of gears M and M3 and C and C3 using a dial gauge and V-blocks as shown in **Figure 20**. New parts measure 0.030-0.096mm. More than 0.12mm indicates that replacement is necessary.
5. Check the backlash of transmission gears as shown in **Figure 21**. New parts measure 0.094-0.188mm, except low gear, which is 0.032-0.09mm. Replace if either is in excess of 0.21mm.

CHAPTER FIVE

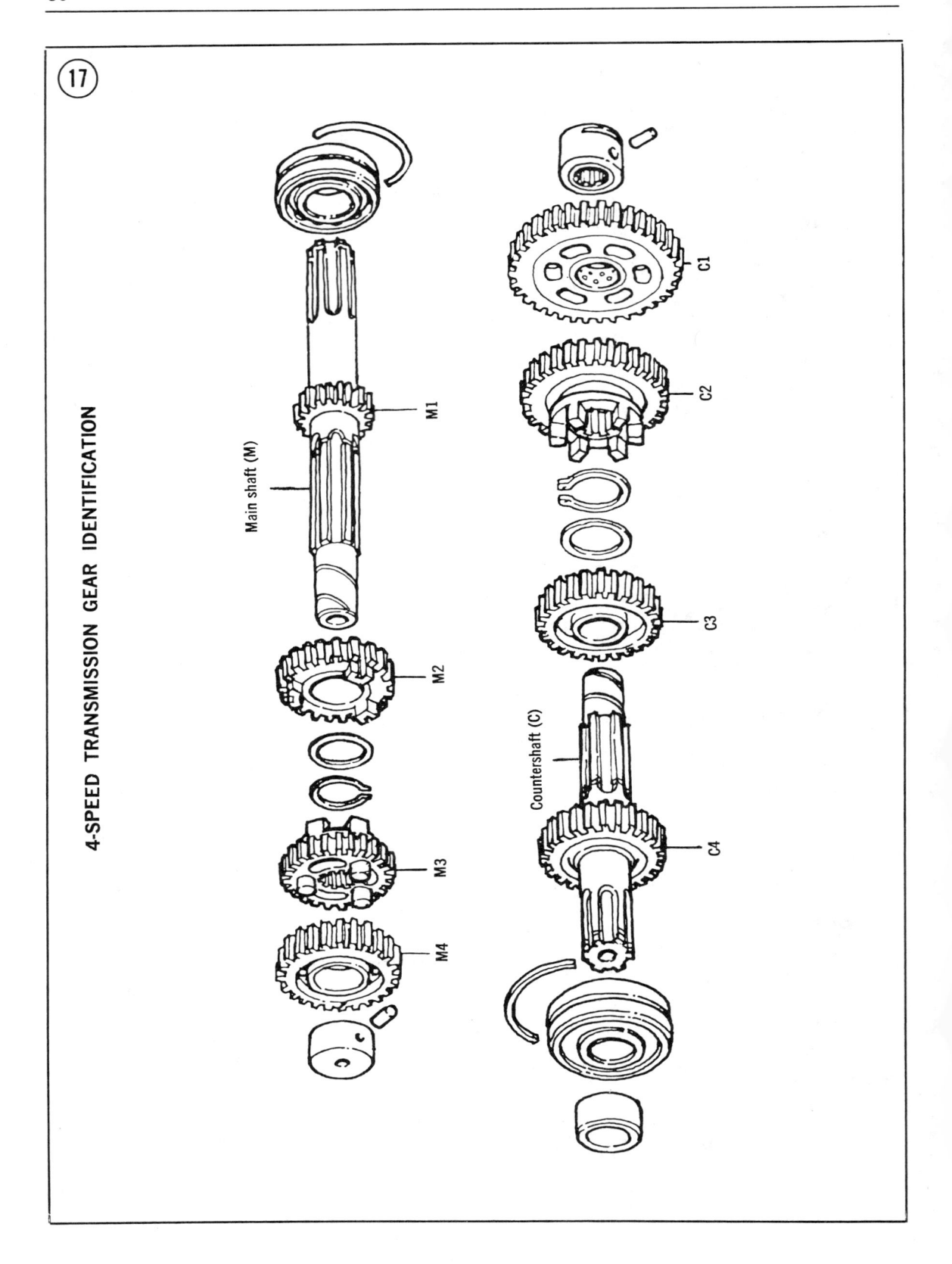

⑰ **4-SPEED TRANSMISSION GEAR IDENTIFICATION**

Main shaft (M), M1, M2, M3, M4

Countershaft (C), C1, C2, C3, C4

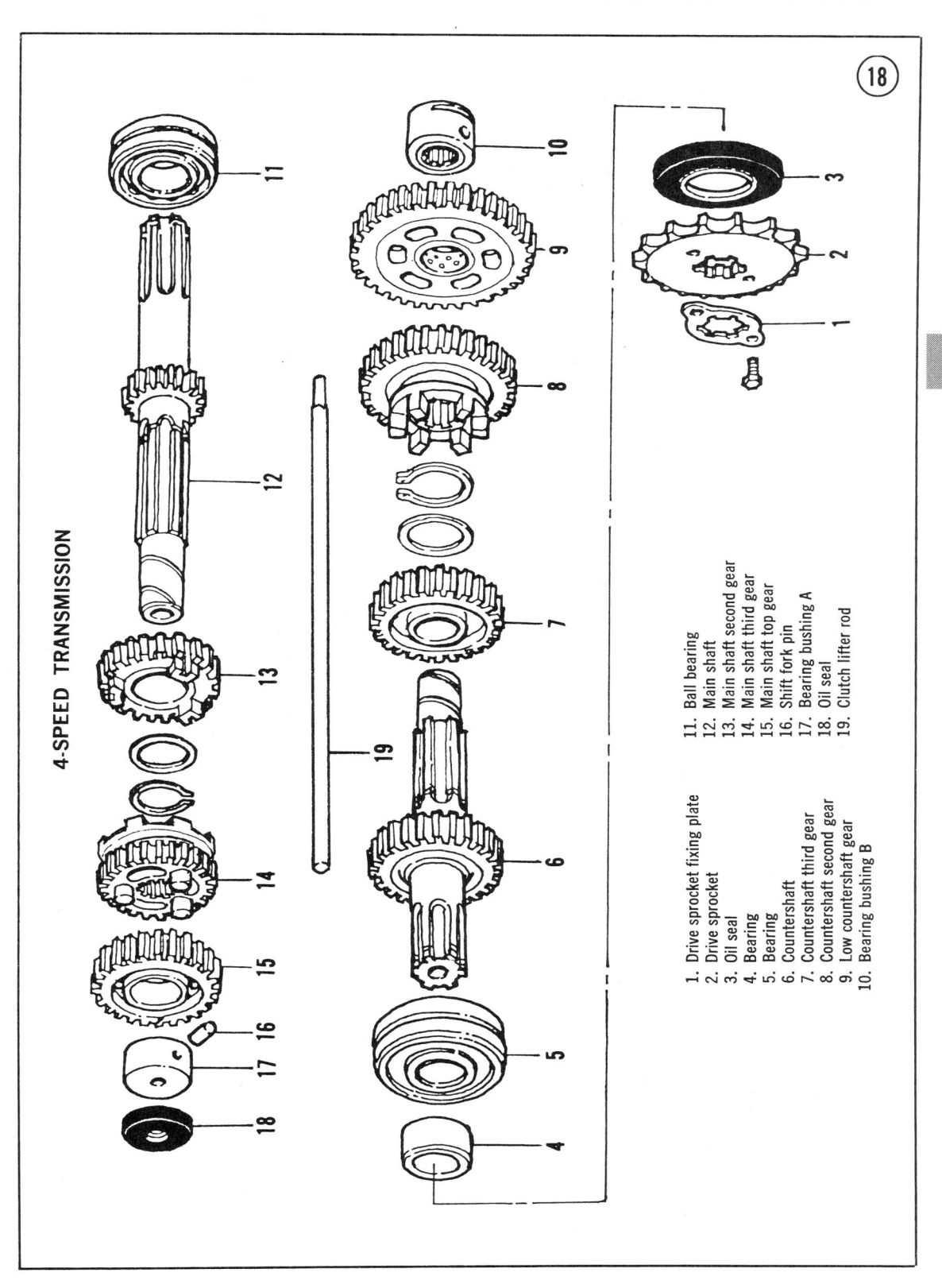

CLUTCH AND TRANSMISSION

4-SPEED TRANSMISSION

1. Drive sprocket fixing plate
2. Drive sprocket
3. Oil seal
4. Bearing
5. Bearing
6. Countershaft
7. Countershaft third gear
8. Countershaft second gear
9. Low countershaft gear
10. Bearing bushing B
11. Ball bearing
12. Main shaft
13. Main shaft second gear
14. Main shaft third gear
15. Main shaft top gear
16. Shift fork pin
17. Bearing bushing A
18. Oil seal
19. Clutch lifter rod

6. Measure the bearing bushing inside diameter of both M and C. New parts measure 20.000-20.028mm for M and 20.000-20.007mm for C. Replace if either is more than 20.06mm.

7. Measure the inside diameter of C1. New parts measure 20.000-20.021mm. Replace if more than 20.08mm.

8. Measure the double-row ball bearing radius direction clearance as shown in **Figure 22**. New parts measure 0.010-0.025mm. Replacement is indicated if measurement exceeeds 0.05mm.

Assembly

Assembly is the reverse of disassembly. Note the following points:

  a. Note the position of the thrust washers and circlips installed next to M2 and C3 gears.
  b. Note that the bearing with the oil groove is installed on the countershaft and bearing without a groove goes on the main shaft.
  c. Check that the bearing set rings and locating pins are aligned and fit in the upper crankcase.
  d. Fit the right side shift fork in gear C2 and the left side shift fork in gear M3. Fit the main shaft and countershaft together.

Gearshift Disassembly

See **Figure 23** for this procedure.

1. Remove the gearshift spindle, separate the upper and lower crankcase halves, and remove the transmission gears. Refer to **Figure 23**.

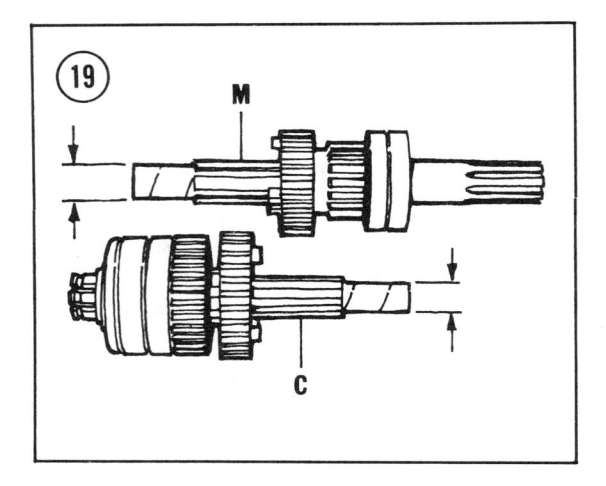

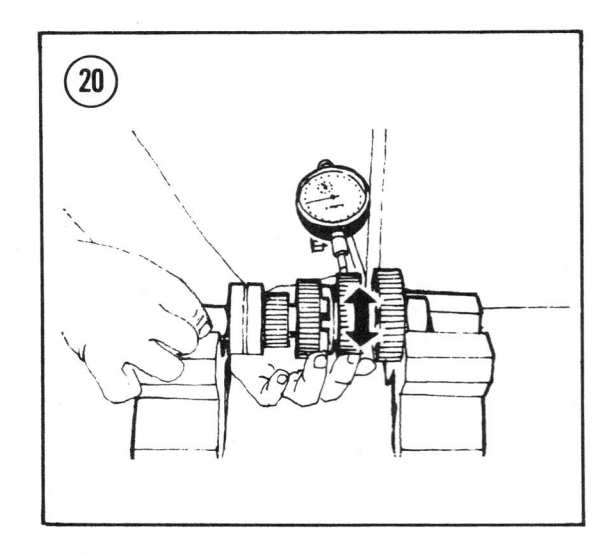

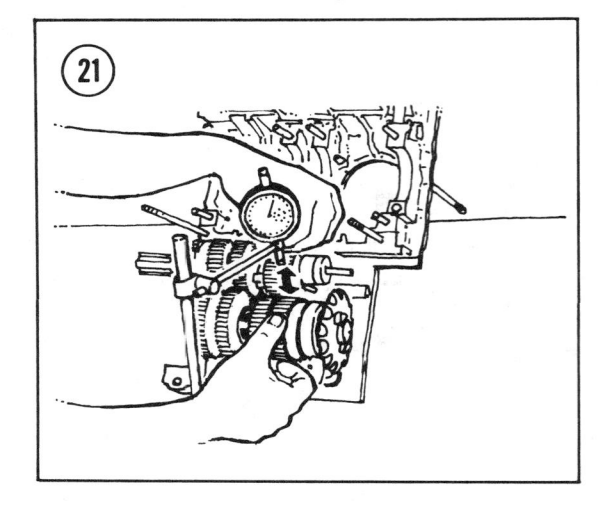

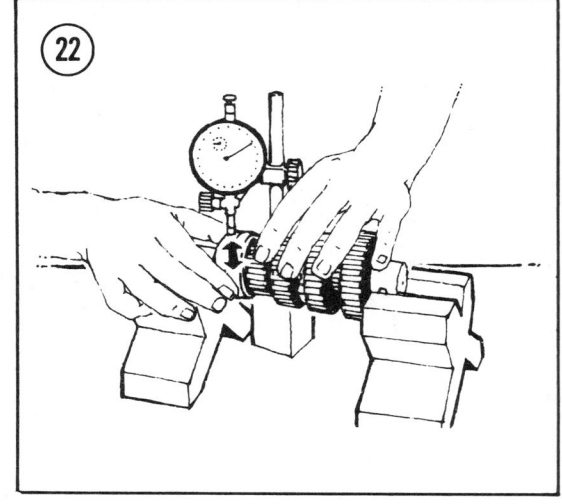

CLUTCH AND TRANSMISSION

SHIFTER DRUM (4-SPEED)

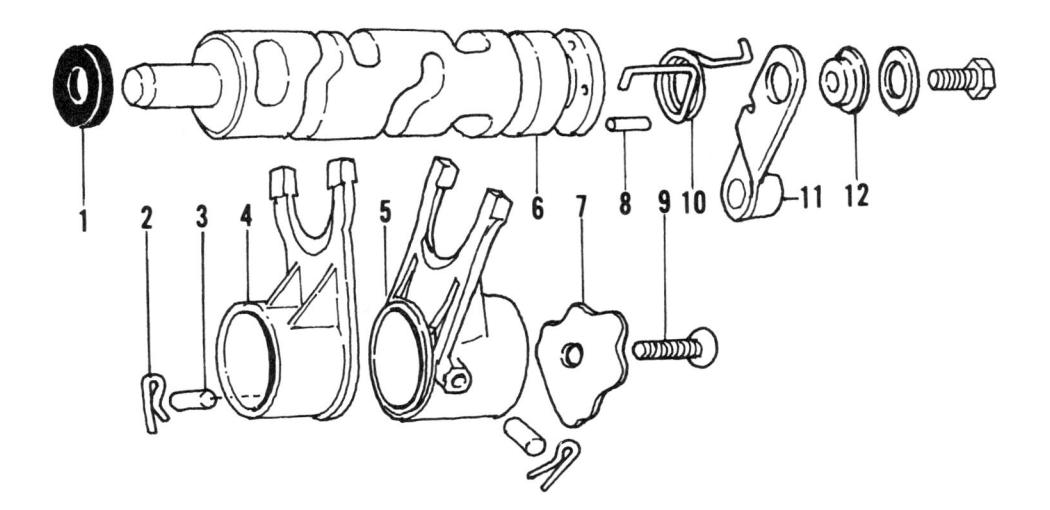

1. Oil seal
2. Gearshift guide pin clip
3. Gearshift fork guide pin
4. Gearshift fork
5. Gearshift fork
6. Gearshift drum
7. Drum stopper cam plate
8. Gearshift drum pin (3)
9. Phillips screw
10. Shift drum stopper spring
11. Shift drum stopper
12. Shift drum stopper collar

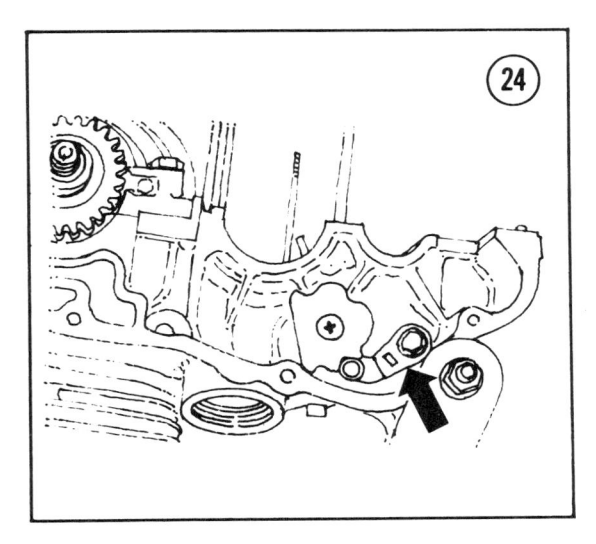

2. Remove the shift drum stop. See **Figure 24**.

3. Remove the shift fork guide pin clip and remove the guide pin. Refer to **Figure 25**.

4. Remove the shift drum guide screw and pull out the shift drum.

Gearshift Inspection

See **Table 2** for correction limits for gearshift forks. All dimensions are in millimeters.

1. Measure the gearshift drum and case clearance with a feeler gauge as shown in **Figure 26**. New parts measure 0.05-0.125mm. Replace if the clearance is more than 0.2mm.

2. The gearshift drum outside diameter must not be less than 11.9mm.

3. The standard gearshift drum groove width is 6.1-6.2mm. Replace if it exceeds 6.5mm.

4. Measure the clearance between the gearshift spindle and the lower case. New parts measure 0.032-0.086mm. Replace if the measurement exceeds 0.13mm.

Gearshift Assembly

Refer to **Figure 23**.

1. Insert the shift drum and shift forks.
2. Insert the shift drum guide screw along with its collar and tighten it.
3. Refer to **Figure 27** and insert the guide pin in the drum groove and set the clip, ensuring that its direction matches that in the diagram.
4. Refer to **Figure 28** for details on the shift drum stop and install.

TRANSMISSION (5-SPEED)

Disassembly

1. Remove engine as described in Chapter Four.
2. Remove left and right crankcase covers as described in Chapter Four.
3. Remove lower crankcase half as described in Chapter Four.
4. Lift each transmission shaft assembly from upper crankcase half.

Table 2   TRANSMISSION SPECIFICATIONS (4-SPEED)

	New	Wear Limit
Gearshift forks		
Inside diameter	34.0-34.025mm	34.1mm
End thickness	4.9-5.0mm	4.6mm
Fork end bending	Within 0.1mm	0.8mm
Main shaft outside diameter	0.7858-0.7866 in. (19.959-19.98mm)	0.785 in. (19.94mm)
Countershaft outside diameter	Same as above	Same as above
Spline clearance[1]	0.0012-0.0038 in. (0.03-0.096mm)	0.0069 in. (0.15mm)
Gear backlash		
1st	0.0013-0.0038 in. (0.032-0.096mm)	0.006 in. (0.15mm)
2nd	0.0035-0.0071 in. (0.089-0.179mm)	0.08 in. (0.2mm)
3rd, 4th, 5th	0.0037-0.0074 in. (0.094-0.188mm)	0.0082 in. (0.21mm)
Main shaft bearing I.D.	0.7882-0.7887 in. (20.02-20.03mm)	0.789 in. (20.06mm)
Countershaft bearing I.D.	Same as above	Same as above
Gear C1 bore	0.7874-0.7882 in. (20.0-20.021mm)	0.789 in. (20.05mm)
Ball bearing clearance[2]	0.0004-0.001 in. (0.01-0.025mm)	0.002 in. (0.05mm)

1. See Figure 34   2. See Figure 36

CLUTCH AND TRANSMISSION

25

Drum guide screw · Shift drum guide collar · Drum · Drum stop · Gearshift fork · Arm · Return spring

GEARSHIFT MECHANISM

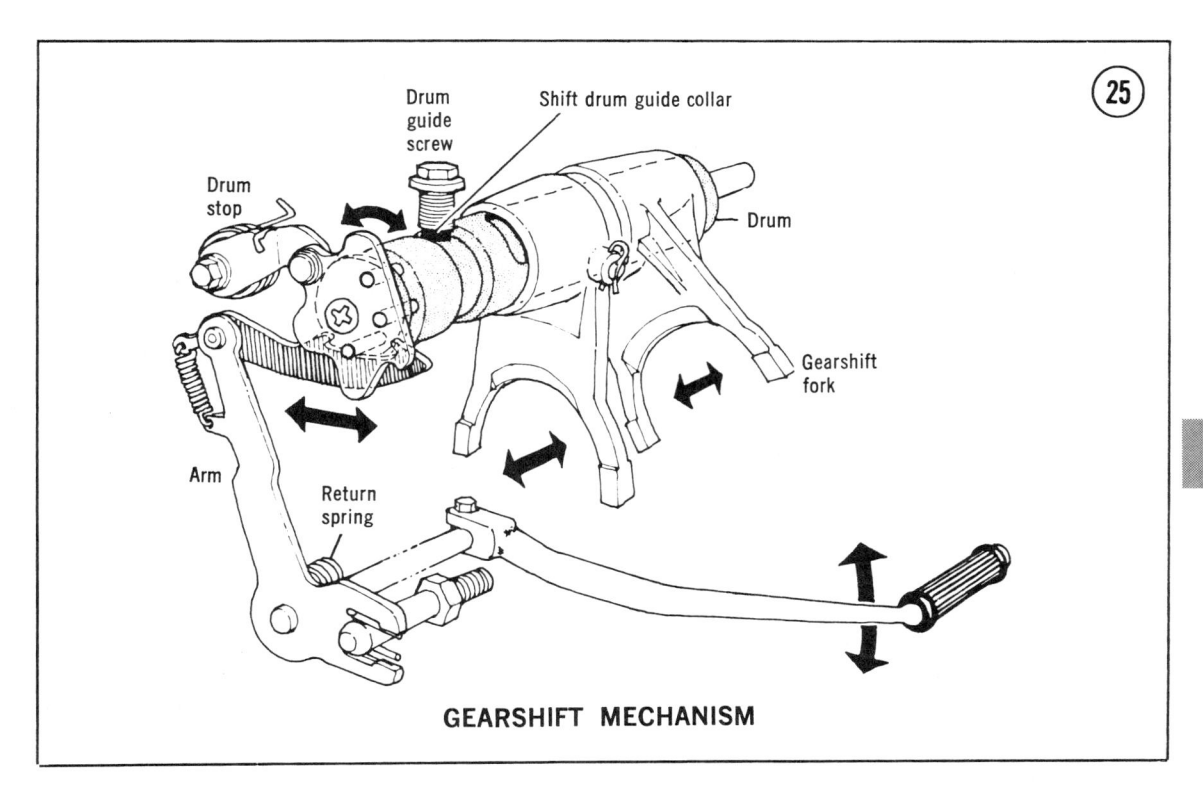

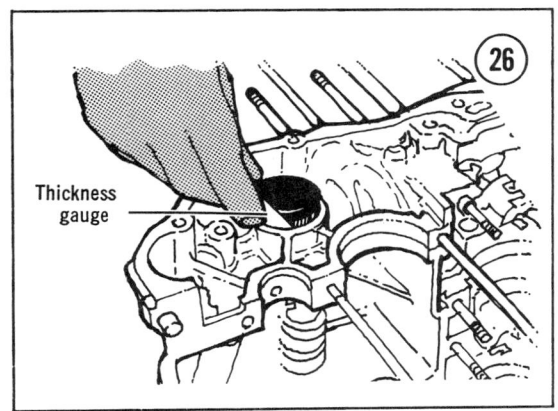

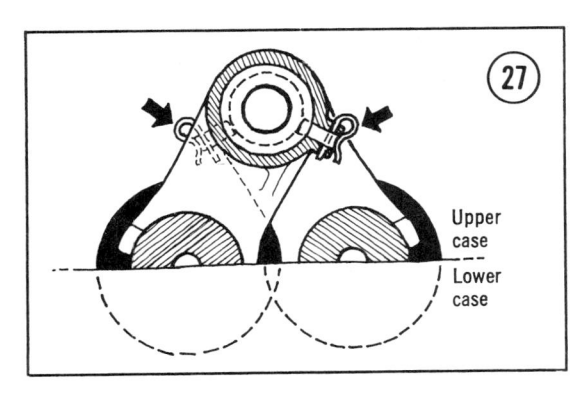

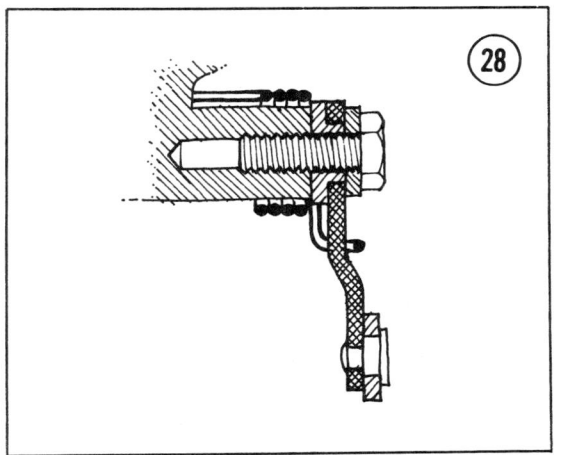

26 Thickness gauge

28

27 Upper case / Lower case

5. Remove each bearing, gear, and thrust washer after first removing the associated circlip. Note carefully the order in which parts are disassembled. Also, note the orientation of each part as it is removed.

NOTE: *Make notes on* **Figures 29**, **30**, **and 31** *to aid reassembly.*

6. Remove oil seals and bearings.
7. Disassemble gear shifter as described later.

CHAPTER FIVE

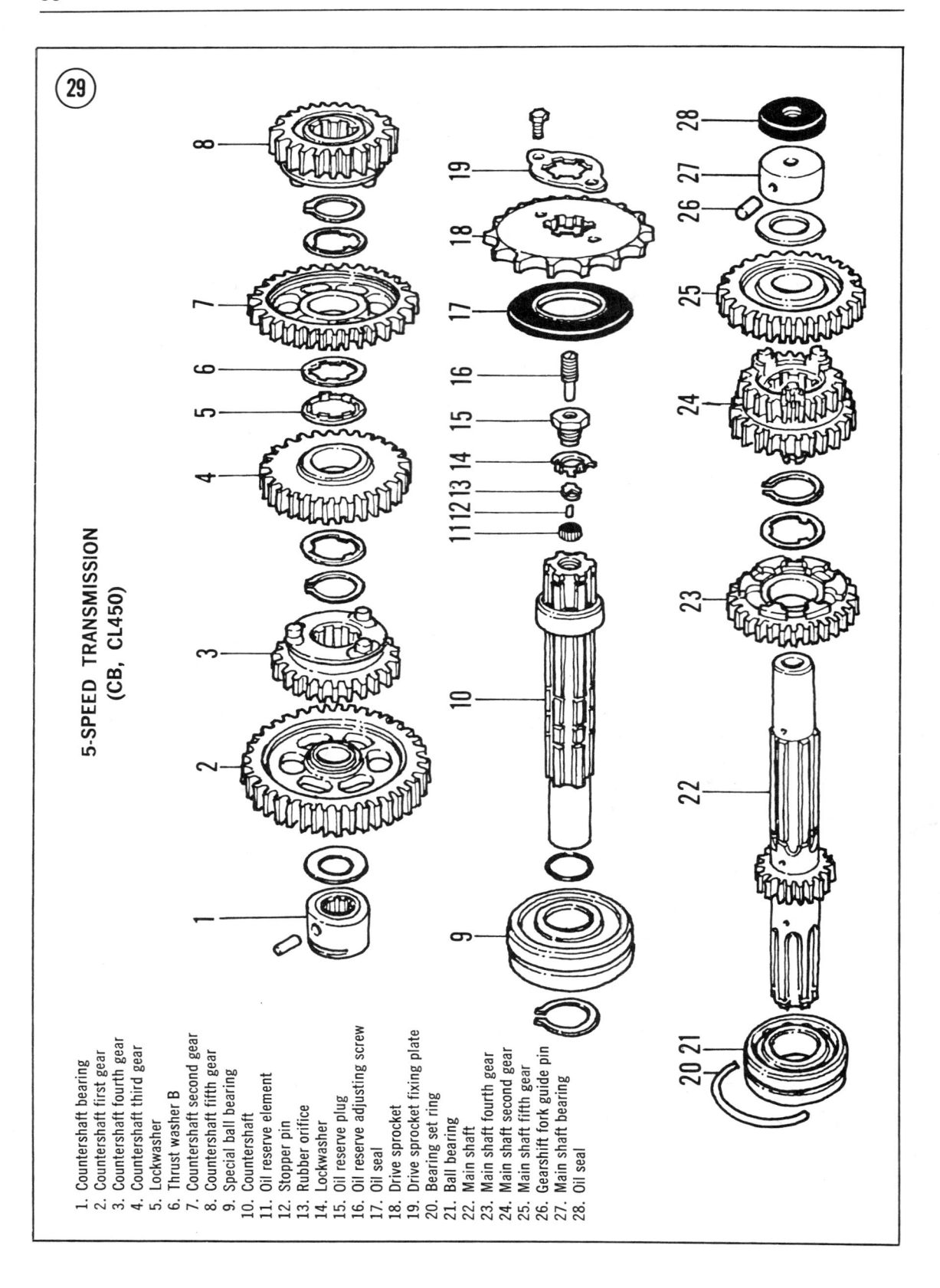

5-SPEED TRANSMISSION (CB, CL450)

1. Countershaft bearing
2. Countershaft first gear
3. Countershaft fourth gear
4. Countershaft third gear
5. Lockwasher
6. Thrust washer B
7. Countershaft second gear
8. Countershaft fifth gear
9. Special ball bearing
10. Countershaft
11. Oil reserve element
12. Stopper pin
13. Rubber orifice
14. Lockwasher
15. Oil reserve plug
16. Oil reserve adjusting screw
17. Oil seal
18. Drive sprocket
19. Drive sprocket fixing plate
20. Bearing set ring
21. Ball bearing
22. Main shaft
23. Main shaft fourth gear
24. Main shaft second gear
25. Main shaft fifth gear
26. Gearshift fork guide pin
27. Main shaft bearing
28. Oil seal

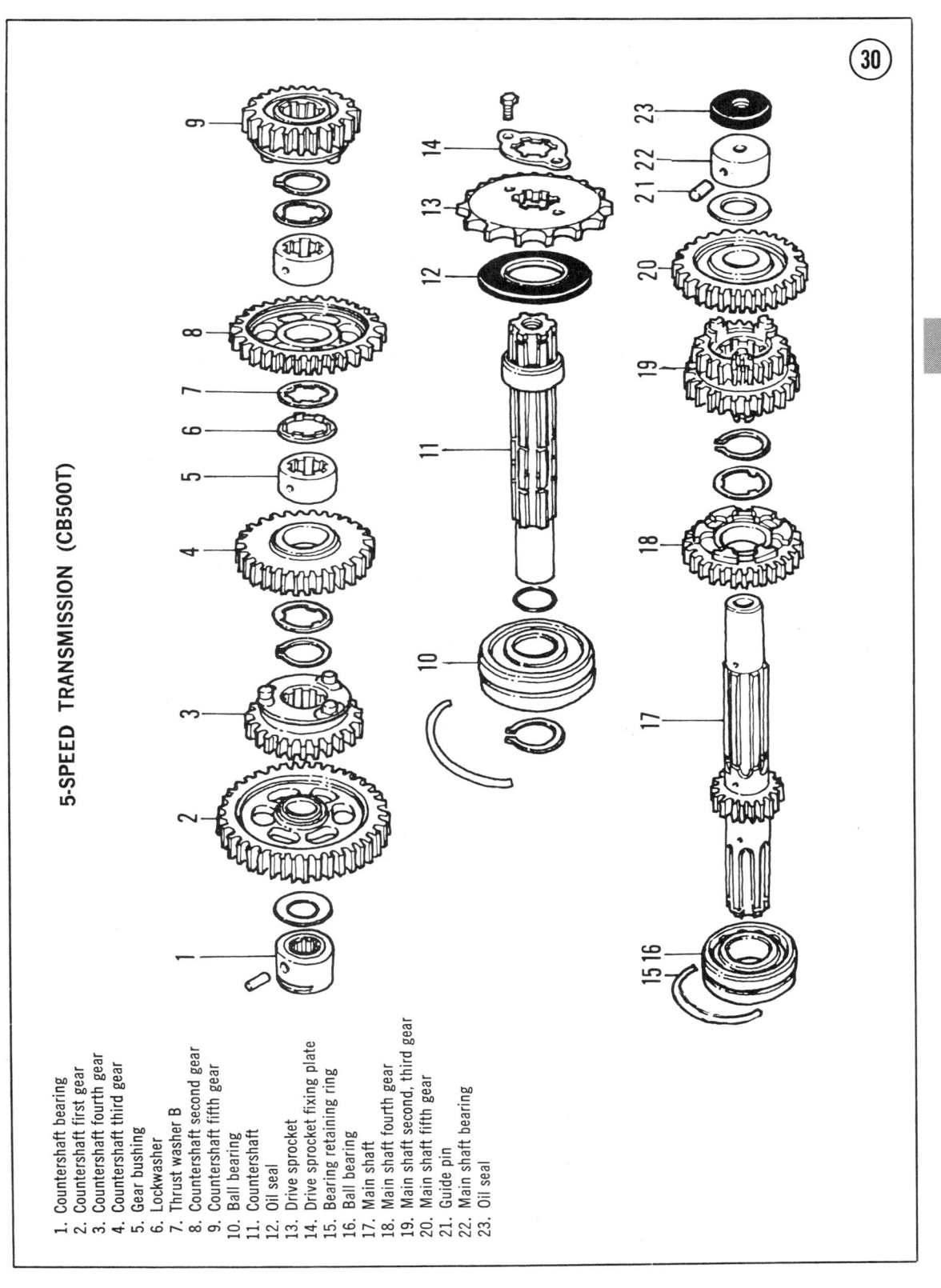

CLUTCH AND TRANSMISSION

5-SPEED TRANSMISSION (CB500T)

1. Countershaft bearing
2. Countershaft first gear
3. Countershaft fourth gear
4. Countershaft third gear
5. Gear bushing
6. Lockwasher
7. Thrust washer B
8. Countershaft second gear
9. Countershaft fifth gear
10. Ball bearing
11. Countershaft
12. Oil seal
13. Drive sprocket
14. Drive sprocket fixing plate
15. Bearing retaining ring
16. Ball bearing
17. Main shaft
18. Main shaft fourth gear
19. Main shaft second, third gear
20. Main shaft fifth gear
21. Guide pin
22. Main shaft bearing
23. Oil seal

CHAPTER FIVE

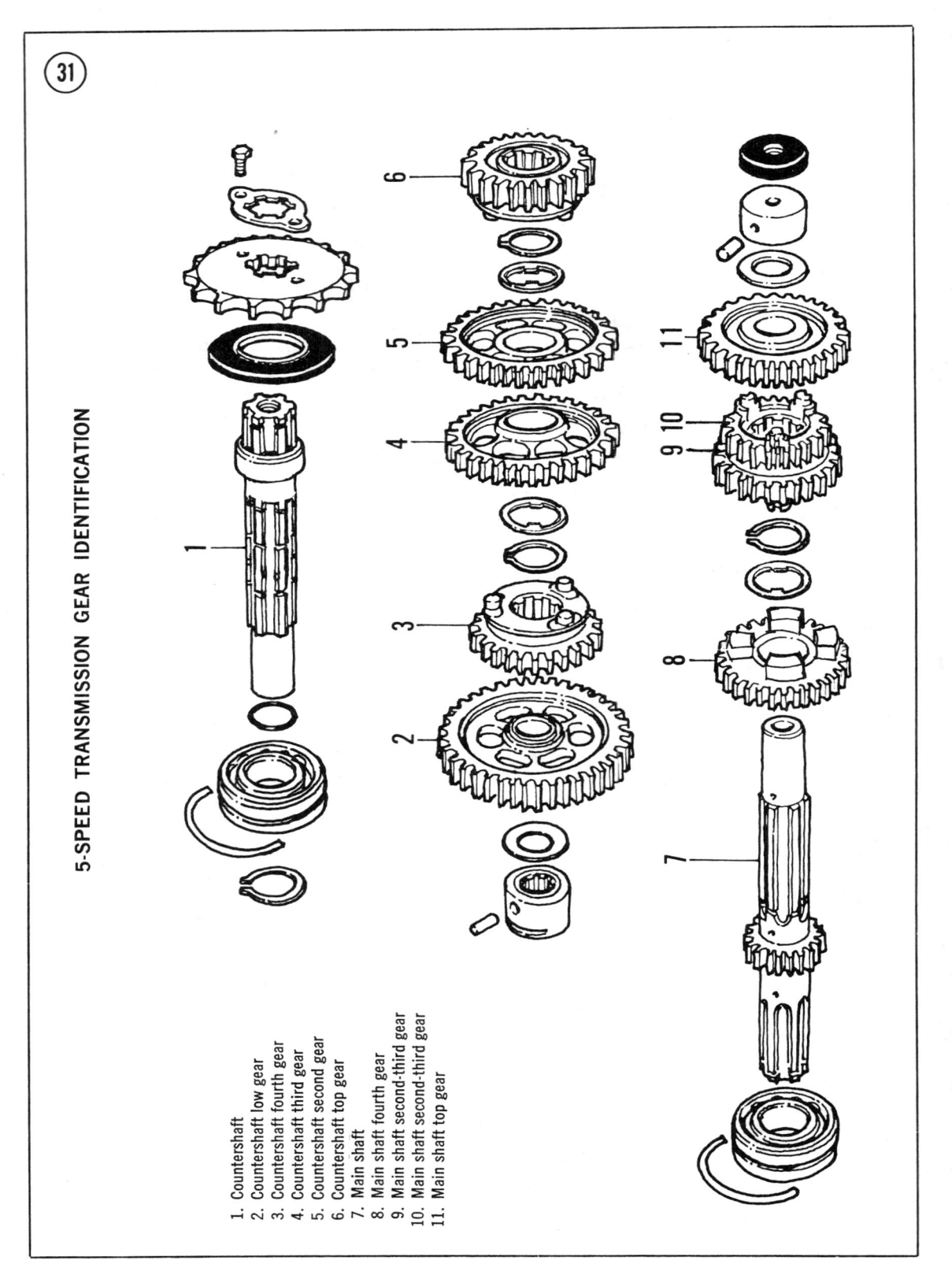

5-SPEED TRANSMISSION GEAR IDENTIFICATION

1. Countershaft
2. Countershaft low gear
3. Countershaft fourth gear
4. Countershaft third gear
5. Countershaft second gear
6. Countershaft top gear
7. Main shaft
8. Main shaft fourth gear
9. Main shaft second-third gear
10. Main shaft second-third gear
11. Main shaft top gear

CLUTCH AND TRANSMISSION

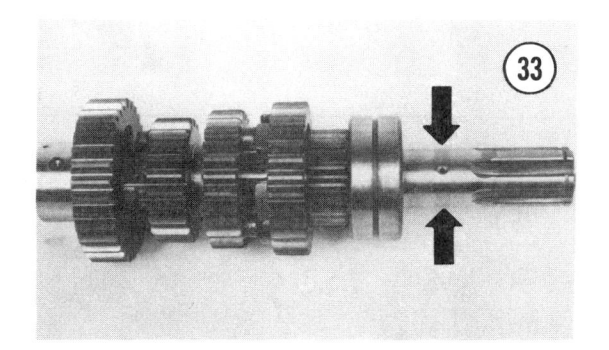

Inspection

Refer to **Figure 31** to identify gears.

1. Measure the main shaft and countershaft outside diameter as shown in **Figures 32 and 33**. Refer to **Table 3** for serviceable limits.

2. Measure spline clearances as shown in **Figure 34**. Refer to **Table 3** for serviceable limits.

3. Measure backlash as shown in **Figure 35**. **Table 3** gives serviceable limits.

4. Measure the main shaft and countershaft bearing inside diameter and compare to **Table 3**.

5. Measure the bore of gear C1 and compare to **Table 3**.

6. Measure the double-row ball bearing clearance (**Figure 36**) and compare to **Table 3**.

Assembly

Assembly is the reverse of disassembly. Note the following points:

    a. Note the thrust washers and circlips on gears M4, C2, and C3.

Table 3   5-SPEED TRANSMISSION DATA

Item	Standard Value	Serviceable Limit 450	Serviceable Limit 500
Shaft outer diameter	0.7858-0.7866 in. (19.959-19.98mm)	Replace if under 0.785 in. (19.94mm)	①
Spline clearance	0.0012-0.0038 in. (0.03-0.096mm)	Replace if over 0.0059 in. (0.15mm)	①
Backlash, low	0.0013-0.0038 in. (0.032-0.096mm)	Replace if over 0.006 in. (0.15mm)	Replace if over 0.0079 in. (0.2mm)
Backlash, 2nd	0.0035-0.0071 in. (0.089-0.179mm)	Replace if over 0.008 in. (0.2mm)	Replace if over 0.0079 in. (0.2mm)
Backlash, 3rd, 4th, top	0.0037-0.0074 in. (0.094-0.188mm)	Replace if over 0.0082 in. (0.21mm)	Replace if over 0.0079 in. (0.2mm)
Bearing inner diameter	0.7882-0.7887 in. (20.02-20.033mm)	Replace if over 0.789 in. (20.06mm)	①
Bore diameter	0.7874-0.7882 in. (20.0-20.021mm)	Replace if over 0.789 in. (20.05mm)	①
Diametrical clearance	0.0004-0.001 in. (0.01-0.025mm)	Replace if over 0.002 in. (0.05mm)	①

① Not specified.

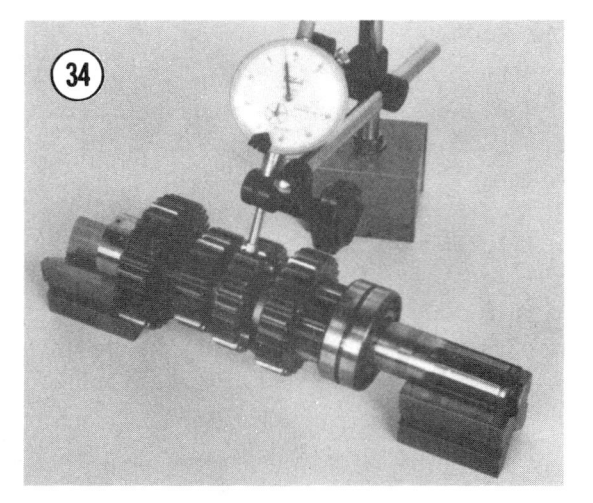

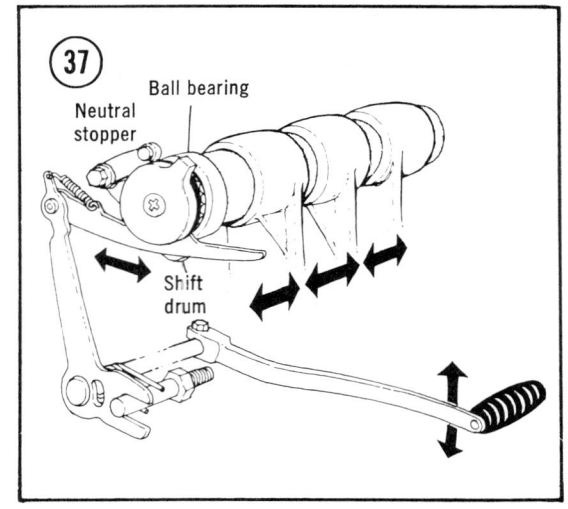

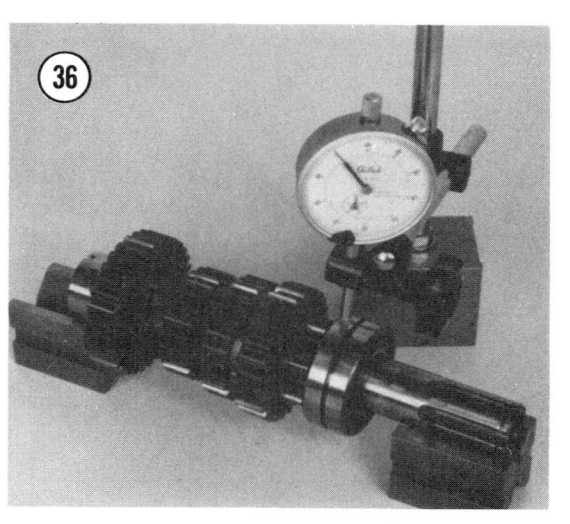

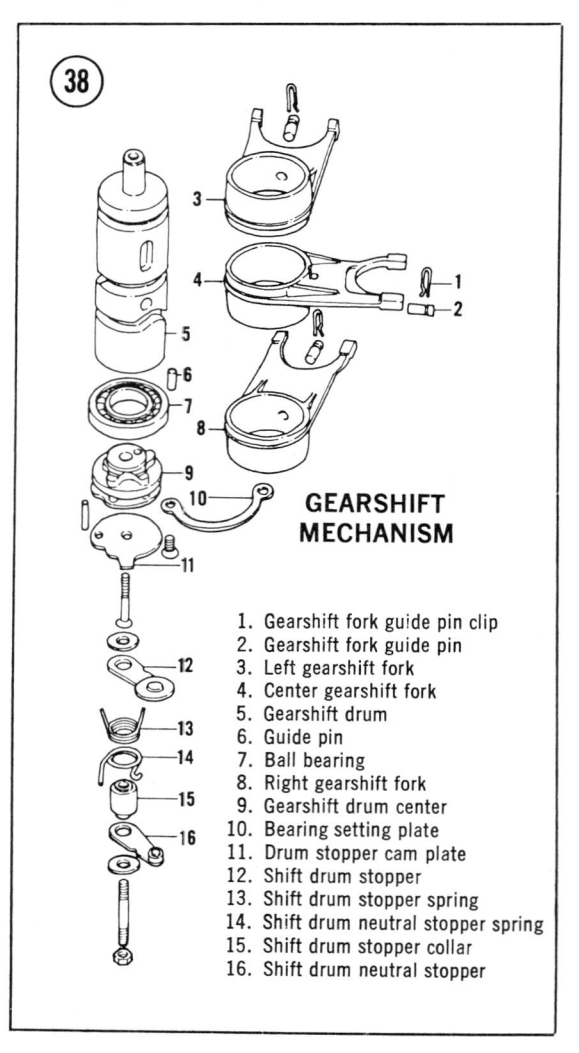

CHAPTER FIVE

③④

③⑤

③⑥

③⑦ Neutral stopper — Ball bearing — Shift drum

③⑧

GEARSHIFT MECHANISM

1. Gearshift fork guide pin clip
2. Gearshift fork guide pin
3. Left gearshift fork
4. Center gearshift fork
5. Gearshift drum
6. Guide pin
7. Ball bearing
8. Right gearshift fork
9. Gearshift drum center
10. Bearing setting plate
11. Drum stopper cam plate
12. Shift drum stopper
13. Shift drum stopper spring
14. Shift drum neutral stopper spring
15. Shift drum stopper collar
16. Shift drum neutral stopper

CLUTCH AND TRANSMISSION

b. The bearing with the oil groove is installed on the countershaft and the plain bearing goes on the main shaft.

c. Do not forget the bearing set ring and the dowel pin.

d. Fit the left shift fork on gear C4, the right shift fork on gear C5, and the center shift fork between gears M2 and M3.

e. Fit the main shaft and countershaft together and install them.

Gearshift Disassembly

Refer to **Figures 37, 38, and 39** for details of the gearshift.

1. Remove the gearshift spindle, separate the crankcase halves, and disassemble the transmission gears.

2. Take out the 6mm bolt and remove the neutral stopper and shift drum stopper.

3. Unscrew the Phillips screw and remove the bearing set plate as shown in **Figure 40**.

4. Take out the shift fork guide pin clip and pull out the guide pin.

5. Remove gearshift drum by gently tapping the case on the side of the neutral switch mount.

Gearshift Inspection

Refer to **Table 4**. Make necessary measurements to determine serviceable limits for the gearshift fork and drum guide grooves. **Figure 41** shows method for measuring fork end bending.

Gearshift Assembly

1. Fit the gearshift drum into the upper case. Check that the shift forks are in their proper locations. Right and left forks are stamped R and L for identification. Use care not to damage the oil seal pressed into the crankcase.

2. Insert the shift fork guide pin into the shift fork and lock it with a clip. Refer to **Figures 42 and 43**. Install the bearing set plate, the neutral stopper, and shift drum stopper.

3. Install the transmission gear assembly.

4. Assemble the crankcase halves.

5. Fit the gearshift spindle, installing a washer on the left side and securing it with the circlip.

6. Check the shift fork action for smoothness and continue assembly of the remaining parts.

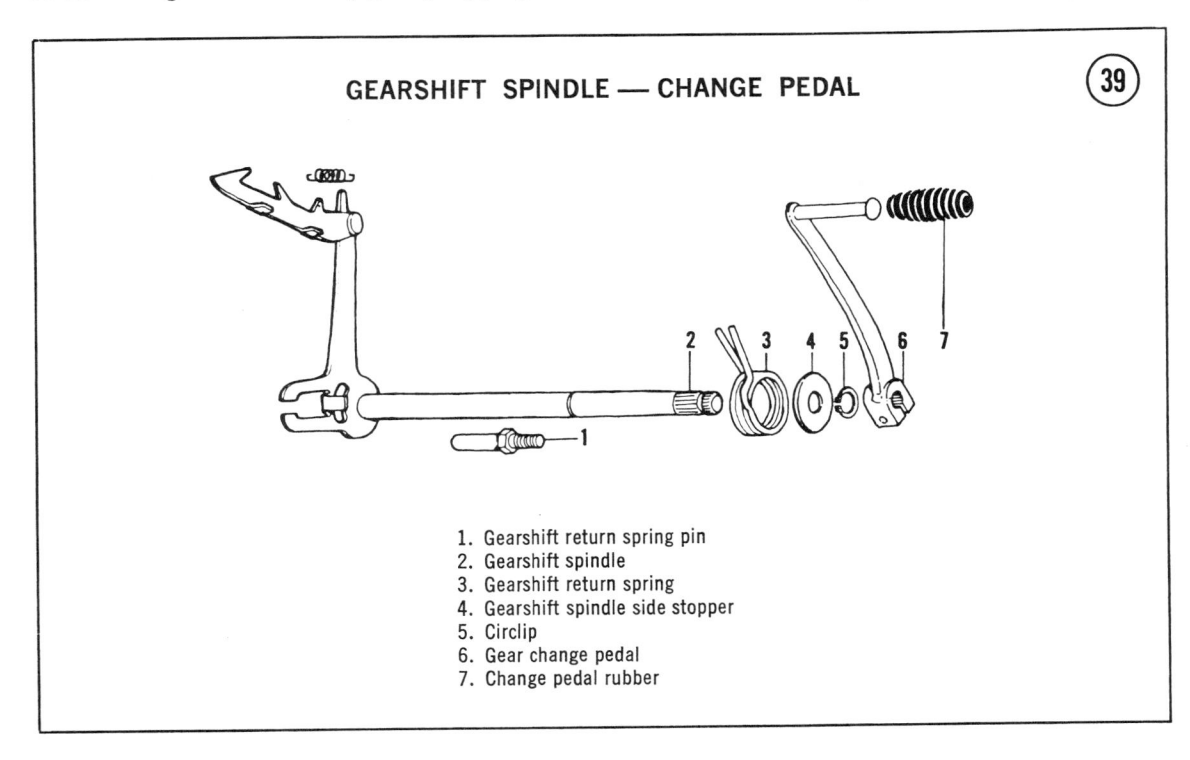

GEARSHIFT SPINDLE — CHANGE PEDAL

1. Gearshift return spring pin
2. Gearshift spindle
3. Gearshift return spring
4. Gearshift spindle side stopper
5. Circlip
6. Gear change pedal
7. Change pedal rubber

CHAPTER FIVE

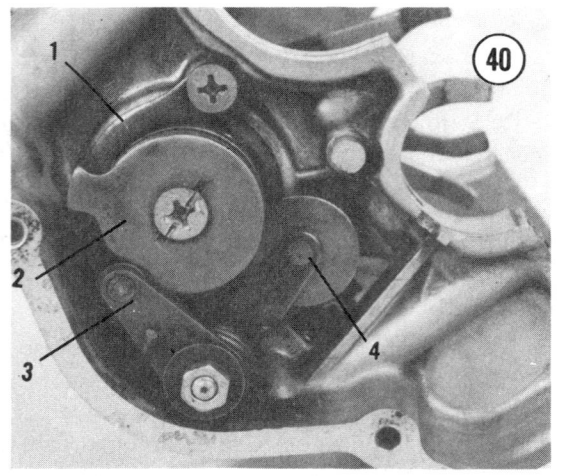

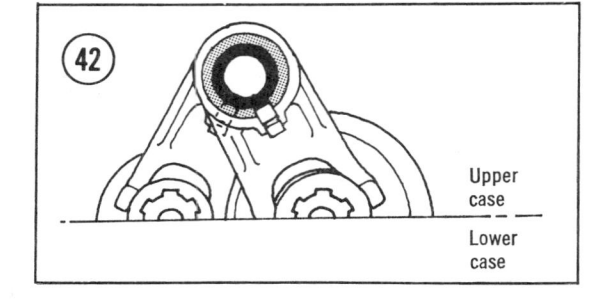

①
1. Plate 2. Drum 3. Drum stop 4. Neutral stop

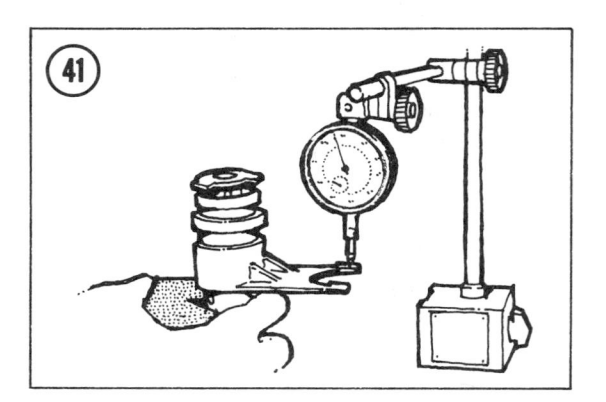

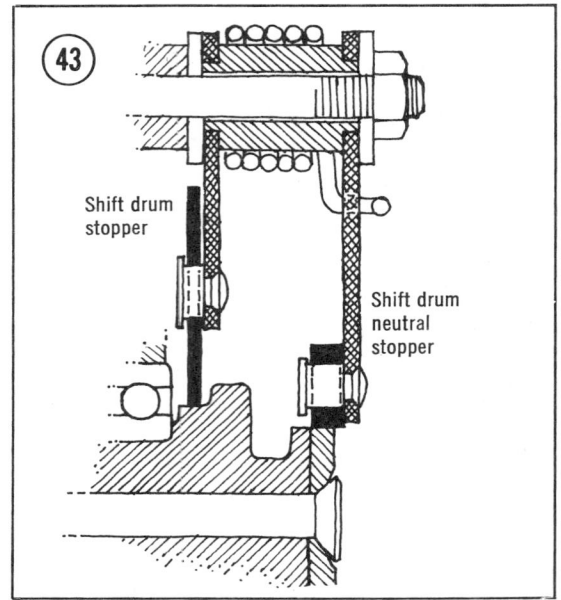

②
Upper case
Lower case

③
Shift drum stopper
Shift drum neutral stopper

④

Table 4   GEARSHIFT FORK AND DRUM LIMITS

Item	Standard value	Serviceable limit
Inside diameter	1.3385-1.339 in. (34.0-34.025mm)	Replace if over 1.3425 in. (34.1mm)
End thickness (left/right)	0.1941-0.1968 in. (4.93-5.0mm)	Replace if under 0.181 in. (4.6mm)
End thickness (center)	0.2334-0.236 in. (5.93-6.0mm)	Replace if under 0.2205 in. (5.6mm)
Bend in fork end (left/right)	Within 0.004 in. (0.1mm)	Replace if over 0.031 in. (0.8mm)
Groove width	0.238-0.242 in. (6.05-6.15mm)	Replace if over 0.256 in. (6.5mm)

CLUTCH AND TRANSMISSION

Figure 44 KICKSTARTER
- Set bolt
- Kickstarter spindle
- Circlip
- Kickstarter pinion
- Countershaft low gear
- Kickstarter spring
- Friction spring

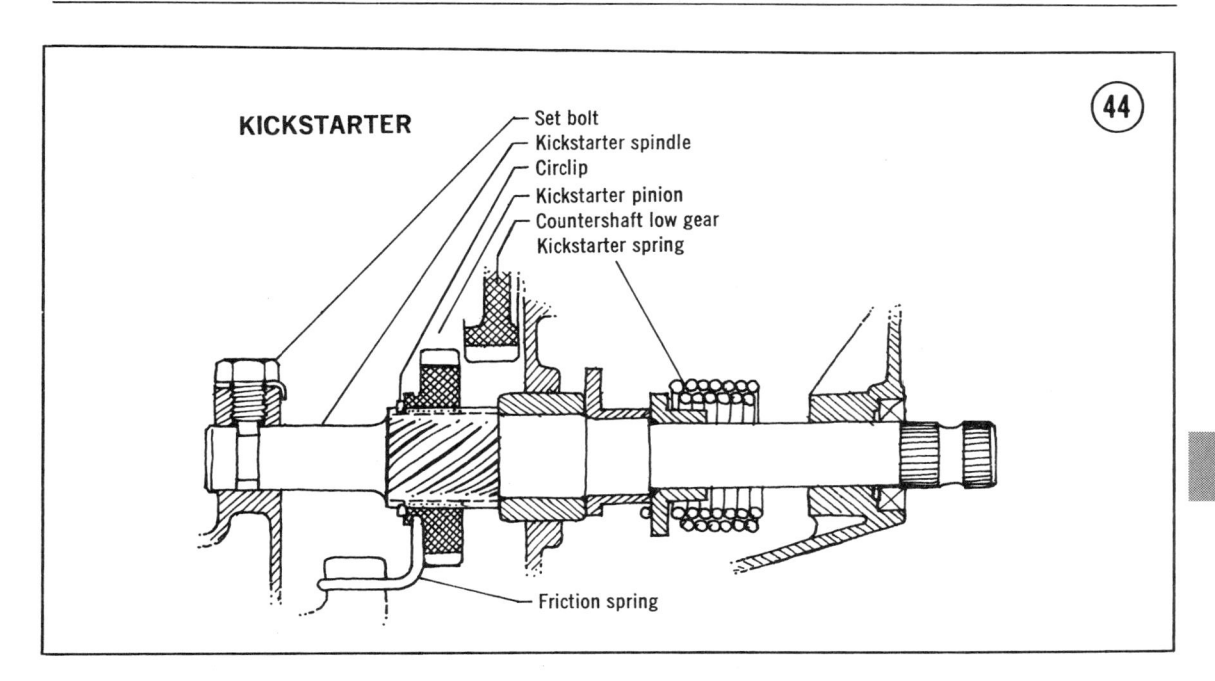

Figure 45 KICKSTARTER
1. Kickstarter rubber
2. Kickstarter arm
3. Kickstarter arm cap
4. Steel ball
5. Kickstarter stopper spring
6. Kickstarter arm bolt
7. Kickstarter spring
8. Kickstarter spindle
9. Lockwasher
10. Kickstarter pinion
11. Friction spring
12. External circlip

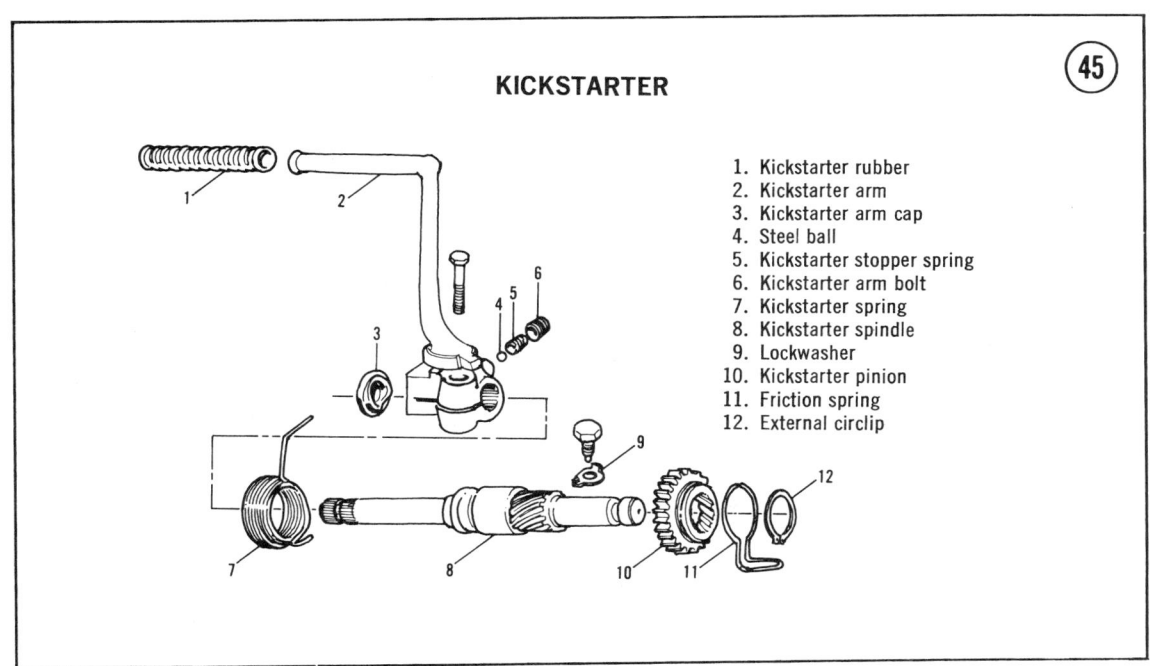

KICKSTARTER

Disassembly/Assembly

1. Split the crankcase halves as described in Chapter Four.

2. Remove the kickstarter spring, the 25mm circlip, unscrew the 8mm lock bolt and remove the washer. Refer to **Figures 44 and 45** for details.

3. Remove the starter spindle.

4. Check pinion and spindle for excessive wear or damage and replace if necessary.

5. Assembly is the reverse of these steps.

CHAPTER SIX

FUEL AND EXHAUST SYSTEMS

The fuel system consists of the fuel tank, shutoff petcock, 2 Keihn carburetors, and 2 air cleaners. The CB500T is equipped with a blow-by gas circulation system. The exhaust system consists of 2 mufflers and connecting exhaust pipes.

This chapter includes service procedures for all parts of the fuel and exhaust system.

AIR CLEANERS

Removal/Installation

Refer to **Figure 1, 2 or 3** for this procedure.

1. Unscrew and remove the side case.

2. Remove air cleaner cover and cover bolt or nuts.

3. Loosen clamp at connecting hose.

4. Remove air cleaner mounting bolt.

5. Remove tool box (**Figure 4**), if so equipped.

6. Remove air cleaners.

7. Tap air cleaners gently on wood block or against your hand. Blow them out with compressed air from the inside out.

8. Installation is the reverse of these steps.

Blow-by Gas Circulation System (CB500T)

Blow-by gas from inside the cylinder head covers is channeled through breather tubes to the breather box, where oil is separated from the gas by the breather element. See **Figure 5**. The gas is then directed into the air cleaners and mixed with fresh air before entering the carburetors, where it is mixed with fuel and reburned in the combustion chambers. This reburning helps reduce the emission of air pollutants.

Breather Element Service

1. Remove the air cleaner elements as described earlier.
2. Remove cover from breather box by removing bolt (**Figure 6**).
3. Remove breather element from breather box (**Figure 7**). Clean element in solvent.

> WARNING
> *Clean element in a well-ventilated area where no open flames, such as pilot lights are present. Do not smoke in the area. Avoid the use of gasoline or other solvents with low flash points. The use of these highly flammable solvents could lead to injury or damage to equipment.*

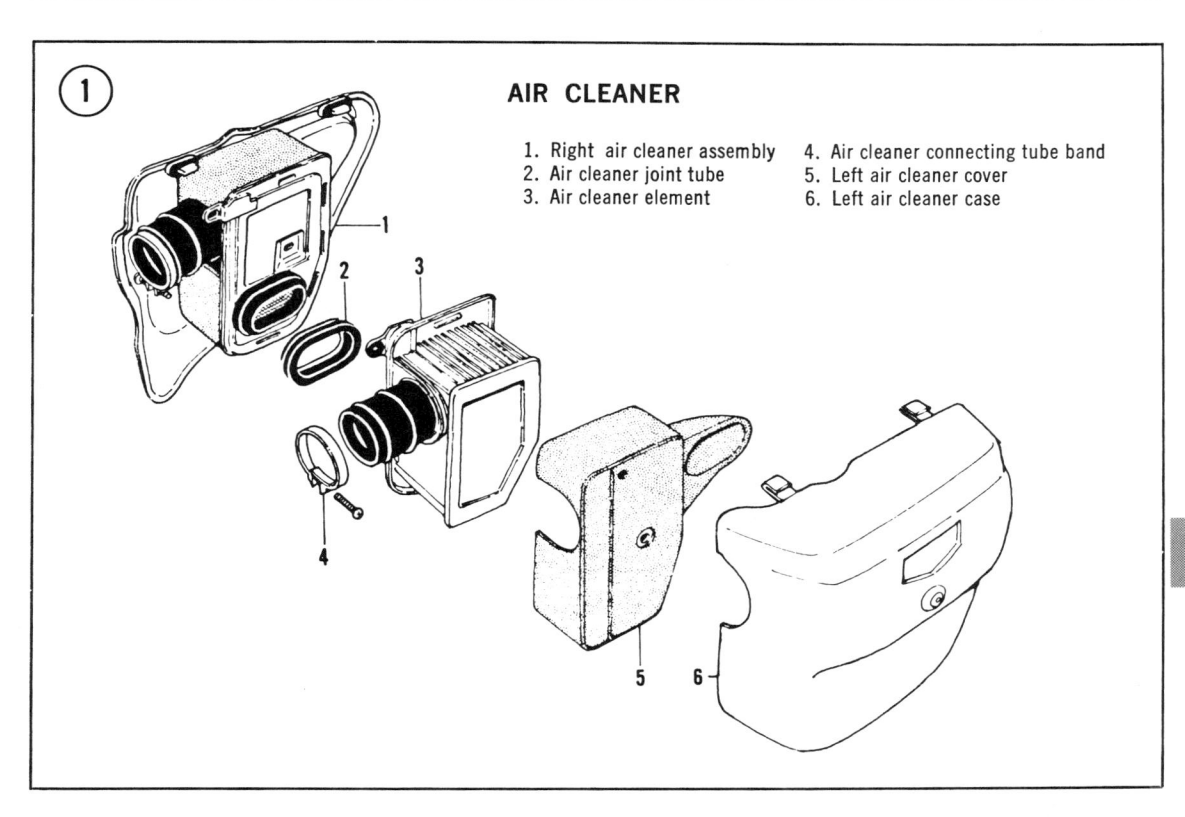

FUEL AND EXHAUST SYSTEMS

AIR CLEANER

1. Right air cleaner assembly
2. Air cleaner joint tube
3. Air cleaner element
4. Air cleaner connecting tube band
5. Left air cleaner cover
6. Left air cleaner case

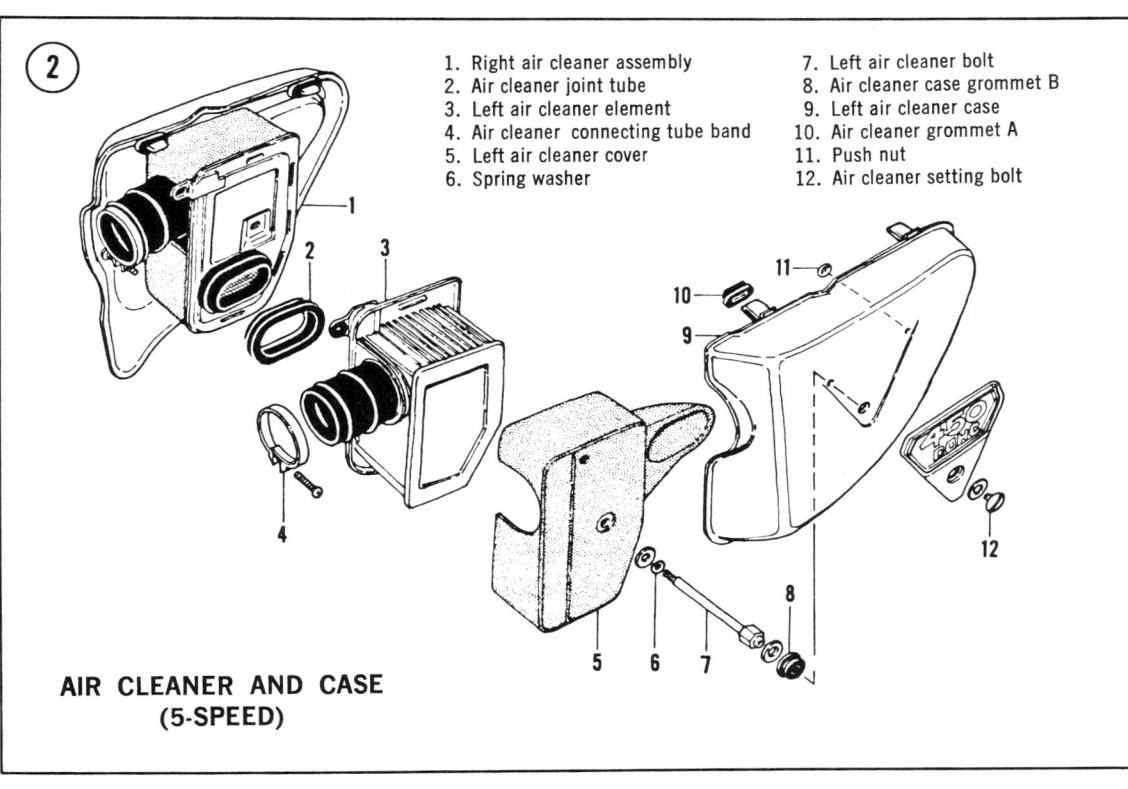

1. Right air cleaner assembly
2. Air cleaner joint tube
3. Left air cleaner element
4. Air cleaner connecting tube band
5. Left air cleaner cover
6. Spring washer
7. Left air cleaner bolt
8. Air cleaner case grommet B
9. Left air cleaner case
10. Air cleaner grommet A
11. Push nut
12. Air cleaner setting bolt

AIR CLEANER AND CASE (5-SPEED)

CHAPTER SIX

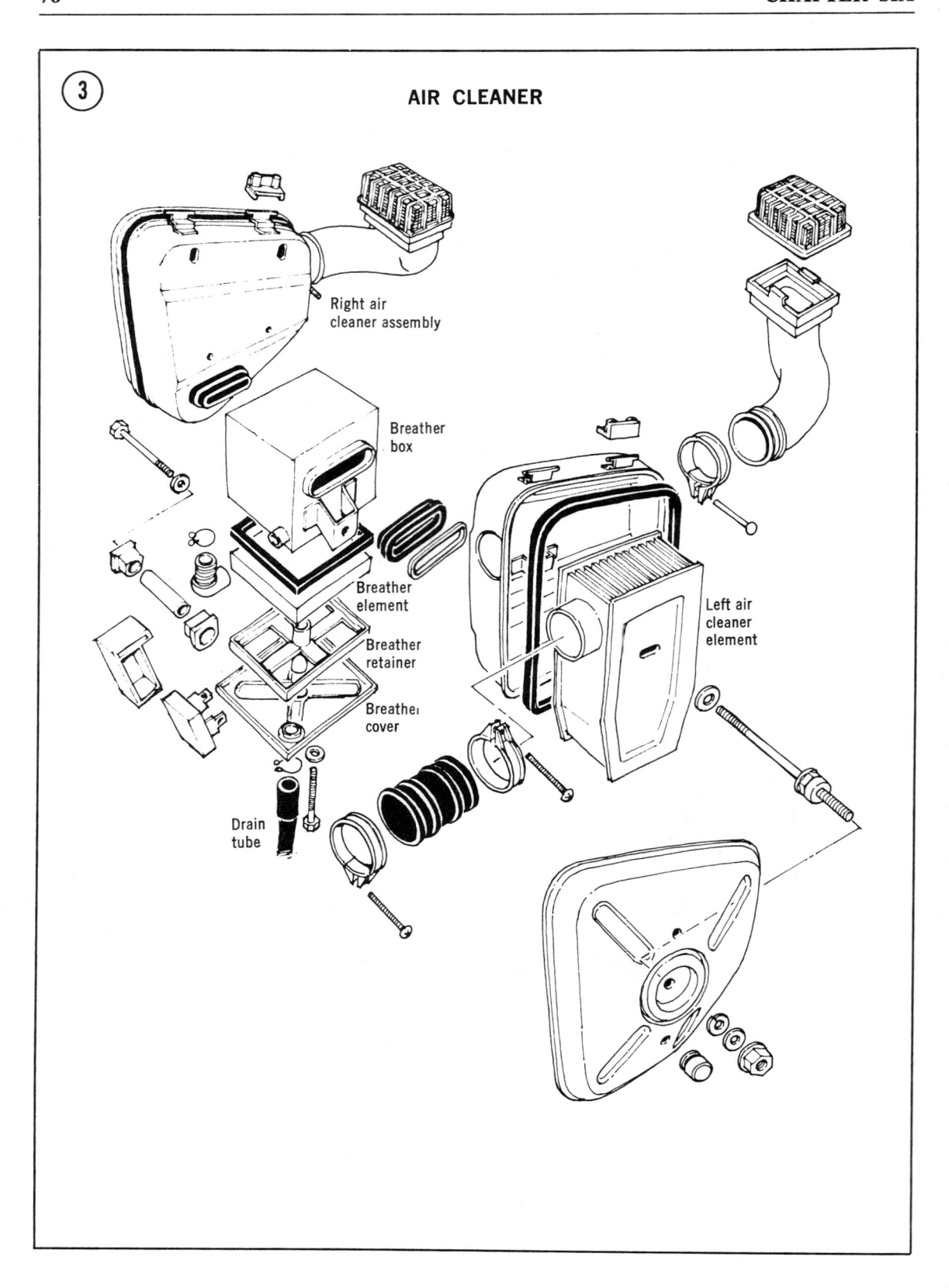

③ **AIR CLEANER**

Right air cleaner assembly

Breather box

Breather element

Breather retainer

Breather cover

Drain tube

Left air cleaner element

FUEL AND EXHAUST SYSTEMS

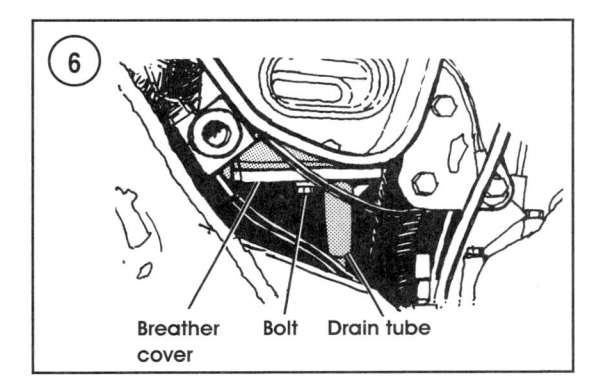

Breather cover   **Bolt**   **Drain tube**

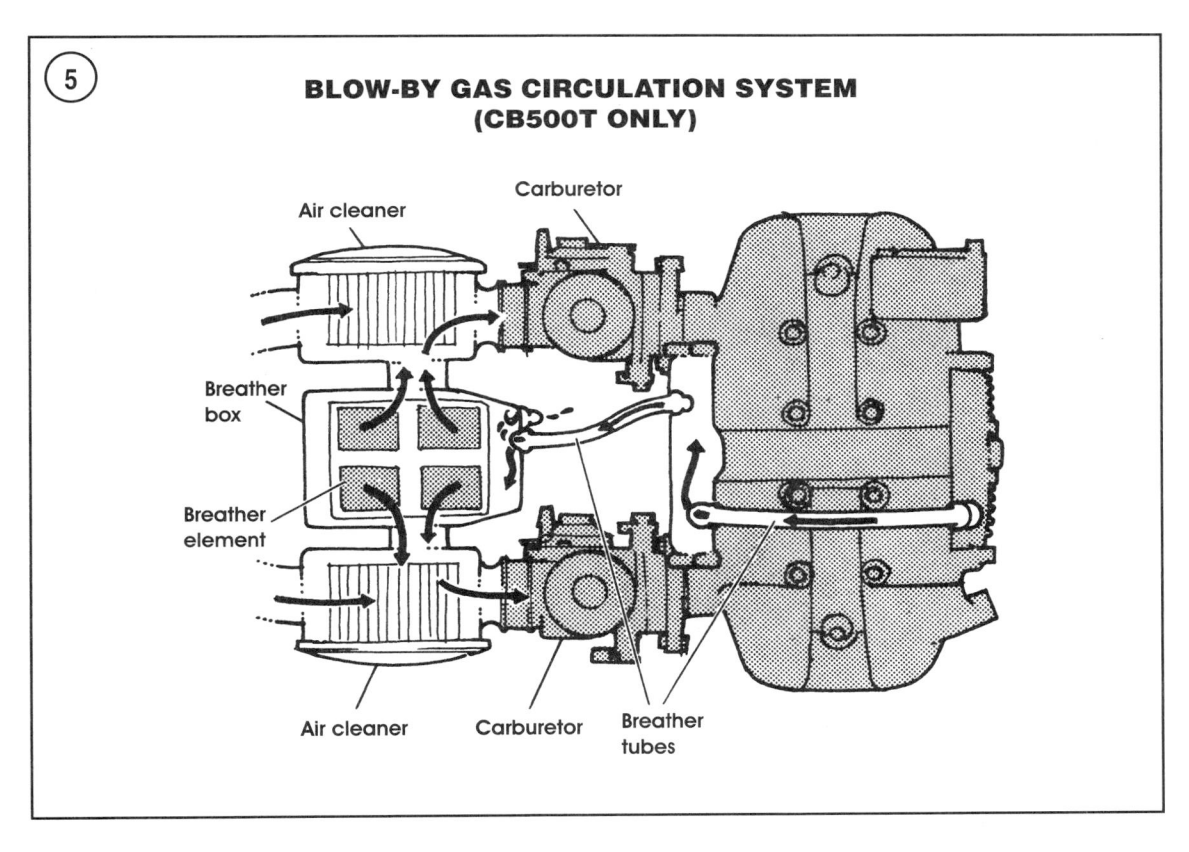

**BLOW-BY GAS CIRCULATION SYSTEM
(CB500T ONLY)**

- Air cleaner
- Carburetor
- Breather box
- Breather element
- Air cleaner
- Carburetor
- Breather tubes

4. Allow element to dry thoroughly, then soak in gear oil or engine oil. Squeeze out excess oil.
5. Clean the breather cover, drain tube, and breather case with solvent. Make sure the slit in the end of the drain tube is not clogged. See **Figure 8**.
6. Assembly is the reverse of disassembly.

CARBURETORS

All Honda 450 and 500 models use a pair of Keihin constant velocity carburetors. The left and right models are similar, but not interchangeable.

Removal/Installation

1. Remove fuel tank.
2. Remove air cleaners.
3. Open throttle valves fully by hand and disconnect throttle cables from lever. If necessary, loosen cable adjusting nut. See **Figure 9**.
4. Loosen the clamping bands that connect the carburetors to the air box (**Figure 10**).
5. Loosen clamps (**Figure 11**) and pull the carburetors off.
6. Installation is the reverse of these steps.
7. Adjust throttle linkage as described elsewhere in this chapter.

Disassembly/Assembly

Refer to **Figure 12, 13, 14, or 15** for this procedure.

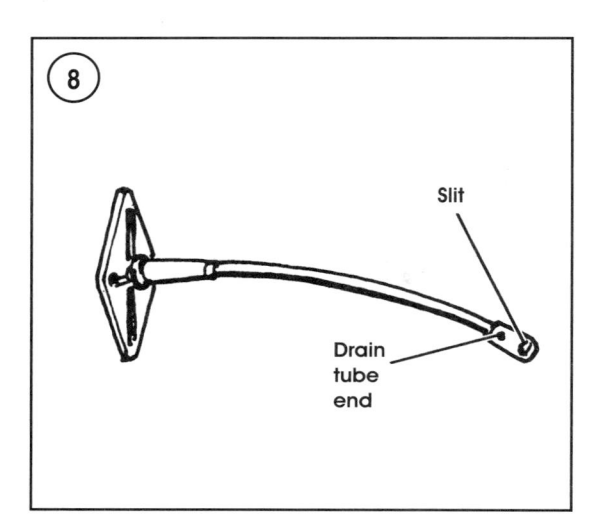

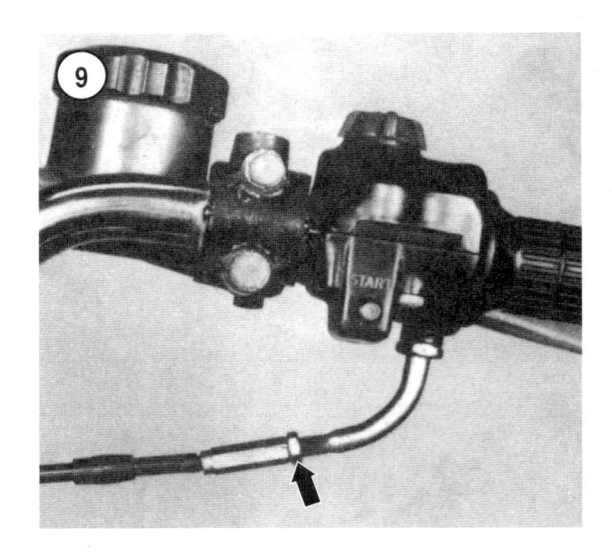

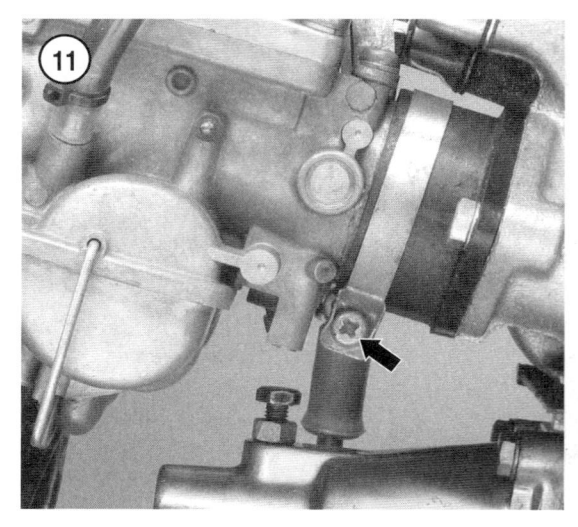

FUEL AND EXHAUST SYSTEMS

RIGHT CARBURETOR ASSEMBLY (5-SPEED — KEIHIN 14H)

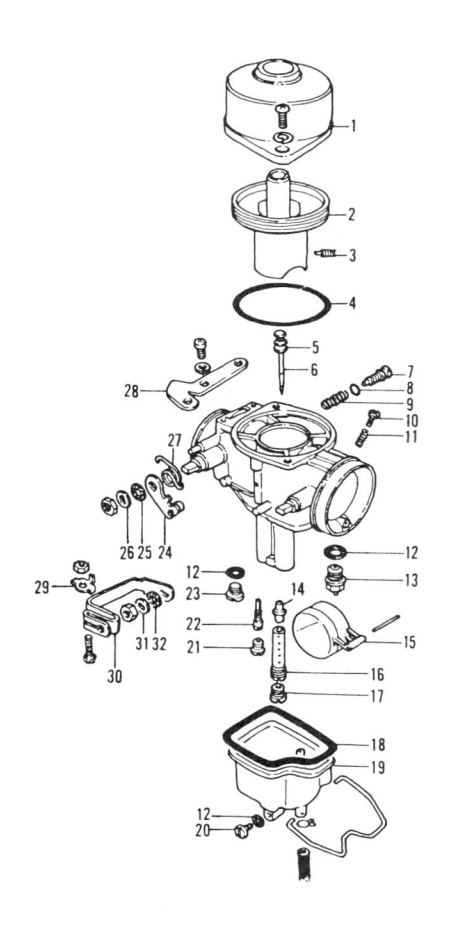

1. Vacuum cylinder
2. Vacuum piston
3. Needle setting screw
4. Vacuum piston stopper
5. Needle clip
6. Needle
7. Pilot screw
8. O-ring
9. Pilot screw spring
10. Throttle stop screw
11. Throttle stop spring
12. Fiber washer
13. Float needle valve
14. Needle jet
15. Float
16. Needle jet holder
17. Main jet
18. Float bowl gasket
19. Float bowl
20. Drain screw
21. Pilot jet
22. Slow jet
23. Plug screw
24. Right throttle lever
25. Serrated lockwasher
26. Lockwasher
27. Right torsion coil spring
28. Right stay plate
29. Tongued washer
30. Connector joint
31. Lockwasher
32. Serrated lockwasher

(12)

RIGHT CARBURETOR — 4-SPEED (KEIHIN 14C AND 14E)

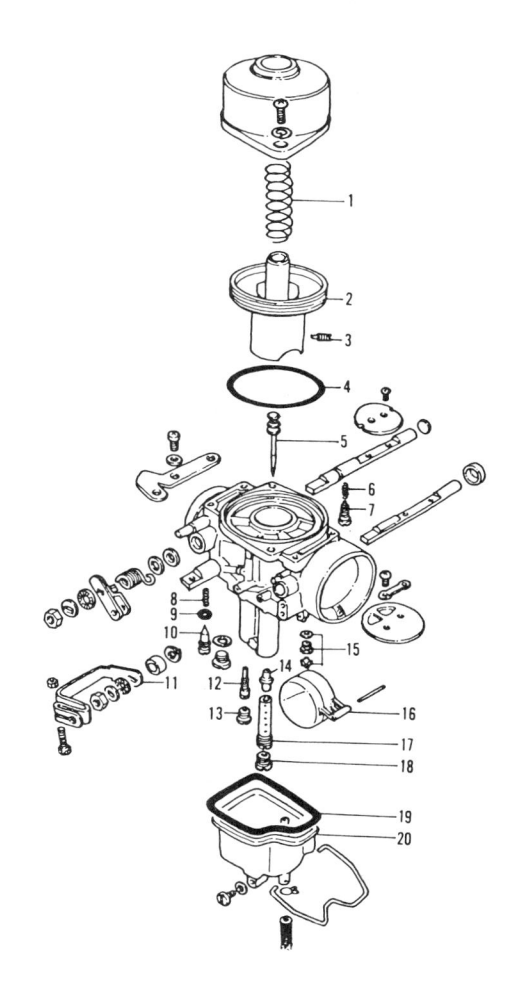

1. Vacuum piston spring
2. Vacuum cylinder
3. Needle setting screw
4. Gasket top
5. Jet needle
6. Air screw spring
7. Throttle stop screw
8. Spring
9. O-ring
10. Pilot screw
11. Connector joint
12. Slow jet
13. Pilot jet
14. Needle jet
15. Needle valve
16. Float
17. Needle jet holder
18. Main jet
19. Float bowl gasket
20. Float bowl

(13)

CHAPTER SIX

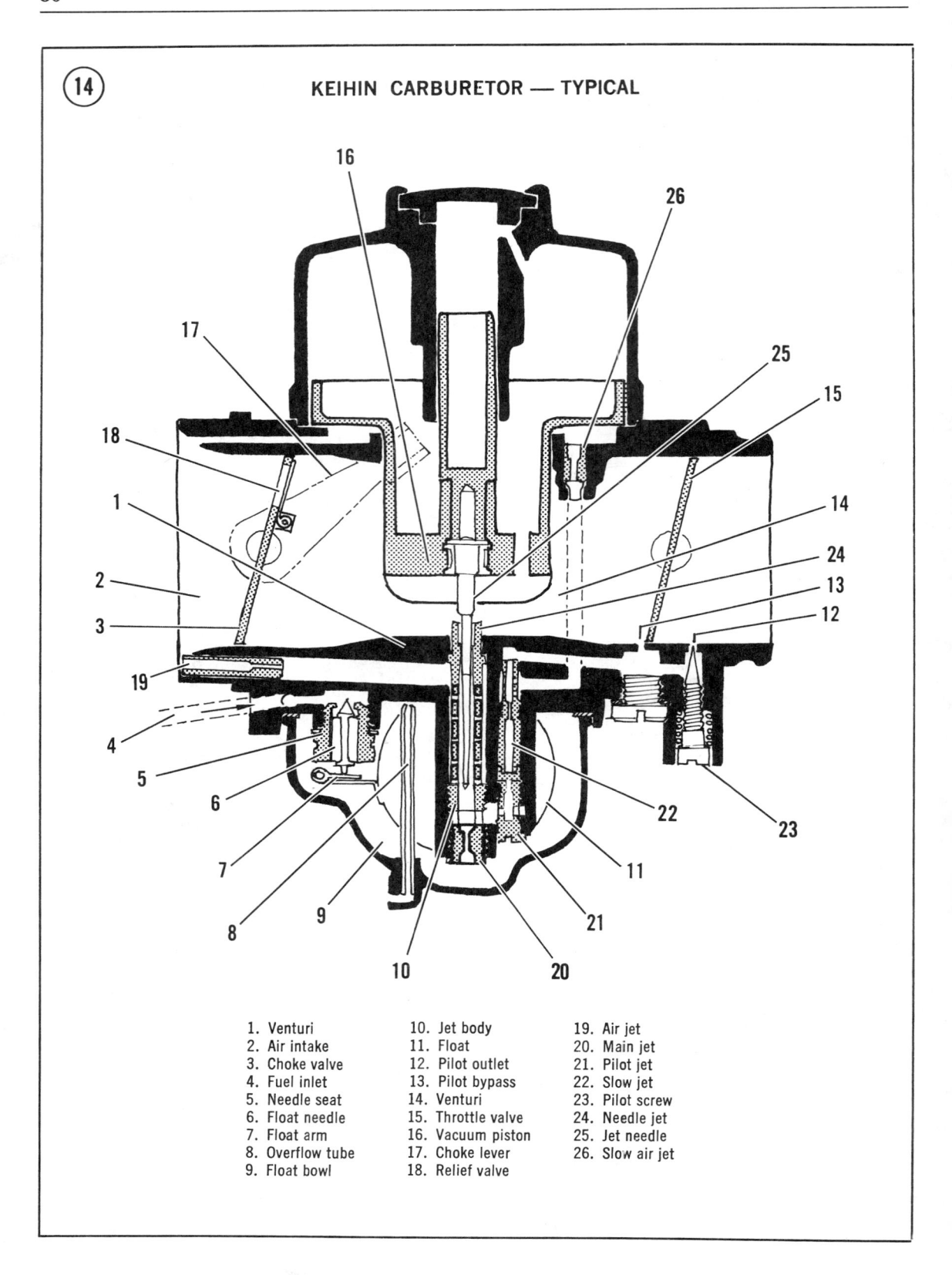

KEIHIN CARBURETOR — TYPICAL

1. Venturi
2. Air intake
3. Choke valve
4. Fuel inlet
5. Needle seat
6. Float needle
7. Float arm
8. Overflow tube
9. Float bowl
10. Jet body
11. Float
12. Pilot outlet
13. Pilot bypass
14. Venturi
15. Throttle valve
16. Vacuum piston
17. Choke lever
18. Relief valve
19. Air jet
20. Main jet
21. Pilot jet
22. Slow jet
23. Pilot screw
24. Needle jet
25. Jet needle
26. Slow air jet

FUEL AND EXHAUST SYSTEMS

RIGHT CARBURETOR (CB500T)

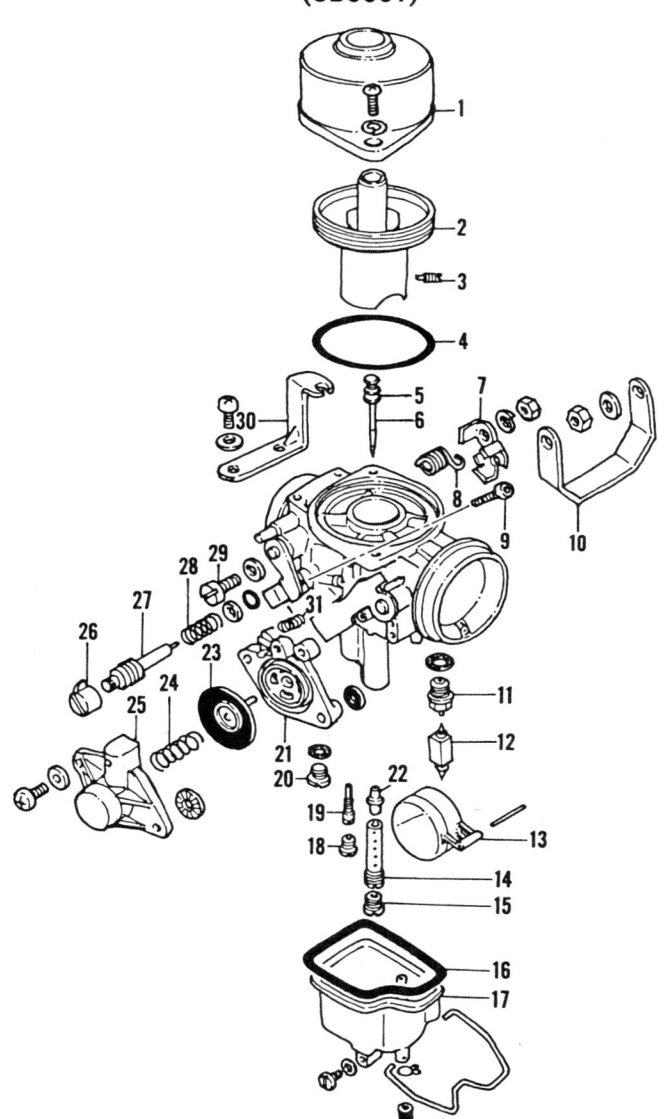

1. Vacuum cylinder
2. Vacuum piston
3. Needle setting screw
4. Vacuum piston stop
5. Jet needle holder
6. Jet needle
7. Throttle lever
8. Torsion spring
9. Throttle stop screw
10. Connecting joint
11. Float valve seat
12. Float valve
13. Float
14. Needle jet holder
15. Main jet
16. Float bowl gasket
17. Float bowl
18. Pilot jet
19. Slow jet
20. Plug
21. Air-cut valve body
22. Needle jet
23. Diaphragm
24. Diaphragm spring
25. Air-cut valve cover
26. Idle limiter
27. Pilot screw
28. Pilot screw spring
29. Vacuum intake hole plug
30. Stay plate
31. Throttle stop spring

1. Remove 2 screws securing top cover (vacuum cylinder). Lift cylinder off.
2. Carefully lift out the piston and the spring (Keihin 14C and E, and CB500T only).

CAUTION
Do not bend needle in piston.

3. Remove the cylinder gasket from the carburetor body.
4. Pull retaining clip aside and lift off float bowl and gasket.
5. Remove float and float pin.
6. Unscrew float valve from carburetor body.
7. Unscrew main jet. Remove main jet, needle jet holder, and needle jet.
8. Remove pilot jet and slow speed jet.
9. Remove pilot screw, seal, and spring.
10. On CB500T, loosen screws and remove air cut valve cover, spring, and diaphragm. Remove additional retaining screws and remove air cut valve body. See **Figure 16**.

> NOTE: *Further disassembly is neither necessary nor advisable. If throttle shafts or butterfly valves are worn or damaged, take the body to your dealer for replacement or repair.*

11. Clean all parts in solvent or special carburetor cleaner.
12. Assembly is the reverse of these steps. Ad-

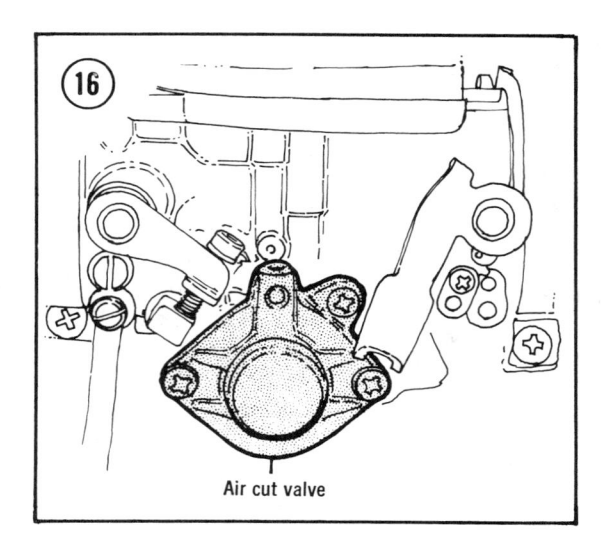

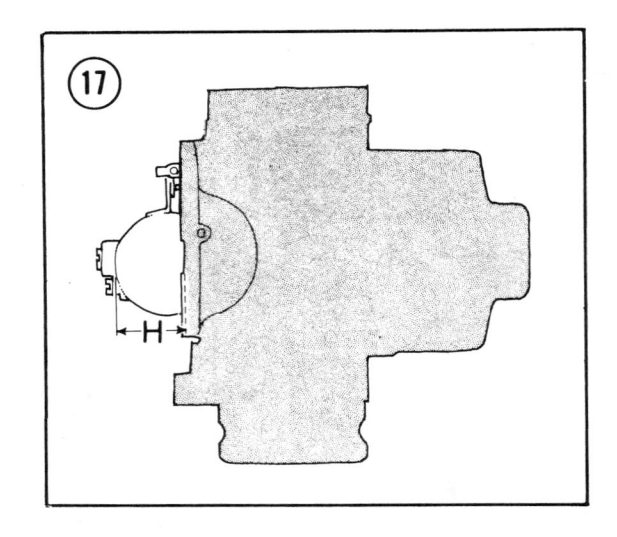

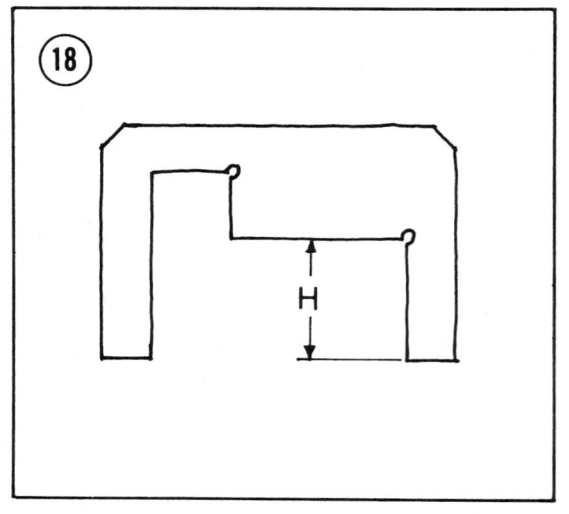

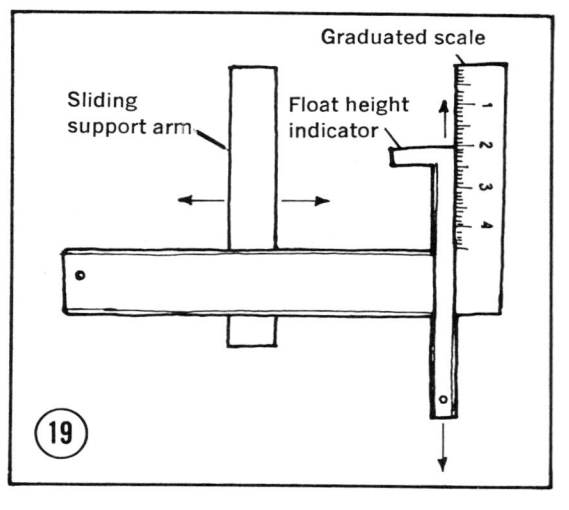

FUEL AND EXHAUST SYSTEMS

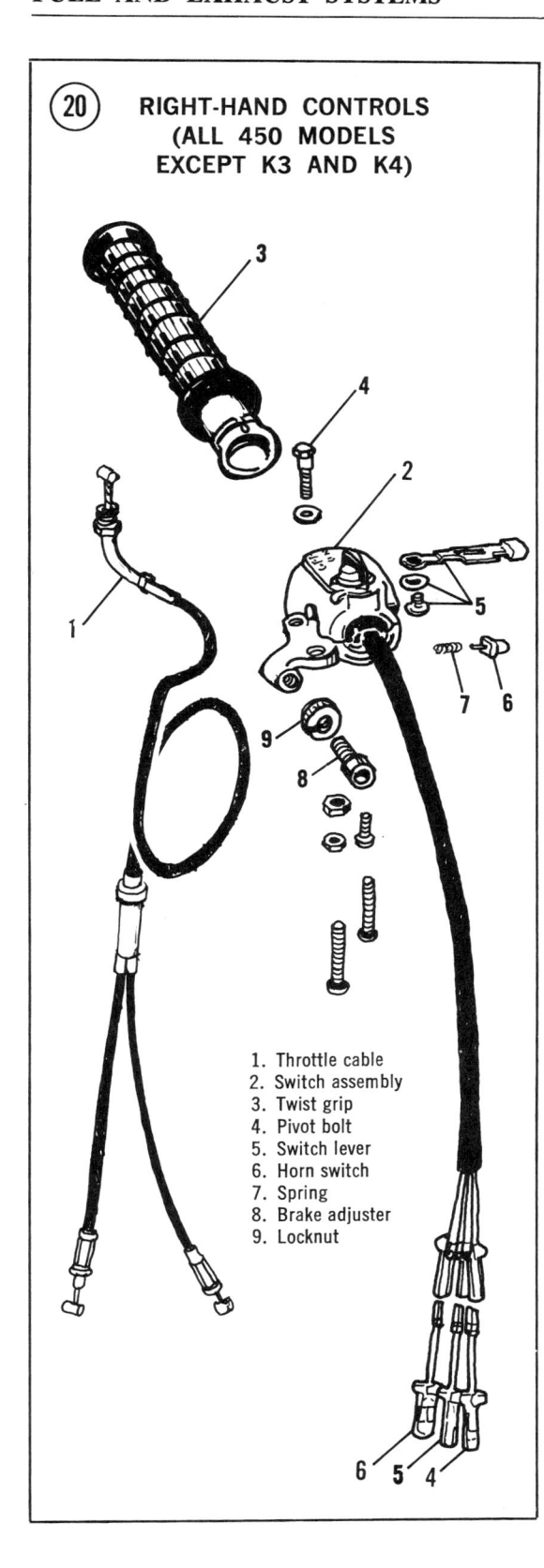

20 RIGHT-HAND CONTROLS (ALL 450 MODELS EXCEPT K3 AND K4)

1. Throttle cable
2. Switch assembly
3. Twist grip
4. Pivot bolt
5. Switch lever
6. Horn switch
7. Spring
8. Brake adjuster
9. Locknut

just float level immediately after installing float, then be careful that you do not disturb the setting while completing the assembly.

Float Level Adjustment

1. Remove float bowl if not removed earlier.
2. Hold carburetor as shown in **Figure 17**.
3. Pull the float gently away from the body, then let it spring back to contact the float valve.
4. Measure distance (H, **Figure 17**) with a special gauge shown in **Figure 18**. Honda also has a universal gauge that can be used (**Figure 19**).
5. Bend the float tang *carefully* to establish distance (H) at 20mm.

THROTTLE LINKAGE

The throttle linkage consists of the twistgrip and cable assembly. See **Figure 20 or 21**.

Throttle Cable Replacement

1. Separate 2 halves of starter switch assembly.
2. Disconnect cable from twistgrip.
3. Unscrew adjuster and pull cable out of switch assembly. See **Figure 22**.
4. Remove fuel tank.
5. Loosen adjusting nut at each carburetor. See **Figure 23**.
6. Disconnect cables from carburetors.

Throttle Cable Adjustment

1. Tighten adjuster at both carburetors just enough to remove cable slack. Both throttle stop screws should still rest on their stops (**Figure 24**).
2. Adjust upper adjuster so that there is 10-15° free play in twistgrip. See **Figure 25**.
3. Adjust carburetors. See Chapter Three.

FUEL TANK

Removal/Installation

1. Drain fuel from tank.
2. Unlock seat and swing out of the way.
3. Shut off fuel petcock.
4. Disconnect fuel lines from petcock; catch fuel from the lines so that it does not spill.

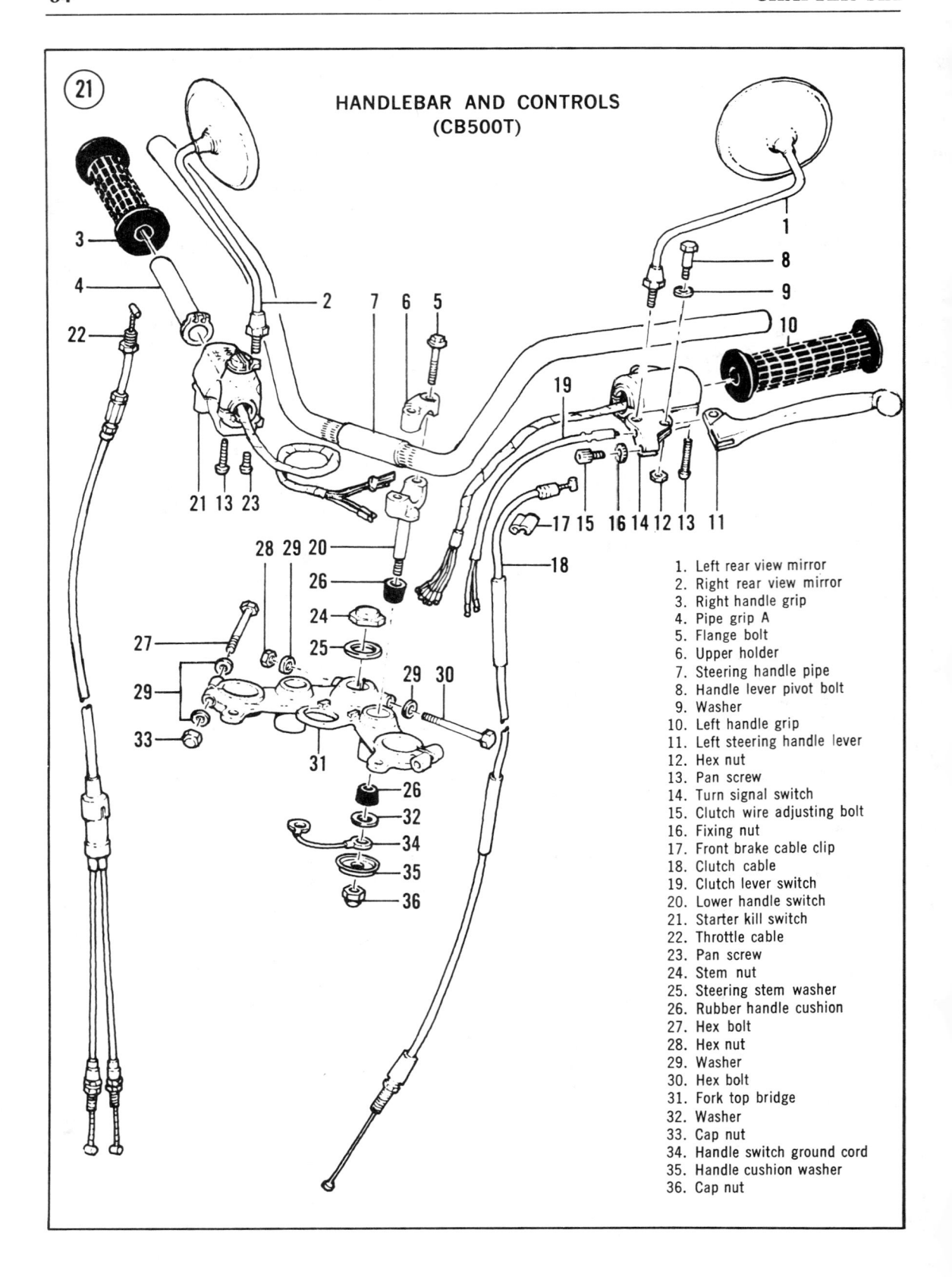

CHAPTER SIX

HANDLEBAR AND CONTROLS (CB500T)

1. Left rear view mirror
2. Right rear view mirror
3. Right handle grip
4. Pipe grip A
5. Flange bolt
6. Upper holder
7. Steering handle pipe
8. Handle lever pivot bolt
9. Washer
10. Left handle grip
11. Left steering handle lever
12. Hex nut
13. Pan screw
14. Turn signal switch
15. Clutch wire adjusting bolt
16. Fixing nut
17. Front brake cable clip
18. Clutch cable
19. Clutch lever switch
20. Lower handle switch
21. Starter kill switch
22. Throttle cable
23. Pan screw
24. Stem nut
25. Steering stem washer
26. Rubber handle cushion
27. Hex bolt
28. Hex nut
29. Washer
30. Hex bolt
31. Fork top bridge
32. Washer
33. Cap nut
34. Handle switch ground cord
35. Handle cushion washer
36. Cap nut

FUEL AND EXHAUST SYSTEMS

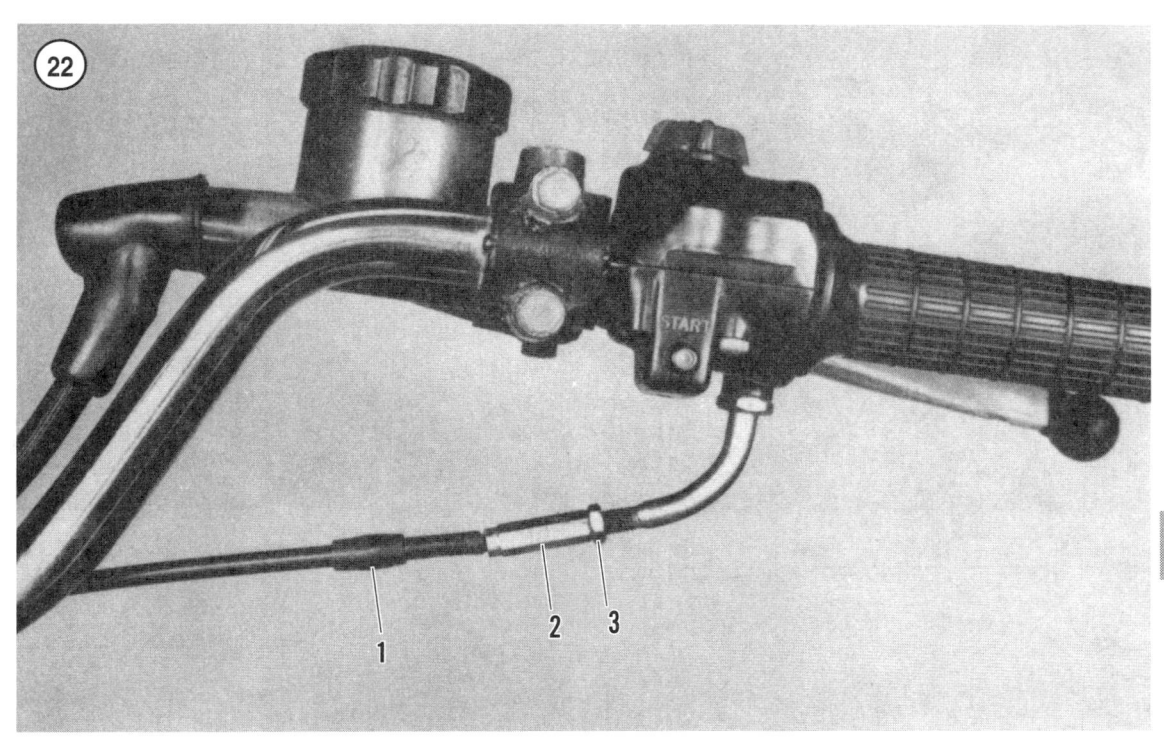

1. Throttle cable   2. Cable adjuster   3. Locknut

CHAPTER SIX

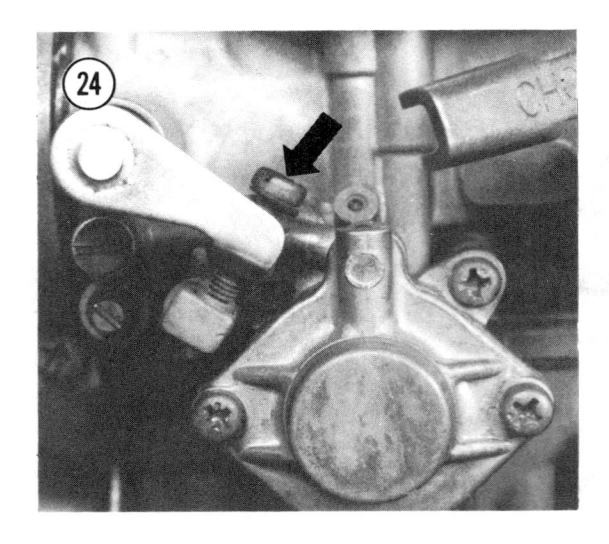

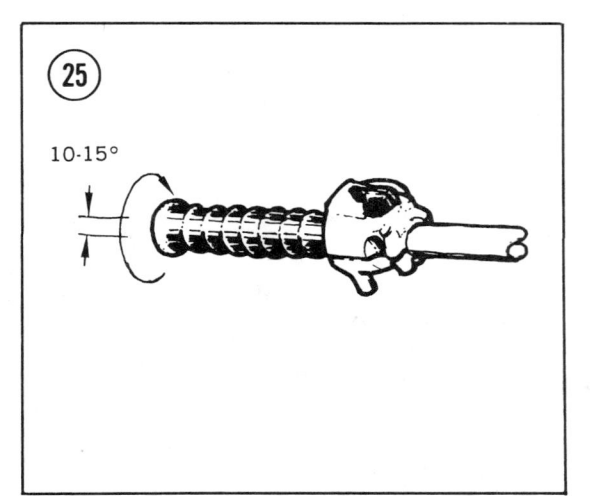

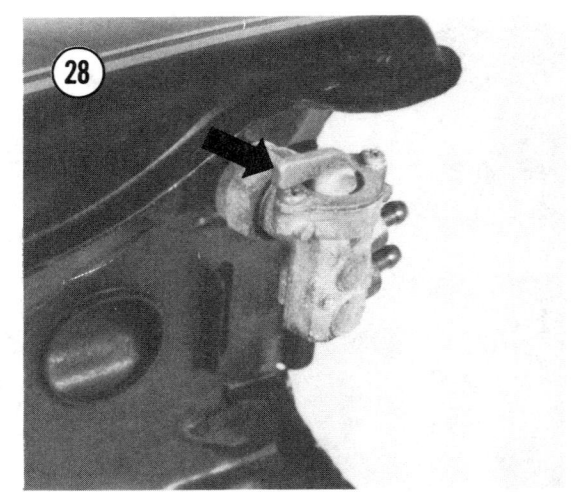

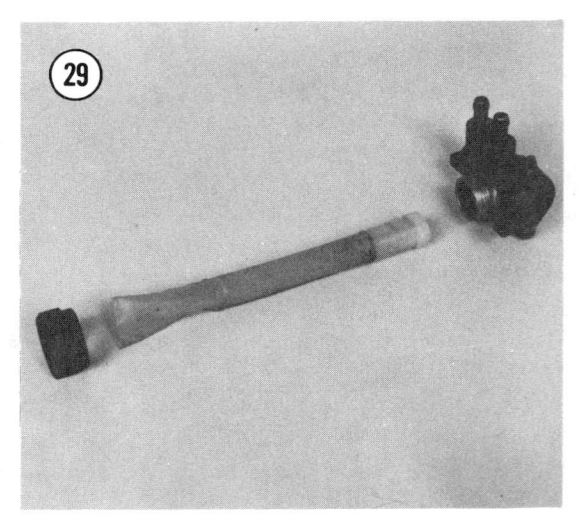

FUEL AND EXHAUST SYSTEMS

5. Disconnect one end of balance line between left and right tank halves, if so equipped. See **Figure 26**.

6. Disconnect fuel tank from rear rubber mount. See **Figure 27**.

7. Lift tank up and toward the rear to remove it.

8. Installation is the reverse of these steps.

Inspection

1. Check the fuel tank for damage or leaks. One way is to close all openings including the cap vent. Immerse it in a tank of hot water. Bubbles will appear wherever there is a leak.

2. Make sure that the filler cap vent is not clogged.

3. Check condition of the filler cap gasket. Replace if necessary.

4. Check all fuel lines for damage or signs of deterioration. Replace if questionable.

Petcock Removal/Installation

1. Drain fuel tank.

2. Remove fuel tank to make job easier.

3. Unscrew the petcock from the fuel tank. See **Figure 28**.

4. On 450 models, remove petcock strainer cover and strainer. See **Figure 29**. Clean both in solvent. On 500 models, see *Fuel Strainer Cleaning*, Chapter Three.

5. Installation is the reverse of these steps. Replace O-ring or strainer if in questionable condition.

EXHAUST SYSTEM

Removal/Installation

See **Figure 30 or 31** for following procedures.

1. Remove nuts securing exhaust pipe(s) to

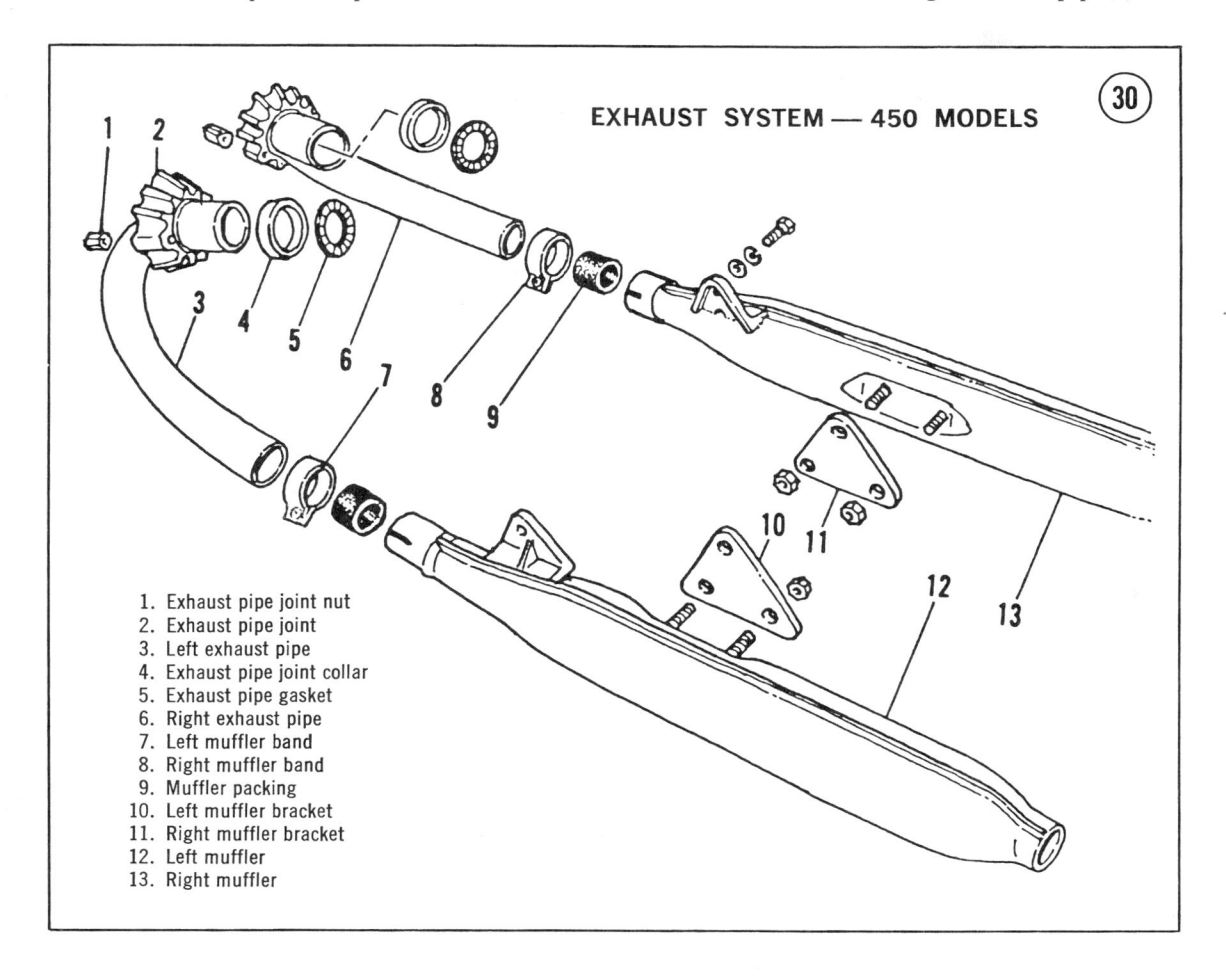

EXHAUST SYSTEM — 450 MODELS (30)

1. Exhaust pipe joint nut
2. Exhaust pipe joint
3. Left exhaust pipe
4. Exhaust pipe joint collar
5. Exhaust pipe gasket
6. Right exhaust pipe
7. Left muffler band
8. Right muffler band
9. Muffler packing
10. Left muffler bracket
11. Right muffler bracket
12. Left muffler
13. Right muffler

CHAPTER SIX

EXHAUST SYSTEM — CB500T

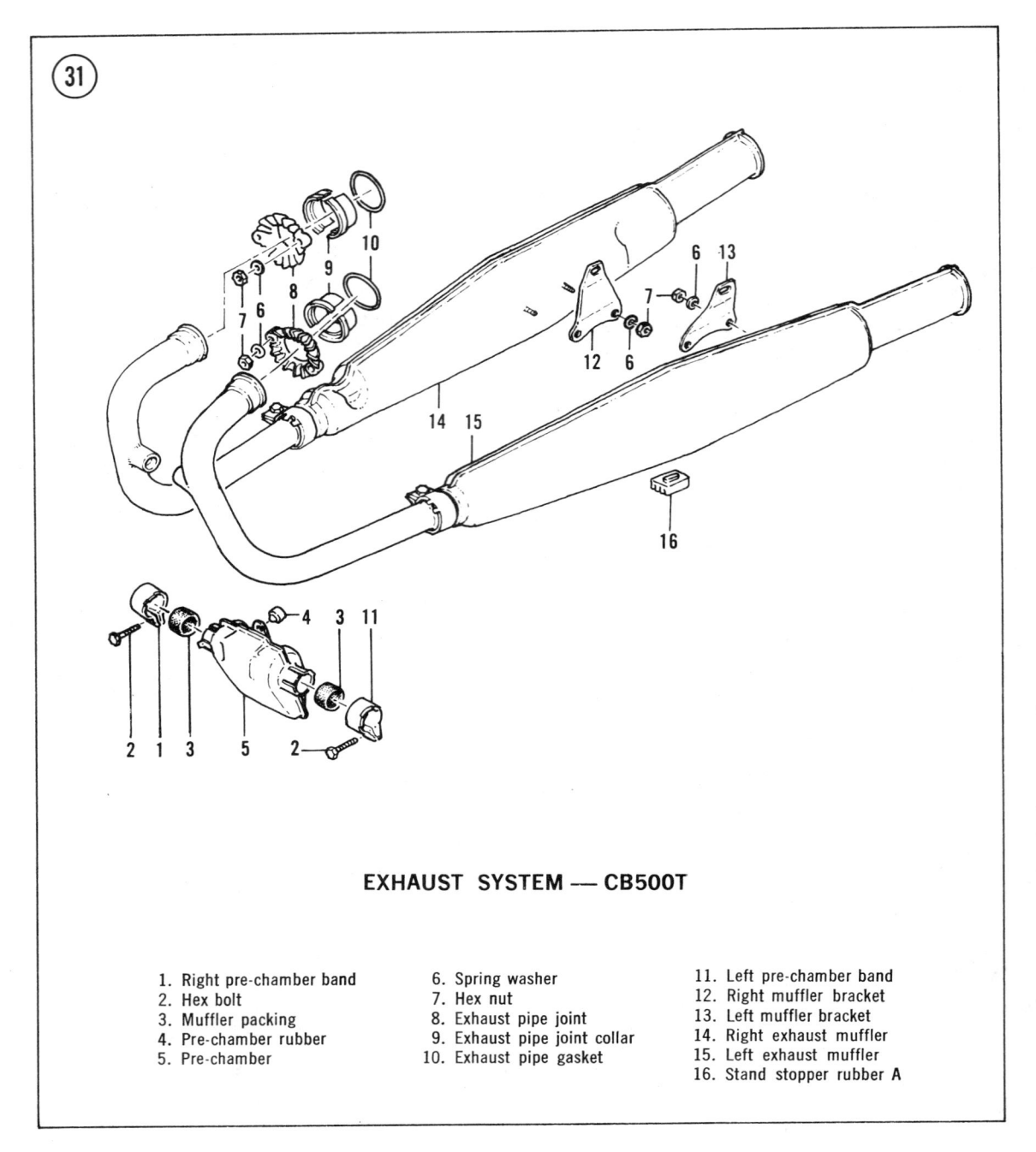

1. Right pre-chamber band
2. Hex bolt
3. Muffler packing
4. Pre-chamber rubber
5. Pre-chamber
6. Spring washer
7. Hex nut
8. Exhaust pipe joint
9. Exhaust pipe joint collar
10. Exhaust pipe gasket
11. Left pre-chamber band
12. Right muffler bracket
13. Left muffler bracket
14. Right exhaust muffler
15. Left exhaust muffler
16. Stand stopper rubber A

cylinder barrels. Remove bolts on pre-chamber bands (**Figure 31**), if so equipped.

2. Remove the nuts that attach the mufflers to the rear brackets. On 450 models, remove the nuts from the forward brackets as well.

3. Remove muffler and exhaust pipe assembly.

4. Remove pre-chamber, if so equipped.

5. Loosen clamp between muffler and exhaust pipe. Separate muffler from exhaust pipe.

6. Installation is the reverse of these steps. Use a new packing between muffler and exhaust pipe. Do not tighten exhaust pipe flange nuts until muffler is in place and mounting nuts snugged down.

CHAPTER SEVEN

ELECTRICAL SYSTEM

The electrical system includes the following systems (each is described in detail in this chapter):

a. Charging system
b. Ignition system
c. Lighting system
d. Directional signals
e. Horn

CHARGING SYSTEM

The charging system consists of the battery, alternator, rectifier, and regulator. See **Figure 1**.

The alternator generates an alternating current (AC) which the rectifier converts to direct current (DC). The regulator maintains the voltage to the battery and load (lights, ignition, etc.) at a constant voltage regardless of variations in engine speed and load.

Testing Charging System

Whenever a charging system trouble is suspected, make sure the battery is good before going any further. Clean and test the battery as described below.

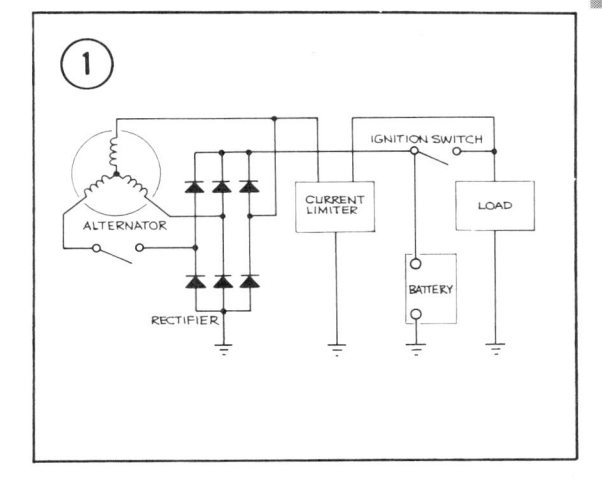

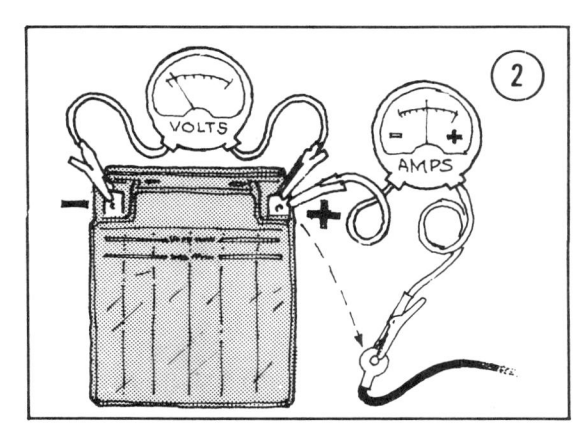

To test the charging system, connect a 0-15 DC voltmeter and a 0-10 DC ammeter as shown in **Figure 2**. Connect the positive ammeter terminal in series to the rectifier wire and the negative ammeter terminal to the positive battery terminal. Connect the positive voltmeter terminal to the positive battery terminal and negative voltmeter terminal to ground.

CAUTION
If the ammeter is connected between the positive battery terminal and the starter cable, the ammeter will burn out if the electric starter is used.

Start the engine and run it at the speeds listed in **Table 1**. Observe the voltmeter and ammeter and compare their indications with the specifications. All of the measurements are made with the lights on.

If charging current is considerably lower than specified, check the alternator and rectifier. Less likely is that the charging current is too high; in that case, the regulator is probably at fault.

Test the separate charging system components as described under appropriate heading.

BATTERY

Care and Inspection

1. Lift seat
2. Remove battery hold-down strap.
3. Disconnect battery cables and vent line.

CAUTION
Do not start engine with battery removed or the rectifier will be damaged.

4. Clean top of battery with baking soda solution. Scrub with a stiff bristle brush. Wipe battery clean with a cloth moistened in ammonia solution, then flush with clean water.

CAUTION
Keep cleaning solution out of battery cells or the electrolyte will be seriously weakened.

5. Clean the battery terminals with a stiff wire brush.
6. Examine entire battery case for cracks.
7. Install the battery and reconnect battery cables. Observe battery polarity.
8. Coat the battery connections with light mineral grease or Vaseline after tightening.
9. Check the electrolyte level and top up if it is necessary.

Testing

Hydrometer testing is the best way to check battery condition. See **Figure 3**. Use a hydrometer with numbered graduations from 1.100-1.300 rather than one with color-coded bands. To use the hydrometer, squeeze the rubber ball, insert the tip in the cell, and release the ball. Draw enough electrolyte to float the weighted float inside the hydrometer. Note the number in line with surface of the electrolyte; this is the specific gravity for this cell. Return the electrolyte to the cell from which it came.

Table 1   CHARGING RPM

Load	Charging Starts at	Charging Current Amps			
		3,000 rpm	5,000 rpm	8,000 rpm	10,000 rpm
450cc					
All lights off	1,000 rpm max.	3.0-4.0	4.0-5.0	—	5.7 max.
Lights on (high beam)	1,800 rpm max.	1.0-1.6	1.6-2.4	—	3.2 max.
Lights on (low beam)	1,500 rpm max.	1.6-2.6	2.4-3.4	—	4.0 max.
500cc					
High beam	2,800 rpm max.	—	1.2 max.	3.5 max.	—

ELECTRICAL SYSTEM

The specific gravity of the electrolyte in each battery cell is an excellent indication of that cell's condition. A fully-charged cell will read 1.275-1.380, while a cell in good condition may read from 1.250-1.280. A cell in fair condition reads from 1.225-1.250, and anything below 1.225 is practically dead.

Specific gravity varies with temperature. For each 10° that electrolyte temperature exceeds 80°F, add 0.004 to reading indicated on the hydrometer. Subtract 0.004 for each 10° below 80°F.

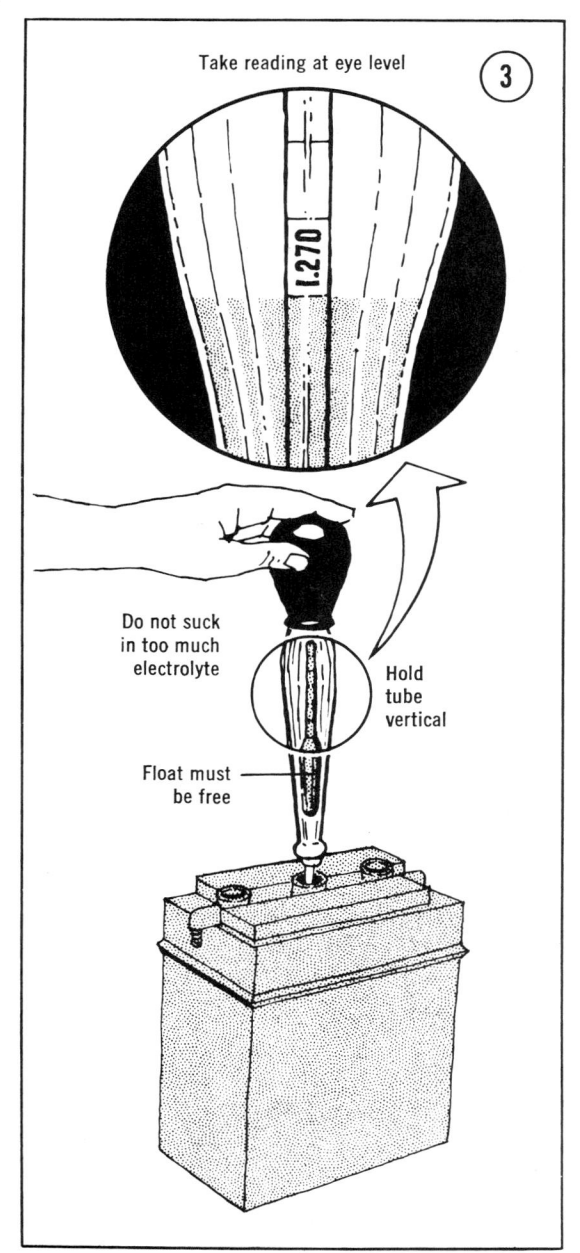

If the cells test in the poor range, the battery requires recharging. The hydrometer is useful for checking the progress of the charging operation. **Table 2** shows approximate state of charge.

> CAUTION
> *Always disconnect both battery connections before connecting charging equipment.*

ALTERNATOR

Removal/Installation

1. Drain engine oil.
2. Remove gearshift lever and left foot peg.
3. Remove left crankcase cover with stator. Disconnect wires from harness.
4. Remove the bolts that attach the alternator stator to the crankcase cover (**Figure 4**). Remove the stator from the cover.

Table 2 STATE OF CHARGE

Specific Gravity	State of Charge
1.110 - 1.130	Discharged
1.140 - 1.160	Almost discharged
1.170 - 1.190	One-quarter charged
1.200 - 1.220	One-half charged
1.230 - 1.250	Three-quarters charged
1.260 - 1.280	Fully charged

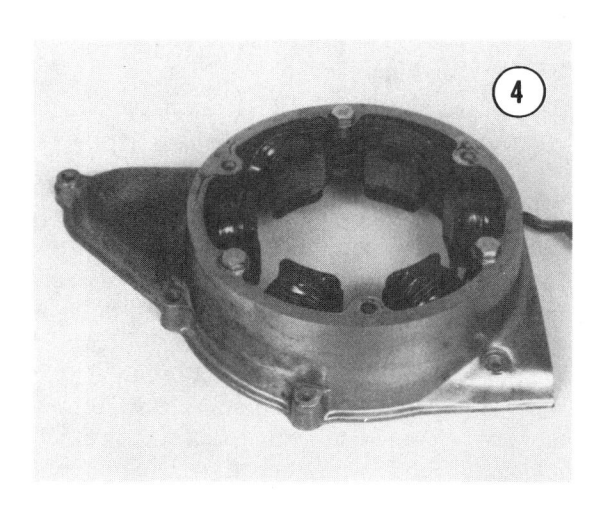

5. Remove alternator rotor (**Figure 5**). If a puller is not available, a suitable substitute can be fabricated by grinding away some of the threads from a CB350 rear axle shaft, then welding the other end to a discarded socket wrench or hex bolt.

6. Test and inspect as described below.

7. Installation is the reverse of these steps.

Testing

Remove stator and rotor as described above.

Check stator for shorts and open circuits with an ohmmeter. See **Figure 6**. Measure between yellow and pink leads; resistance should be about 1.1 ohms. Measure between white and pink leads; resistance should be about 0.55 ohms. Significantly lower readings indicate a short. Significantly higher or an "infinity" reading indicates an open circuit. In either case, replace the stator.

The rotor is permanently magnetized and cannot be tested except by replacement with a rotor known to be good. A rotor can lose magnetism from old age or a sharp blow. If defective, the rotor must be replaced.

Check all wiring to the stator for chafe or broken connections. Also check condition of stator windings for damaged insulation.

RECTIFIER

Removal/Installation

1. Lift the seat.
2. Loosen the nut securing rectifier to battery bracket. See **Figure 7**.
3. Pull rectifier out and disconnect cable.
4. Installation is the reverse of these steps.

Testing

All models are equipped with full wave bridge rectifiers. There are 3 principal types of rectifiers; both operate the same, but they differ in lead colors and connections.

Some rectifiers mount by one terminal. The other terminals are leads, colored yellow, brown, and red/white. To test this rectifier, disconnect it from the motorcycle, then using an ohmmeter,

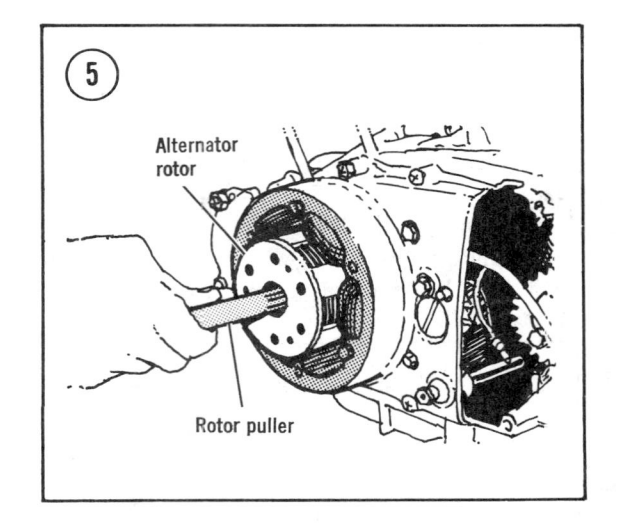

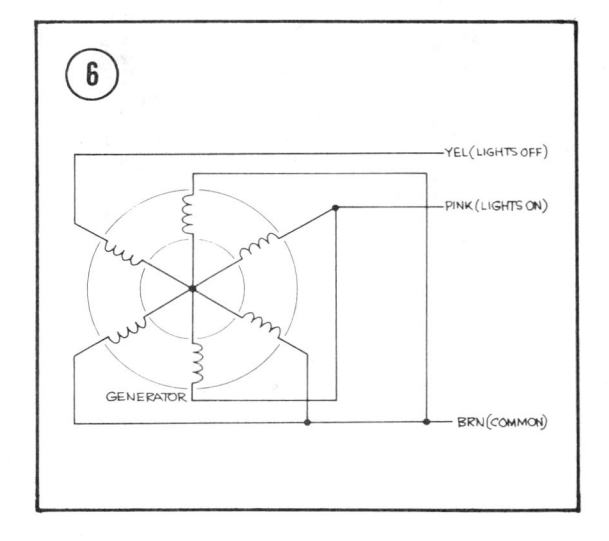

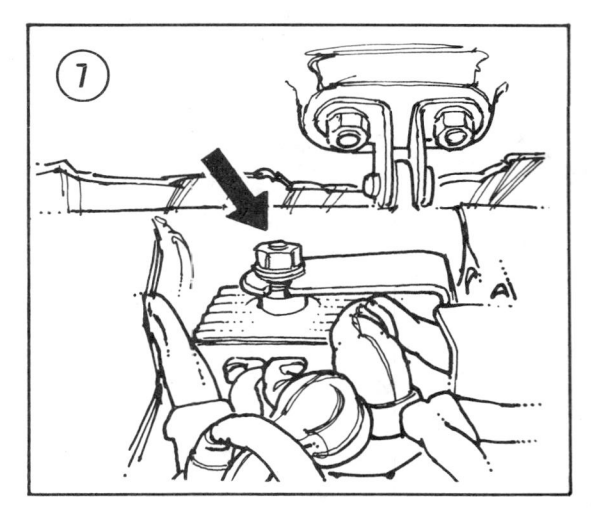

ELECTRICAL SYSTEM

measure resistance in both directions between the following pairs of terminals:

a. Yellow-ground
b. Brown-ground
c. Yellow-red/white
d. Brown-red/white

The second type rectifier has 4 leads colored green, yellow, red/white or brown/white, and pink. To test this rectifier, measure resistance between each pair of wires listed:

a. Green-yellow
b. Green-pink
c. Yellow-red/white or brown/white
d. Pink-red/white or brown/white

On either of the above rectifiers, resistance between each pair should be very high in one direction and low in the other. If resistance is either very high or very low in either direction, replace the rectifier assembly.

The third type is the silicon diode rectifier used on the CB500T. Check each diode by connecting the negative probe of an ohmmeter to the green lead (terminal one) and the positive lead to the red/white, yellow, and pink leads in turn (terminals 2, 3, and 4, respectively). Then reverse the leads and repeat the test. Resistance should be very high in one direction and very low in the other. Continuity should not exist between any other combination of leads.

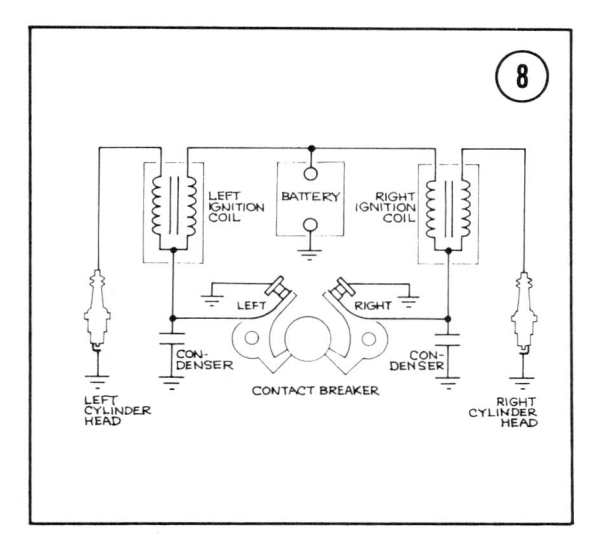

CAUTION
Do not use a megger for this test, as the high voltage involved could damage the diodes.

Always handle the rectifier assembly carefully. Do not bend or try to rotate the wafers. Do not loosen the screw which holds the assembly together. Moisture can damage the assembly, so keep it dry.

REGULATOR

Removal/Installation

1. Remove tool box, if so equipped.
2. Remove 2 bolts securing regulator.
3. Disconnect 3 electrical wires and remove regulator.
4. Installation is the reverse of these steps.

Testing

Test charging system as described earlier. If charging current is too high, replace regulator.

IGNITION SYSTEM

The ignition system consists of a coil spark plug and point set for each cylinder (**Figure 8**). Some models have a single coil and point set and 2 spark plugs (**Figure 9**), but these have never been imported into the U.S.

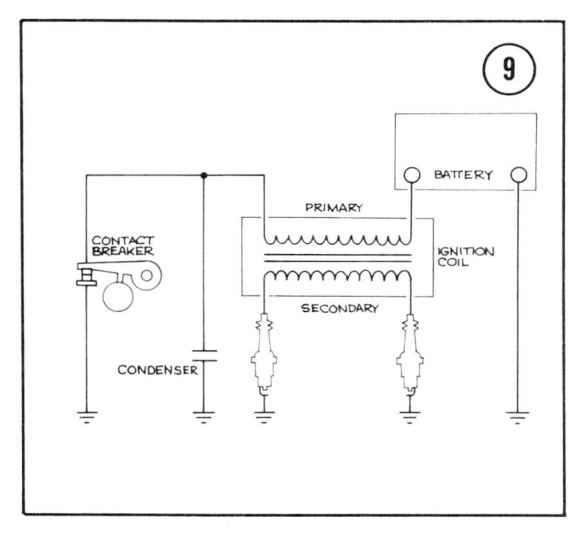

IGNITION COILS

Removal/Installation

The coils are located under the fuel tank. See **Figure 10** for the 450 models. The CB500T uses the same system, except that the ignition switch has been moved to the fork top bridge and also serves as a fork lock.

1. Remove fuel tank, described in Chapter Six.
2. Disconnect leads at spark plugs.
3. Disconnect 4 small wires at the harness connectors.
4. Remove screw securing coil assembly and remove coil assembly.
5. Installation is the reverse of these steps.

Testing

The best test for a suspected coil is to replace it with a known good coil. Another way is to check it for continuity as follows.

1. Short both black/white wires together with a small jumper wire.
2. Connect black ohmmeter lead to common connection of black/white wires.
3. Connect red ohmmeter lead to each spark plug lead. The 2 measurements should be nearly equal. If one reads significantly higher or lower, replace the coil assembly.
4. Connect red ohmmeter lead to the blue, then the yellow lead. Both measurements should be nearly equal. If one reads significantly higher or lower than the other, replace the coil assembly.

CONDENSERS

Removal/Installation

Both condensers are in the same case, mounted directly over coil assembly (**Figure 10**).
1. Remove fuel tank, described in Chapter Six.
2. Disconnect condenser wires from harness.
3. Remove 2 screws securing condenser to coil assembly and remove condenser.
4. Installation is the reverse of these steps.

Testing

The condenser can be tested with ohmmeters which have an internal battery of 12 volts or less. Ohmmeters with larger batteries can destroy a good condenser as soon as connected.
1. Connect one lead of ohmmeter to metal case of condenser.
2. Touch other ohmmeter lead to one condenser lead and watch the ohmmeter needle. If condenser is good, needle will initially drop to a very low resistance, then start climbing higher and higher. Eventually, it may reach infinity. Touch condenser lead to case (**Figure 11**) to discharge it.
3. Repeat Step 2 on the other lead.
4. If the needle drops to a low value and stays there, or climbs very slightly, the condenser is shorted. If the needle never drops to a low value, but remains high, the condenser is open. In either case, replace the condenser assembly.

BREAKER POINTS

Breaker point maintenance is fully described in Chapter Three under *Engine Tune-up*.

STARTING SYSTEM

The starting system consists of the starter motor, chain, sprockets, starter clutch, and solenoid (magnetic switch).

STARTER MOTOR

The starter motor is mounted on the forward part of the engine.

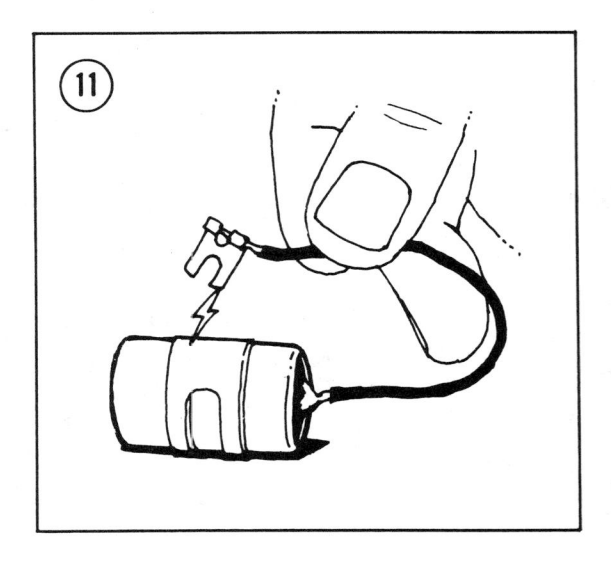

ELECTRICAL SYSTEM

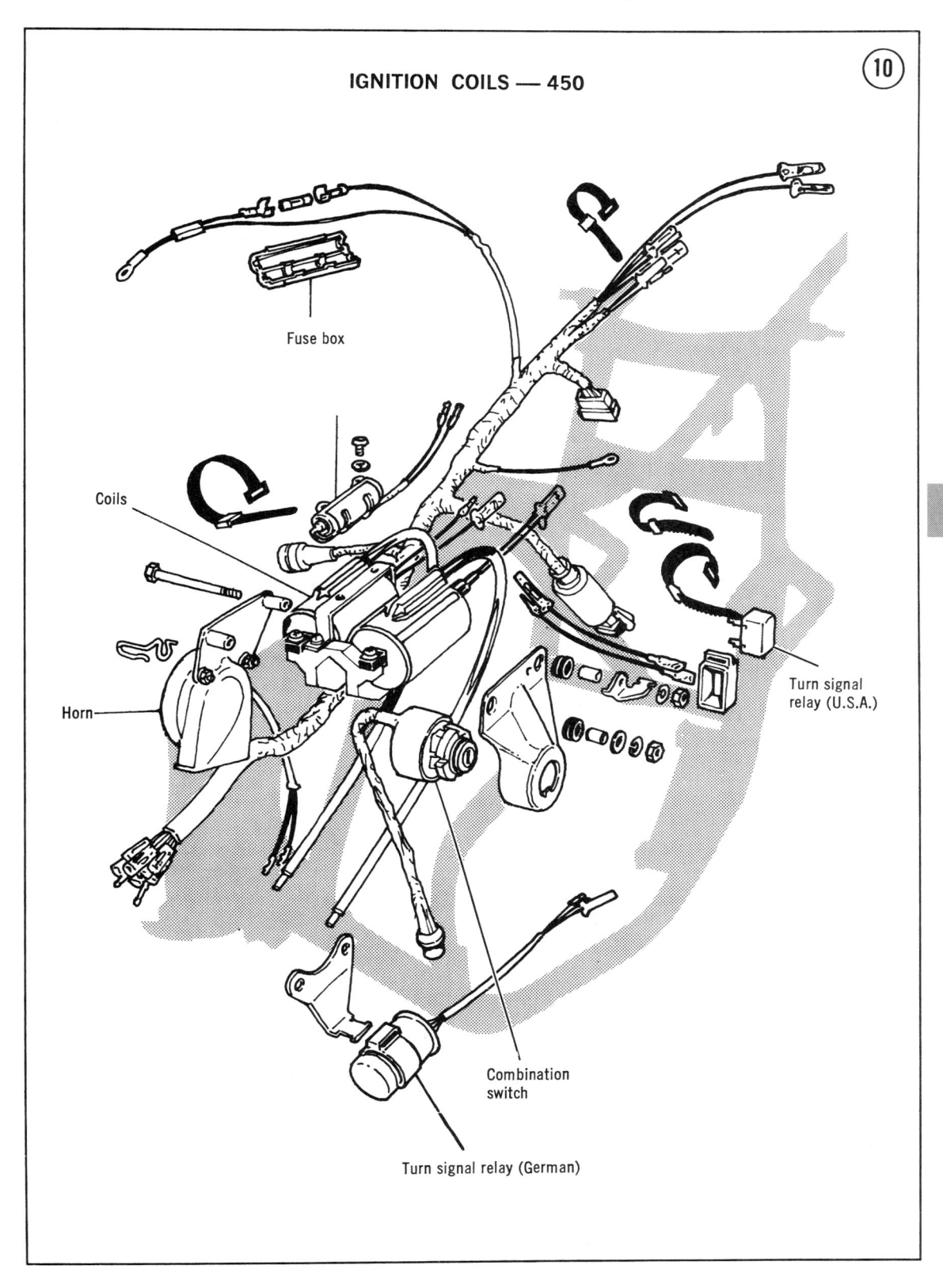

IGNITION COILS — 450

- Fuse box
- Coils
- Horn
- Turn signal relay (U.S.A.)
- Combination switch
- Turn signal relay (German)

Removal/Installation

1. Remove left crankcase cover.
2. Disconnect starter cable at starter terminal.
3. On early CB450's, remove side cover shown in **Figure 12**.
4. Remove 2 bolts from right side and remove motor while carefully disengaging chain from sprocket.
5. Installation is the reverse of these steps.

Disassembly/Assembly

Refer to **Figures 13 and 14**.

1. Remove 2 through bolts.
2. Separate end bracket from motor.
3. Loosen 3mm screw securing brush holder.
4. Remove brushes from holder.
5. Remove gearcase.
6. Remove 3 gears from case.
7. Remove armature.
8. Assembly is the reverse of these steps. Grease gears thoroughly; use new gaskets and O-rings.

Inspection

1. Check the condition of the commutator (**Figure 15**). The mica in a good commutator is cut below the level of the copper (A). If the copper is worn down to the mica (B), the mica must be cut down. This is a job for your dealer or an automotive electrical specialist.
2. Clean all grease, dirt, and carbon dust from armature, case, end bracket, and gearcase.

> **CAUTION**
> Do not *immerse brushes of the wire windings in solvent or the insulation might be damaged. Wipe windings with a cloth lightly moistened with solvent.*

STARTER CLUTCH

The starter clutch is part of the alternator rotor.

Removal/Installation

1. Remove starter motor as described above.

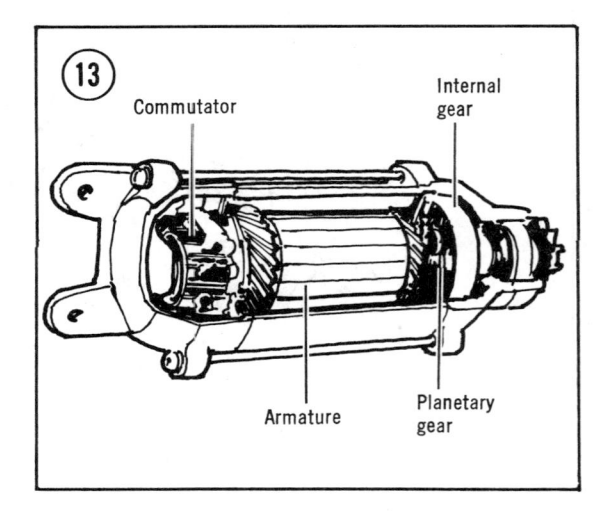

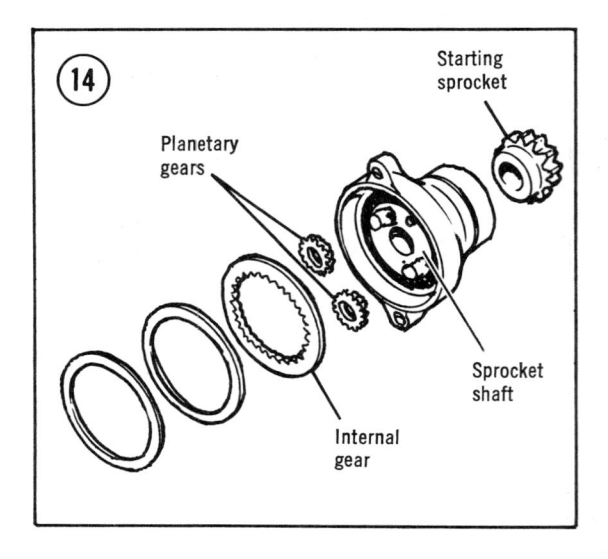

ELECTRICAL SYSTEM

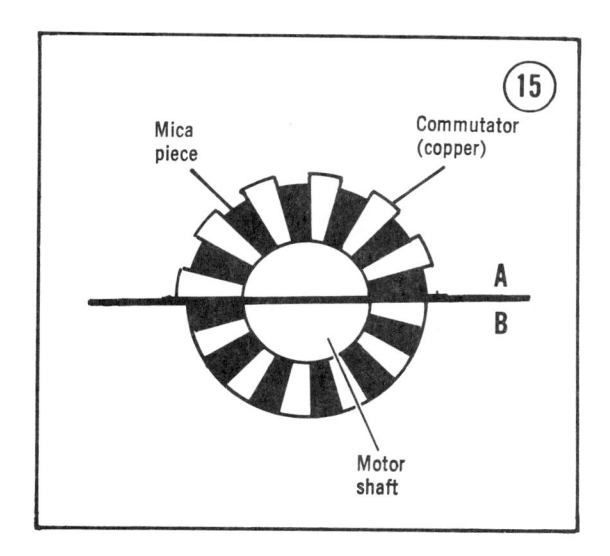

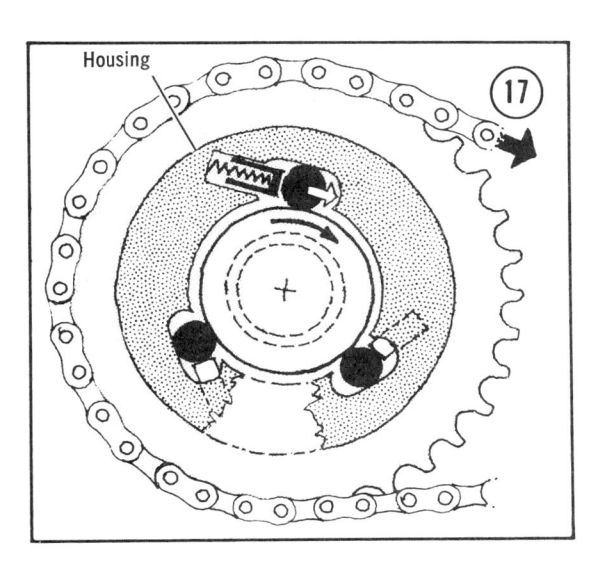

2. Remove alternator rotor as described elsewhere in this chapter.

3. Remove 3 screws securing side plate. See **Figure 16**.

4. Remove clutch parts. Note orientation before removing and compare to **Figure 17**.

5. Clean all parts in solvent.

6. Make sure clutch parts are not magnetized. If they show magnetic attraction for each other, replace them, otherwise the clutch will act erratically.

7. Grease clutch parts with silicone (high temperature) grease and reassemble.

8. Install side plate with 3 screws.

9. Install alternator rotor/clutch assembly over sprocket.

10. Install starter rotor.

STARTER SOLENOID

Removal/Installation

The starter solenoid is mounted near the battery under the seat.

1. Lift the seat.
2. Disconnect negative battery cable at battery.
3. Disconnect wires from solenoid.
4. Pull solenoid out of rubber mount.
5. Installation is the reverse of these steps.

Cleaning

1. Remove 2 screws securing solenoid cover and lift cover. See **Figure 18**.

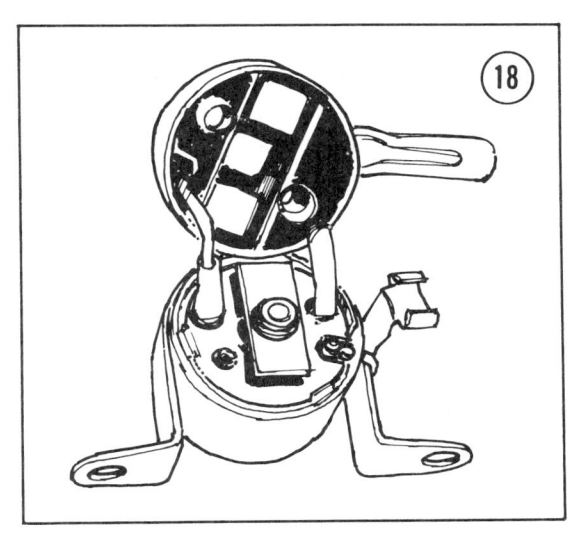

2. File contacts, if necessary, to clean them.

3. Wipe off any oil from contacts.

4. Check condition of the O-ring. Replace if necessary.

5. Install cover.

LIGHTING SYSTEM

The lighting system consists of the following components:

a. Headlight
b. Taillight
c. Directional signals
d. Warning lights
e. Stoplights

Table 3 lists replacement bulbs for the above components.

HEADLIGHT

Replacement (U.S. Models)

1. Remove 3 screws and remove headlight from case. See **Figure 19**.

2. Disconnect socket from sealed beam.

3. Remove 2 retaining lock pins and screws from rim.

4. Remove sealed beam.

5. Installation is the reverse of these steps. Adjust headlight as described below.

Replacement (U.K. Models)

U.K. models use a prefocused headlamp bulb and a city (pilot) lamp. To replace either bulb:

1. Unscrew the 3 crosshead screws from the headlight rim (**Figure 19**) and remove the rim from the housing.

2. Pull the city lamp out of the housing (**Figure 20**). Insert a new bulb and push it back into the housing.

3. Disconnect the spring that holds the headlight socket in place (**Figure 21**). Remove the old bulb from the socket. Install a new bulb, making sure the offset pins line up with their respective slots so the prefocusing will not be disturbed. Note also that the socket can be installed only one way. Reconnect the spring.

NOTE: Do not touch *the glass portion of the bulb with your fingers. Should you do so, wipe the bulb clean before installing it. Grease or oil from your fingers will shorten the life of the bulb.*

Table 3　REPLACEMENT BULBS

Headlight	12v—35/50W
Tail/stoplight	SAE 1157 (12v—3/32cp)
Directional signals	SAE 1073 (12v—32cp)
Instrument lights	SAE 57 (12v—2cp)
Neutral indicator	SAE 57 (12v—2cp)
Directional signal indicator	SAE 57 (12v—2cp)
High beam indicator	SAE 57 (12v—2cp)

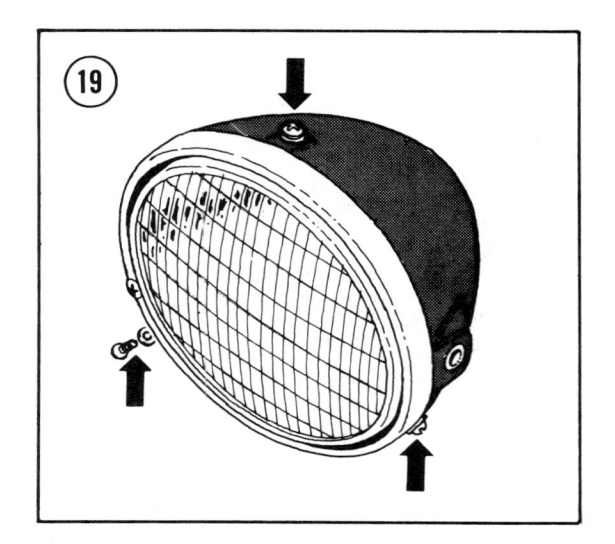

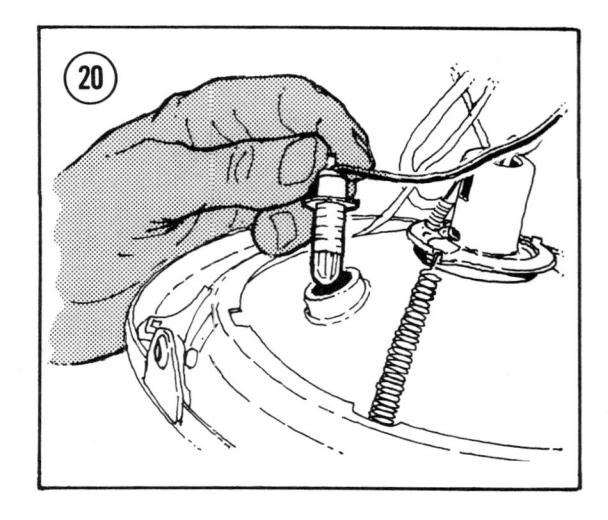

ELECTRICAL SYSTEM

4. Install the headlamp unit in the housing, install the rim, and screw in and tighten the crosshead screws.

5. Adjust the headlight as described below.

Adjustment

Adjust headlight horizontally and vertically, according to Department of Motor Vehicle regulations in your state (**Figure 22**).

To adjust headlight horizontally, turn the screw illustrated in **Figure 23**. To adjust vertically, loosen the bolts on either side of the case. Move the headlight to the desired position, then tighten bolts.

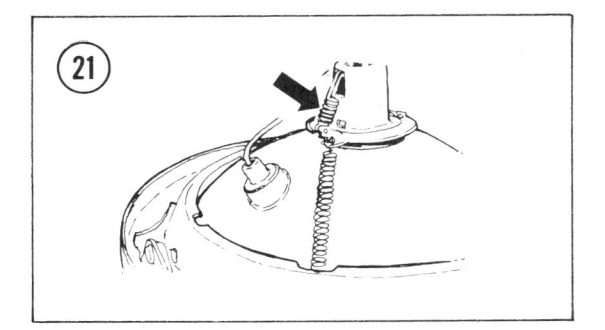

TAIL/STOPLIGHTS

Taillight Replacement

A single bulb performs as a taillight, license plate light, and stoplight. To replace the bulb, remove the lens and turn bulb counterclockwise. See **Table 3** for replacement type.

Front Stoplight Switch Replacement

The front stoplight switch operates from hydraulic brake pressure. It is located just above the bottom triple clamp. See **Figure 24**.

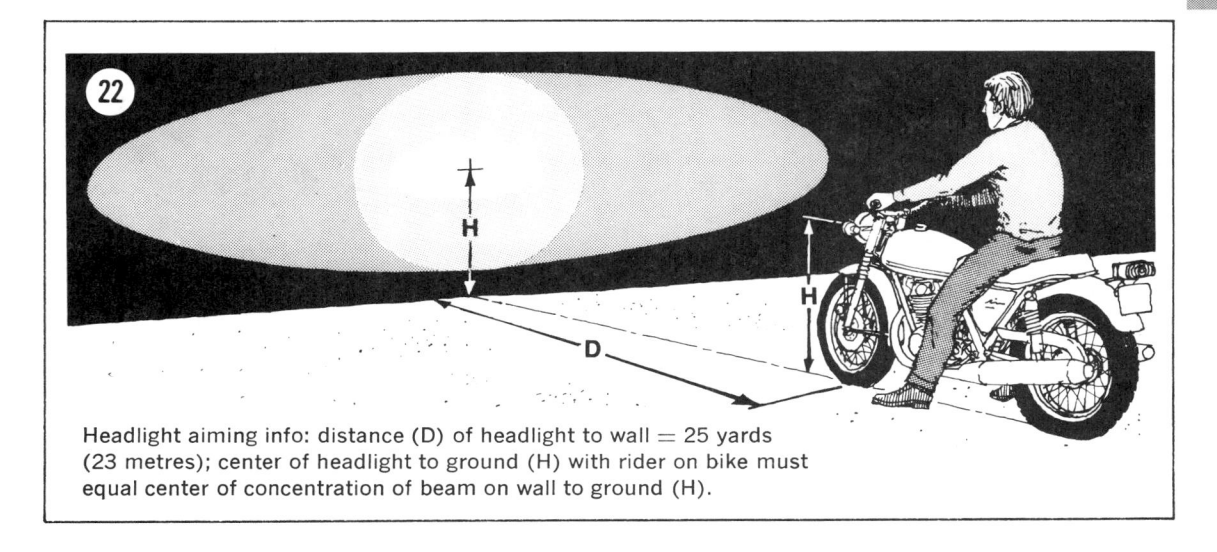

Headlight aiming info: distance (D) of headlight to wall = 25 yards (23 metres); center of headlight to ground (H) with rider on bike must equal center of concentration of beam on wall to ground (H).

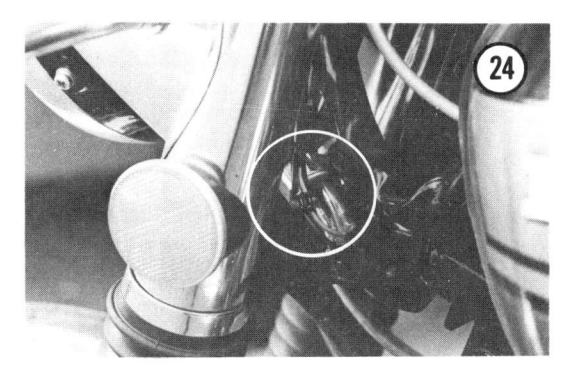

1. Disconnect electrical wires.
2. Siphon brake fluid from reservoir with a siphon used only for brake fluid.

> **WARNING**
> *Do not suck brake fluid out with your mouth. Brake fluid is poisonous.*

3. Unscrew the stoplight switch.

> **CAUTION**
> *Catch dripping brake fluid before it spills on painted surfaces. Brake fluid can damage paint. If brake fluid does spill, flush it off with mild detergent and water immediately.*

4. Installation is the reverse of these steps.
5. Fill brake reservoir and bleed brakes as described in Chapter Ten.

Rear Stoplight Switch

The rear stoplight switch is located near the tool box. See **Figure 25** to adjust switch.

1. Make sure rear brake is properly adjusted. See Chapters Three and Ten.
2. Turn ignition switch on.
3. Depress brake pedal. Light should come on just as the brake begins to work.
4. To make light come on sooner, hold switch body and turn adjusting nut clockwise as viewed from top. Turn the nut counterclockwise to delay the light.

> *NOTE: Some riders prefer the light to come on a little early. This way, they can tap the pedal without braking to warn drivers who follow too closely.*

To replace the switch, disconnect spring and wires and pull switch with locknut out of bracket. Installation is the reverse. Adjust as described above.

NEUTRAL SWITCH AND INDICATOR

The neutral switch is located under the left crankcase cover. See **Figure 26**.

To replace the switch:
1. Remove 2 screws securing switch.
2. Disconnect wire from harness.

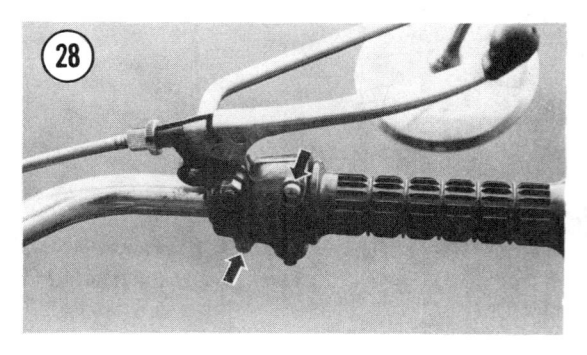

ELECTRICAL SYSTEM

3. Remove switch.

4. Installation is the reverse of these steps.

To replace indicator lamp, remove lens panel as described under *Directional Signals*.

DIRECTIONAL SIGNALS

Switch Removal

1. Remove headlight as shown in **Figure 27**.
2. Disconnect wires from harness.
3. Disconnect the clutch cable as described in Chapter Five.
4. Remove mirror and clutch lever.
5. Remove 2 screws securing switch assembly (**Figure 28**) and separate 2 halves.
6. Tie ends of switch wires to a piece of small rope (1/8-1/4 in.) about 2-3 feet long.
7. Pull switch wires out of handlebars. Leave the rope in place in the handlebars with one end sticking out of the center hole and the other end sticking out of the end hole.

Switch Installation

1. Tape end of switch wires to rope sticking out of end hole.
2. Pull on rope at center hole and pull wires through handlebars. Untape rope.
3. Secure switch to handlebars.
4. Mount mirror and clutch lever.
5. Connect the clutch cable and adjust the lever free play.
6. Insert switch wires into headlight housing and reconnect to harness.
7. Install headlight.

Indicator Light Replacement

1. On 450 models, remove 3 screws and remove headlight rim with sealed beams. See **Figure 27**.
2. Remove headlight case mounting bolts and lower case.
3. Remove 2 screws securing indicator lens panel and pull lens panel off. See **Figure 29**.
4. On 500 models, remove 3 self-tapping screws and remove lens panel. See **Figure 30**.
5. Replace defective bulb.
6. Install lens panel and headlight (if removed).

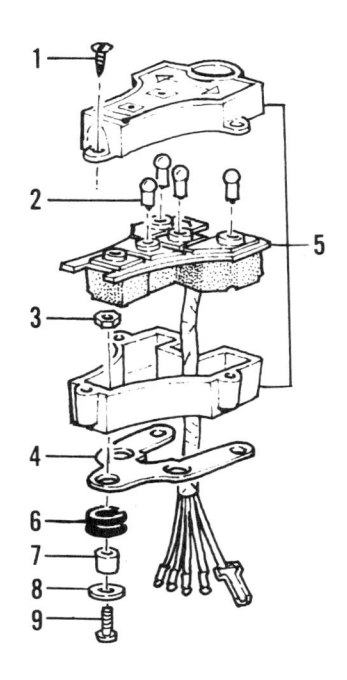

INDICATOR LIGHT — CB500T

1. Self tapping screw
2. Dash bulb
3. Hex nut
4. Pilot plate A
5. Combination pilot
6. Rubber rear fender cushion
7. Rear fender collar
8. Washer
9. Pan screw

7. Adjust headlight as described elsewhere (if removed).

Signal Light Replacement

To replace any of the 4 directional signal lamps, remove lens and replace bulb. Install lens, but do not overtighten screws.

Flasher Relay Replacement

The flasher relay is located under the fuel tank on the CB450. See **Figure 31**. On the CB500T, the relay is located in the connector case (**Figure 32**). Pull old flasher relay out of rubber mount. Transfer wires to new relay and install new relay in rubber mount.

HORN

Removal/Installation

1. Disconnect horn wires from harness.

   NOTE: *Sometimes it is easier to remove the fuel tank first in order to gain better access to connectors.*

2. Remove 2 nuts securing horn to bracket.
3. Installation is the reverse of these steps.

Horn Testing

1. Disconnect horn wires from harness.
2. Connect horn wires to 12-volt battery. If it is good, it will sound.

Horn Switch Removal/Installation

The horn switch is part of the directional signal assembly.

FUSE

There is only one fuse on the Honda 450. This 15 ampere fuse is located near the battery in a holder. See **Figure 33**. It protects the ignition and lighting circuits. If it fails, none of the electrical components on the bike will work.

The Honda 500 has 3 fuses located in a fuse box under the seat. These include a 15 ampere main fuse, a 7 ampere headlight fuse, and a 7 ampere taillight fuse. See **Figure 34**.

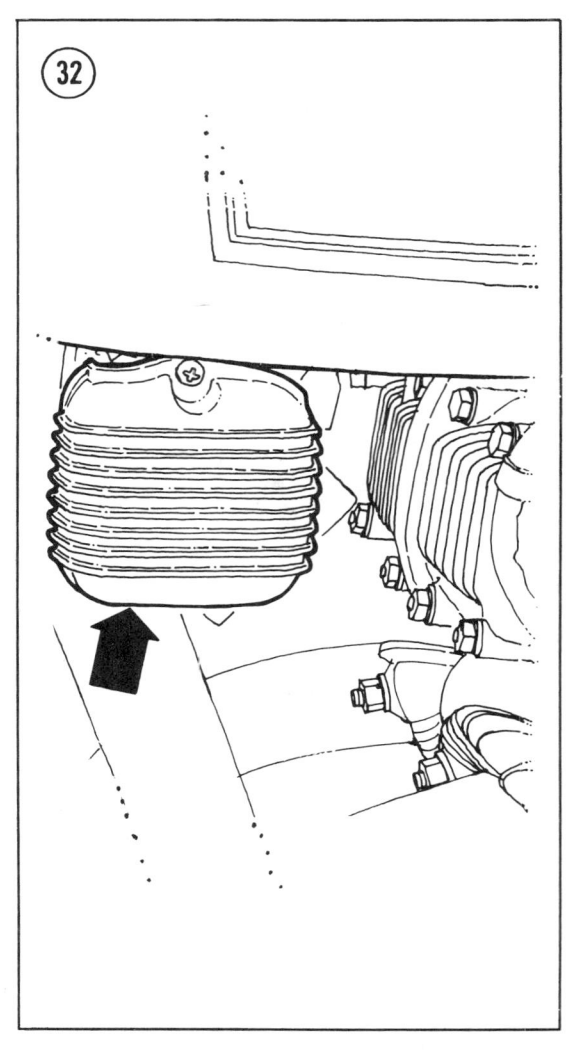

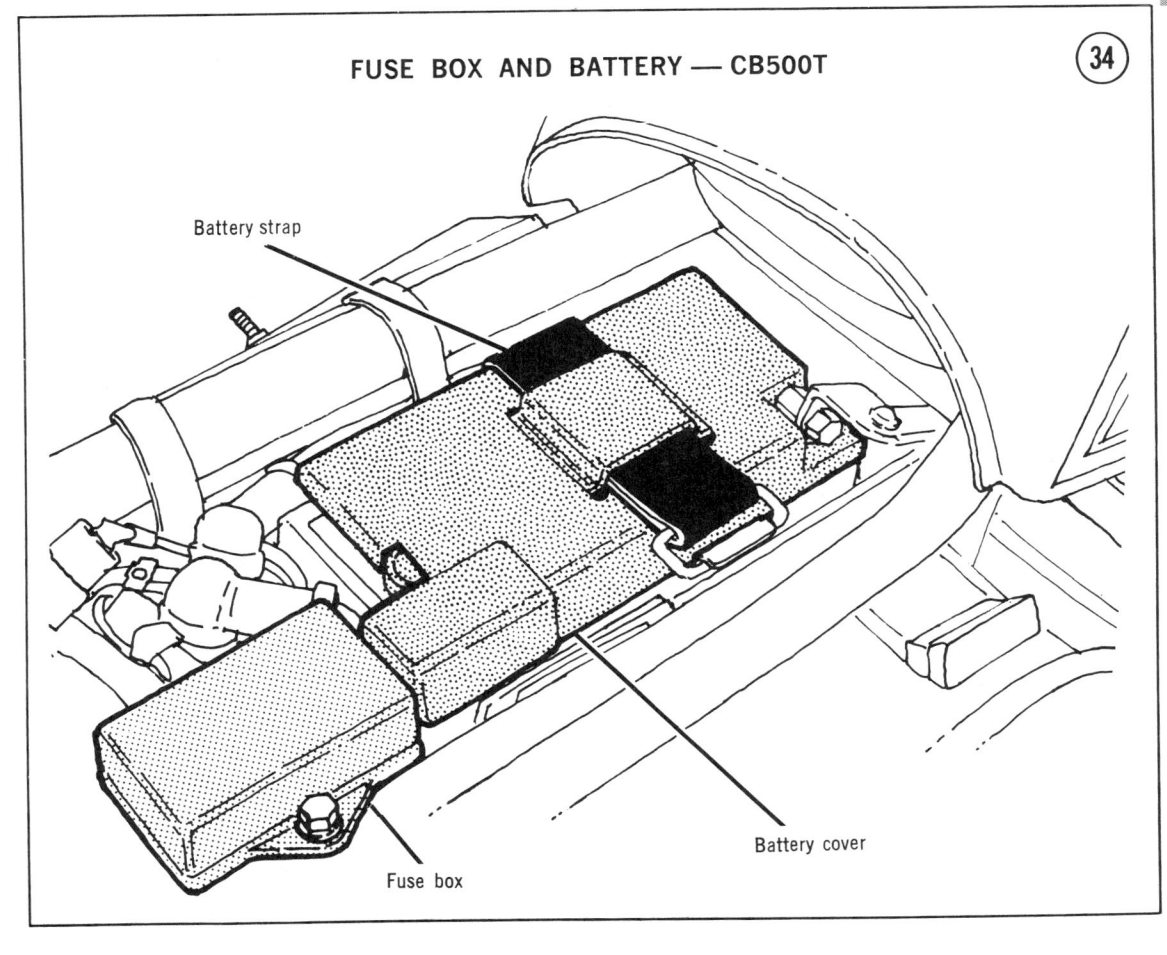

ELECTRICAL SYSTEM

(33)

FUSE BOX AND BATTERY — CB500T (34)

Battery strap

Battery cover

Fuse box

Carry at least one spare for each fuse in the tool box. Wrap it carefully to protect it from breakage.

Whenever a fuse blows, find out the reason for the failure before replacing the fuse. Usually the trouble is related to a short circuit in the wiring. This may possibly be caused by worn-through insulation or a disconnected wire shorting to ground.

CAUTION
Never substitute a tinfoil or wire for a fuse. Never use a higher amperage fuse than specified. An overload could result in fire and complete loss of bike.

WIRING HARNESS

Figure 35 shows routing of wiring harness for the 450; **Figure 36** for the 500. Follow this routing whenever installing harness after painting frame or when replacing defective harness. Routing is important so that connecting wires will reach various components.

Wiring diagrams for the 450 and 500 are on pages 107-109.

ELECTRICAL SYSTEM

105

CHAPTER SEVEN

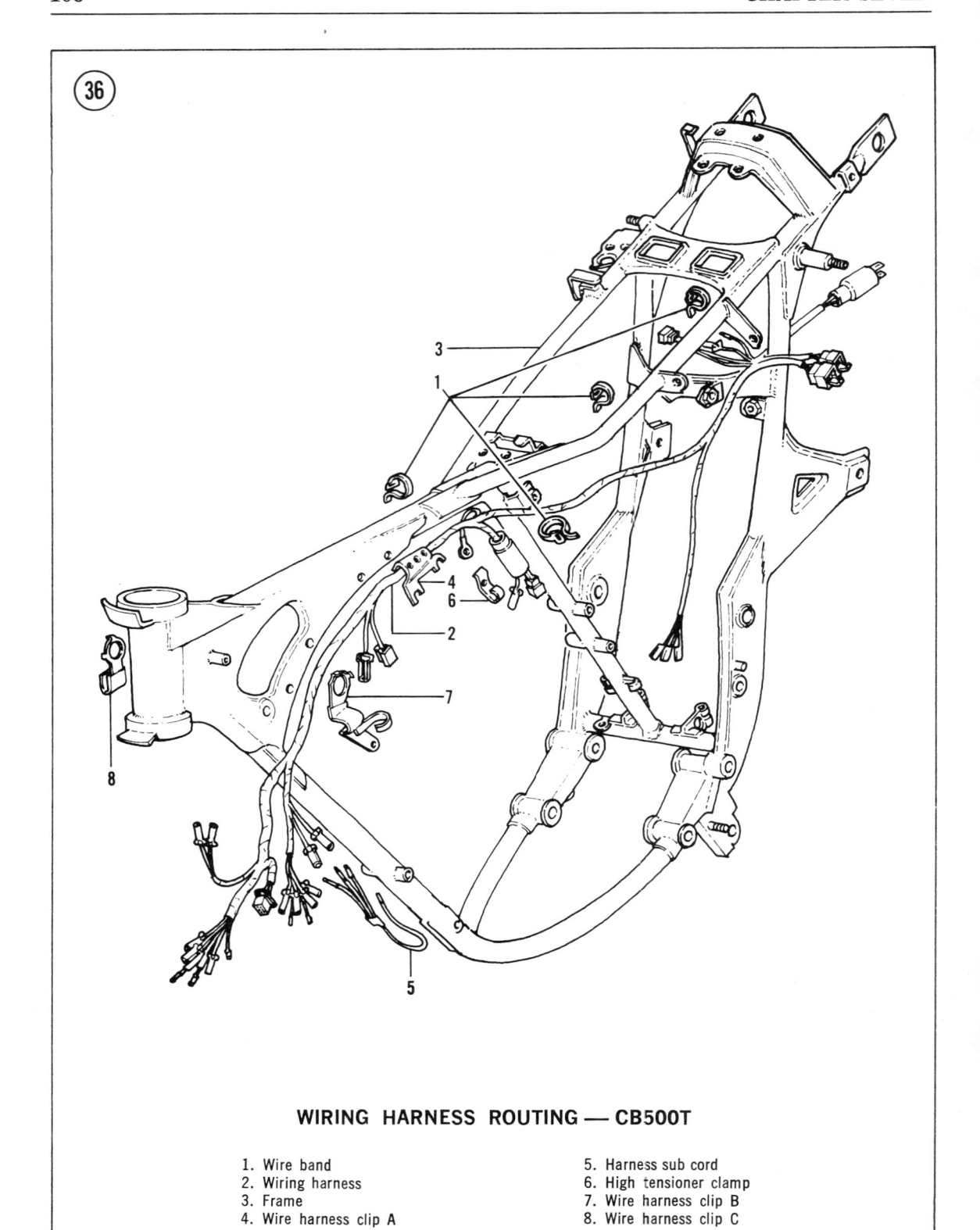

WIRING HARNESS ROUTING — CB500T

1. Wire band
2. Wiring harness
3. Frame
4. Wire harness clip A
5. Harness sub cord
6. High tensioner clamp
7. Wire harness clip B
8. Wire harness clip C

ELECTRICAL SYSTEM

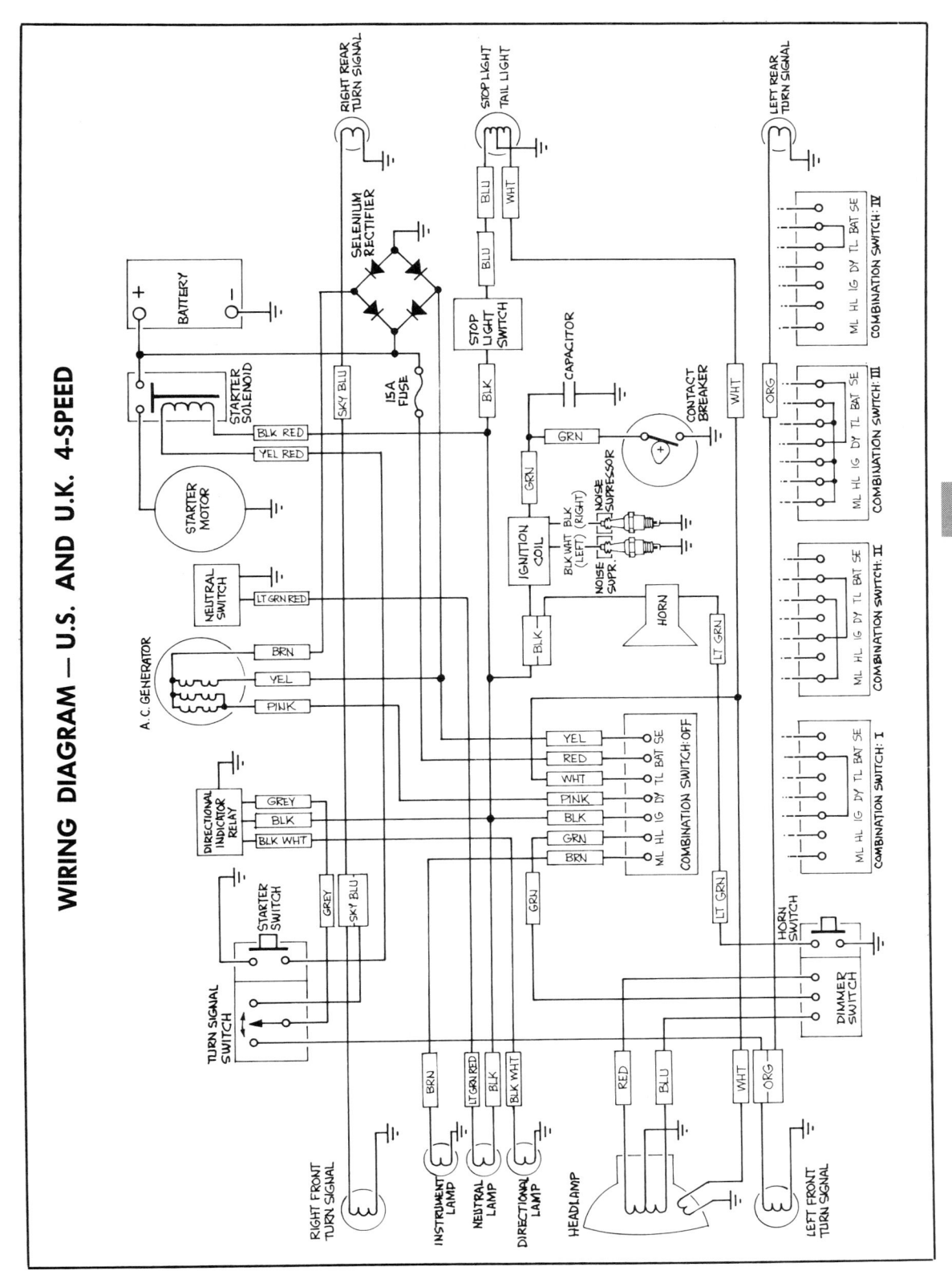

WIRING DIAGRAM — U.S. AND U.K. 4-SPEED

CHAPTER SEVEN

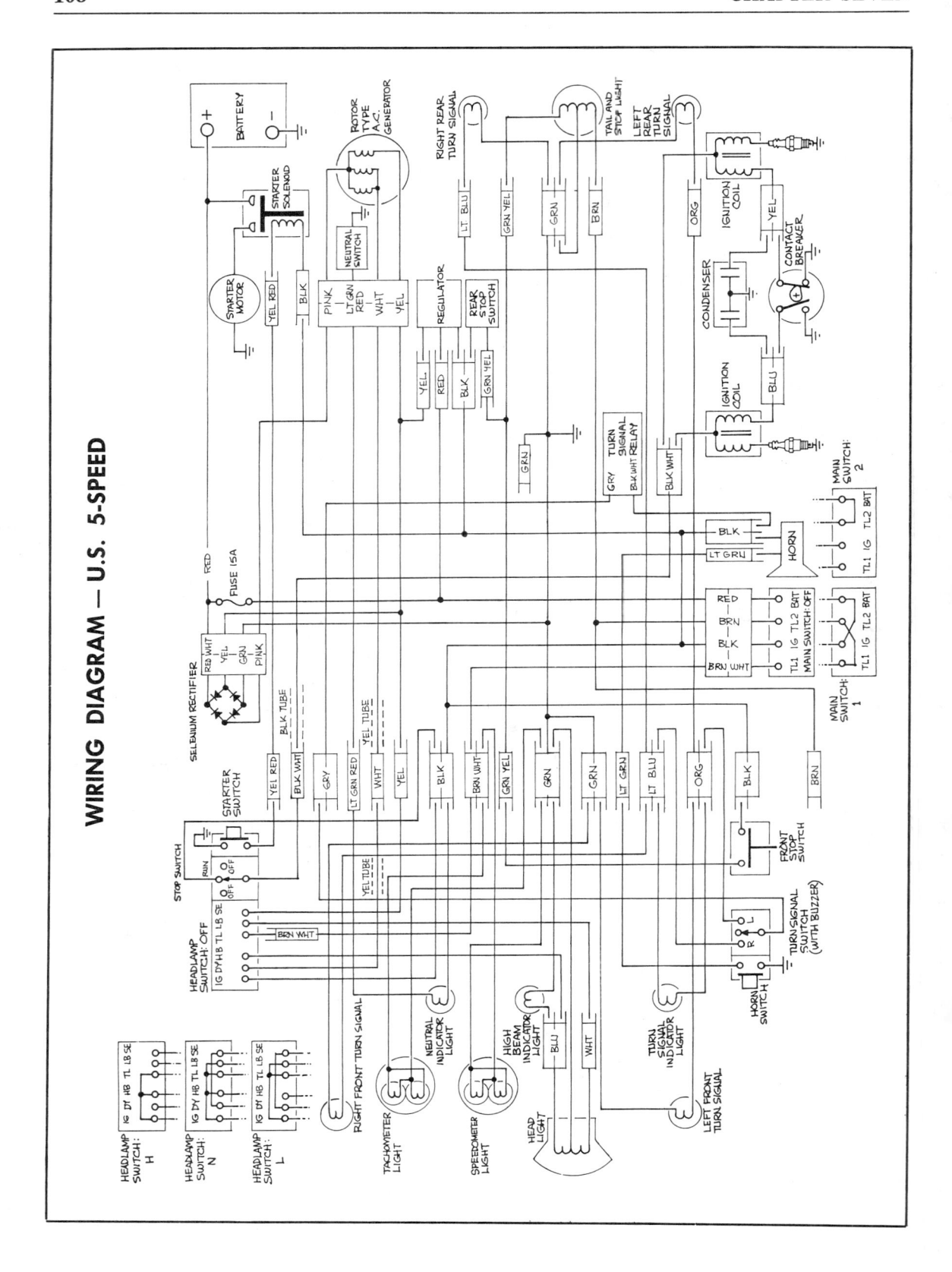

WIRING DIAGRAM — U.S. 5-SPEED

ELECTRICAL SYSTEM

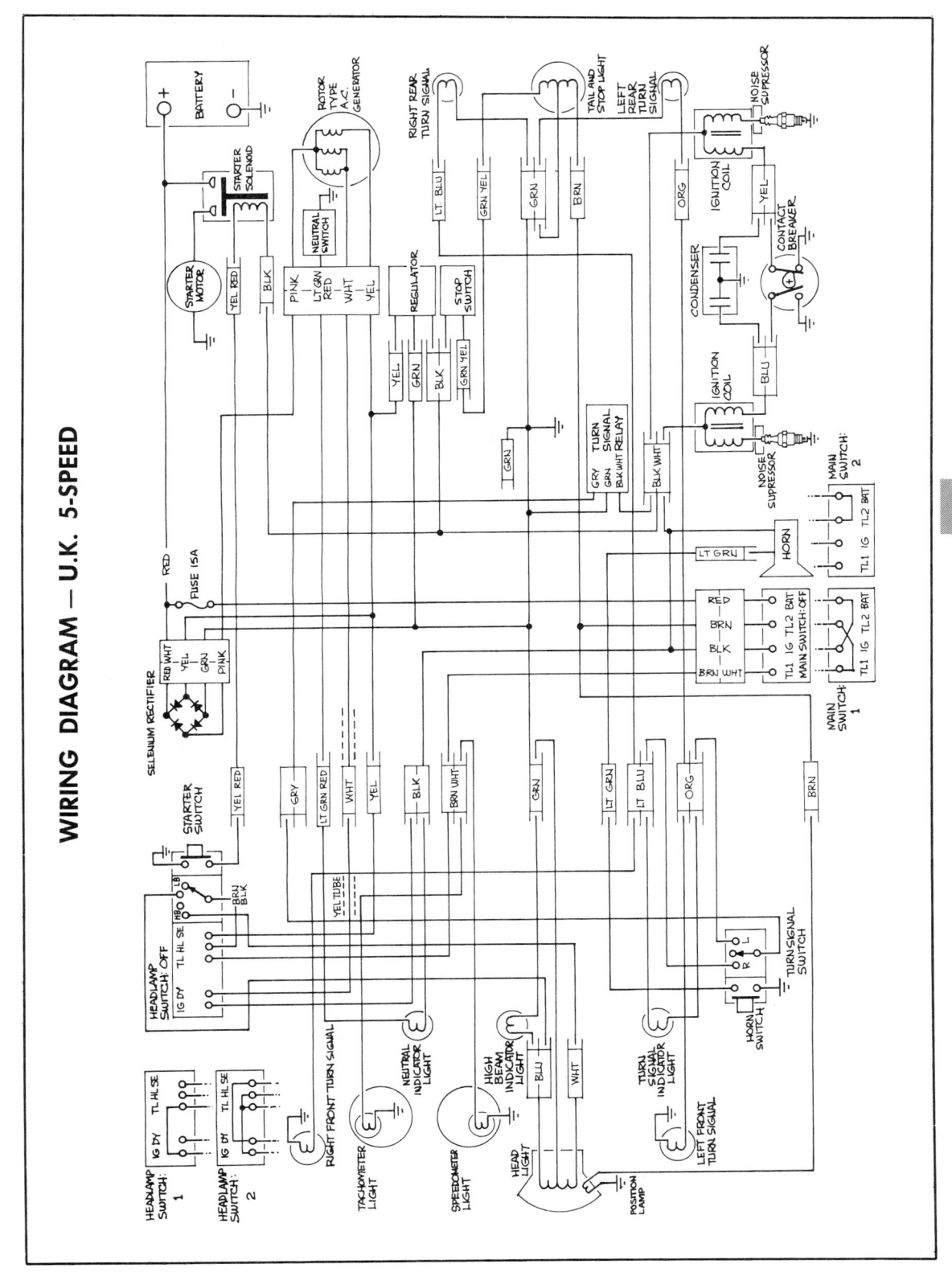

109

CHAPTER EIGHT

FRONT SUSPENSION AND STEERING

This chapter includes repair and replacement procedures for the front wheel, forks, and steering components. **Figures 1, 2, and 3** show the front wheels used.

FRONT WHEELS (DRUM BRAKE)

Removal/Installation

1. Rest bike on centerstand.
2. Place jack under engine and raise front wheel clear of ground.
3. Disconnect brake cable and brake torque link. See **Figure 4**.
4. Disconnect speedometer cable.
5. Remove axle holder nuts on both sides and remove wheel.
6. Installation is the reverse of these steps. Adjust brake lever free play as described in Chapter Two.

Disassembly

See **Figure 1** (CB) or **Figure 3** (CL).

1. Remove axle nut and pull axle out.
2. Lift off complete brake panel.
3. On CB450, remove gearbox retainer cover and retainer. See **Figure 5**.
4. Remove bearing retainer and dust seal. See **Figure 6**.
5. Remove bearings and spacer.

Inspection

1. Check brake components as described in Chapter Ten.
2. Clean bearings thoroughly in solvent.
3. Clean hub inside and out with solvent.
4. Turn each bearing by hand. Make sure bearings turn smoothly. Check balls for evidence of wear, pitting, or excessive heat (bluish tint). Replace bearings if questionable.
5. Check the axle for wear and straightness. **Figure 7** shows one method.
6. Check brake drum surface in hub for out-of-round, scoring, and excessive wear.

Assembly

1. Pack bearings thoroughly with multipurpose grease. Work grease in between balls thoroughly.
2. Pack wheel hub with grease.
3. Insert spacer.
4. Install bearings with the sealed side facing outward.

> **CAUTION**
> *When tapping the bearings into place, tap on outer race only. Do not tap on inner race or the bearing might be damaged.*

FRONT SUSPENSION AND STEERING

① FRONT WHEEL — CB450 K1-K2

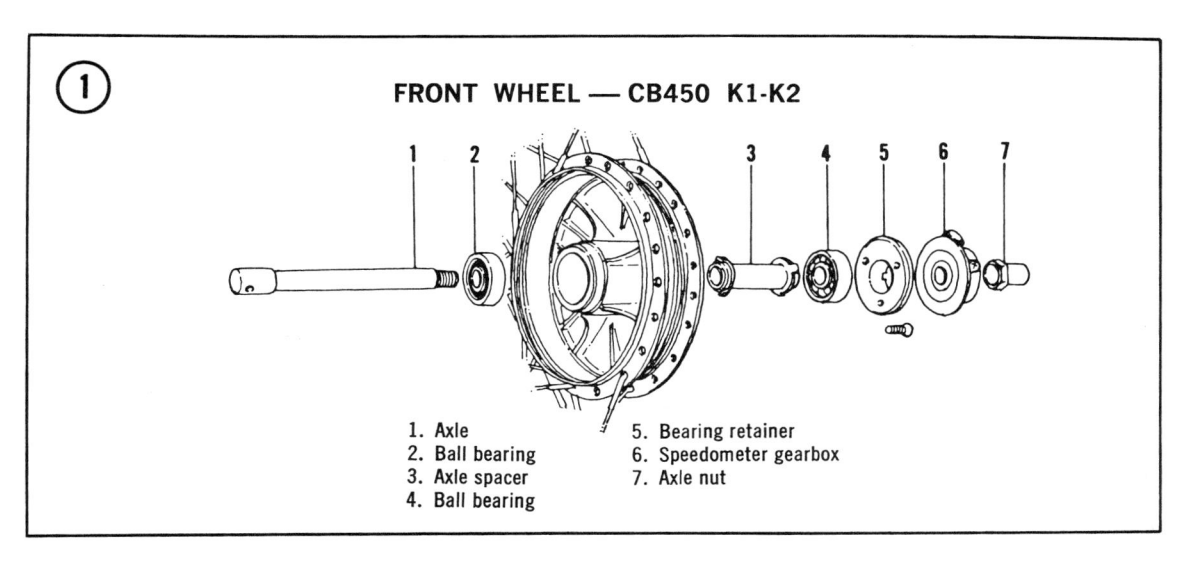

1. Axle
2. Ball bearing
3. Axle spacer
4. Ball bearing
5. Bearing retainer
6. Speedometer gearbox
7. Axle nut

② FRONT WHEEL — CB450 K3-K7 AND CB500T

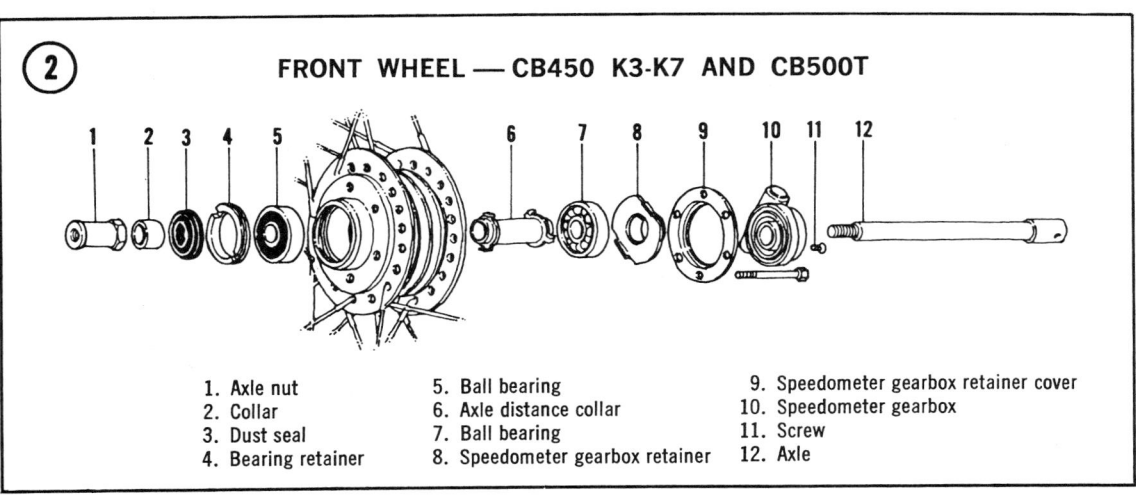

1. Axle nut
2. Collar
3. Dust seal
4. Bearing retainer
5. Ball bearing
6. Axle distance collar
7. Ball bearing
8. Speedometer gearbox retainer
9. Speedometer gearbox retainer cover
10. Speedometer gearbox
11. Screw
12. Axle

③ FRONT WHEEL — CL450

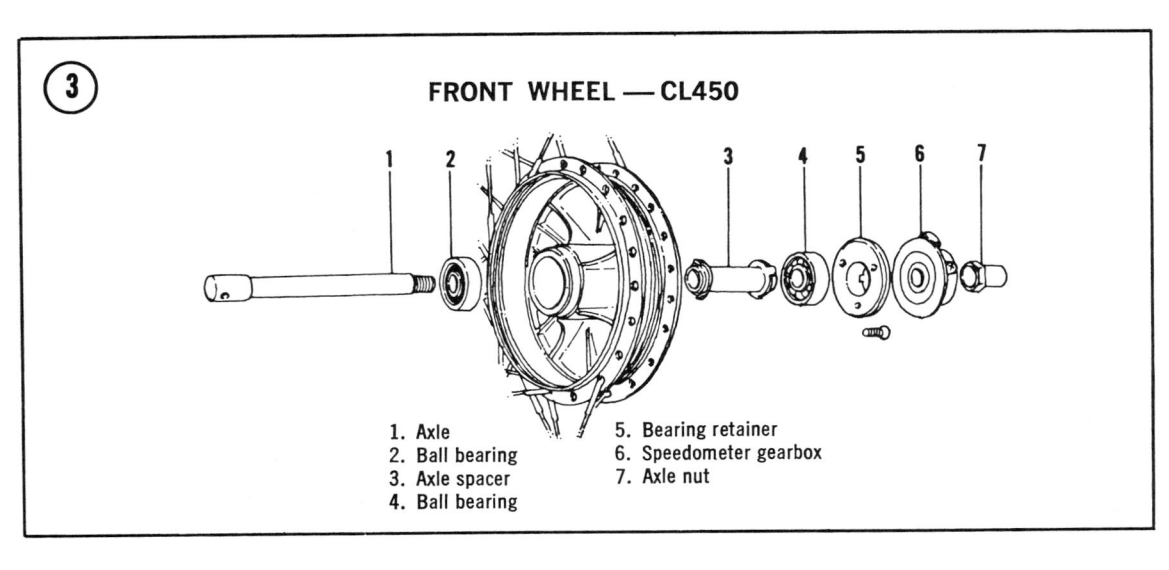

1. Axle
2. Ball bearing
3. Axle spacer
4. Ball bearing
5. Bearing retainer
6. Speedometer gearbox
7. Axle nut

5. Install bearing retainer and dust seal.

6. On CB450, install speedometer gearbox retainer and cover.

7. Install brake panel.

8. Install axle and secure with axle nut.

Wheel Balancing

An unbalanced wheel can be dangerous. Depending on the degree of unbalance and speed, the rider may experience anything from mild vibration to violent shimmy. In severe cases, the rider can lose control.

Wheels are relatively easy to balance without special equipment. Your dealer has an assortment of balance weights which attach to the spokes. They are crimped onto the light side of the wheel with ordinary gas pliers. See **Figure 8**. Buy a couple of each weight available (**Figure 9**). If undamaged, you can return unused weights.

Before balancing a wheel, make sure bearings are in good condition and properly lubricated. Use the wheel disassembly/inspection/assembly procedures in this chapter to be sure. In addition, make sure that the brakes do not drag. The wheel must rotate freely.

1. Rest bike on centerstand.

2. Place jack under engine and raise front wheel clear of ground.

3. Rotate rear wheel slowly and allow it to come to rest by itself. Note position of valve stem.

4. Repeat Step 3 several times. If the valve stem stops at a different position each time, the wheel is balanced. If the valve stem stops near the same position each time, add weight at the 12 o'clock position (light side) until valve stem no longer favors one position when the wheel stops.

5. Road test bike on smooth, straight road.

FRONT WHEEL (DISC BRAKE)

Removal/Installation

1. Rest bike on centerstand.

2. Place jack under engine and raise front wheel clear of ground.

3. Disconnect speedometer cable from hub.

4. Remove axle holder nuts and remove wheel.

NOTE: *Do not operate brake lever while wheel is off. The caliper piston will be forced out, requiring brake system bleeding (see Chapter Ten) and possible disassembly of cylinder.*

5. Installation is the reverse of these steps.

Disassembly

Refer to **Figure 10** during disassembly.

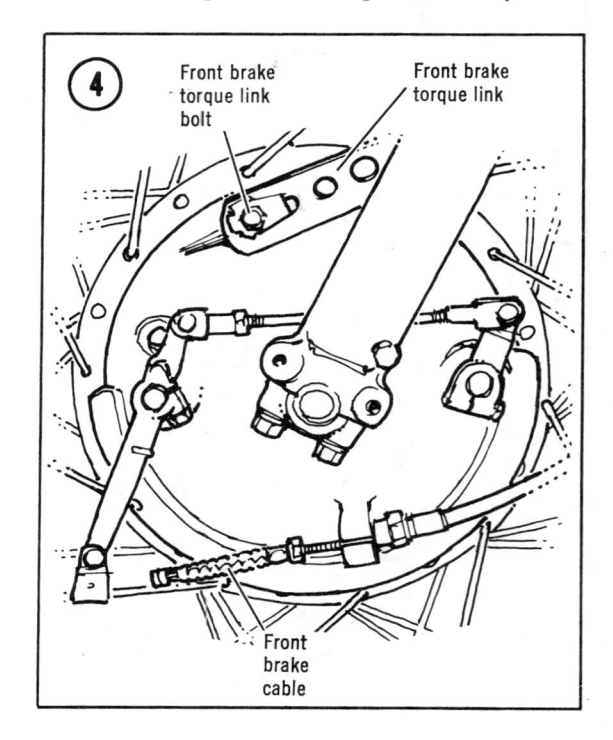

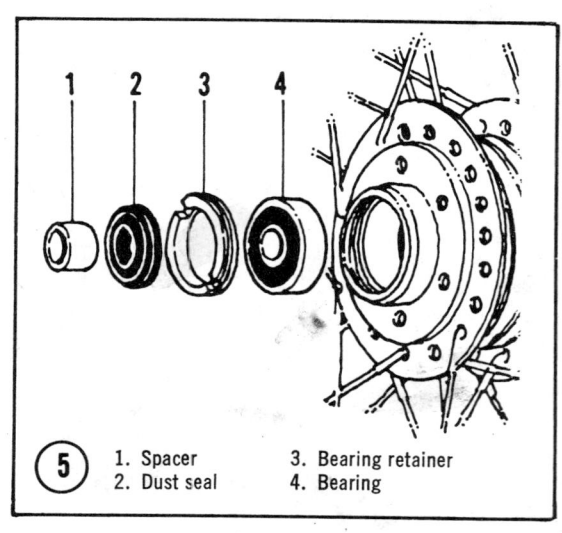

④ Front brake torque link bolt / Front brake torque link / Front brake cable

⑤
1. Spacer
2. Dust seal
3. Bearing retainer
4. Bearing

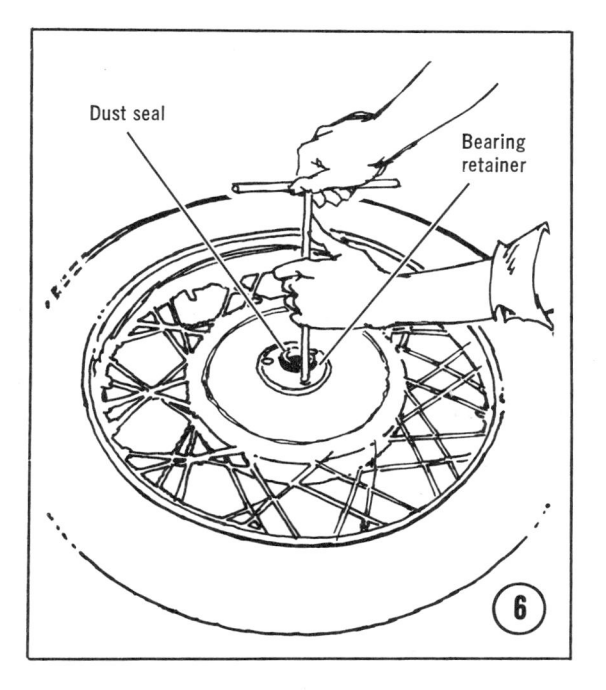

FRONT SUSPENSION AND STEERING

113

- Dust seal
- Bearing retainer

⑥

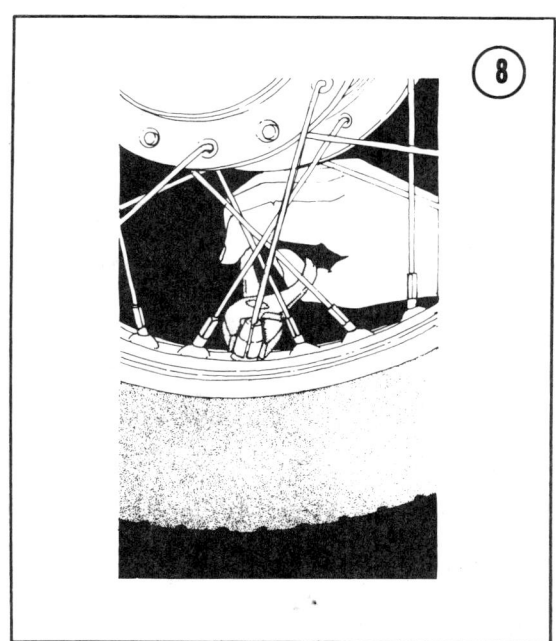

⑧

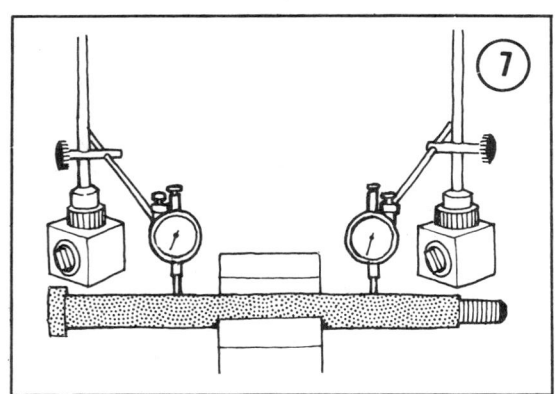

⑦

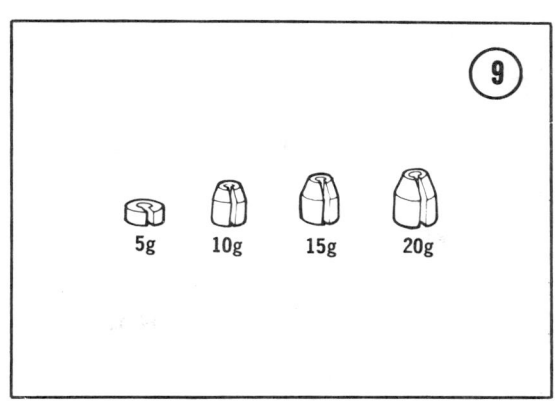

⑨

5g 10g 15g 20g

FRONT WHEEL — CB450 K3-K7 AND CB500T ⑩

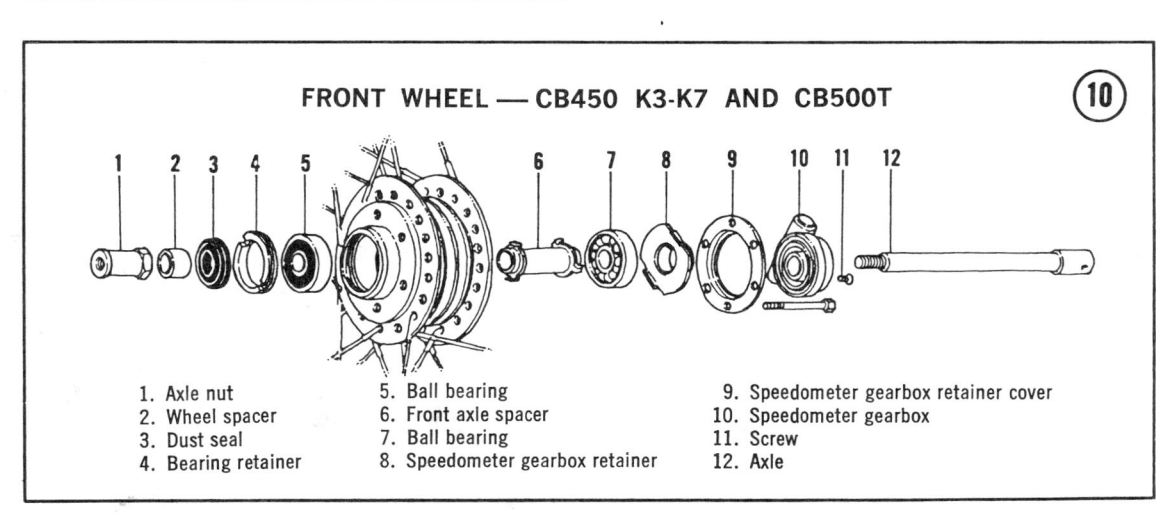

1. Axle nut
2. Wheel spacer
3. Dust seal
4. Bearing retainer
5. Ball bearing
6. Front axle spacer
7. Ball bearing
8. Speedometer gearbox retainer
9. Speedometer gearbox retainer cover
10. Speedometer gearbox
11. Screw
12. Axle

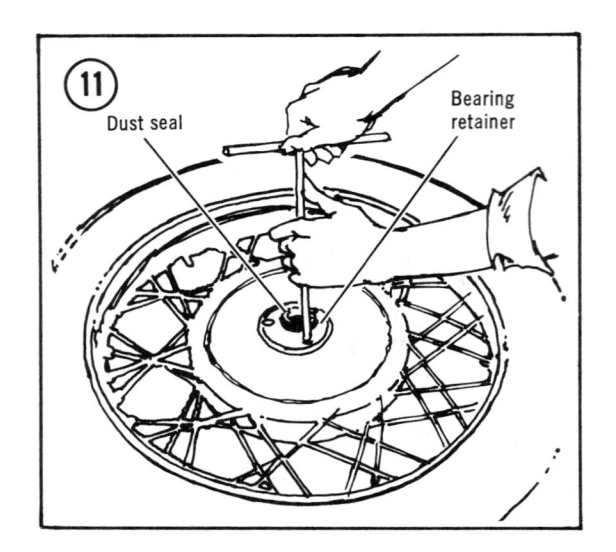

114   CHAPTER EIGHT

⑪
Dust seal
Bearing retainer

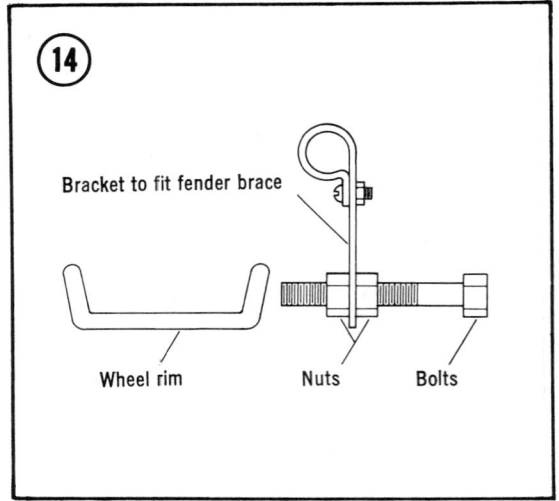

⑭
Bracket to fit fender brace
Wheel rim   Nuts   Bolts

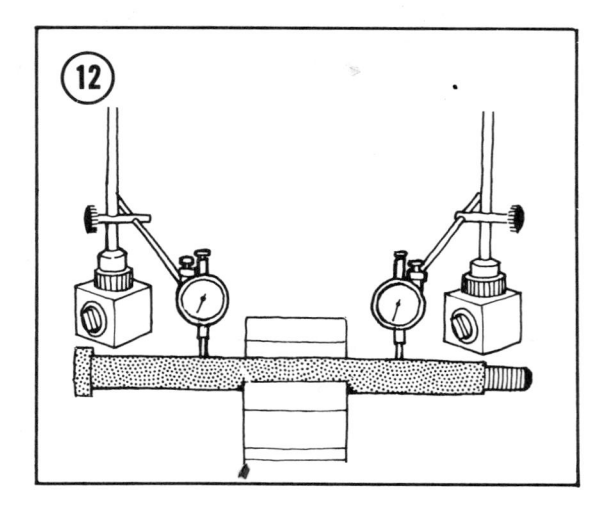

⑫

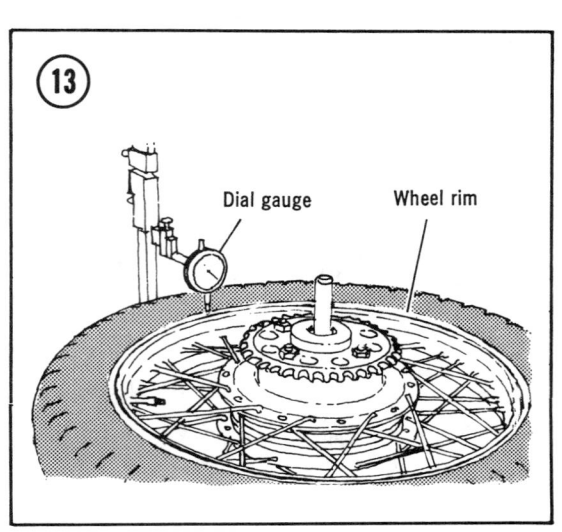

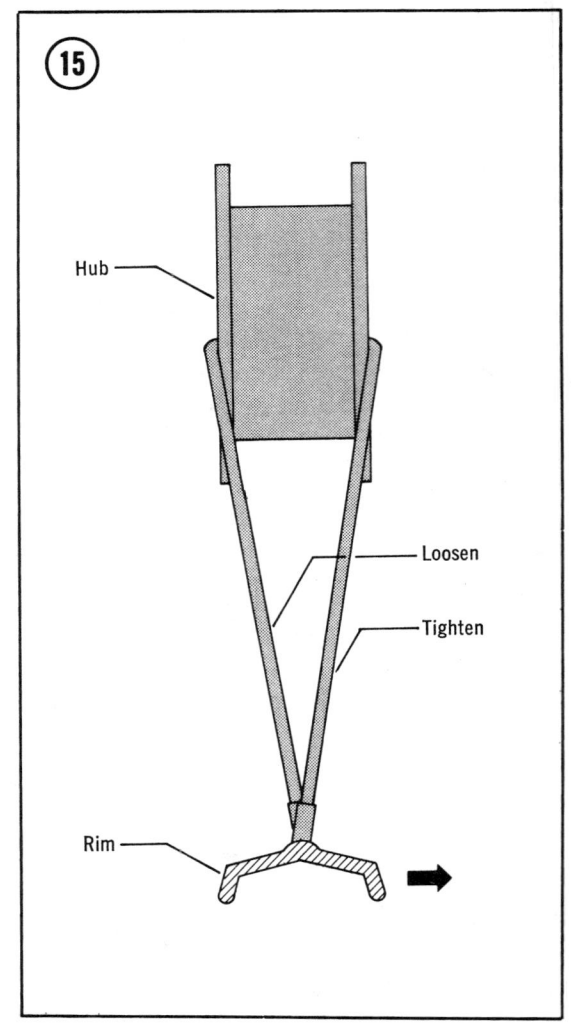

⑮
Hub
Loosen
Tighten
Rim

⑬
Dial gauge   Wheel rim

FRONT SUSPENSION AND STEERING

1. Remove axle nut and pull out axle.
2. Remove speedometer gearbox.
3. Bend up tabs on lockwashers and remove nuts securing brake disc. Lift off disc.
4. Remove gearbox retainer cover and retainer.
5. Remove bearing retainer and dust seal. See **Figure 11**.
6. Remove wheel bearings and spacer.

Inspection

1. Check brake disc, described in Chapter Ten.
2. Clean bearings thoroughly in solvent.
3. Clean hub inside and out with solvent.
4. Turn each bearing by hand. Make sure bearings turn smoothly. Check balls for evidence of wear, pitting, or excessive heat (bluish tint). Replace bearings if questionable.
5. Check the axle for wear and straightness. **Figure 12** shows one method.

Assembly

1. Pack bearings thoroughly with multipurpose grease. Work grease in between balls thoroughly.
2. Pack wheel hub with grease.
3. Insert spacer.
4. Install bearings with the sealed side facing outward.

> **CAUTION**
> *When tapping the bearing into place, tap on outer race only. Tapping on inner race might damage bearing.*

5. Install bearing retainer and dust seal.
6. Install speedometer gearbox retainer and cover.
7. Install brake disc with new lockwashers.
8. Install axle and secure with axle nut.

Wheel Balancing

Balance disc brake wheels in same manner described for drum brake wheels in this chapter.

Spoke Adjustment

Spokes loosen with use and should be checked periodically. The "tuning fork" method of checking spoke tightness is simple and works well. Tap each spoke with a spoke wrench or shank of a screwdriver and listen to the tone. A tightened spoke will emit a clear, ringing tone, and a loose spoke will sound flat. All spokes in a correctly tightened wheel will emit tones of similar pitch but not exactly the same pitch.

Bent or stripped spokes should be replaced as soon as they are detected. Unscrew the nipple from the spoke and depress the nipple into the rim far enough to free the end of the spoke; take care not to push the spoke all the way in. Remove the damaged spoke from the hub and use it to match a new spoke of identical length. If necessary, trim the new spoke to match the original and dress the end of the threads with a die. Install the new spoke in the hub and screw on the nipple, tightening it until the spoke's tone is similar to the tone of the other spokes on the wheel. Periodically check the new spoke; it will stretch and must be retightened several times before it takes its final set.

Wheel Runout

After tightening spokes, check rim runout to be sure you have not pulled the rim out of shape.

One way to check rim runout is shown in **Figure 13**. Another way is to mount the dial indicator on the front fork so that it bears on the rim.

If you do not have a dial indicator, improvise as shown in **Figure 14**. Adjust position of bolt until it just clears rim. Rotate rim and note whether clearance increases or decreases. Mark the tire with chalk or crayon at areas that produce significantly large or small clearance. Clearance must not *change* by more than 0.08 in. (2mm).

To pull rim out, tighten spokes which terminate on same side of hub and loosen spokes which terminate on opposite side of hub. See **Figure 15**. In most cases, only a slight amount of adjustment is necessary to true the rim. After adjustment, rotate rim and make sure another area has not been pulled out of true. Continue adjustment and checking until runout does not exceed 0.08 in. (2mm).

STEERING

Handlebar Removal/Installation

1a. On front drum brake models, slacken brake cable and disconnect it from hand lever.

1b. On front disc brake models, remove master cylinder as described in Chapter Ten.

2. Slacken clutch cable and disconnect from hand lever. See **Figure 16**.

3. Separate 2 halves of starter switch assembly. Disconnect throttle cable from twistgrip.

4. Remove 3 screws around headlight and pull headlight forward to expose wiring (**Figure 17**).

5. Disconnect electrical connections for horn, starter, headlight switch, and directional signals.

6. Remove 4 bolts securing handlebars and lift them off.

7. Installation is the reverse of these steps. Adjust brake free play and clutch free play as described in Chapter Three. Adjust throttle cable as described in Chapter Six.

Fork Crown (Top Triple Clamp) Removal/Installation

1. Remove handlebars.
2. Remove instruments.
3. Remove fork cap bolts. See **Figure 18**.
4. Remove steering stem nut.
5. Loosen fork clamp bolts.
6. Pull fork crown off.
7. Installation is the reverse of these steps.

Steering Stem Removal

1. Remove handlebars as described earlier.
2. Remove front wheel.
3. Remove forks, fork crown (top triple clamp), and fork tube covers.
4. Remove speedometer and tachometer.
5. Remove the top bridge.
6. Remove stem adjuster as shown in **Figure 19**.
7. Pull stem out of head tube.

> NOTE: *Do not lose ball bearings. There are 37 of them, uncaged, between top and bottom.*

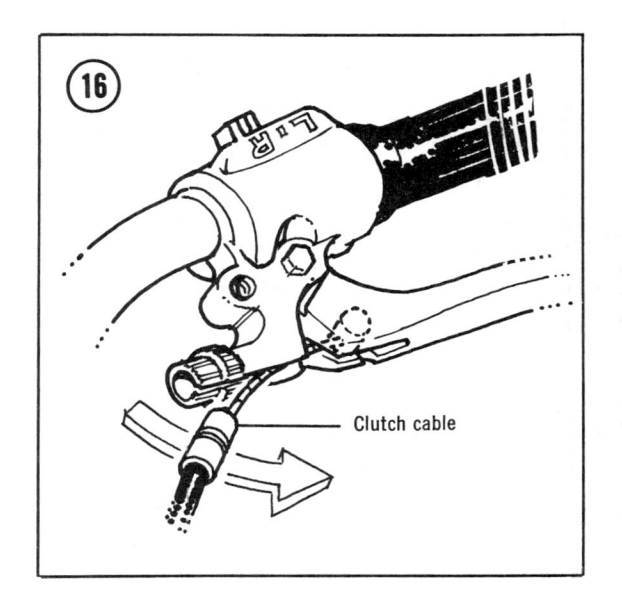

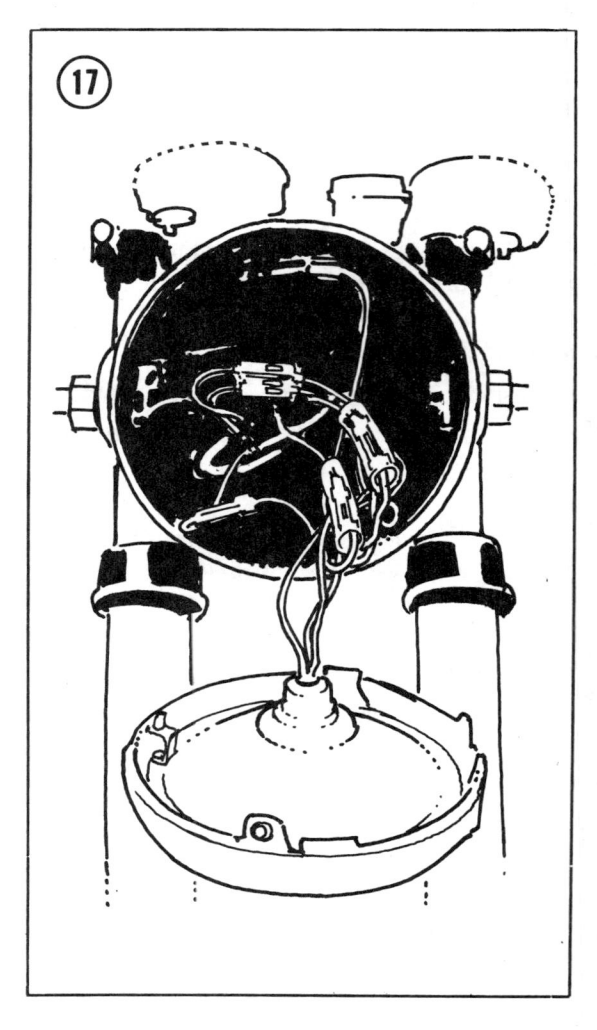

FRONT SUSPENSION AND STEERING

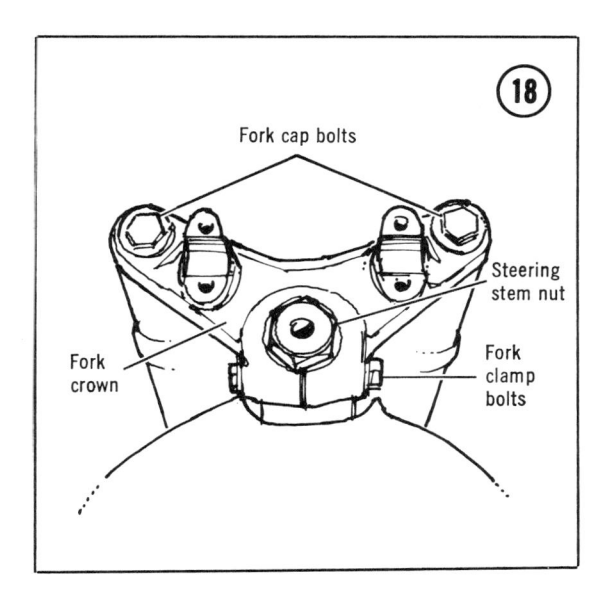

8. Remove top bearing race cone and remove the top ball bearings.

9. Remove bearings, bottom bearing race cone, dust seal, and washer from stem.

Steering Stem Inspection

1. Clean all parts except dust seal in solvent.

2. Check each ball bearing for wear and pitting. Replace if necessary.

3. Inspect the bearing race cones for wear and pitting.

4. Inspect bearing races in head tube for wear and pitting. If damaged, tap them out from the inside with a long punch, or a hardwood stick and a hammer. See **Figure 20**.

5. Check steering stem for cracks.

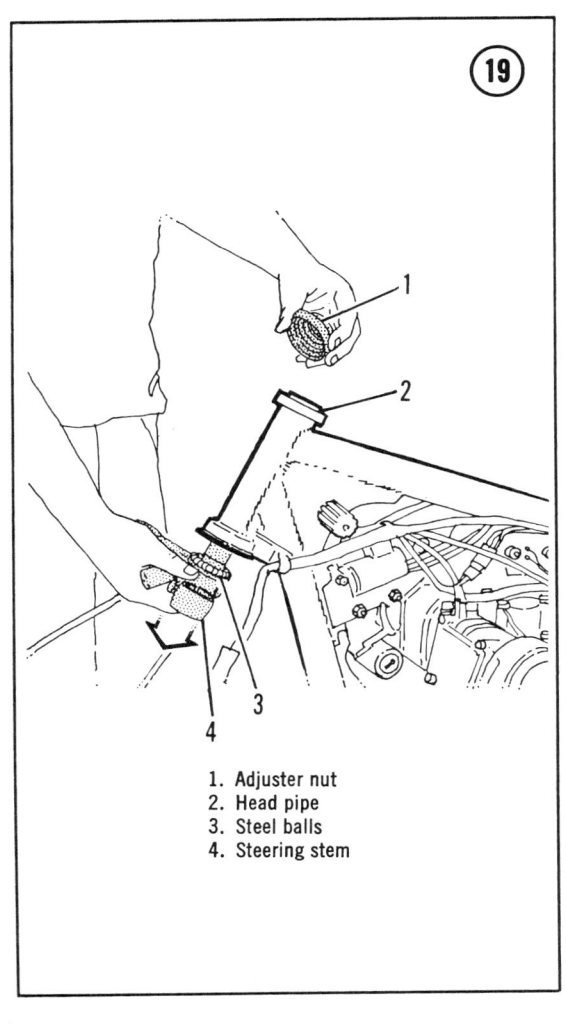

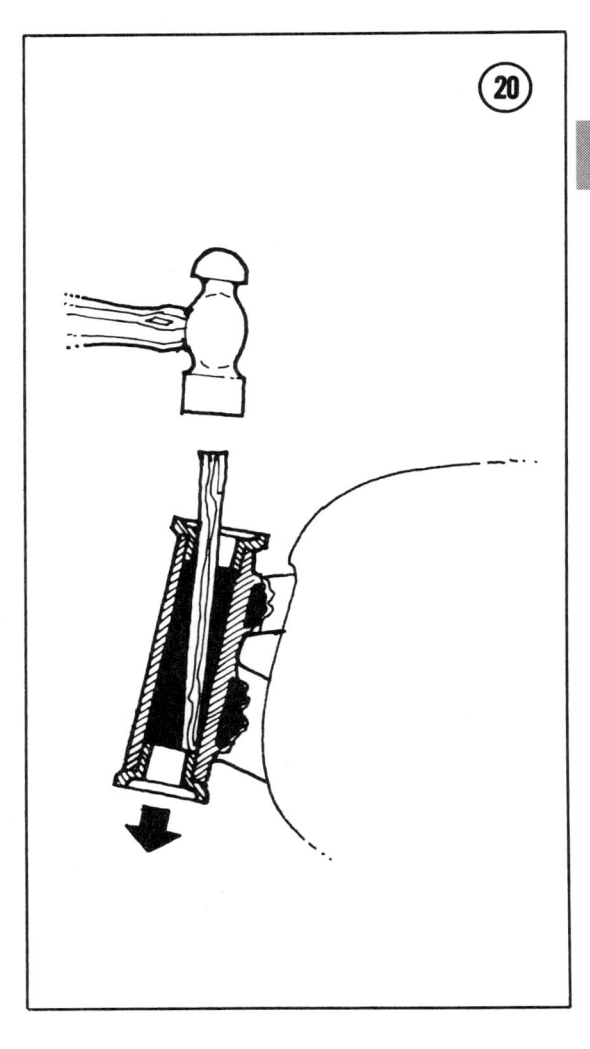

1. Adjuster nut
2. Head pipe
3. Steel balls
4. Steering stem

CHAPTER EIGHT

Steering Stem Assembly

Refer to **Figure 21** for this procedure.

1. Tap new races into head tube if removed during *Inspection*, Step 4. Grease them with multipurpose grease.
2. Place washer and new dust seal over the steering stem.
3. Place bottom bearing race cone over steering stem. Slide down to the bottom.
4. Apply coat of grease to bottom race cone and fit 19 ball bearings (18 on CB500T) around it. The grease will hold them in place.
5. Fit ball bearings into top race in head tube. Grease will hold them in place.
6. Insert steering stem into head tube. Hold it firmly in place.
7. Install top bearing race cone.
8. Screw steering stem adjuster onto stem.
9. Tighten adjuster firmly with 48mm pin spanner to seat bearings. See **Figure 22**.
10. Loosen adjuster until there is noticeable play in stem. See **Figure 23**.
11. Tighten adjuster just enough to remove all play, both horizontal and vertical, yet loose enough so that the assembly will turn to the locks under its own weight after an initial assist.

Steering Stem Adjustment

If play develops in the steering stem, it may only require adjustment. However, do not take a chance on it. Disassemble the stem and look for possible damage. Then reassemble and adjust as described above.

FRONT FORKS
(EARLY, 2-SPRING)

Early CB and CL forks have 2 internal springs. See **Figure 24**.

Removal

1. Remove front wheel as described elsewhere.
2. Remove the front fender and the front brake stop bolt.
3. Loosen clamp bolt on bottom triple clamp. See **Figure 25**.

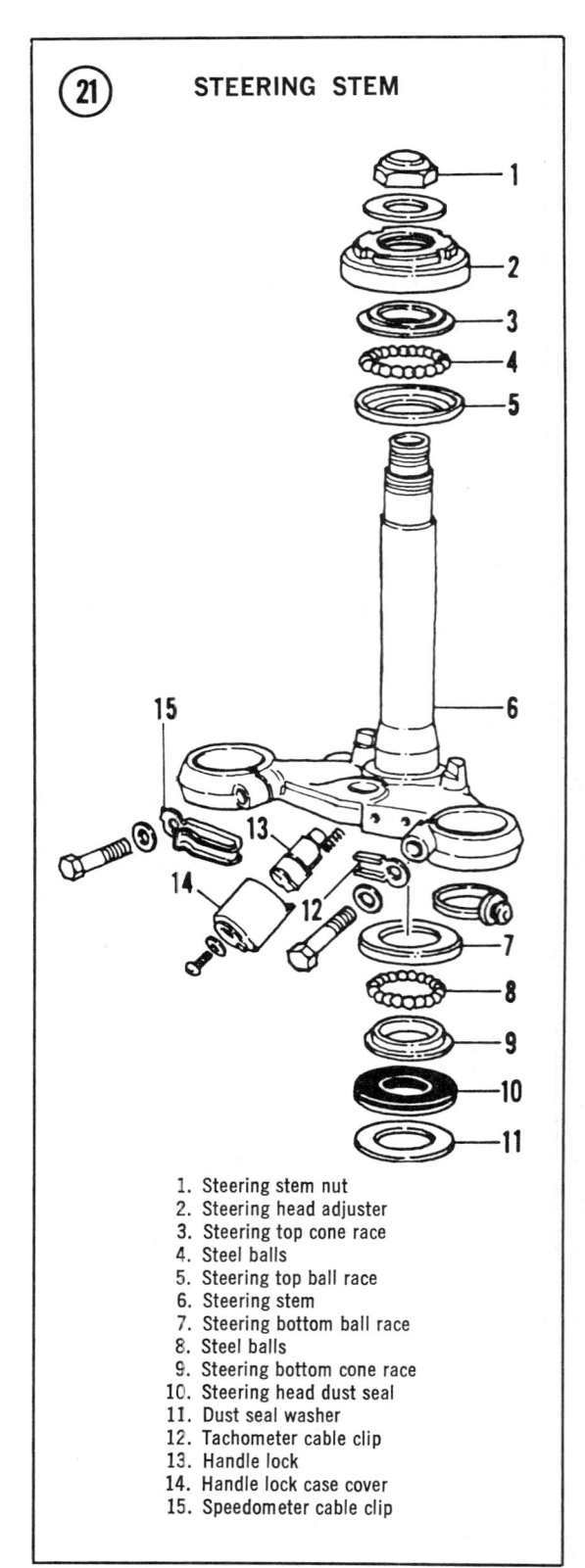

21 STEERING STEM

1. Steering stem nut
2. Steering head adjuster
3. Steering top cone race
4. Steel balls
5. Steering top ball race
6. Steering stem
7. Steering bottom ball race
8. Steel balls
9. Steering bottom cone race
10. Steering head dust seal
11. Dust seal washer
12. Tachometer cable clip
13. Handle lock
14. Handle lock case cover
15. Speedometer cable clip

FRONT SUSPENSION AND STEERING

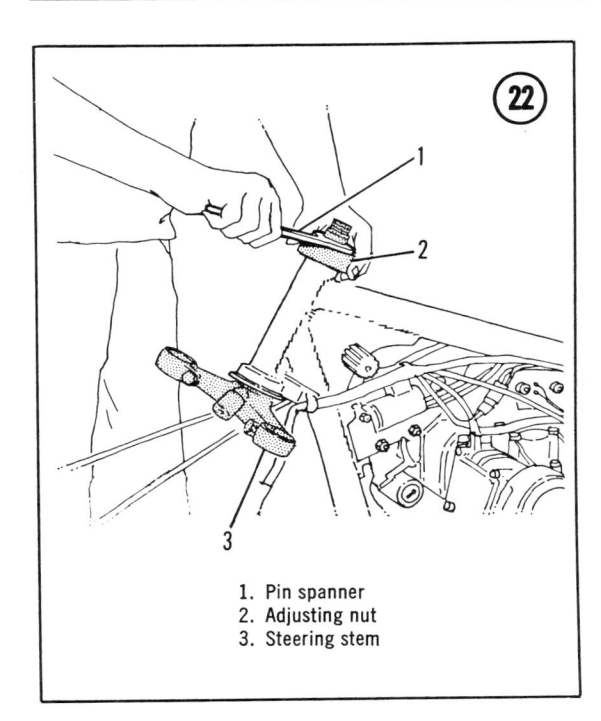

22

1. Pin spanner
2. Adjusting nut
3. Steering stem

4. Remove top fork cap.
5. Pull fork downward and out.
6. Drain oil from fork.

Disassembly

Refer to **Figure 24** for this procedure.

1. Unscrew fork seal housing. See **Figure 26**.
2. Remove fork pipe assembly.
3. Remove 2 springs, washers, and center spring seat (joint piece).
4. Remove snap ring, piston, damper valve, stop ring, guide, and seal housing.
5. Remove seal retainer and seal from housing. See **Figure 27**.

Inspection

1. Clean all parts in solvent.
2. Measure parts and compare to specifications in **Table 1**.

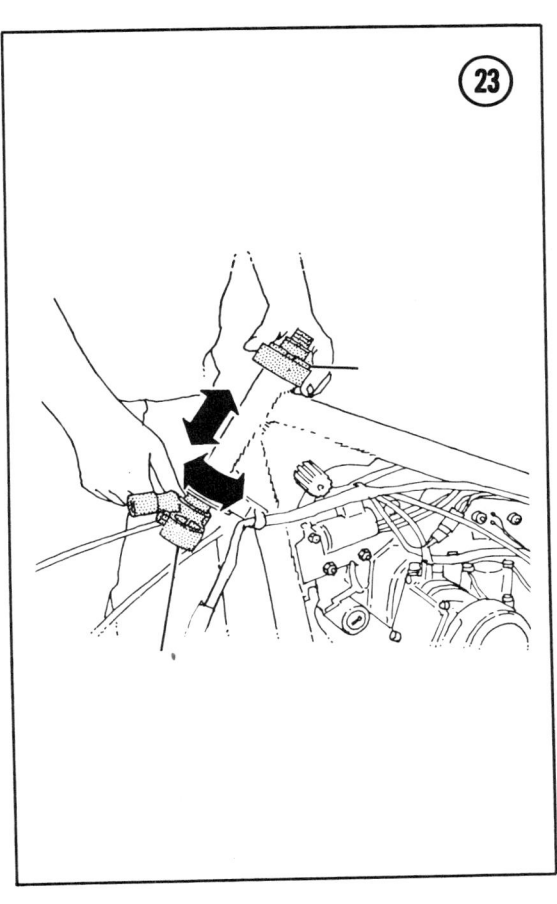

23

25

㉔ FRONT FORK — EARLY, 2-SPRING

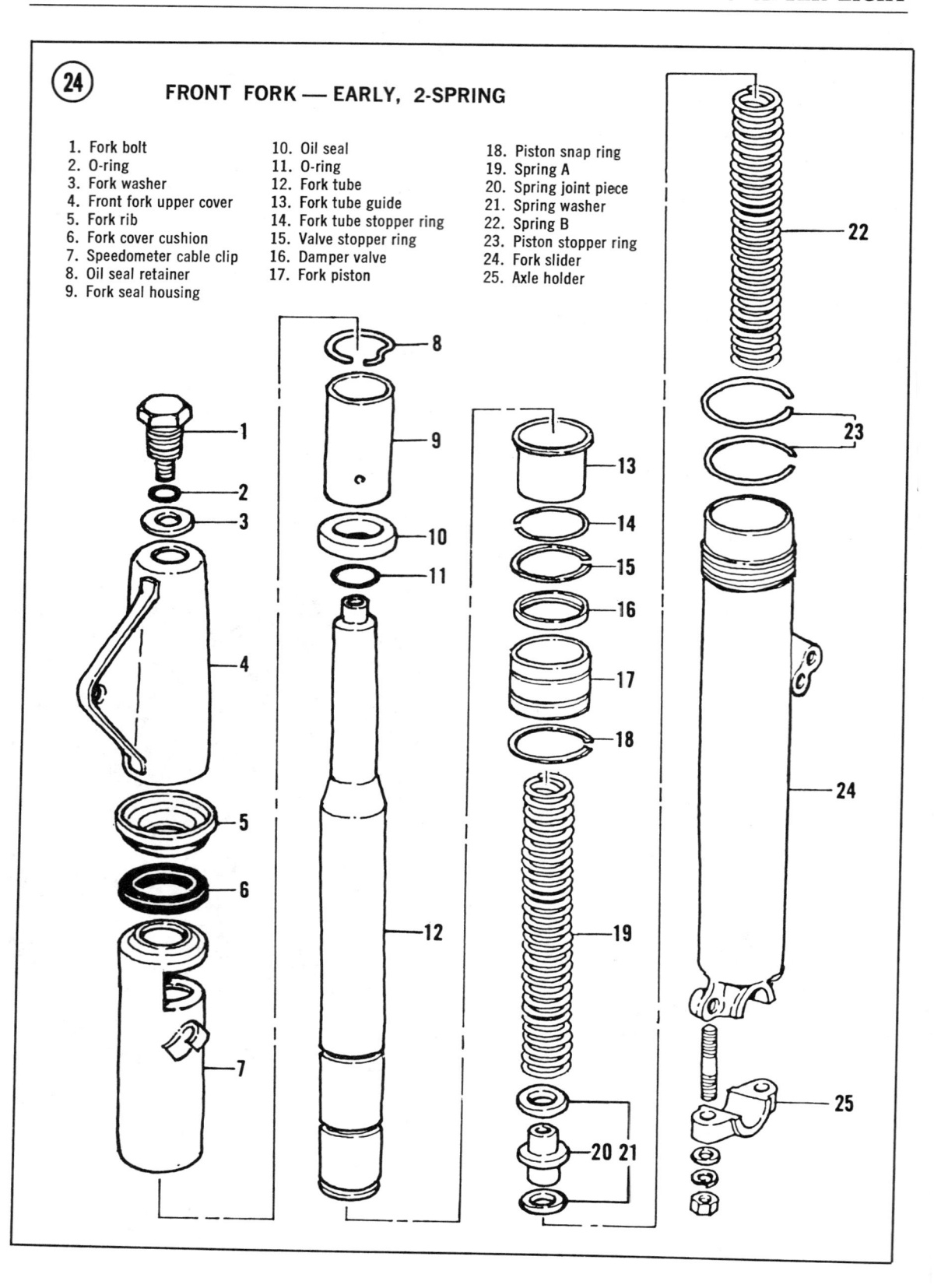

1. Fork bolt
2. O-ring
3. Fork washer
4. Front fork upper cover
5. Fork rib
6. Fork cover cushion
7. Speedometer cable clip
8. Oil seal retainer
9. Fork seal housing
10. Oil seal
11. O-ring
12. Fork tube
13. Fork tube guide
14. Fork tube stopper ring
15. Valve stopper ring
16. Damper valve
17. Fork piston
18. Piston snap ring
19. Spring A
20. Spring joint piece
21. Spring washer
22. Spring B
23. Piston stopper ring
24. Fork slider
25. Axle holder

FRONT SUSPENSION AND STEERING

Figure 26 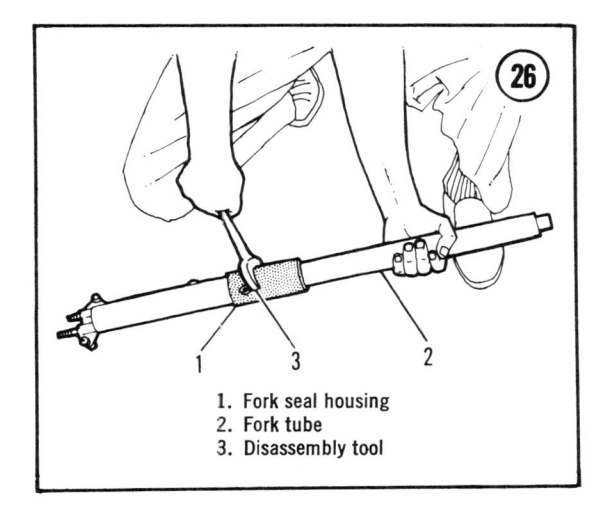
1. Fork seal housing
2. Fork tube
3. Disassembly tool

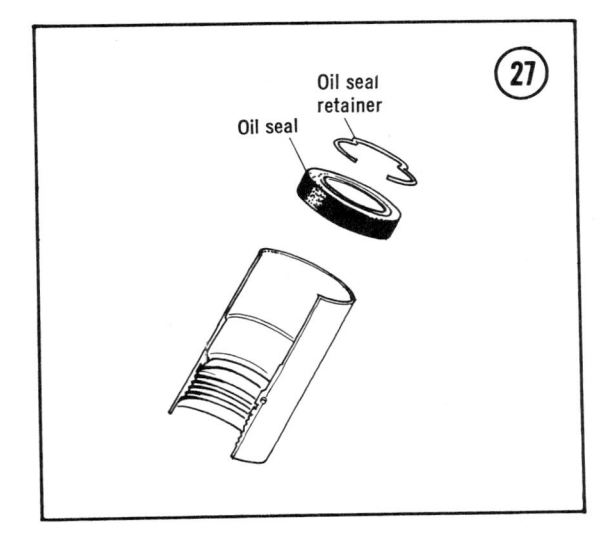

Figure 27
Oil seal
Oil seal retainer

Figure 28
1. Oil seal 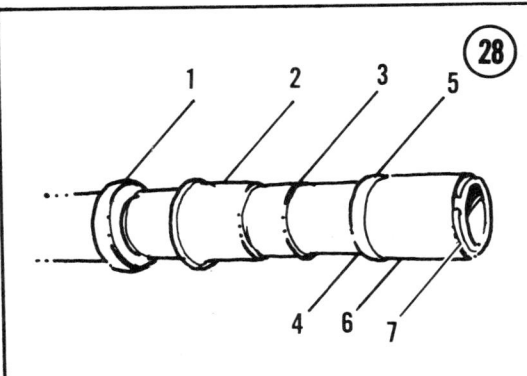
2. Fork tube guide
3. Fork tube stopper ring
4. Fork valve stopper ring
5. Damper valve
6. Fork piston
7. Fork piston snap ring

Assembly

Refer to **Figure 24**.
1. Install new seal in seal housing. Install retainer. See **Figure 27**.
2. Install seal housing, guide, stop ring, damper valve, piston and snap ring. See **Figure 28**.
3. Install springs, washers, and center spring seat in bottom case.
4. Install fork pipe into bottom case.
5. Tighten seal housing.

Installation

Installation is the reverse of removal. Fill each fork leg with the quantity of 10W-30 oil listed in the *QRD* at the front of the manual.

FRONT FORK (EARLY, 1-SPRING)

Some early CB models use a single internal spring, rather than 2 springs. Some early CL models use a single external spring.

Removal/Installation

1. Remove front wheel.
2. Remove fender and front brake stop arm bolt.
3. Unbolt headlight housing.
4. Remove clamp bolt on lower triple clamp.
5. Remove top fork cap.
6. Pull fork fownward and out.
7. Drain oil from fork.
8. Installation is the reverse of removal. Fill each fork with 9.6-10.0 ounces (285-295 cc) of 10W-30 engine oil.

Disassembly/Assembly

Refer to **Figure 29** (CB450) or **Figure 30** (CL450) for this procedure.
1. Remove fork cover and rubber boot.
2. Remove spring
3. Remove circlip as shown in Figure 31.
4. Separate fork pipe and bottom case.
5. Remove snap ring, piston, piston stopper ring, damper valve, valve stopper ring, fork pipe stopper ring, and guide. See **Figure 32**.
6. Assembly is the reverse of disassembly.

Inspection

1. Clean all parts in solvent.
2. Measure parts and compare with **Table 1**.
3. Check bottom surface of damper valve and upper surface of piston for scratches.

FRONT FORKS
(CB450 K3 AND K4)

Removal

1. Remove front wheel as described elsewhere.
2. Remove the brake caliper as described in Chapter Ten.
3. Remove front fender.
4. Remove side bolts securing headlight housing to fork covers.
5. Remove filler caps at top of forks.
6. Pull the fork tubes downward and out.
7. Invert fork and pour oil out.

Disassembly

Refer to **Figure 33** for this procedure.

1. Remove circlip shown in **Figure 34** and separate bottom case from fork pipe.
2. Remove snap ring (1, **Figure 35**). Pull off front fork piston and damper valve from the fork pipe.

Inspection

1. Clean all parts thoroughly in solvent.
2. Measure piston diameter with a micrometer as shown in **Figure 36**. Replace if diameter is less than 1.551 in. (39.4mm) or there is uneven wear or scoring.
3. Measure inside diameter of bottom case with an inside micrometer. See **Figure 37**. Replace if greater than 1.562 in. (39.68mm).

Assembly

1. Clean all parts again in solvent.
2. Assemble pipe guard, stopper rings, damper valve, piston, and snap ring on front fork pipe. See **Figure 38**.

3. Install fork pipe on bottom case and install oil seal with special tools shown in **Figure 39**.

> NOTE: *These tools can be improvised. Start the seal by hand, then lay a large washer over it. Drive the seal in with a piece of pipe, which can slide over the fork pipe. Make sure the pipe does not mar fork pipe surface.*

4. Install circlip at top of bottom case. See **Figure 40**.

Installation

1. Install upper fork tube covers between upper and lower rubber cushions.
2. Push fork tubes upward into place.
3. Tighten lower clamp bolt just enough to hold fork tube.
4. Fill fork tubes with 7.0-7.3 oz. (220-230cc) of 10W-30 engine oil. Install caps.
5. Tighten both clamp bolts.
6. Install the brake caliper as described in Chapter Ten.
7. Install front wheel.

FRONT FORKS
(CB450 K5-K7)

Removal

1. Drain fork oil.
2. Remove front wheel as described elsewhere.
3. Remove the brake caliper as described in Chapter Ten.
4. Loosen clamp bolts on steering stem and fork crown.
5. Pull forks downward and out.

Disassembly

Refer to **Figure 41** for this procedure.

1. Remove front fork bolt.
2. Loosen locknut (11, **Figure 41**).
3. Remove spring and spring seat.
4. Remove the bolt securing damper (3, **Figure 41**).
5. Remove fork pipe and damper.
6. Remove circlip and oil seal (6 and 7, **Figure 41**).

FRONT SUSPENSION AND STEERING

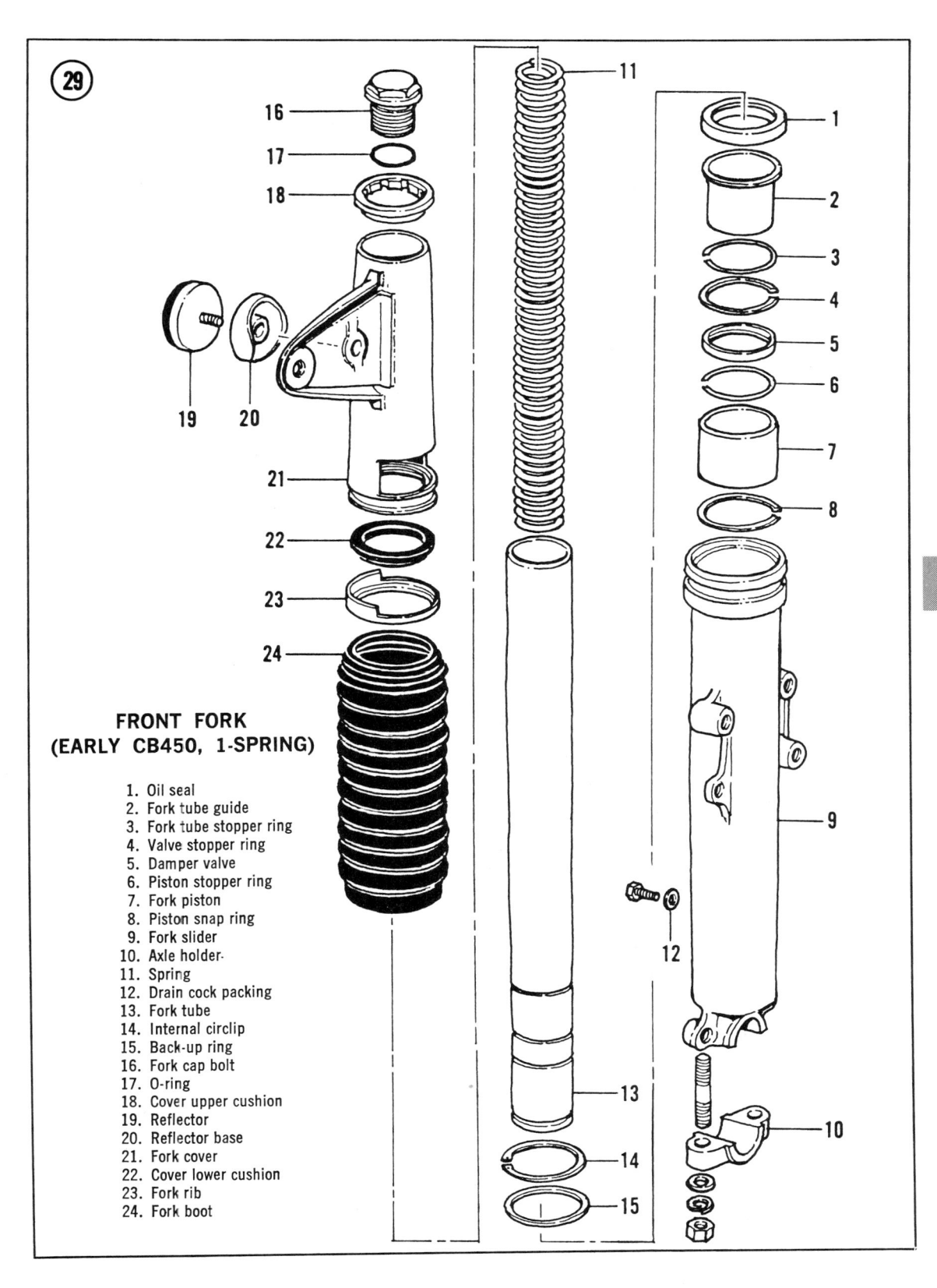

**FRONT FORK
(EARLY CB450, 1-SPRING)**

1. Oil seal
2. Fork tube guide
3. Fork tube stopper ring
4. Valve stopper ring
5. Damper valve
6. Piston stopper ring
7. Fork piston
8. Piston snap ring
9. Fork slider
10. Axle holder
11. Spring
12. Drain cock packing
13. Fork tube
14. Internal circlip
15. Back-up ring
16. Fork cap bolt
17. O-ring
18. Cover upper cushion
19. Reflector
20. Reflector base
21. Fork cover
22. Cover lower cushion
23. Fork rib
24. Fork boot

CHAPTER EIGHT

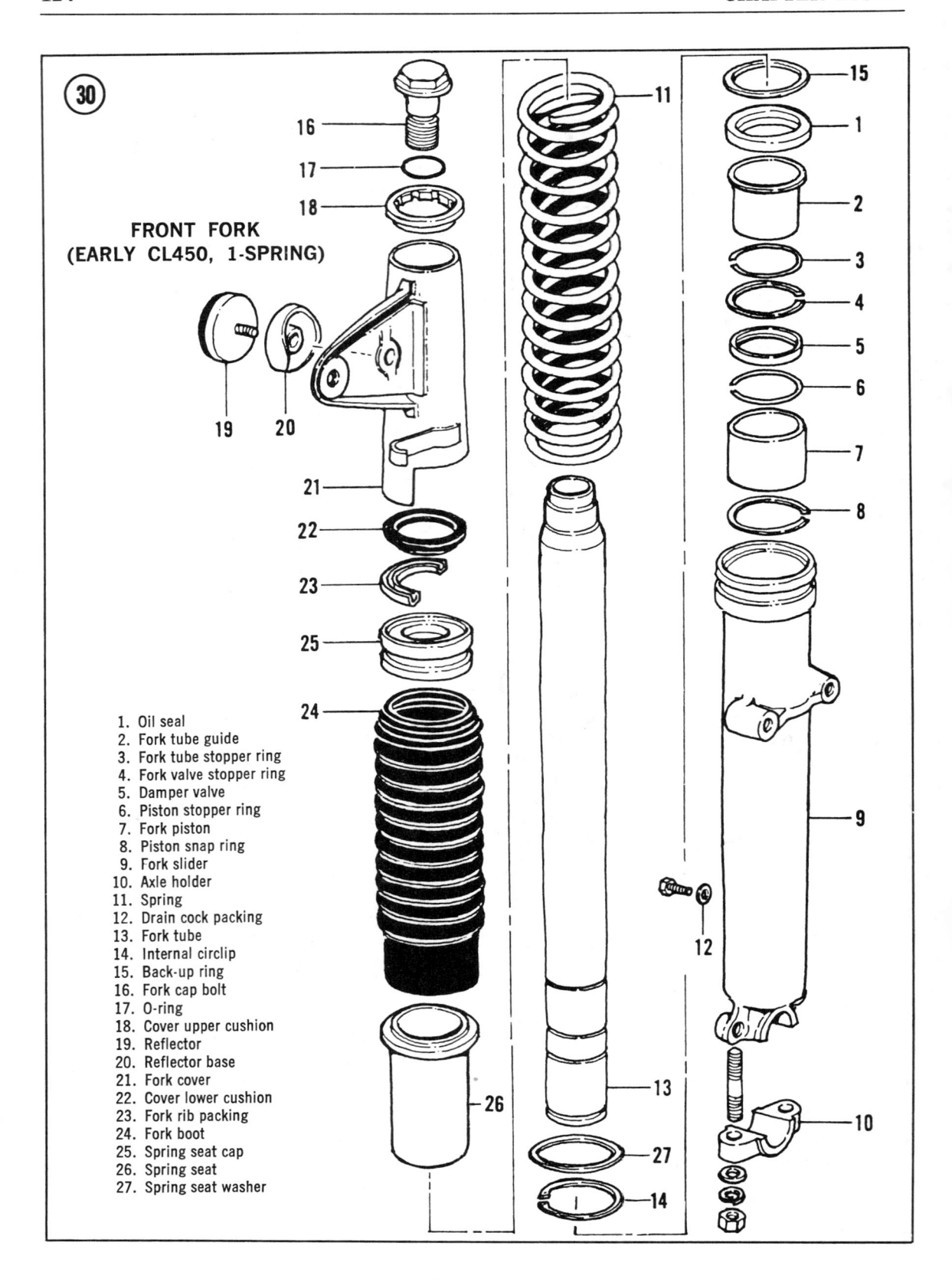

FRONT FORK (EARLY CL450, 1-SPRING)

1. Oil seal
2. Fork tube guide
3. Fork tube stopper ring
4. Fork valve stopper ring
5. Damper valve
6. Piston stopper ring
7. Fork piston
8. Piston snap ring
9. Fork slider
10. Axle holder
11. Spring
12. Drain cock packing
13. Fork tube
14. Internal circlip
15. Back-up ring
16. Fork cap bolt
17. O-ring
18. Cover upper cushion
19. Reflector
20. Reflector base
21. Fork cover
22. Cover lower cushion
23. Fork rib packing
24. Fork boot
25. Spring seat cap
26. Spring seat
27. Spring seat washer

FRONT SUSPENSION AND STEERING

Table 1   FRONT FORK

Springs	
Unloaded length (upper)	197mm
Unloaded length (lower)	215mm
Front fork piston	
Outside diameter	37.5mm
Inside diameter	0.008mm
Taper	0.015mm
Front fork pipe	
Outside diameter	33.0mm
Elliptic wear	0.015mm
Deflection	Within 0.04mm
Front fork pipe guide	
Full length	36mm
Inside diameter	33.0mm
Outside diameter	37.5mm

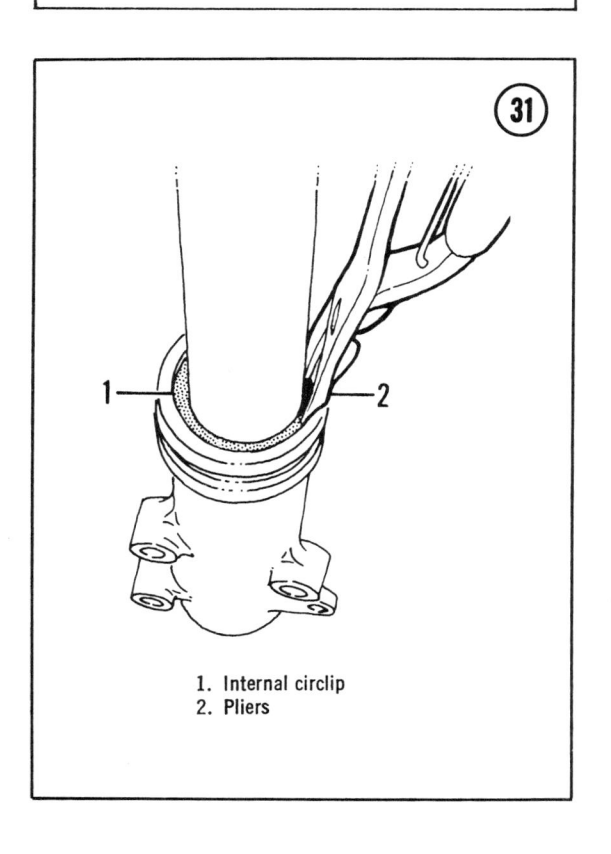

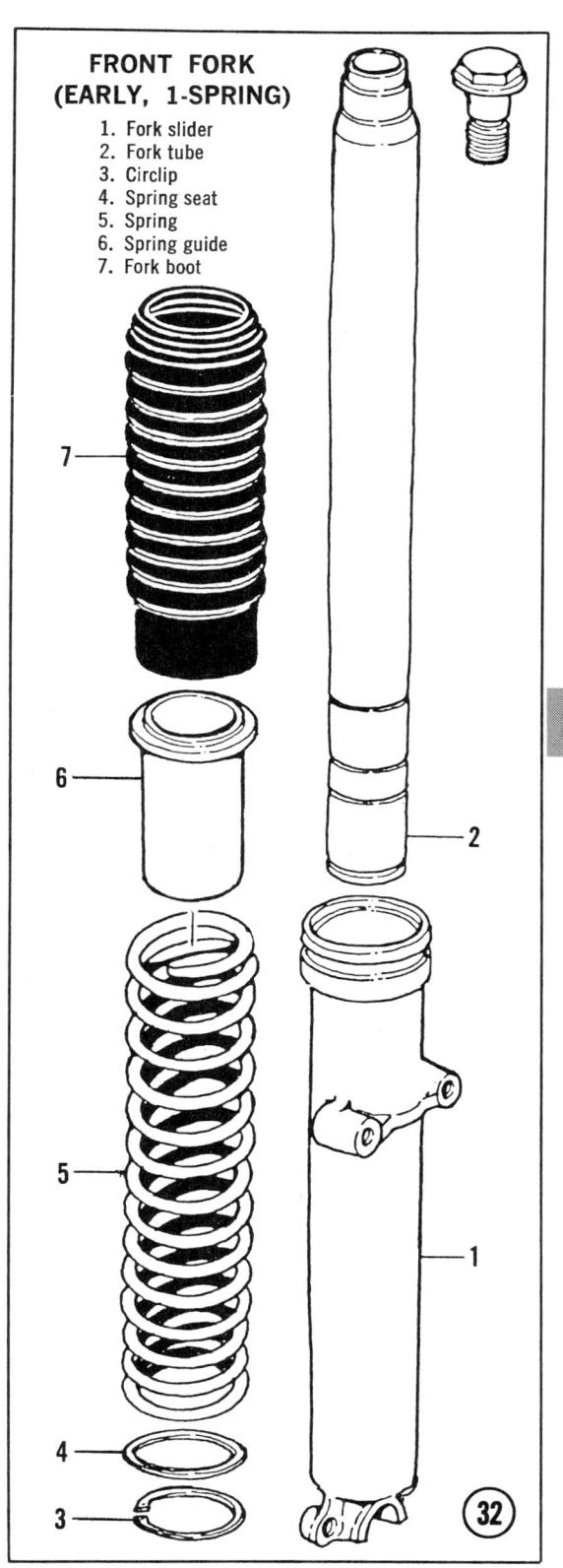

FRONT FORK (EARLY, 1-SPRING)
1. Fork slider
2. Fork tube
3. Circlip
4. Spring seat
5. Spring
6. Spring guide
7. Fork boot

(32)

(31)
1. Internal circlip
2. Pliers

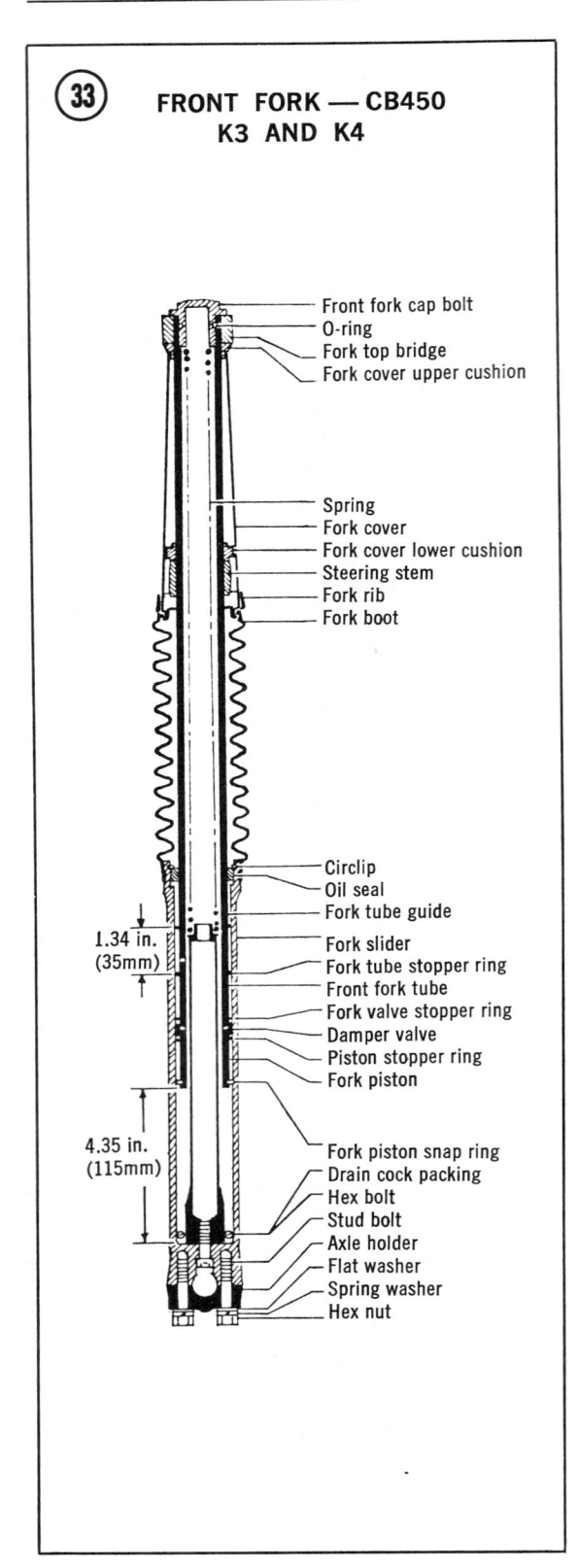

CHAPTER EIGHT

33 FRONT FORK — CB450 K3 AND K4

- Front fork cap bolt
- O-ring
- Fork top bridge
- Fork cover upper cushion
- Spring
- Fork cover
- Fork cover lower cushion
- Steering stem
- Fork rib
- Fork boot
- Circlip
- Oil seal
- Fork tube guide
- Fork slider
- Fork tube stopper ring
- Front fork tube
- Fork valve stopper ring
- Damper valve
- Piston stopper ring
- Fork piston
- Fork piston snap ring
- Drain cock packing
- Hex bolt
- Stud bolt
- Axle holder
- Flat washer
- Spring washer
- Hex nut

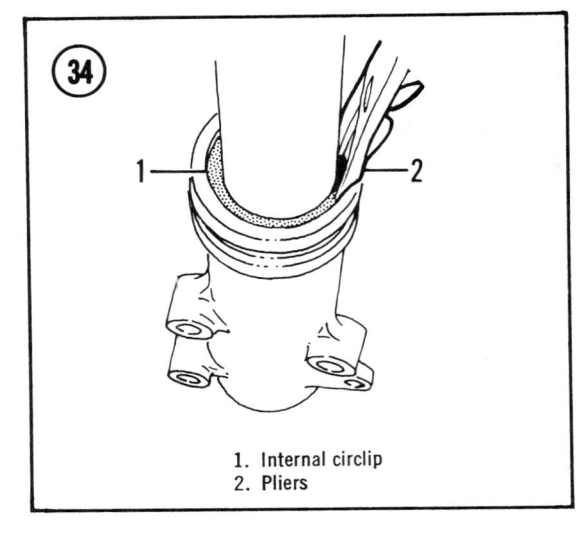

1.34 in. (35mm)

4.35 in. (115mm)

34

1. Internal circlip
2. Pliers

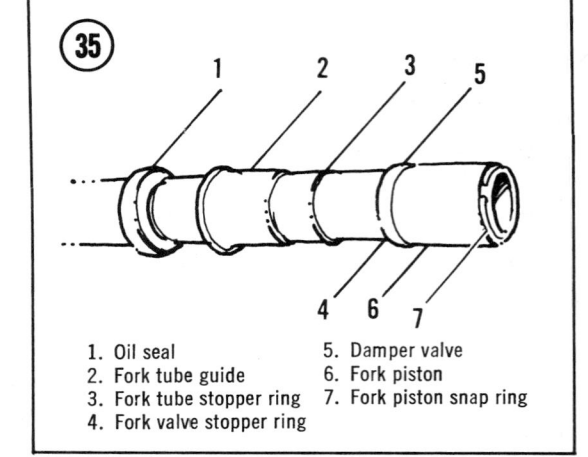

35

1. Oil seal
2. Fork tube guide
3. Fork tube stopper ring
4. Fork valve stopper ring
5. Damper valve
6. Fork piston
7. Fork piston snap ring

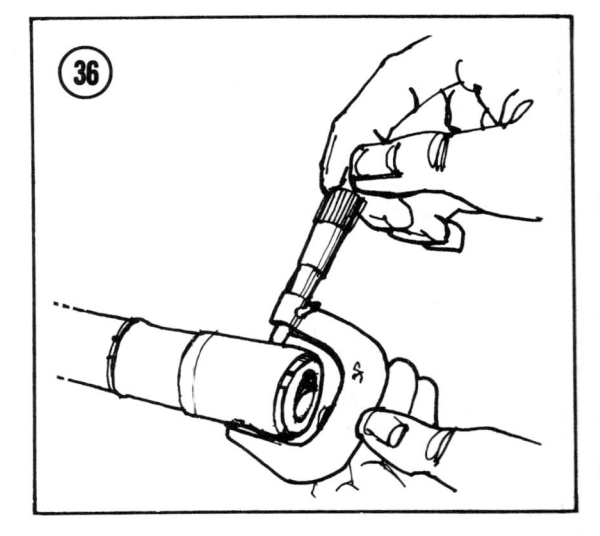

36

FRONT SUSPENSION AND STEERING

Inspection

1. Measure free length and distoriton (tilt) of spring as shown in **Figure 42**. Compare with **Table 2** replace if necessary.
2. Check fork pipe and bottom case for damage or wear.
3. Inspect oil seal for damage and try to determine the cause. Then discard it.
4. Check damper unit for wear or damage.

Assembly

Assembly is the reverse of disassembly. Note the following points:

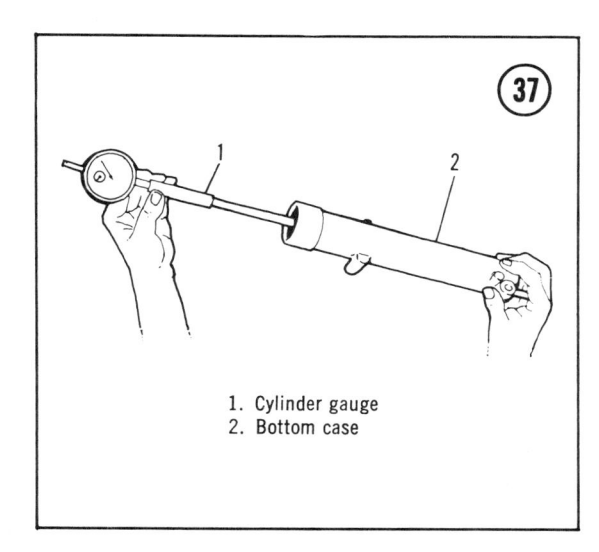

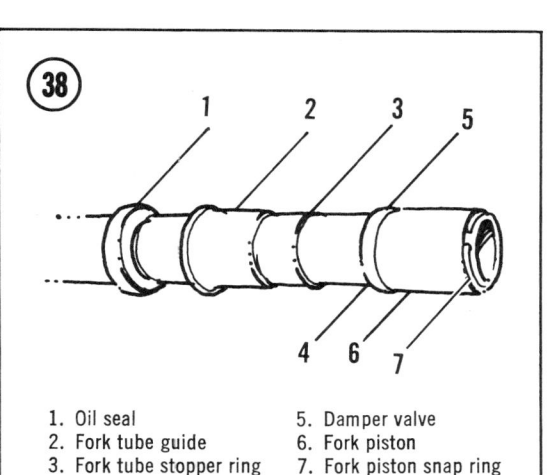

a. Use Loctite on piston threads before installing locknut.
b. Use a new oil seal.
c. Adjust brake caliper clearance as described in Chapter Ten.
d. Fill each fork with 5.3-5.6 oz. (155-165cc) of automatic transmission fluid.

FRONT FORKS (CB500T)

Removal

1. Drain fork oil.
2. Remove front wheel as described under

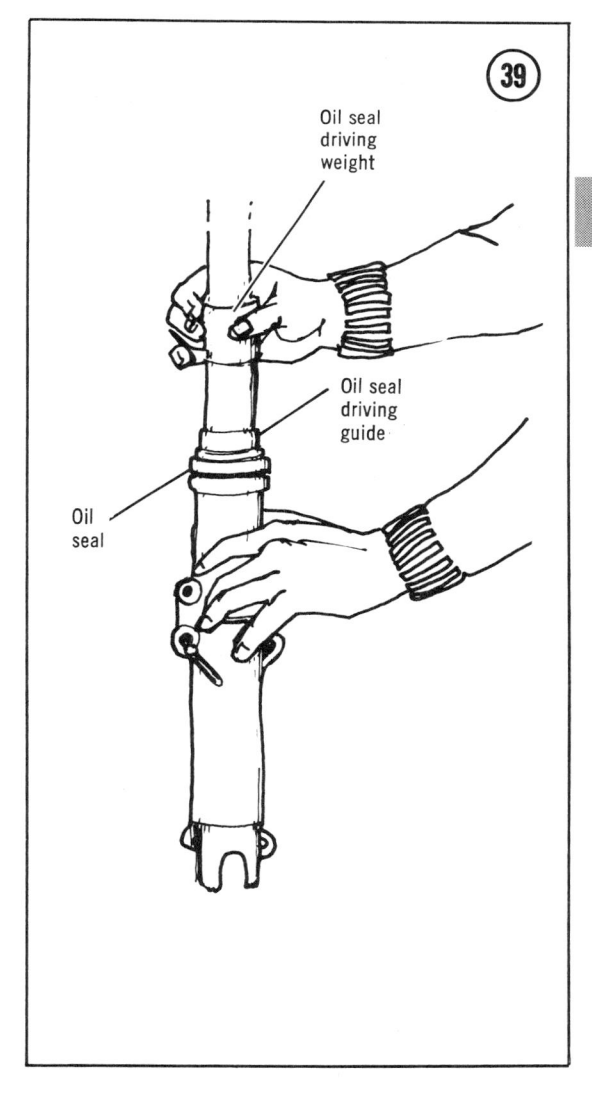

37
1. Cylinder gauge
2. Bottom case

38
1. Oil seal
2. Fork tube guide
3. Fork tube stopper ring
4. Fork valve stopper ring
5. Damper valve
6. Fork piston
7. Fork piston snap ring

39
Oil seal driving weight
Oil seal driving guide
Oil seal

CHAPTER EIGHT

Front Wheel (Disc Brake), Removal/Installation, this chapter.

3. Remove brake caliper as described in Chapter Ten, *Front Disc Brake, Caliper Removal/Installation*.

4. Loosen front fork bolt, then loosen clamp bolts at fork top bridge and steering stem.

5. Pull forks downward and out. Remove all external rust with crocus or very fine emery cloth.

Disassembly

Refer to **Figure 43** for this procedure.

1. Remove the damper retainer bolt (7, **Figure 43**) and separate the fork slider (5) from front fork tube (9) and oil lock piece. See **Figure 44**, which shows a special Allen-head wrench being used to remove the bolt.

> NOTE: *A vise with soft jaws may be used to hold fork parts during this procedure. Additional finish protection can be provided by wrapping parts in several thicknesses of heavy cloth before clamping them in the vise.*

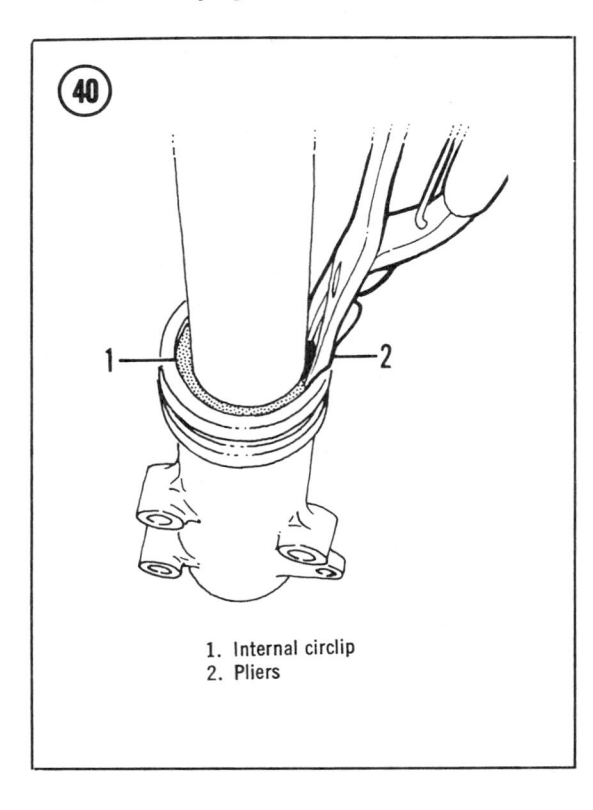

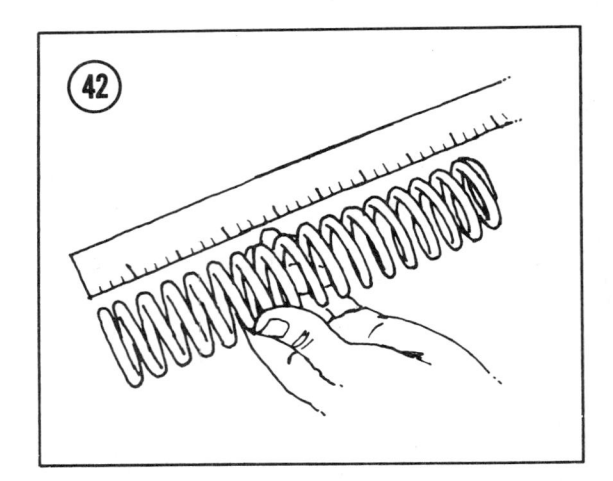

1. Internal circlip
2. Pliers

Table 2 FRONT FORK (K5-K7 AND CB500T)

Spring	
Free length	8.35 in. (211.9mm)
Tilt	Within 1.5°
Front fork piston	
Outside diameter	1.552-1.553 in. (39.425-39.45mm)
Inside diameter	Within 0.0003 in. (0.008mm)
Taper	Within 0.0059 in. (0.015mm)
Front fork pipe	
Outside diameter	1.551-1.552 in. (34.90-34.915mm)
Elliptic wear	0.00059 in. (0.015mm)
Deflection	Within 0.0016 in. (0.04mm)
Front fork pipe guide	
Full length	1.378 in. (35.0mm)
Inside diameter	1.378-1.380 in. (35.0-35.039mm)
Outside diameter	1.551-1.556 in. (39.466-39.539mm)
Front fork bottom case	
Inside diameter	1.555-1.557 in. (39.5-39.539mm)

FRONT SUSPENSION AND STEERING

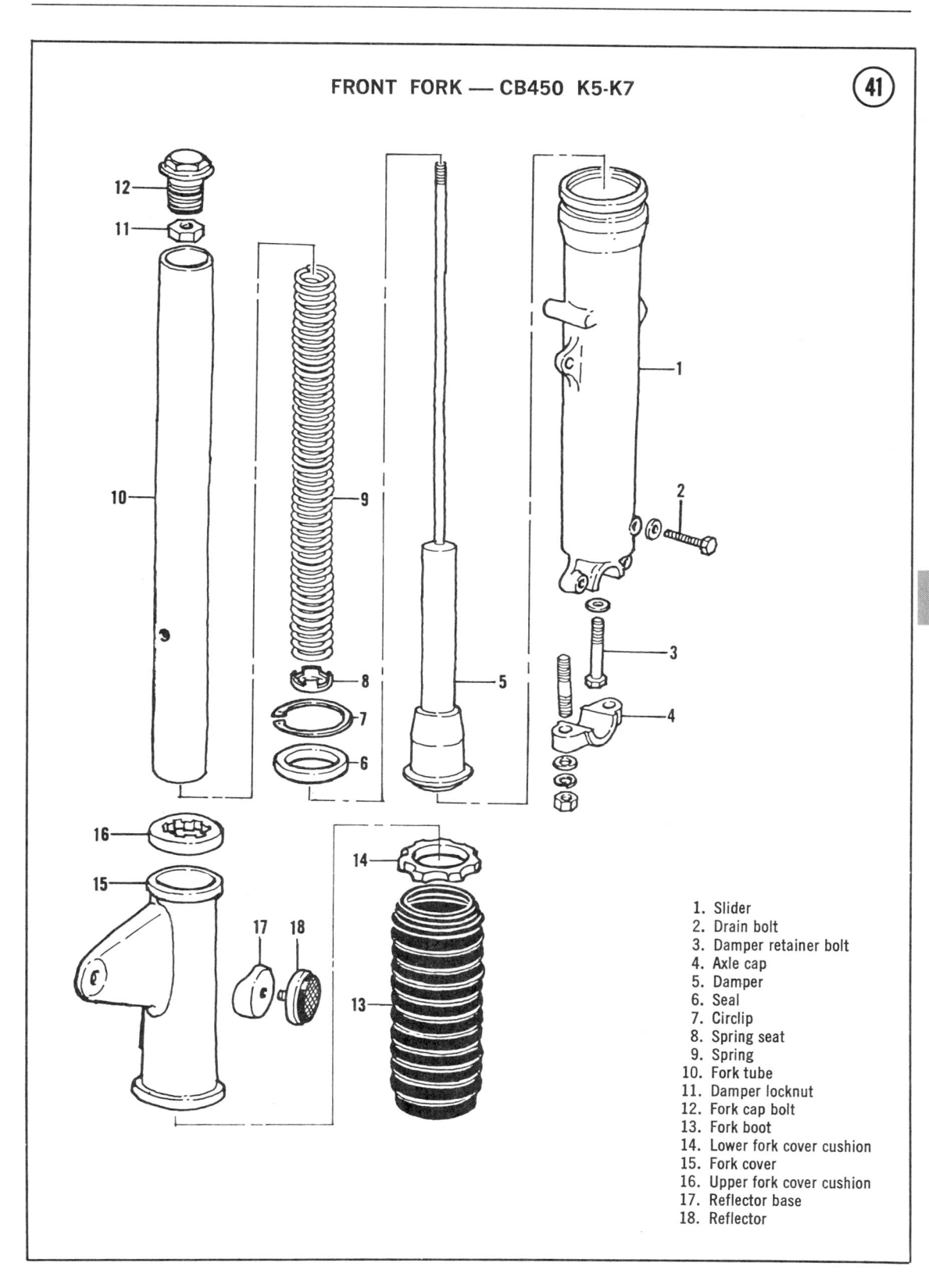

FRONT FORK — CB450 K5-K7

1. Slider
2. Drain bolt
3. Damper retainer bolt
4. Axle cap
5. Damper
6. Seal
7. Circlip
8. Spring seat
9. Spring
10. Fork tube
11. Damper locknut
12. Fork cap bolt
13. Fork boot
14. Lower fork cover cushion
15. Fork cover
16. Upper fork cover cushion
17. Reflector base
18. Reflector

CHAPTER EIGHT

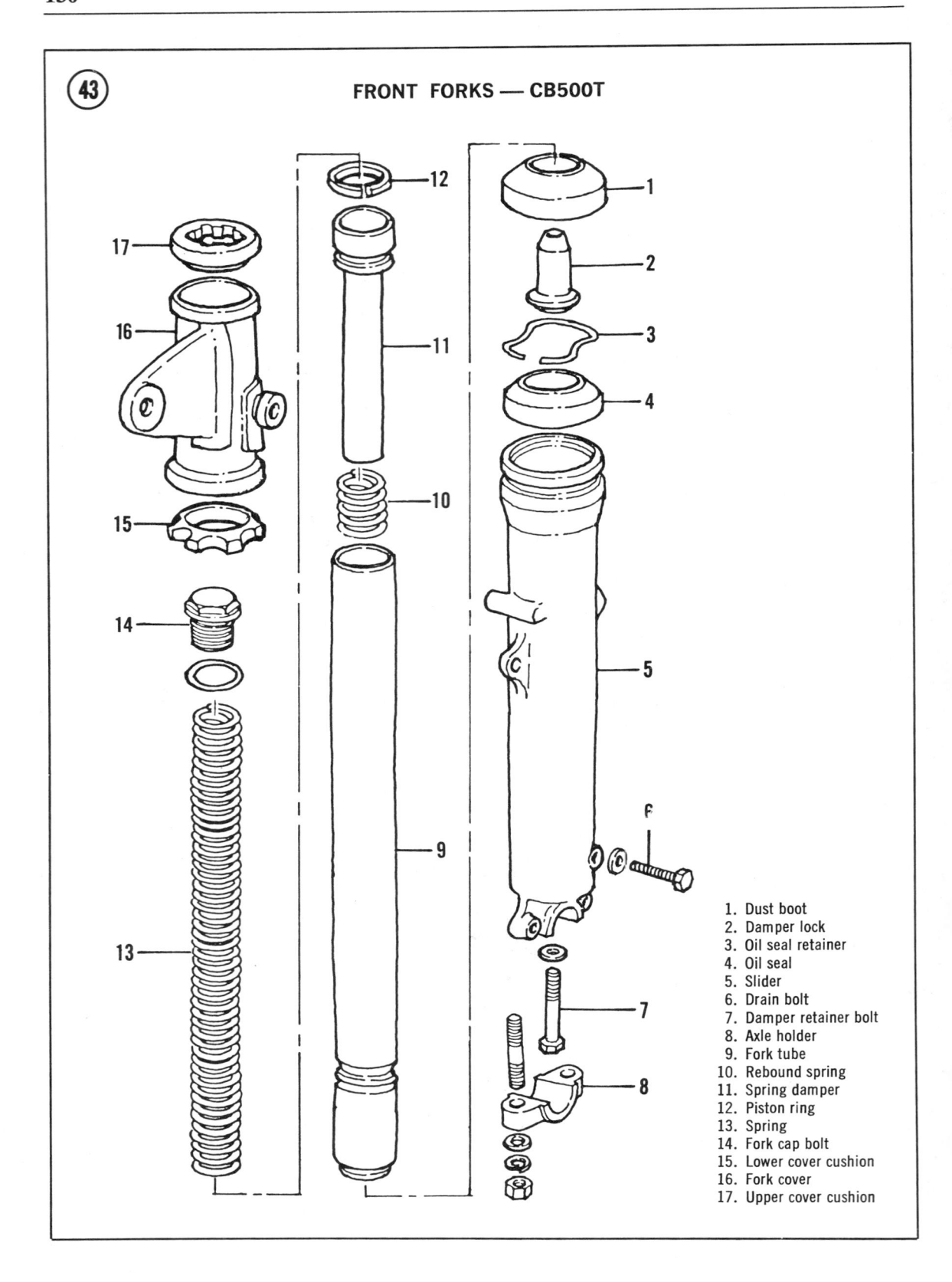

43 FRONT FORKS — CB500T

1. Dust boot
2. Damper lock
3. Oil seal retainer
4. Oil seal
5. Slider
6. Drain bolt
7. Damper retainer bolt
8. Axle holder
9. Fork tube
10. Rebound spring
11. Spring damper
12. Piston ring
13. Spring
14. Fork cap bolt
15. Lower cover cushion
16. Fork cover
17. Upper cover cushion

FRONT SUSPENSION AND STEERING

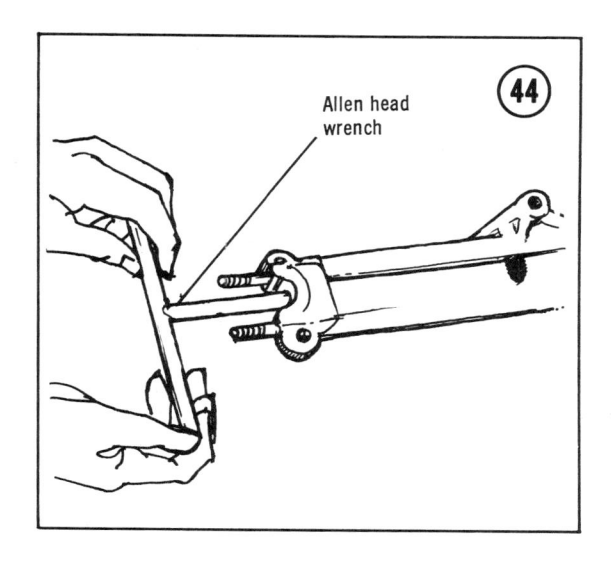

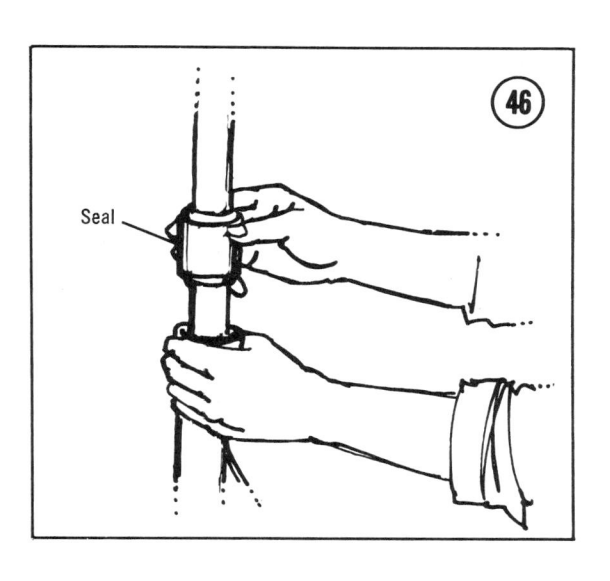

2. Remove the front fork bolt (14, **Figure 43**), then remove front shock absorber spring (13), spring damper (11), and rebound spring (10).

3. Remove the bottom case cover (5) and then remove the oil seal stop (3). Remove the oil seal (4). See **Figure 45**.

Inspection

1. Clean all parts in solvent, then check the free length of the front shock absorber spring. Replace if shorter than 17.32 in. (440mm). Standard length is 18.35 in. (466mm).

2. Check the underseat pipe for piston ring wear or damage. Replace if worn or damaged.

3. Measure the inside diameter of the bottom case at several places and replace if any measurement is more than 1.3859 in. (35.20mm). Standard inside diameter is 1.3790-1.3810 in. (35.025-35.064mm).

4. Measure the outside diameter of the front fork pipe (where it fits inside the bottom case) in several places. Replace if any measurement is less than 1.3729 in. (34.87mm). Standard is 1.3740-1.3772 in. (34.90-34.98mm).

5. Check bottom case and fork pipe for cracks or other damage. Replace if necessary.

6. Check oil seal for wear or damage. It is a good idea to replace oil seals whenever they are removed, regardless of whether or not they seem damaged.

Assembly

1. Coat all surfaces of the new oil seal with automatic transmission fluid and install seal in the bottom case. See **Figure 46**. Make sure the seal is properly seated. Install the oil seal stop (snap ring) and the bottom case cover.

2. Insert the rebound spring and the underseat pipe into the front fork pipe, then insert the shock absorber spring with the large pitch (coils farther apart) toward the bottom.

3. Install the oil lock piece, then install the front fork pipe in the bottom case and secure with the socket head bolt. Use Loctite or other liquid sealant on the threads.

4. Fill each fork with 6.2-6.5 oz. (185-191cc)

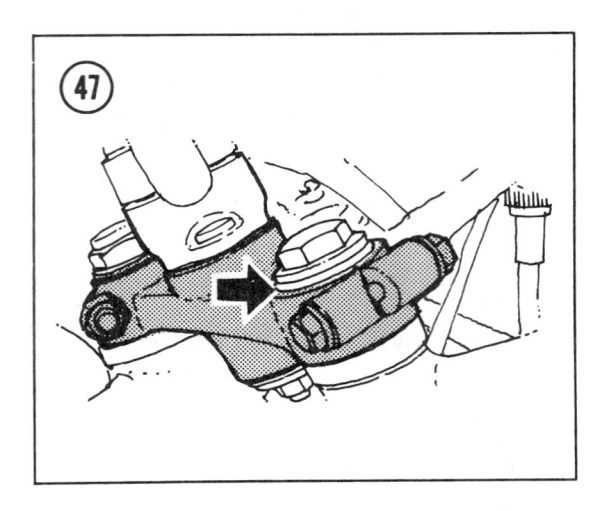

of automatic transmission fluid and install the fork bolts.

5. Install each front fork assembly so that the chamfered edge of the fork pipe is aligned with the upper surface of the fork top bridge. See **Figure 47**.

6. Securely tighten all clamp bolts. Check shock absorber action by grasping handlebars and moving forks up and down. Check oil seal for signs of leaks.

7. Reinstall brake caliper following procedures given in Chapter Ten. Reinstall the front wheel. See *Front Wheel (Disc Brake), Removal/Installation*, given earlier in this chapter.

CHAPTER NINE

REAR SUSPENSION

This chapter includes repair and replacement procedures for the rear wheel, drive chain, and rear suspension components.

REAR WHEEL

Removal/Installation

1. Disconnect drive chain as described elsewhere in this chapter.
2. Remove brake rod adjusting nut. See **Figure 1**. Separate rod from brake arm.
3. Remove backing plate stop nut (see **Figure 2**) and free stop arm from backing plate.
4. Remove cotter pin and axle nut.
5. Lift up wheel to take strain off axle and pull axle out.

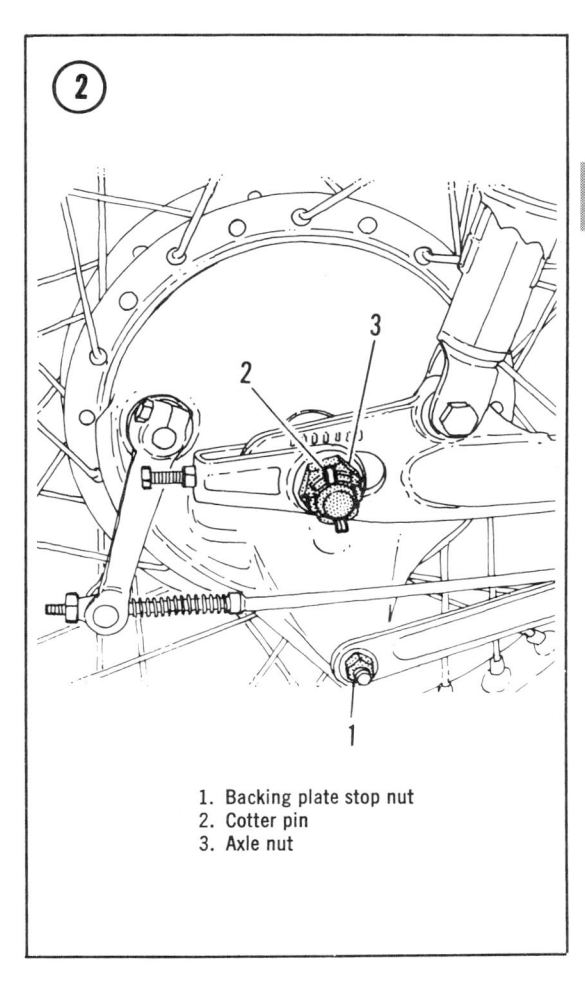

1. Backing plate stop nut
2. Cotter pin
3. Axle nut

6. Lower wheel. See **Figure 3**.

7. Installation is the reverse of these steps.

8. Adjust drive chain tension and brake pedal free play.

Disassembly

Refer to **Figures 4 and 5**.

1. Lift off brake panel.
2. Remove bearing retainer cap.
3. Remove circlip.
4. Straighten tabs on drive sprocket retaining nuts and remove nuts. See **Figure 6**. Lift sprocket off.
5. Unscrew wheel bearing retainer with a special tool made for this purpose. See **Figure 7**.

NOTE: *This tool is easily improvised.* **Figure 8** *shows one method.*

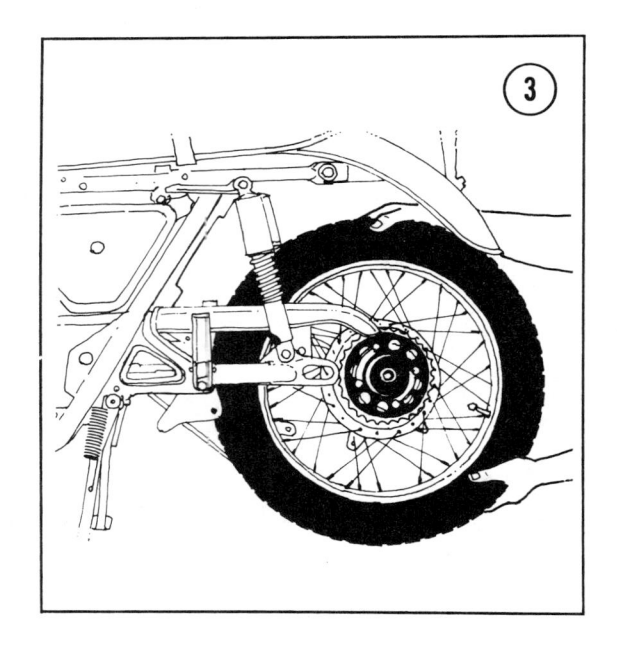

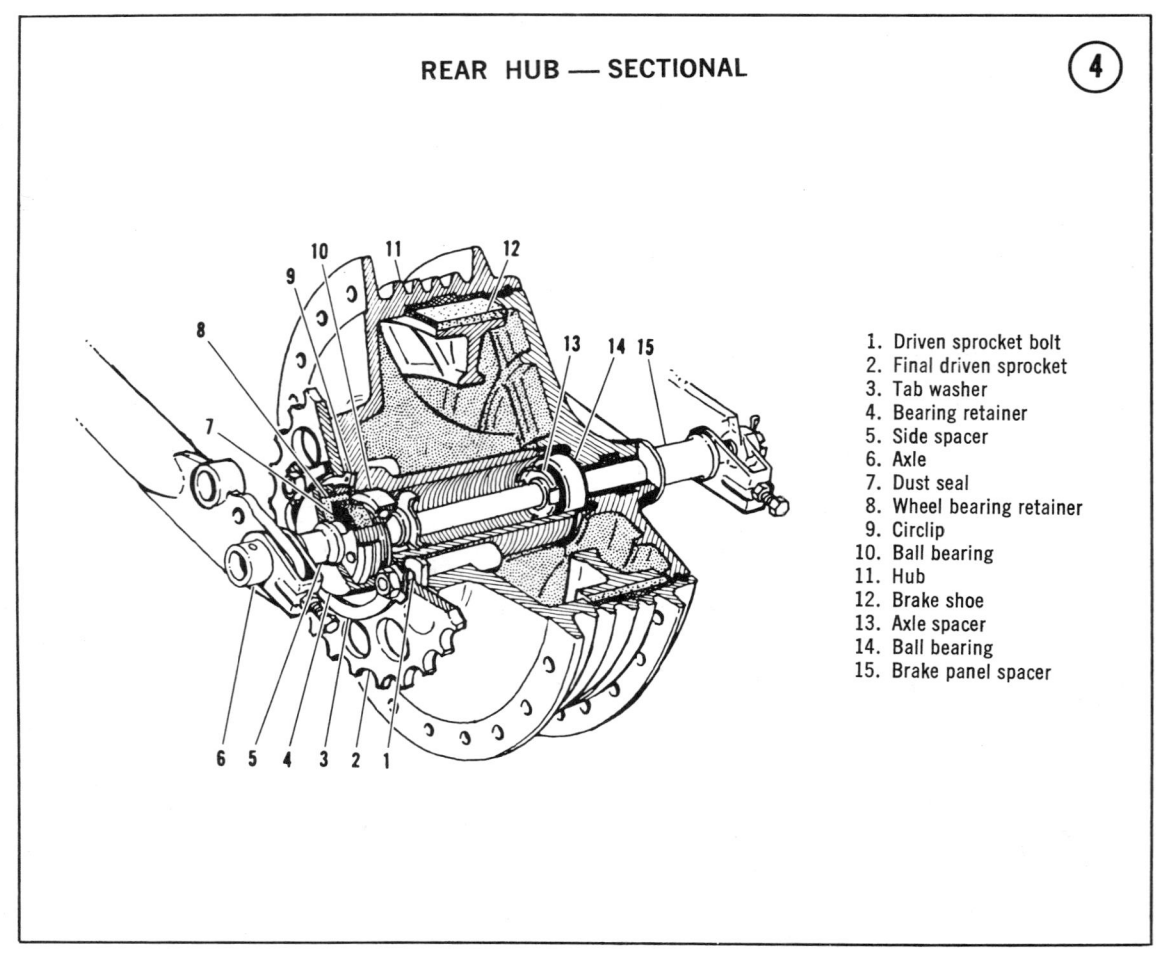

REAR HUB — SECTIONAL

1. Driven sprocket bolt
2. Final driven sprocket
3. Tab washer
4. Bearing retainer
5. Side spacer
6. Axle
7. Dust seal
8. Wheel bearing retainer
9. Circlip
10. Ball bearing
11. Hub
12. Brake shoe
13. Axle spacer
14. Ball bearing
15. Brake panel spacer

REAR SUSPENSION

135

REAR HUB — EXPLODED ⑤

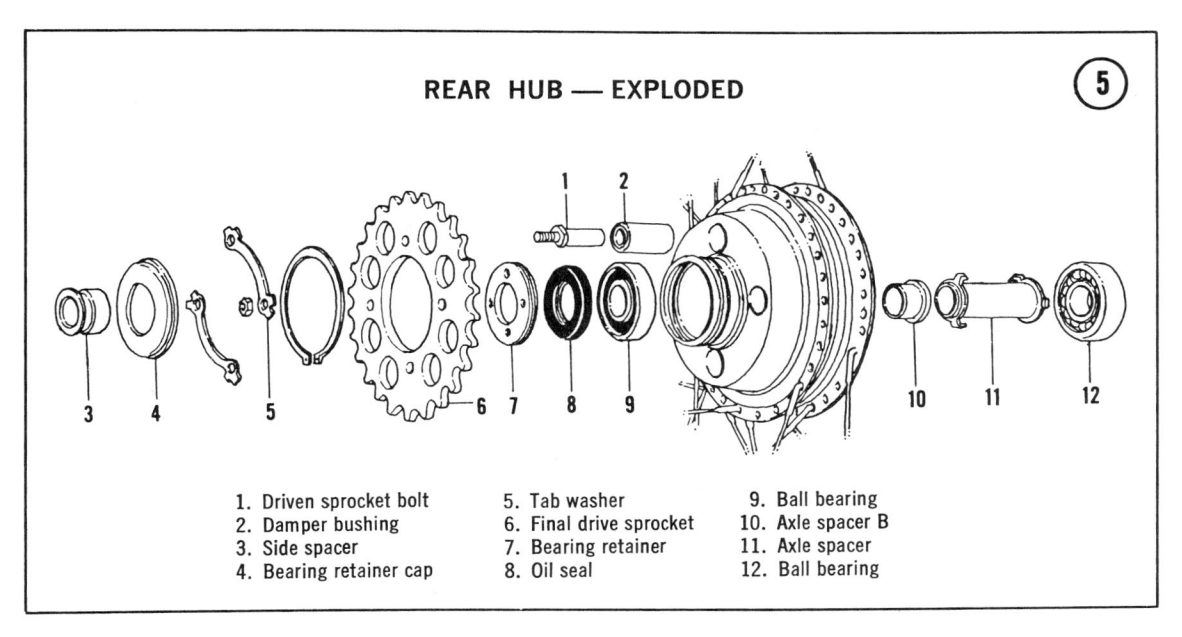

1. Driven sprocket bolt
2. Damper bushing
3. Side spacer
4. Bearing retainer cap
5. Tab washer
6. Final drive sprocket
7. Bearing retainer
8. Oil seal
9. Ball bearing
10. Axle spacer B
11. Axle spacer
12. Ball bearing

⑥

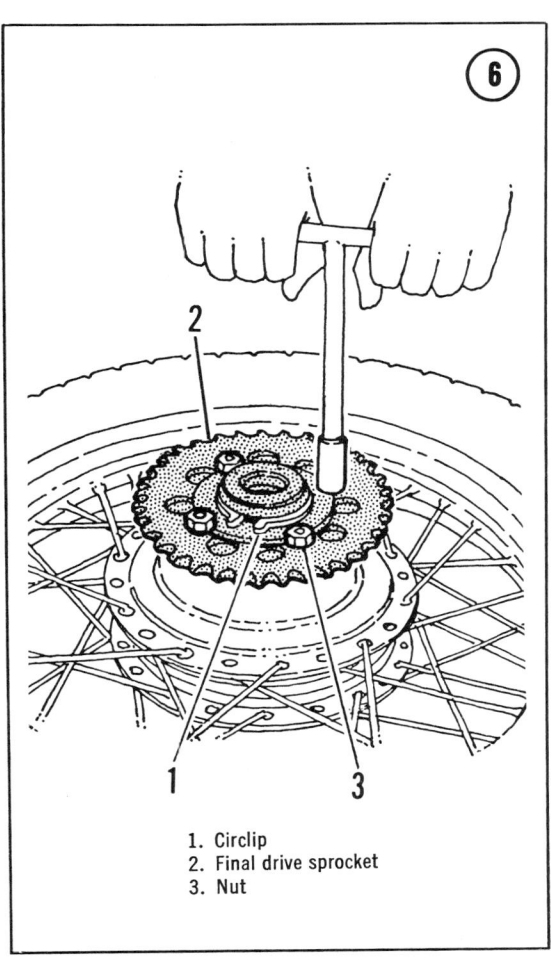

1. Circlip
2. Final drive sprocket
3. Nut

⑦

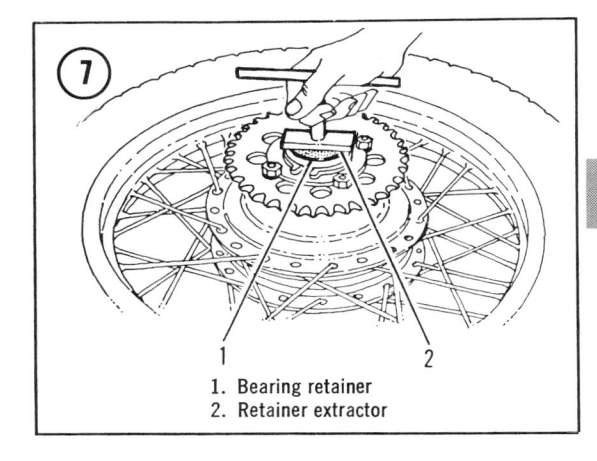

1. Bearing retainer
2. Retainer extractor

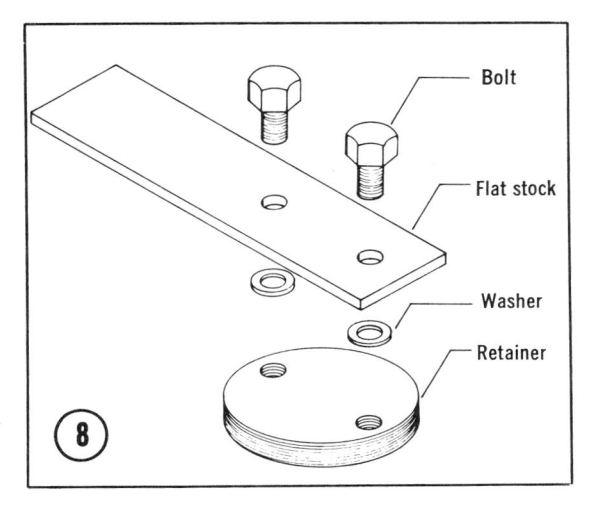

⑧

- Bolt
- Flat stock
- Washer
- Retainer

6. Remove both bearings and spacer.

Inspection

1. Clean all parts in solvent.

2. Check brake components as described in Chapter Ten.

3. Turn each bearing by hand. Make sure that bearings turn smoothly. Check balls for evidence of wear, pitting, or excessive heat (bluish tint). Replace questionable bearings.

4. Check axle for wear and straightness. **Figure 9** shows one method.

5. Check brake drum surface in hub for out-of-round, scoring, and excessive wear.

6. Check for bent or broken spokes.

Assembly

1. Pack bearings thoroughly with multipurpose grease. Work grease in between balls thoroughly.

2. Pack wheel hub with grease.

3. Insert spacer.

4. Install the bearings with the sealed side facing outward.

> **CAUTION**
> *When tapping bearings into place, tap on outer race only. Do not tap on inner race or bearing might be damaged.*

5. Install new oil seal and screw in bearing retainer.

6. Install sprocket. Use new lock tabs.

7. Install circlip.

8. Install bearing retainer cap.

9. Install brake panel.

Wheel Balancing

An unbalanced wheel can be dangerous. Depending on the degree of unbalance and speed, the rider may experience anything from mild vibration to violent shimmy. In severe cases, the rider can lose control.

Wheels are relatively easy to balance without special equipment. Your dealer has an assortment of balance weights which attach to the spokes. They are crimped onto the light side of the wheel with ordinary gas pliers. See **Figure 10**. Buy a couple of each weight available.

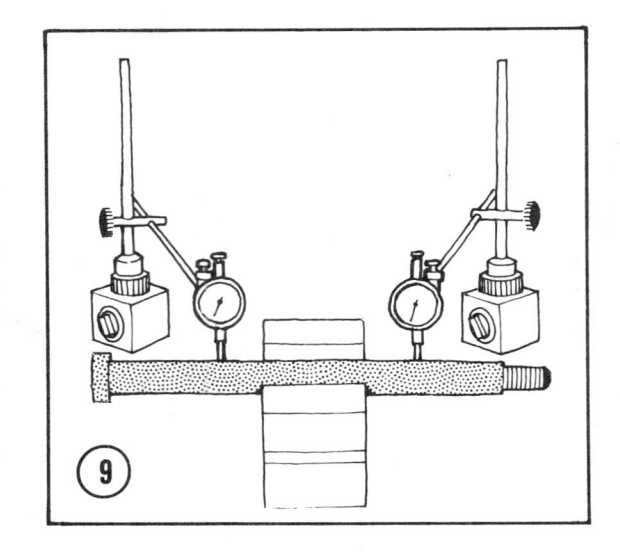

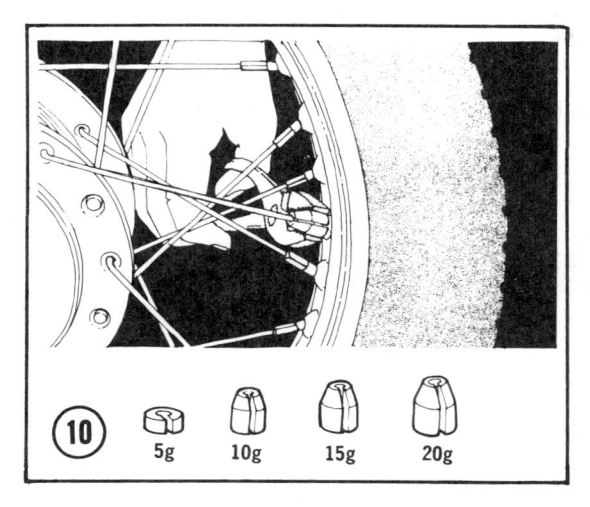

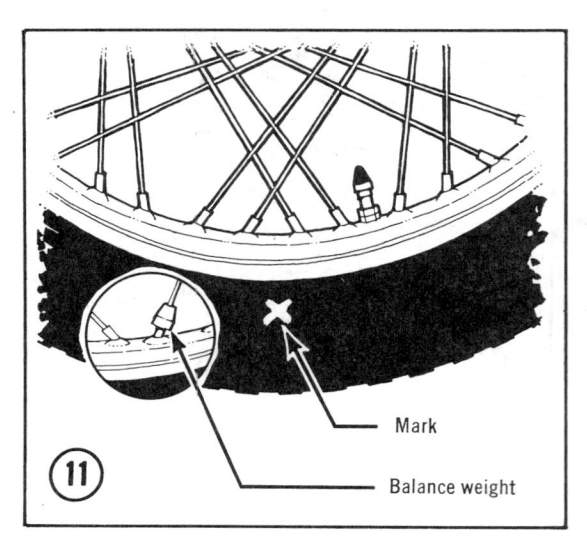

REAR SUSPENSION

If undamaged, you can return unused weights.

Before balancing a wheel, make sure bearings are in good condition and properly lubricated. Use the wheel disassembly/inspection/assembly procedures in this chapter to be sure. In addition, make sure that the brakes do not drag. The wheel must rotate freely.

1. Rest bike on centerstand.
2. Disconnect drive chain.
3. Rotate rear wheel slowly and allow it to come to rest by itself. Note the position of valve stem (**Figure 11**).
4. Repeat Step 3 several times. If the valve stem stops at a different position each time, the wheel is balanced. If the valve stem stops near the same position each time, add weight at the 12 o'clock position (light side) until valve stem no longer favors one position when the wheel stops.
5. Reconnect drive chain and road test bike on smooth, straight road.

Spoke Adjustment

Spokes loosen with use and should be checked periodically. Follow the procedure described in Chapter Eight.

DRIVE CHAIN

Removal

Early CB and CL models have a master link which can be disconnected. Later bikes have an endless drive chain; a special tool is required to separate links.

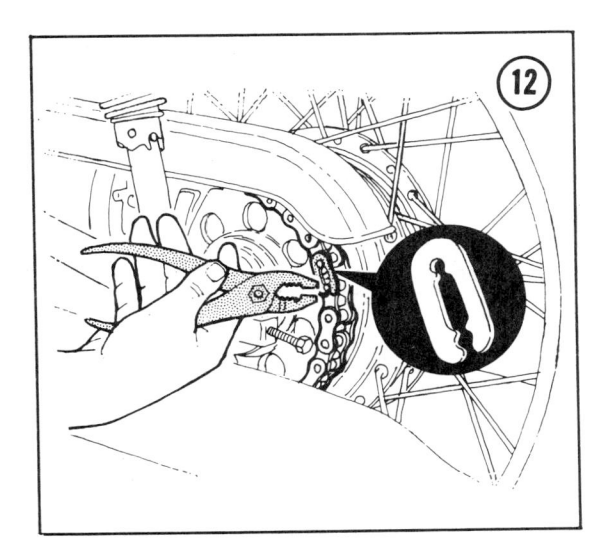

1a. On chains with master link, remove master link with pliers (**Figure 12**) and separate chain.
1b. On endless chains, separate any link in chain with a chain breaker tool available at your dealer.
2. Remove gearshift lever and left foot peg. Remove front chain cover.
3. Remove chain.

> NOTE: *Some mechanics join the new chain to the old before removing the old. As the old chain rotates off the drive sprocket, the new one rotates on. While it saves time, it is not a good practice. If the chain requires replacement, the drive sprocket should be fully inspected. A damaged sprocket will simply damage the new chain and you are back where you started.*

Inspection

1. Clean chain thoroughly in solvent. Let it soak for several minutes and scrub it well with a bristle brush.
2. Check each and every link and roller for cracks and wear. If questionable, replace chain.
3. Check front and rear sprockets for wear and damage.

Installation

1. Lubricate chain thoroughly. One good way is to soak the chain in hot oil for several minutes.

> WARNING
> *Be careful when heating oil. Do not let it get too hot or it can burst into flame. Keep a fire extinguisher nearby which is rated for oil fires.*

2. Install chain around sprockets.
3. Connect ends of chain. Slacken chain adjusters if necessary.

> CAUTION
> *On chains with master link, the master link must be installed with the* closed *end pointing in the direction of chain travel. See* **Figure 13**.

4. Install front chain cover, foot peg, and gearshift lever.

5. Adjust chain tension.

6. Adjust clutch lever free play.

7. Adjust rear brake pedal free play.

SPROCKET

Removal/Installation

1. Remove rear wheel as described elsewhere.

2. Remove bearing retainer cap.

3. Remove circlip.

4. Straighten locking tabs on sprocket retaining nuts. Remove nuts (**Figure 14**) and lift the sprocket off.

5. Installation is the reverse of these steps. Use new locking tabs.

REAR SHOCKS

Removal/Installation

1. Rest bike on centerstand and set shock to its softest setting.

2. Remove upper mounting nut and lower mounting bolt.

3. Pull shock off.

4. Installation is the reverse of these steps.

Disassembly/Assembly (450)

WARNING
Without the proper tool, this procedure can be dangerous. The spring can fly loose, causing injury. For a small bench fee, your dealer can do the job for you.

1. Compress shock as shown in **Figure 15** and remove spring seat stops.

2. Release compression.

3. Remove cover and spring from damper unit.

4. Measure free length of springs. They should be 195mm or more in length.

5. Check damper unit for leakage and make sure damper rod is straight.

NOTE: *The damper cannot be rebuilt, it must be replaced as a unit.*

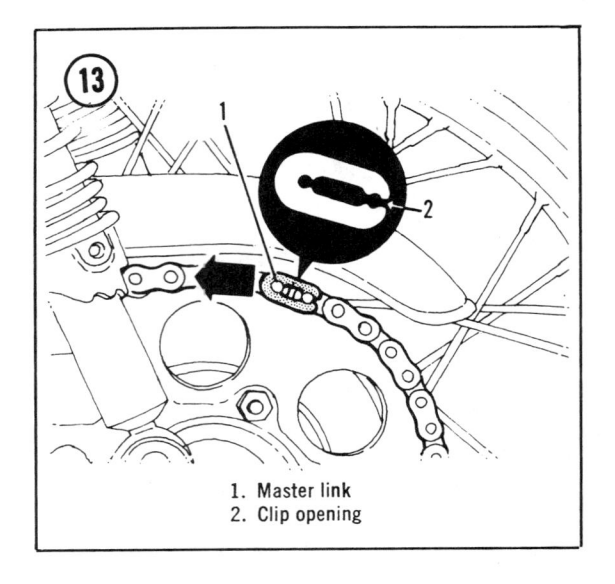

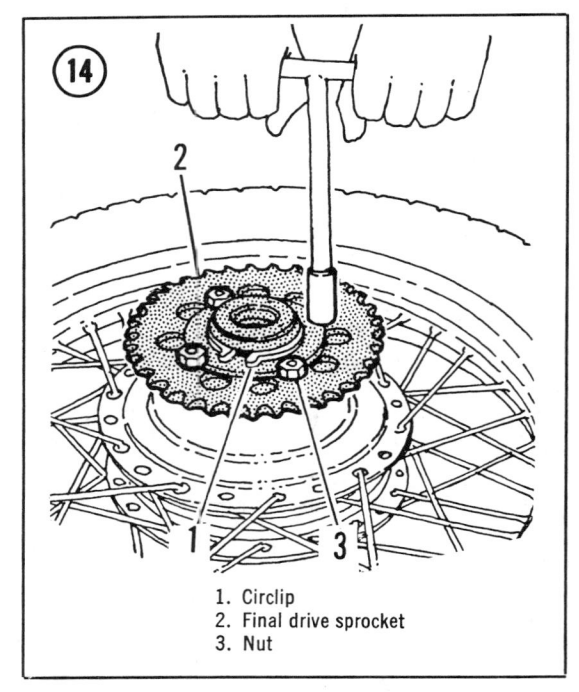

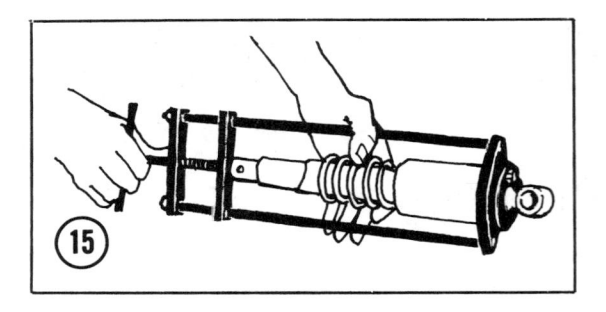

1. Master link
2. Clip opening

1. Circlip
2. Final drive sprocket
3. Nut

REAR SUSPENSION

REAR SHOCK ABSORBERS — 450

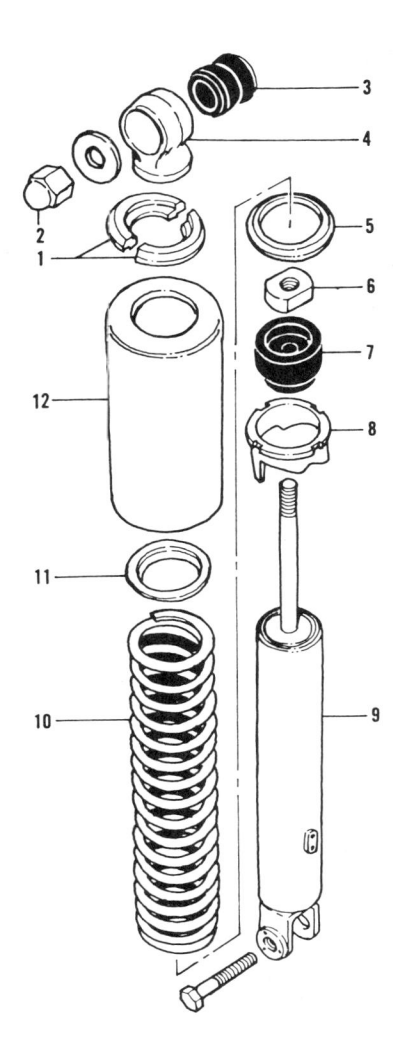

1. Spring lock
2. Upper nut
3. Joint rubber
4. Upper joint
5. Spring seat
6. Locknut
7. Stopper rubber
8. Spring adjuster
9. Damper
10. Spring
11. Spring seat
12. Upper case

Figure 16

6. Assembly is the reverse of disassembly. Note order of parts shown in **Figure 16**.

Disassembly/Assembly (500)

1. Compress the rear shock absorber as shown in **Figure 17**.

> **WARNING**
> *If the proper tool is not available, do not attempt this procedure. An improperly compressed spring could fly off, causing injury. Your Honda dealer will do the job for a small bench fee.*

2. Remove the spring seat stoppers (**Figure 18**).

3. Loosen the locknut, then remove the upper spring seat, the upper joint, the locknut, and the rubber stopper.

4. Release the tension on the spring and remove the spring, spring underseat, and the spring adjuster. Measure free length of spring. Replace if not at least 8.07 in. (205mm) long.

5. Assembly is the reverse of these steps. Make certain end of spring with the large pitch is at the bottom.

SWINGING ARM

Removal/Installation

Refer to **Figure 19** (early 450 models),

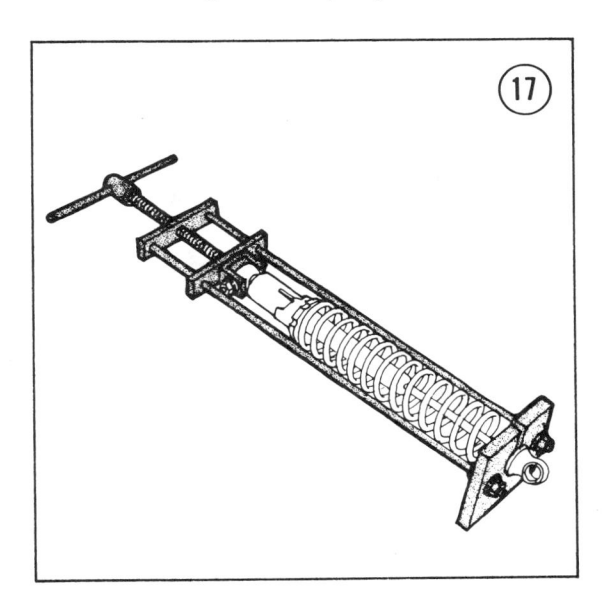

Figure 17

CHAPTER NINE

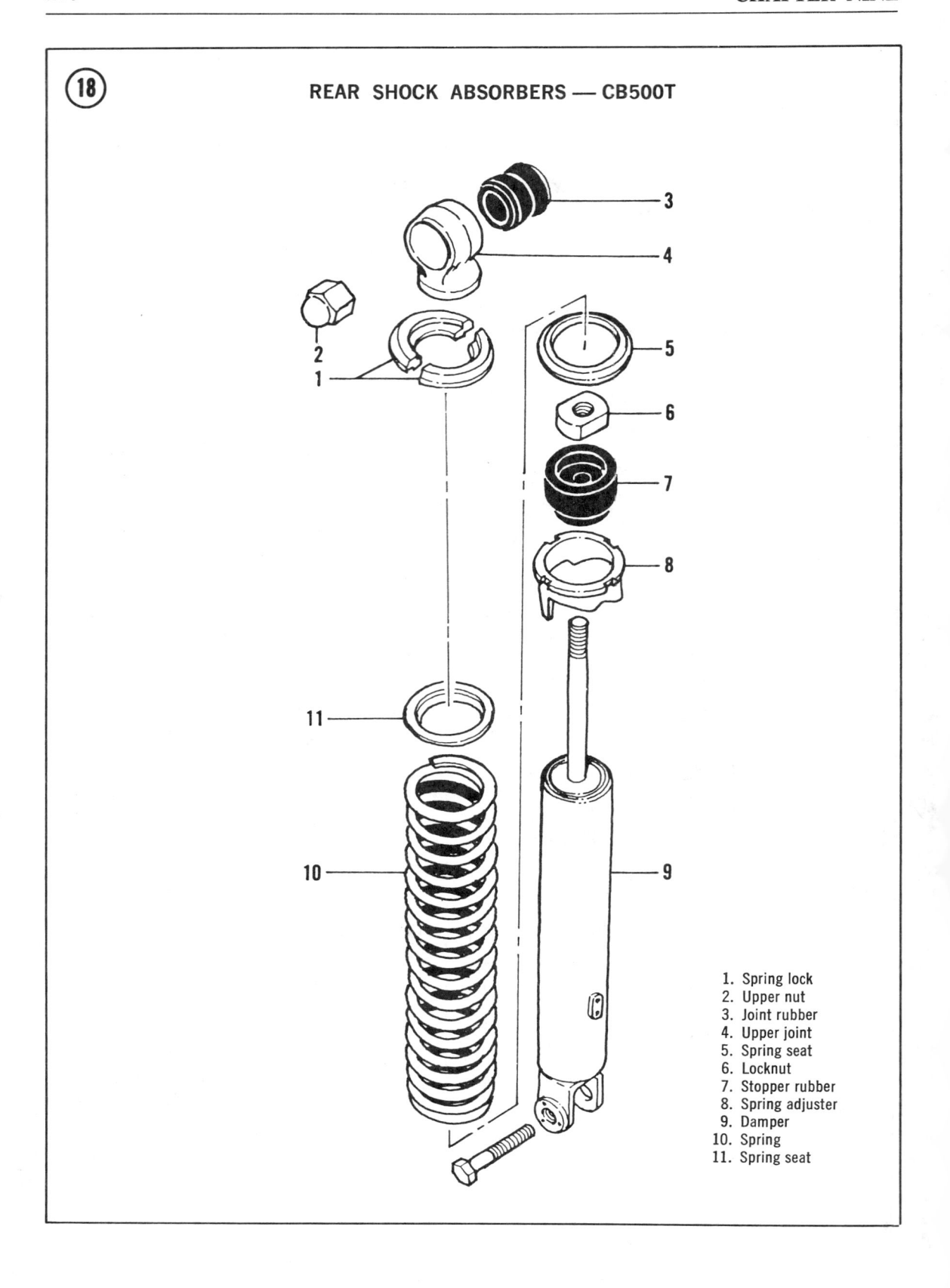

REAR SHOCK ABSORBERS — CB500T

1. Spring lock
2. Upper nut
3. Joint rubber
4. Upper joint
5. Spring seat
6. Locknut
7. Stopper rubber
8. Spring adjuster
9. Damper
10. Spring
11. Spring seat

REAR SUSPENSION

SWINGING ARM (EARLY 450 MODELS)

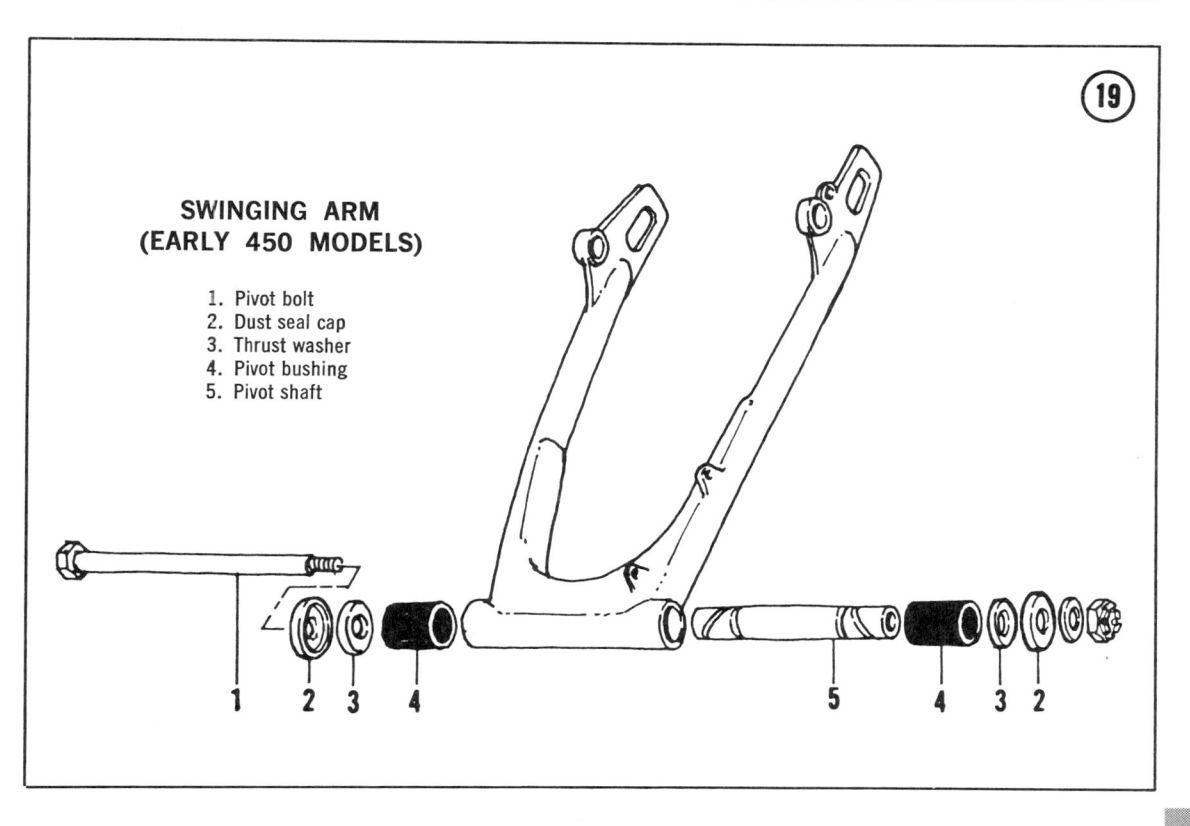

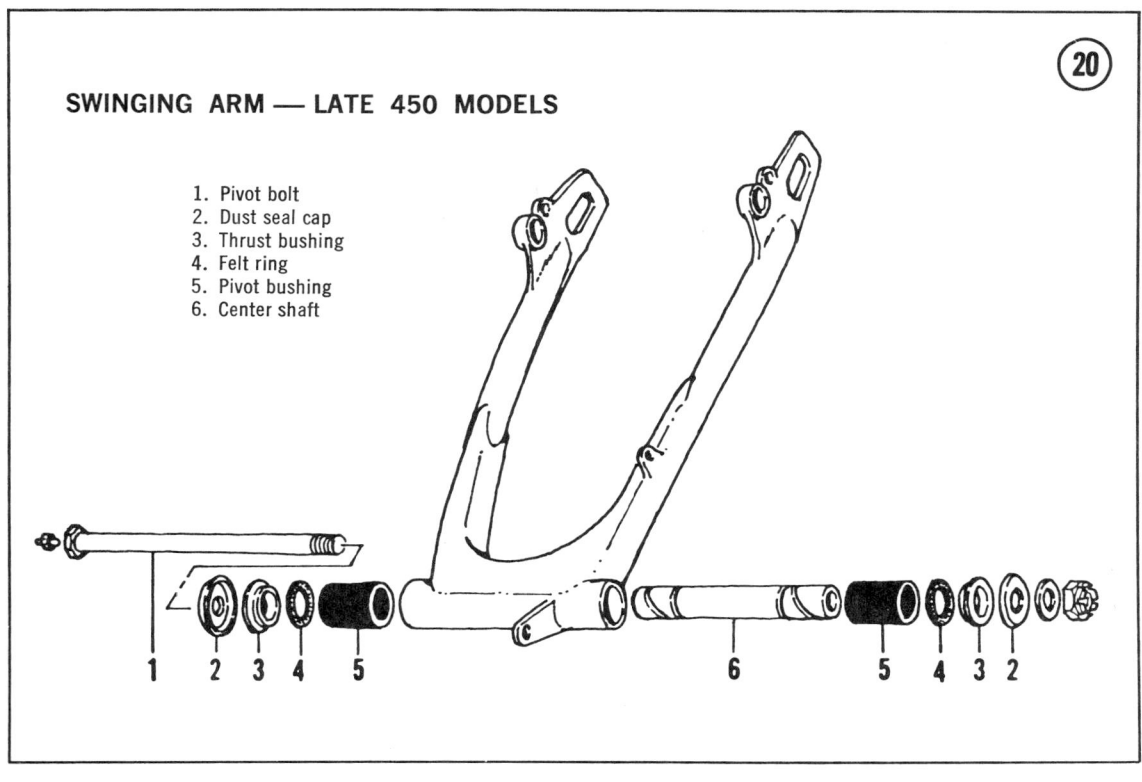

1. Pivot bolt
2. Dust seal cap
3. Thrust washer
4. Pivot bushing
5. Pivot shaft

SWINGING ARM — LATE 450 MODELS

1. Pivot bolt
2. Dust seal cap
3. Thrust bushing
4. Felt ring
5. Pivot bushing
6. Center shaft

Figure 20 (late 450 models), or **Figure 21** (500 models).

1. Remove rear wheel as described earlier in this chapter.
2. Remove rear shock absorbers.
3. Remove self-locking nut on end of pivot bolt. See **Figure 22**.
4. Pull out bolt.
5. Tap out center collar and bushings.
6. Inspect components as described below.
7. Installation is the reverse of these steps. Soak felt dust seals in oil before installation.

Inspection

1. Take the swing arm to a dealer or machine shop. Have swing arm twist measured with center collar and bushings in place (**Figure 23**).
2. Measure center collar, bushings, and pivot bolt and compare with specifications in **Table 1**.

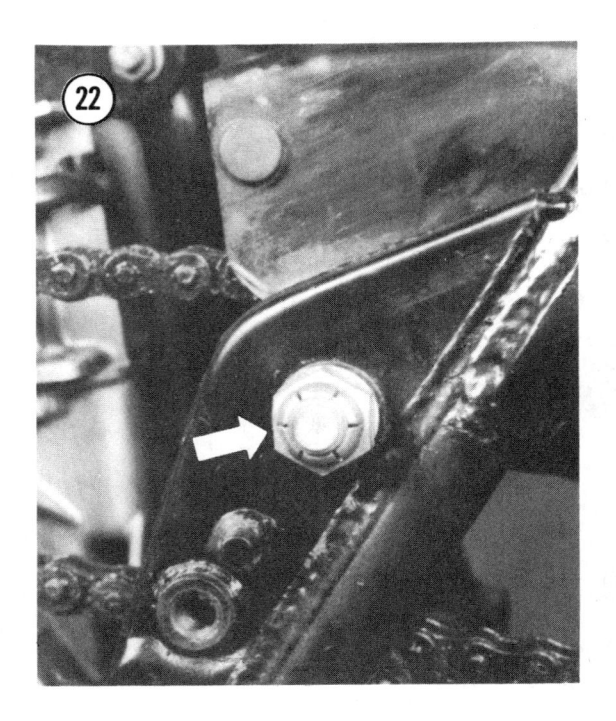

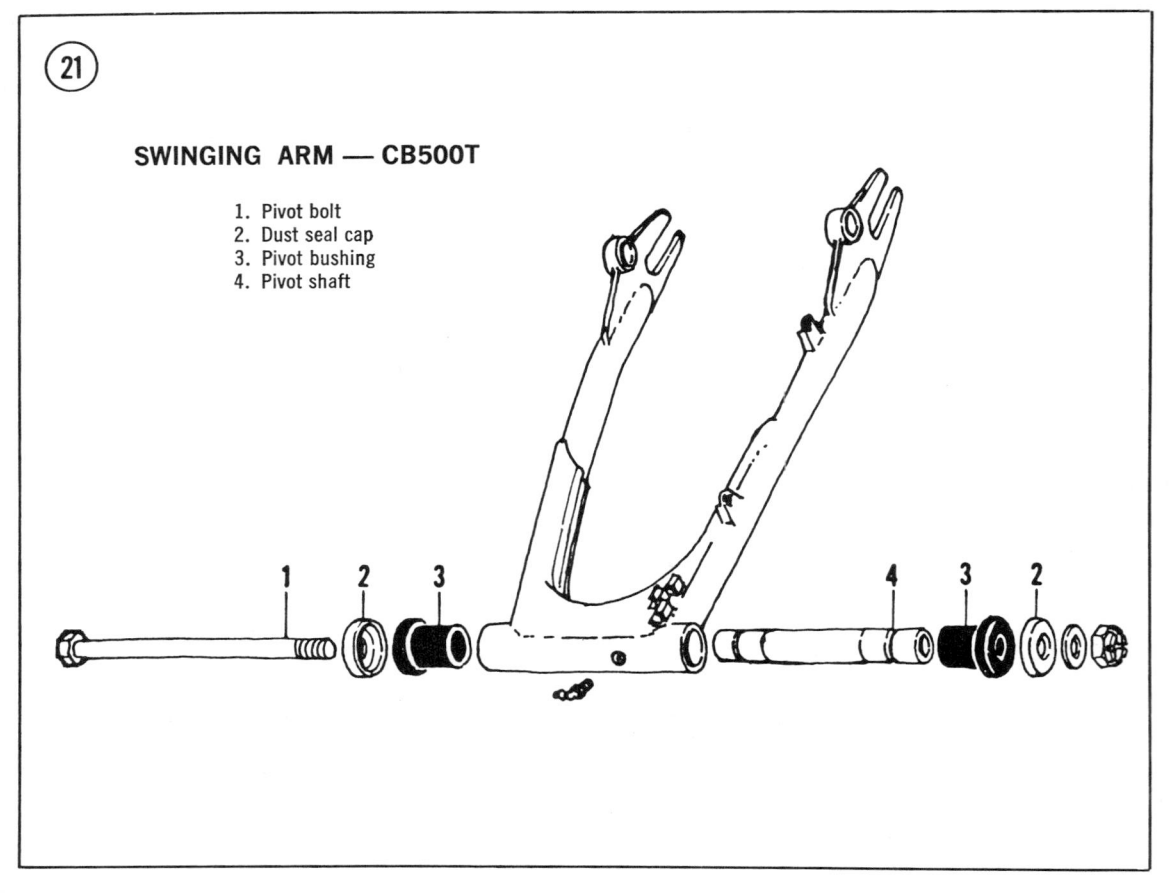

SWINGING ARM — CB500T

1. Pivot bolt
2. Dust seal cap
3. Pivot bushing
4. Pivot shaft

REAR SUSPENSION

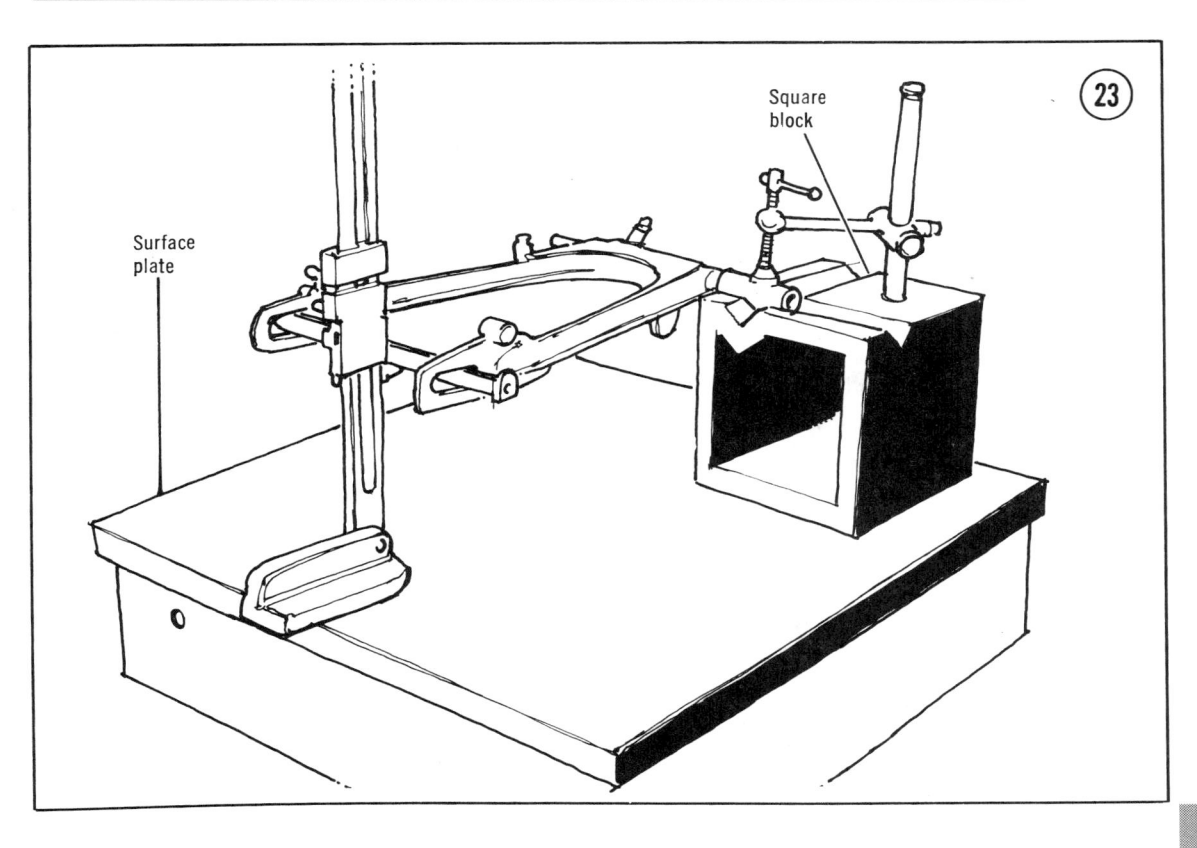

(Figure 23: Rear fork measurement setup with surface plate and square block)

Table 1 REAR FORK SPECIFICATIONS

	Nominal Value*	Service Limit*
Center collar		
Full length	189.9 + 0 / − 0.3	Replace when less than 18.96
Inside diameter	14.0 + 0.027 / − 0	Replace when more than 14.1
Outside diameter	21.5 − 0.007 to − 0.028	Replace when less than 21.4
Pivot bushing		
Inside diameter	21.5 + 0.033 / − 0 (After pressing in)	Replace when more than 21.6
Inside width	33.0 − 0.1 to − 0.2	
Pivot bolt		
Outside diameter	14.0 − 0.032 to − 0.075	
Bending	0.01mm in 100mm	0.02mm in 100mm

* Dimensions are given in millimeters

CHAPTER TEN

BRAKES

All CL450 and CB450 K1 and K2 models use a drum type front brake, cable-operated by right-hand lever. Later CB450's and CB500T's use a hydraulically operated front disc brake.

The rear brake on all CB, CL450, and CB500T models is operated by levers from the brake pedal.

This chapter describes repair and replacement procedures for all brake components used on CB, CL450, and CB500T models.

FRONT DRUM BRAKE

Disassembly

Refer to **Figures 1 and 2**.
1. Remove the front wheel as described in Chapter Eight.
2. Remove axle nut and take out axle.
3. Pull brake panel with speedometer gearbox away from hub.
4. Remove front brake arm and actuating cam.
5. Lift up the brake shoes together to disengage them from the brake cam and pivot (**Figure 3**).

Inspection

1. Make sure that the anchor pin is straight.
2. Check brake drum surface in hub for scoring, out-of-round, and excessive wear.
3. Check condition of return springs and compare free length with **Table 1**.
4. Check condition and thickness of linings. Replace if less than 0.08 in. (2mm).

Assembly

Refer to **Figures 1 and 2** for this procedure.
1. Install brake arm and cam. Punch marks on the arm and cam must line up as shown in **Figure 4**.
2. Install brake shoes and return springs.
3. Install brake panel in hub.
4. Install axle.
5. Align the speedometer gearbox parallel with the brake rod. See **Figure 5**. Tighten axle nut.
6. Install the front wheel as described in Chapter Eight.
7. Adjust brake lever free play to 0.6-1.2 in. (15-30mm). See Chapter Two.

FRONT DISC BRAKE

Caliper Removal/Installation

1. Remove the front wheel as described in Chapter Eight.
2. Disconnect hydraulic line. See **Figure 6**.
3. Remove the caliper mounting bolts (**Fig-**

BRAKES

FRONT BRAKE — CL450 MODELS

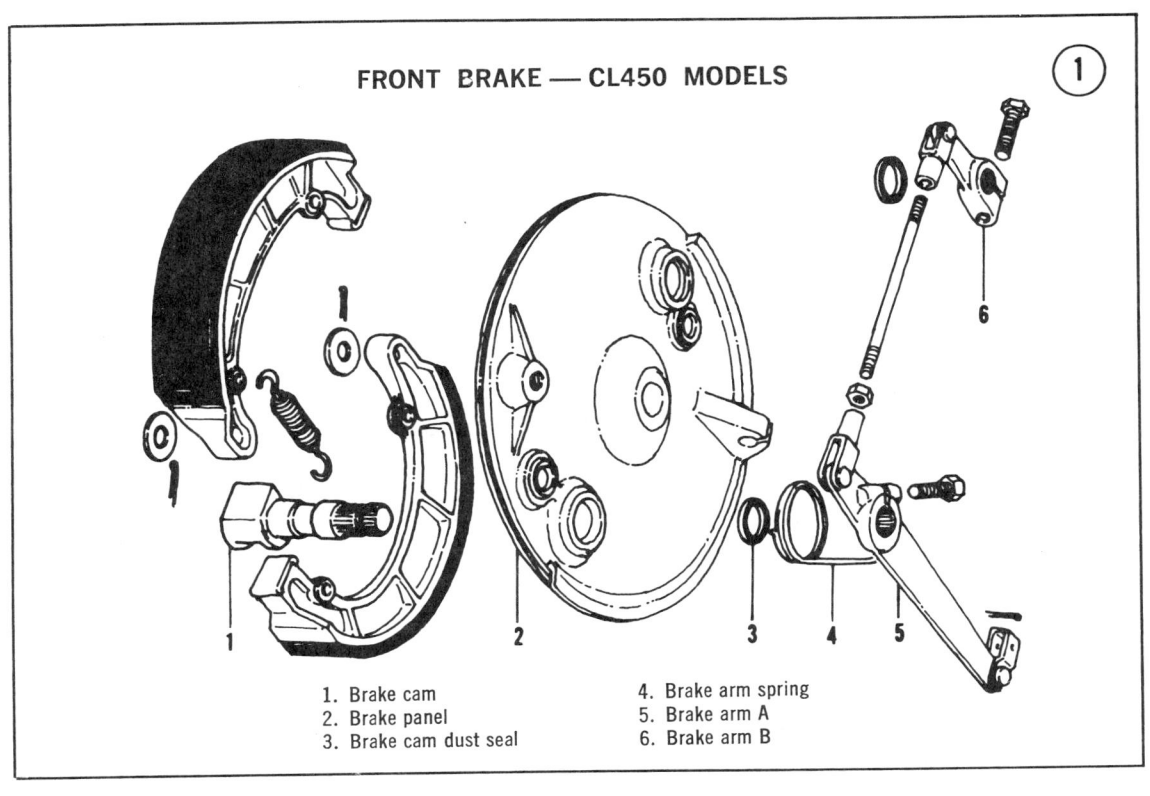

1. Brake cam
2. Brake panel
3. Brake cam dust seal
4. Brake arm spring
5. Brake arm A
6. Brake arm B

FRONT BRAKE — CB MODELS

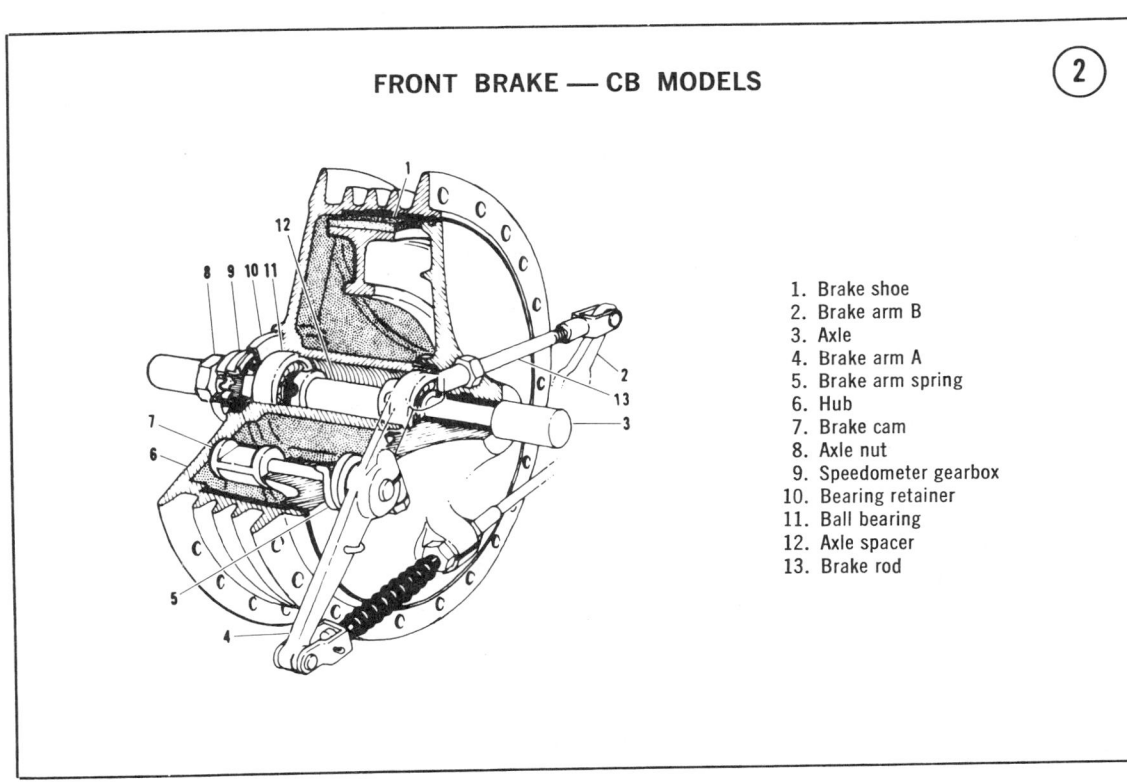

1. Brake shoe
2. Brake arm B
3. Axle
4. Brake arm A
5. Brake arm spring
6. Hub
7. Brake cam
8. Axle nut
9. Speedometer gearbox
10. Bearing retainer
11. Ball bearing
12. Axle spacer
13. Brake rod

ure 7) and remove the caliper from the fork tube.

4. Installation is the reverse of these steps.

5. Bleed brake as described later.

6. Adjust the brake caliper clearance as described below.

Caliper Clearance Adjustment

1. Rest bike on centerstand.

2. Place jack under engine and raise front wheel clear of ground.

3. Loosen locknut on stopper bolt. See **Figure 8**.

4. Turn stopper bolt clockwise until friction pad contacts disc and some resistance can be felt when turning front wheel.

5. Turn bolt counterclockwise until resistance just disappears, then an additional ⅛-¼ turn.

6. Tighten locknut.

Caliper Disassembly

Refer to **Figure 9** (K3, K4) or **Figure 10** (K5-K7 and CB500T) for this procedure.

1. Remove caliper as described above.

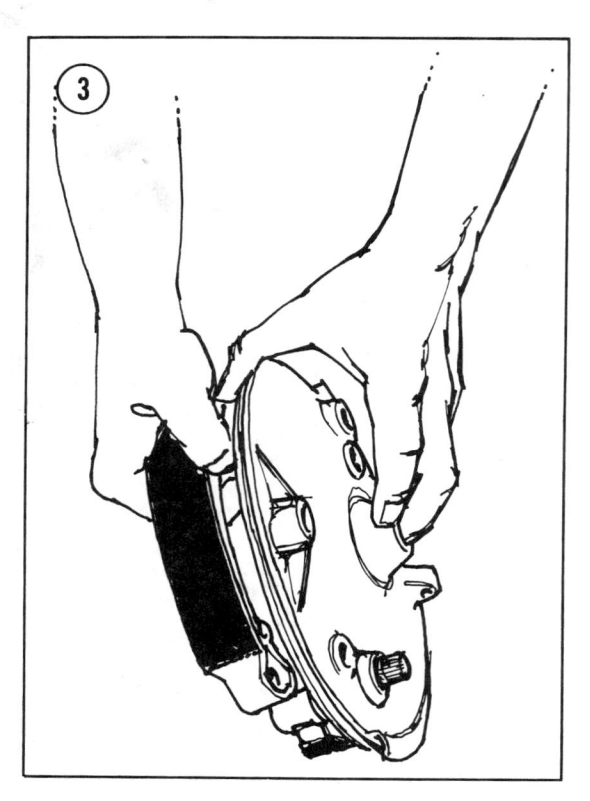

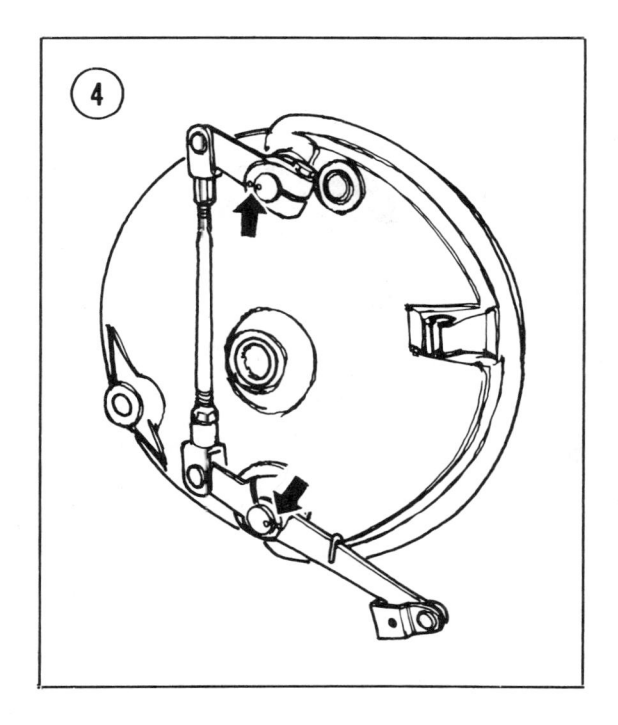

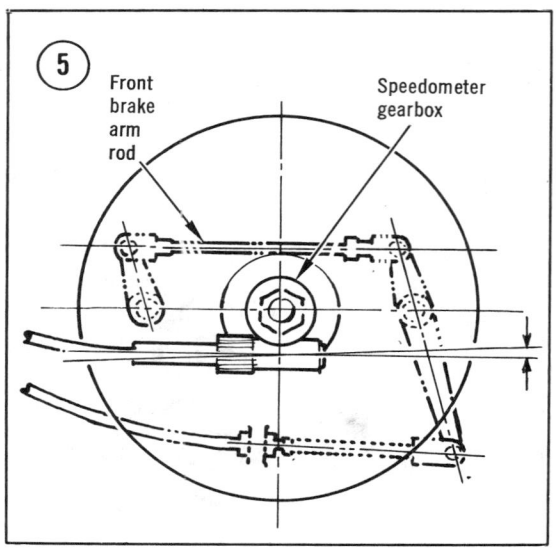

Table 1 FRONT DRUM BRAKE

Brake shoe spring	
Free length	2.65 in. (67.4mm)
Length @ load	2.95 in @ 13.3 lbs. (75mm @ 6kg)
Brake shoes	
Thickness	0.17 in. (4.5mm)
Diameter	7.84-7.86 in. (199.8-200mm)
Cam thickness	0.394 in. (10mm)

BRAKES

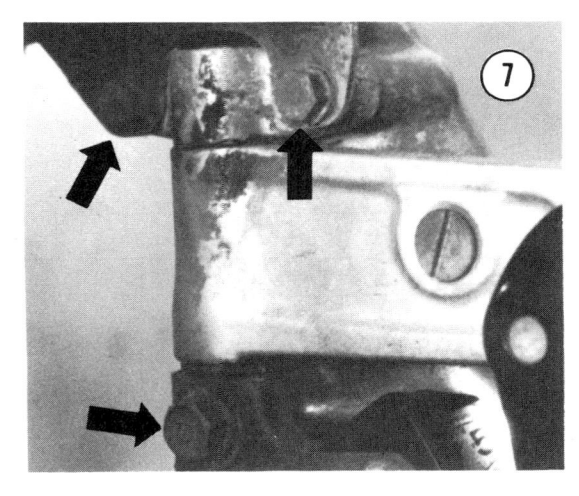

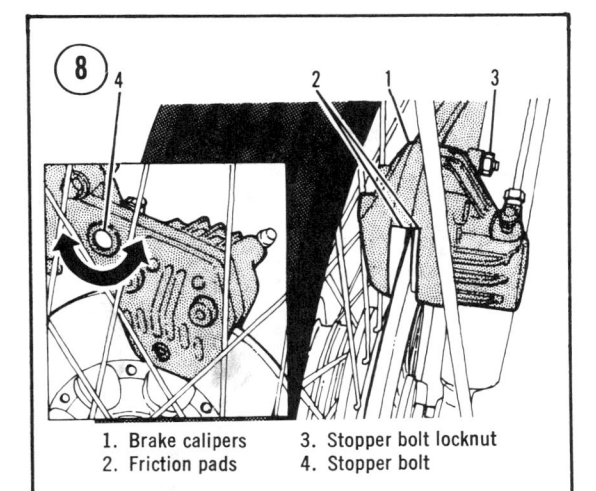

2. Remove 2 Allen screws (2, **Figure 7**) and remove both calipers.

3. Remove pad, pad seat, and piston from caliper A.

4. Remove cotter pin and pad from caliper B.

5. Assembly is the reverse of these steps. Apply a small amount of silicone grease to calipers where shown in **Figure 11**.

> **WARNING**
> Do not *get grease on braking surfaces of pads or brakes will not work. Pads cannot be cleaned; if contaminated, they must be replaced.*

Caliper Inspection

1. Clean all parts except brake pads in denatured alcohol or clean brake fluid.

2. Measure caliper piston-to-cylinder clearance. Clearance should not exceed 0.004 in. (0.11mm). Replace cylinder if larger than 1.504 in. (38.215mm) and piston if smaller than 1.5 in. (38.105mm).

3. Check piston seal. Replace if damaged.

Brake Disc Removal/Installation

1. Remove the front wheel as described in Chapter Eight.

2. Bend up locking plates and remove nuts securing disc to hub.

3. Remove disc.

4. Installation is the reverse of these steps.

Brake Disc Inspection

It is not necessary to remove disc from wheel to inspect it.

1. Remove the front wheel as described in Chapter Eight.

2. Measure thickness at several points around the disc. Compare to **Table 2**.

3. Measure runout with a dial gauge. Use a procedure similar to that described in Chapter Eight for wheel runout.

4. Clean disc thoroughly with non-petroleum solvent such as trichloroethylene.

1. Brake calipers
2. Friction pads
3. Stopper bolt locknut
4. Stopper bolt

CHAPTER TEN

⑨ **FRONT DISC BRAKE (CB450 K3 AND K4)**

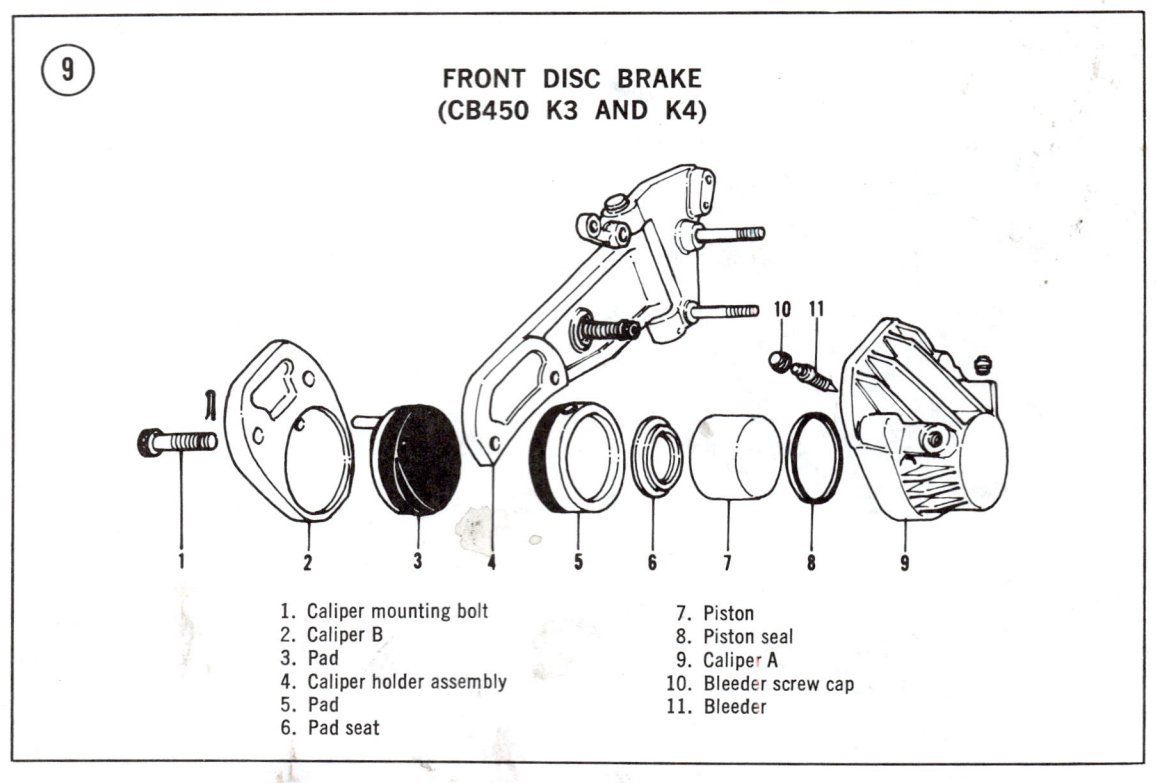

1. Caliper mounting bolt
2. Caliper B
3. Pad
4. Caliper holder assembly
5. Pad
6. Pad seat
7. Piston
8. Piston seal
9. Caliper A
10. Bleeder screw cap
11. Bleeder

⑩ **FRONT DISC BRAKE (CB450 K5-K7 AND CB500T)**

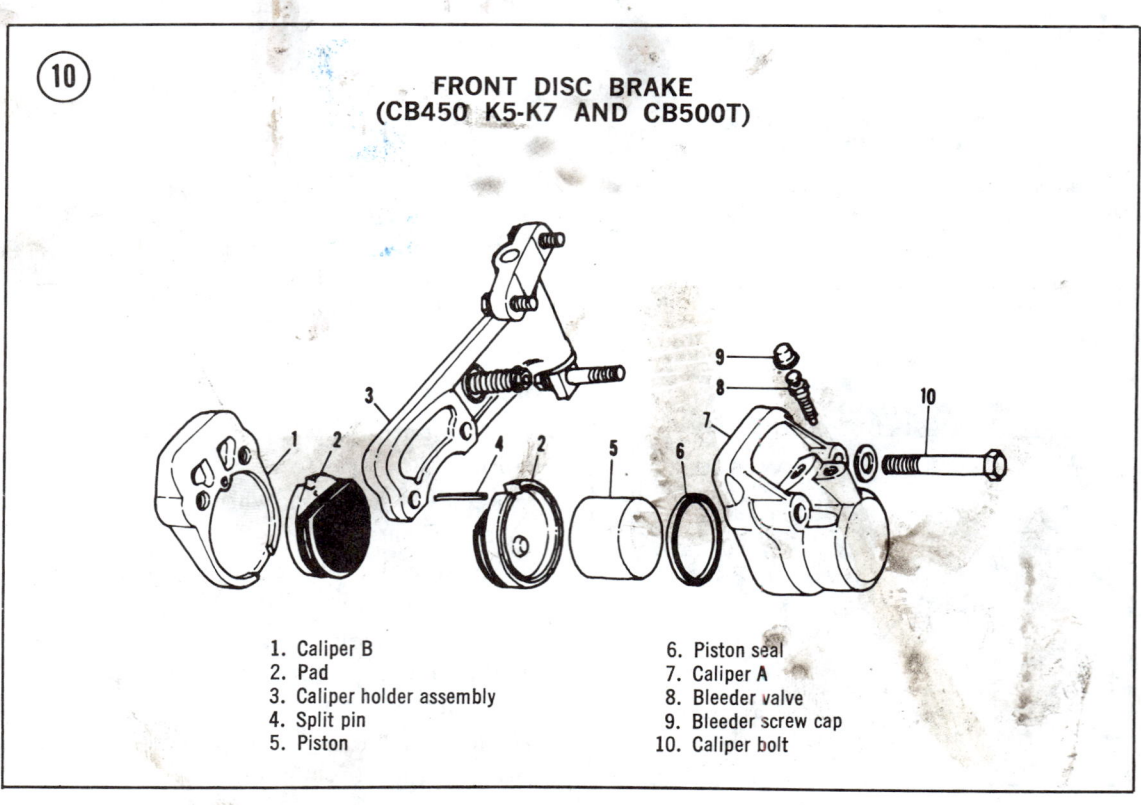

1. Caliper B
2. Pad
3. Caliper holder assembly
4. Split pin
5. Piston
6. Piston seal
7. Caliper A
8. Bleeder valve
9. Bleeder screw cap
10. Caliper bolt

BRAKES

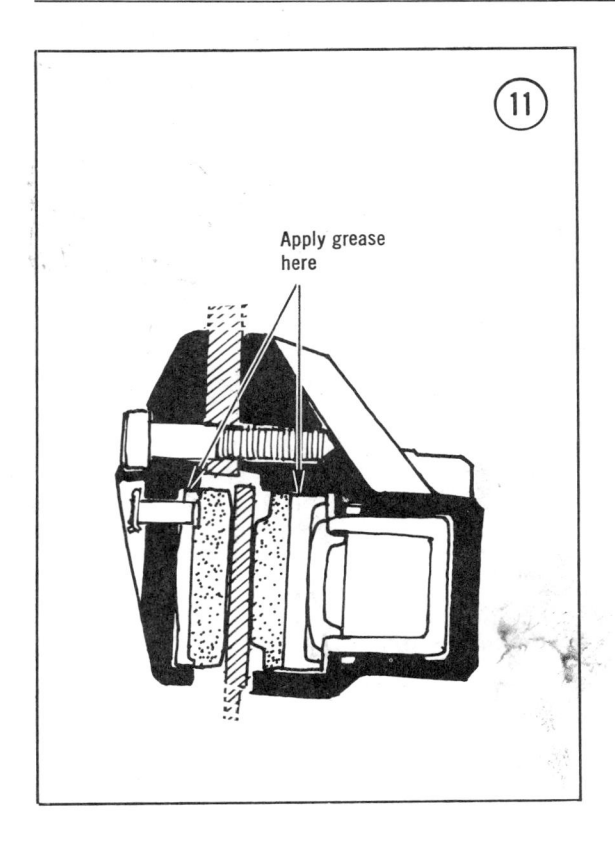

Master Cylinder Removal/Installation

1. Remove bolt (**Figure 12**) securing brake hose to master cylinder.
2. Remove 2 clamp bolts securing master cylinder to handlebars.
3. Installation is the reverse of these steps.
4. Bleed brake as described later.

Master Cylinder Disassembly/Assembly

Refer to **Figure 13** for this procedure.

1. Remove master cylinder as described above.
2. Remove top cap and diaphragm. Pour the fluid out.
3. Remove the snap ring and boot (**Figure 13**).
4. Remove circlip as shown in **Figure 14**.
5. Remove washer, piston, spring, and the check valve.
6. Clean all parts thoroughly in denatured alcohol or clean brake fluid.
7. Measure cylinder bore and piston. Cylinder bore must not exceed 0.553 in. (14.015mm) and the piston must not be smaller than 0.549 in. (13.940mm). Replace badly worn parts.
8. Replace primary and secondary cups with new ones.
9. Install check valve, spring, piston, washer, and circlip.
10. Install boot and snap ring.
11. Install diaphragm and top cap.

Bleeding the System

1. Remove dust cap from bleeder valve and

Table 2   DISC BRAKE SERVICE LIMITS

	Inch	Millimeters
Disc		
Thickness	0.217	5.5
Lateral runout	0.012	0.3
Rim runout	0.08	2.0
Caliper		
Piston diameter	1.5002	38.105
Cylinder diameter	1.5045	38.215

CHAPTER TEN

MASTER CYLINDER

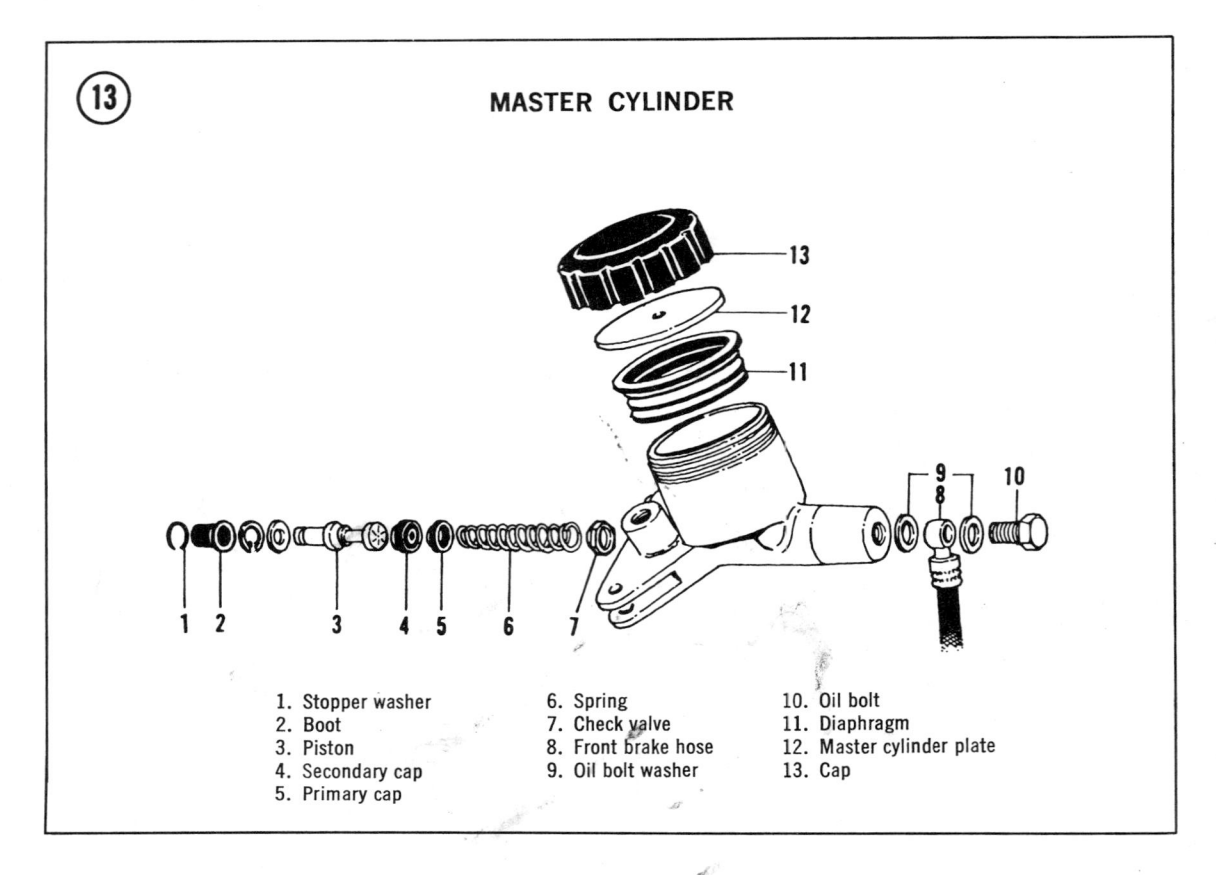

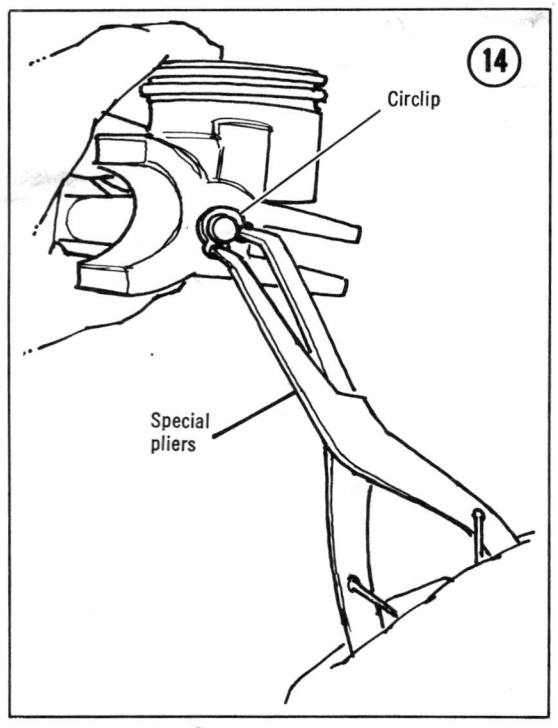

1. Stopper washer
2. Boot
3. Piston
4. Secondary cap
5. Primary cap
6. Spring
7. Check valve
8. Front brake hose
9. Oil bolt washer
10. Oil bolt
11. Diaphragm
12. Master cylinder plate
13. Cap

Table 3 REAR DRUM BRAKE

Brake shoe spring	
Free length	0.2205 in. (56.4mm)
Brake shoes	
Thickness	0.197 in. (5mm)
Diameter	7.078-7.087 in. (179.8-180.0mm)
Cam thickness	0.39 in. (10mm)

attach a small plastic hose as shown in **Figure 15**.

2. Immerse the other end of the hose in a clean jar about ¼ full of *clean* brake fluid.

3. Fill the reservoir with clean fluid clearly marked SAE 70R3, DOT 3, or J1703.

> NOTE: *During the entire procedure, make certain the reservoir never runs dry or you will have to start over again.*

4. Pump brake lever several times until some resistance is felt, then hold it tight.

5. Open the bleeder valve and squeeze lever all the way.

BRAKES

6. Close bleeder valve *before* releasing lever.

7. Repeat Steps 4-6 as many times as necessary until no more bubbles emerge from bleeder tube. Keep reservoir topped up.

> **WARNING**
> *Do not reuse brake fluid from bleeder jar. This fluid could be contaminated, causing brake failure.*

8. When no more air bubbles are in the system, tighten the bleeder valve, remove the tube, and install the dust cap.

9. Top up the reservoir if necessary.

REAR DRUM BRAKE

Disassembly

Refer to **Figures 16 through 19** for the following procedure.

1. Remove the rear wheel as described in Chapter Nine.
2. Lift off brake panel.
3. Remove cotter pins securing brake shoes. Also remove return springs.
4. Remove brake arm.
5. Remove brake shoes.

Inspection

1. Make sure that the anchor pin is straight.
2. Check brake drum surface in hub for scoring, out-of-round, and excessive wear.
3. Check condition of return springs and compare free length with **Table 3**.
4. Check condition and thickness of linings. Replace if less than 0.08 in. (2mm).

Assembly

1. Install brake shoes. Secure with cotter pins, washer, and return springs.
2. Install brake arm.
3. Install brake panel over hub.
4. Install rear wheel, described in Chapter Nine.

REAR WHEEL

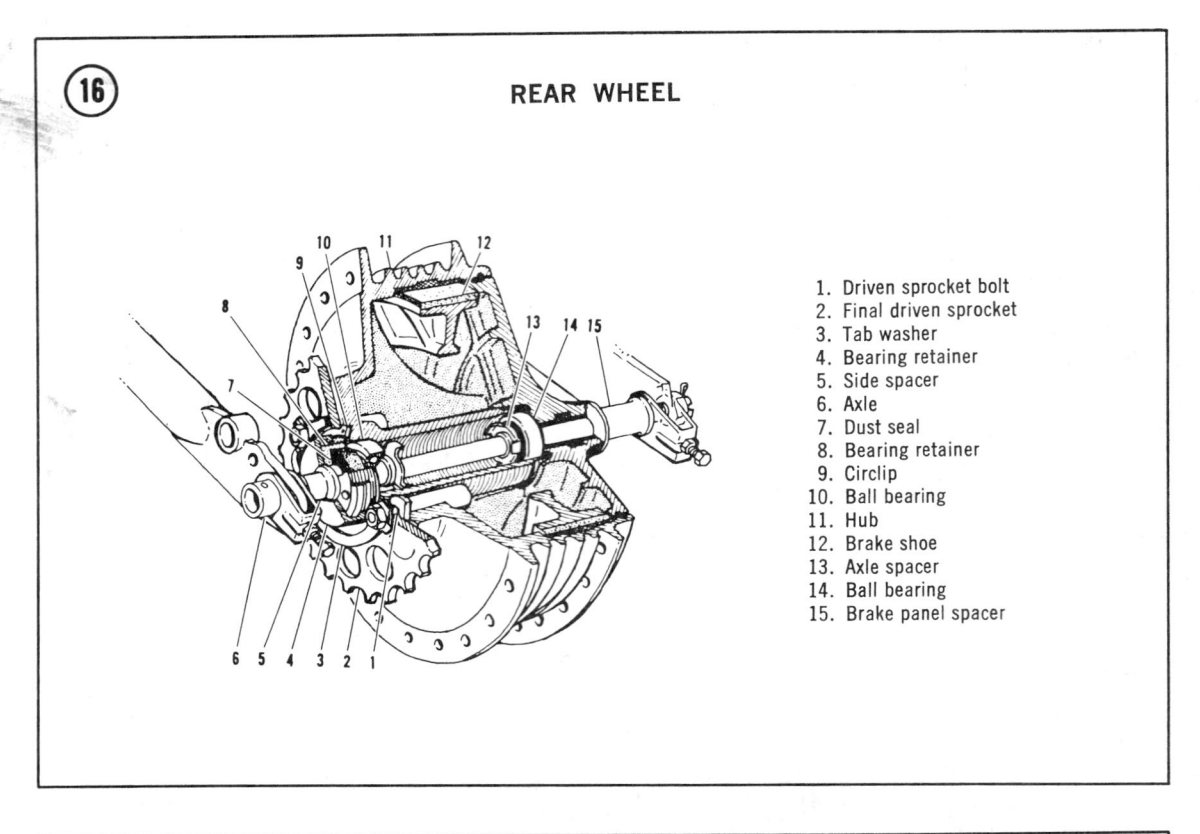

1. Driven sprocket bolt
2. Final driven sprocket
3. Tab washer
4. Bearing retainer
5. Side spacer
6. Axle
7. Dust seal
8. Bearing retainer
9. Circlip
10. Ball bearing
11. Hub
12. Brake shoe
13. Axle spacer
14. Ball bearing
15. Brake panel spacer

REAR BRAKE — PANEL

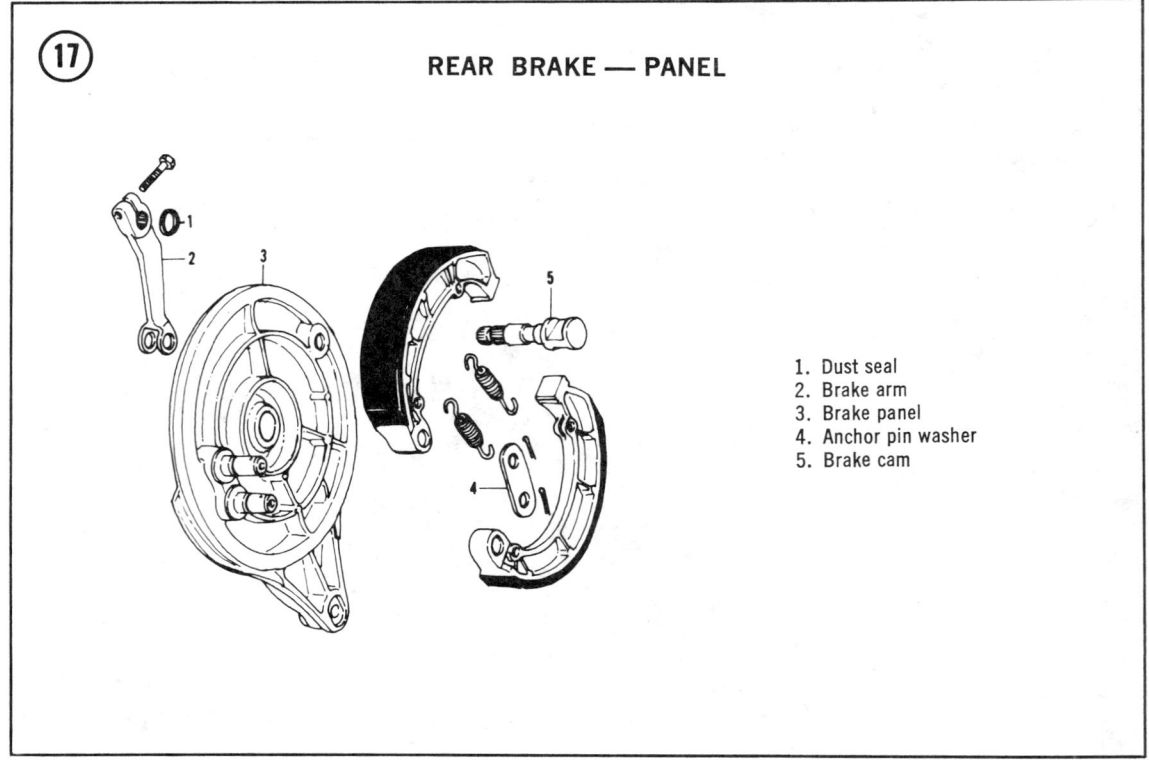

1. Dust seal
2. Brake arm
3. Brake panel
4. Anchor pin washer
5. Brake cam

BRAKES

REAR WHEEL ASSEMBLY

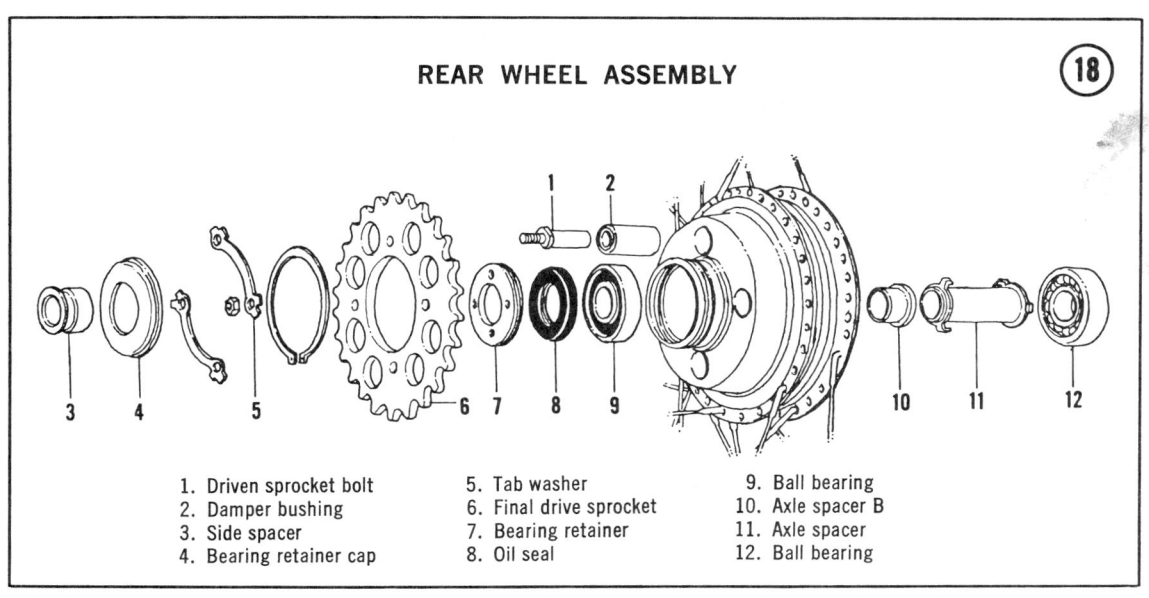

1. Driven sprocket bolt
2. Damper bushing
3. Side spacer
4. Bearing retainer cap
5. Tab washer
6. Final drive sprocket
7. Bearing retainer
8. Oil seal
9. Ball bearing
10. Axle spacer B
11. Axle spacer
12. Ball bearing

REAR WHEEL AND HUB

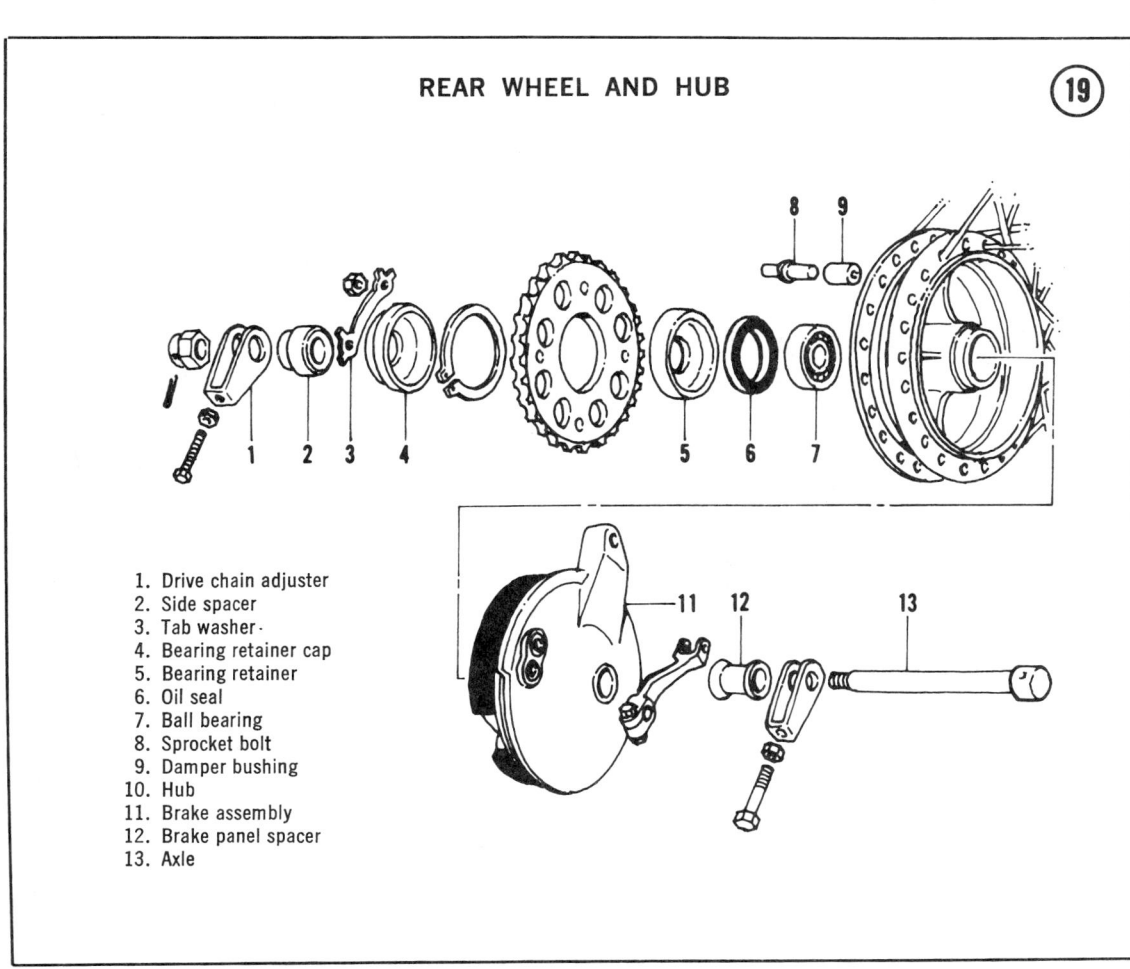

1. Drive chain adjuster
2. Side spacer
3. Tab washer
4. Bearing retainer cap
5. Bearing retainer
6. Oil seal
7. Ball bearing
8. Sprocket bolt
9. Damper bushing
10. Hub
11. Brake assembly
12. Brake panel spacer
13. Axle

CHAPTER ELEVEN

FRAME

The frame does not require periodic maintenance. However, all welds should be examined immediately after any accident, even a slight one.

This chapter describes procedures for completely stripping and inspecting the frame. In addition, recommendations are provided for repainting the stripped frame.

This chapter also includes procedures for the kickstand, centerstand, and foot pegs.

KICKSTAND (SIDE STAND)

Removal/Installation

1. Support bike on centerstand.
2. Disconnect kickstand return spring from kickstand.
3. Unbolt kickstand from frame.
4. Installation is the reverse of these steps.

CENTERSTAND

Refer to **Figure 1** for this procedure.
1. Support bike on kickstand.
2. Remove the right muffler on CB450. See Chapter Six.
3. Disconnect stand return spring and brake pedal return spring.
4. Remove the cotter pin on the end of centerstand shaft.
5. Loosen 2 clamp bolts. See **Figure 2**.
6. Slide shaft out and remove stand.
7. Installation is the reverse of these steps. Use a new cotter pin. Fill shaft with grease.

CAUTION
Do not overtighten clamp bolts.

8. Make sure that rear brake and stoplight work properly.

STRIPPING THE FRAME

1. Remove the fuel tank, seat, and battery. Disconnect negative terminal *first*.
2. Remove engine as described in Chapter Four.
3. Remove front wheel, steering, and suspension as described in Chapter Eight.
4. Remove rear wheel and suspension components. See Chapter Nine.
5. Remove lighting and other electrical equipment. Remove wiring harness. See Chapter Seven.
6. Remove the kickstand.
7. Remove bearing races from steering head tube with a wooden drift. See **Figure 3**.

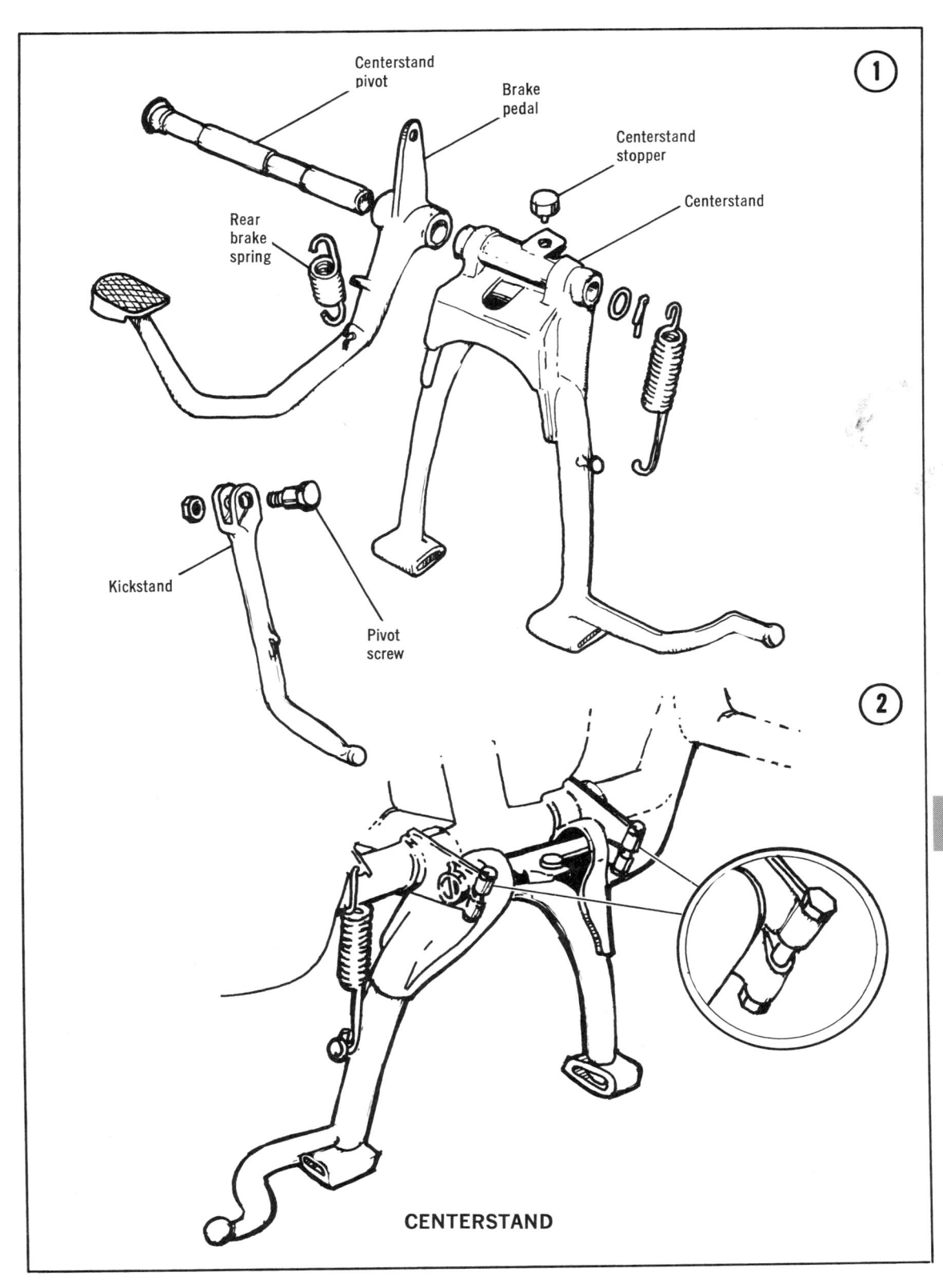

FRAME

155

①

Centerstand pivot
Brake pedal
Centerstand stopper
Centerstand
Rear brake spring
Kickstand
Pivot screw

②

CENTERSTAND

11

PAINTING THE FRAME

Strip *all* components from the frame. Thoroughly strip all old paint. The best way is to have it sandblasted down to bare metal. If this is not possible, you can use a liquid paint remover and steel wool.

When the frame is down to bare metal, have it inspected for hairline and internal cracks. Magnafluxing is the most common process.

Spray one or two coats of primer as smoothly as possible. Use a fine grade of wet sandpaper to remove flaws. Carefully clean the surface, then spray on either lacquer or enamel, following the manufacturer's instructions.

A shop specializing in painting will probably do the best job. However, you can do a surprisingly good job with spray-can paint with this trick. First, shake the can thoroughly—at least as long as stated on the can. Then immerse the can upright in a pot or bucket of *warm* water (not over 120°F).

WARNING
Higher temperature could cause the can to burst.

Leave the can in for several minutes. When thoroughly warmed, shake the can again and spray the frame. Several light mist coats are better than one heavy coat.

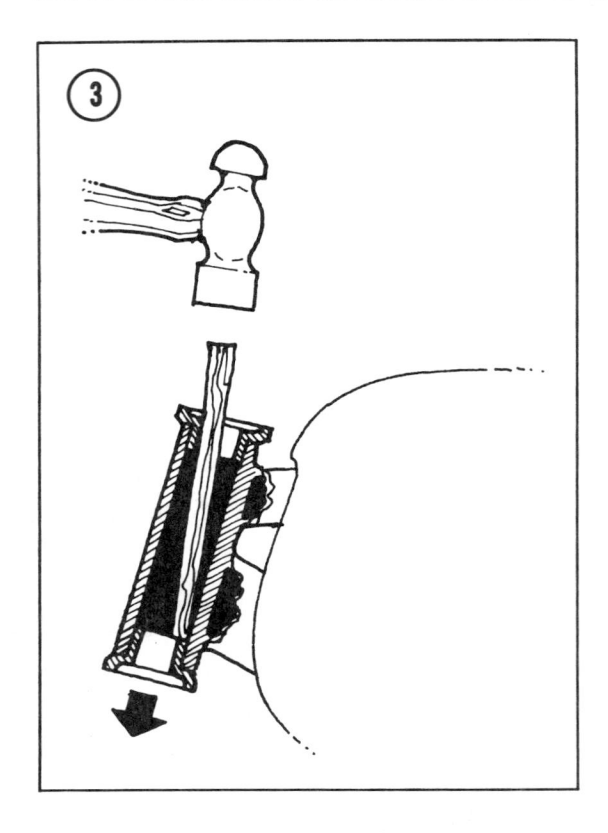

8. Check the frame for bends, cracks, or other damage, especially around welded joints and areas which are rusted.

9. Assembly is the reverse of these steps.

APPENDIX

GENERAL SPECIFICATIONS

Table 1 GENERAL SPECIFICATIONS — 450cc

	CB450	CL450
DIMENSION		
Overall length	82.7 in. (2,100mm)	82.0 in. (2,080mm)
Overall width	31.5 in. (800mm)	33.6 in. (860mm)
Overall height	44.9 in. (1,100mm)	45.5 in. (1,155mm)
Wheelbase	54.3 in. (1,300mm)	54.0 in. (1,375mm)
Seat height	32.1 in. (815mm)	32.1 in. (815mm)
Ground clearance	5.3 in. (135mm)	5.3 in. (135mm)
Curb weight	430 lb. (195kg)	414.5 lb. (188 kg)
FRAME		
Type	Semi-double cradle	Semi-double cradle
Suspension, front	Telescopic fork	Telescopic fork
Suspension, rear	Swing arm	Swing arm
Tire size, front	3.25—19 (4 PR)	3.25—19 (4 PR)
Tire size, rear	3.50—18 (4 PR)	3.50—18 (4 PR)
Brake type		
Front	Disc	Drum
Rear	Drum	Drum
Fuel capacity	3.6 U.S. gal. (13.5 lit., 3.0 Imp. gal.)	2.4 U.S. gal. (9.0 lit., 2.0 Imp. gal.)
Fuel reserve capacity	3.8 U.S. pt. (1.8 lit., 3.2 Imp. pt.)	3.4 U.S. pt. (1.6 lit., 2.8 Imp. pt.)
Caster angle	62.5°	62.5°
Trail	4.1 in. (104mm)	4.5 in. (115mm)
ENGINE		
Type	DOHC, air-cooled, 4-stroke	DOHC, air-cooled, 4-stroke
Cylinder arrangement	Vertical, parallel twin	Vertical, parallel twin
Bore and stroke	2.756 x 2.276 in. (70 x 57.8mm)	2.756 x 2.276 in. (70 x 57.8mm)
Displacement	27.09 cid (444cc)	27.09 cid (444cc)
Compression ratio	9.0 : 1	9.0 : 1
Carburetor	Constant velocity type	Constant velocity type
Valve train	Chain-driven DOHC	Chain-driven DOHC
Oil capacity	5.9 U.S. pt. (2.8 lit., 4.9 Imp. pt.)	5.9 U.S. pt. (2.8 lit., 4.9 Imp. pt.)
Lubrication system	Forced and wet sump	Forced and wet sump
DRIVE TRAIN		
Clutch	Wet, multi-plate type	Wet, multi-plate type
Transmission	5-speed, constant mesh	5-speed, constant mesh
Primary reduction ratio	3.304	3.304
Gear ratio: 1st	2.412	2.412
2nd	1.636	1.636
3rd	1.269	1.269
4th	1.000	1.000
5th	0.844	0.844
Final reduction ratio	2.333	2.333
ELECTRICAL		
Ignition	Battery and coil	Battery and coil
Starting system	Start motor and kickstarter	Start motor and kickstarter
Charging system	Alternator	Alternator
Battery	12V 12AH	12V 12AH

SPECIFICATIONS

Table 1 GENERAL SPECIFICATIONS — CB500T

DIMENSION

Overall length	84.3 in. (2,140mm)
Overall width	32.9 in. (836mm)
Overall height	44.7 in. (1,135mm)
Wheelbase	55.5 in. (1,410mm)
Seat height	31.9 in. (810mm)
Ground clearance	5.3 in. (135mm)
Curb weight	425 lb. (193 kg)

FRAME

Type	Semi-double cradle
Suspension, front	Telescopic fork
Suspension, rear	Swing arm
Tire size, front	3.25519
Tire size, rear	3.75518
Brake	
Front	Disc
Rear	Drum
Fuel capacity	4.2 U.S. gal. (15.9 lit., 3.5 Imp. gal.)
Fuel reserve capacity	1.0 U.S. gal. (4.0 lit., 0.9 Imp. gal.)
Caster angle	62.5°
Trail	4.3 in. (109mm)

ENGINE

Type	DOHC, air-cooled, 4-stroke
Cylinder arrangement	Vertical, parallel twin
Bore and stroke	2.756 x 2.551 in. (70 x 64.8mm)
Displacement	30.39 cid (498cc)
Compression ratio	8.5 : 1
Carburetor	Constant velocity type
Valve train	Chain-driven DOHC
Oil capacity	5.9 U.S. pt. (2.8 lit., 4.9 Imp. pt.)
Lubrication system	Forced and wet sump

DRIVE TRAIN

Clutch	Wet, multi-plate type
Transmission	5-speed, constant mesh
Primary reduction ratio	3.304
Gear ratio: 1st	2.277
2nd	1.521
3rd	1.230
4th	1.000
5th	0.844
Final reduction ratio	2.200

ELECTRICAL

Ignition	Battery and coil
Starting system	Start motor and kickstarter
Charging system	Alternator
Battery	12V 12AH

INDEX

A

Air cleaner
    breather element service 74-78
    removal and installation 74
Air filter 16, 18-19
Alternator 91-92

B

Backfiring 7
Battery 14-15, 90-91
Brakes
    adjustment 17
    overhaul, front disc brake 144-151
    overhaul, front drum brake 144
    overhaul, rear drum brake 151-153
    pad inspection, disc brakes 18
    troubleshooting 8
Breaker points 22

C

Cam chain 16
Cam chain guides 40
Camshafts 37-39
Carburetor
    adjustment 25
    disassembly and assembly 78-83
    float level adjustment 83
    removal and installation 78

Centerstand 154
Charging system 89-90
Clutch
    adjustment 16
    inspection 53-58
    removal and installation 53
    slip or drag 7
    specifications 57
    condenser 94
    crankcase 44
    crankcase side covers 44
    crankshaft 44-52
    cylinder head 32-34
    cylinders 34-35

D

Directional signals 101-102
Drive chain 13, 137-138

E

Electrical system
    alternator 91-92
    battery 90-91
    charging system 89-90
    condensers 94
    directional signals 101-102
    fuses 102-103
    headlight 98-99
    horn 102

INDEX

Electrical system (continued)
   ignition coils 94
   lighting system 98
   neutral switch and indicator 100-101
   rectifier 92-93
   regulator 93
   starting system 94
   tail/stoplights 99-100
   wiring diagrams 107-109
   wiring harness 104-106
Engine
   cam chain guides 40
   camshaft 37-39
   crankcase 44
   crankcase side covers 44
   cylinder head 32-34
   cylinders 34-35
   oil filter and pump 43-44
   pistons, pins, and rings 36-37
   removal and installation 27-32
   specifications 175-176
   valves and valve guides 40-43
Exhaust system 87-8

F

Flat spots 7
Fork, front
   oil change 18
   service (CB450 K3 and K4) 122
   service (CB450 K5-K7) 122-127
   service (CB500T) 127-132
   service (early, 1-spring) 121-122
   service (early, 2-spring) 118-121
Fork bushing, rear 15
Fork crown (top triple clamp) 116
Frame 154-156
Fuel system
   air cleaners 74-78
   carburetors 78-83
   fuel strainer cleaning 15
   fuel tank 83-87
   throttle linkage 83
Fuses 102-103

G

Gearing, performance modification 161
Gearshift (4-speed) 62-64
Gearshift (5-speed) 71-72
General information 1-4

H

Handlebar 116
Handling 8
Headlight 98-99
Horn 102

I

Idling, poor 6
Ignition system
   coils 94
   condensers 94
   description 93
   tune-up 22-25

K

Kickstand 154
Kickstarter 73

L

Lighting system 8, 11, 98-102
Lubricants, recommended 12

M

Maintenance (*also see* Tune-up)
   air filter 16, 18-19
   battery 14-15
   brakes 17-18
   cam chain 16
   clutch 16
   drive chain 13
   front fork oil 18
   fuel strainer 15
   lights 11
   lubricants, recommended 12
   maintenance schedule 11
   nuts, bolts, and fasteners 11-13
   oil and filter, engine 10, 14, 18
   rear fork bushing 15
   routine checks 10
   throttle cable 15
   tires 14
   wheels 15-16
   500-mile/monthly maintenance 11-14
   1,500-mile/3-month maintenance 14, 15
   3,000-mile/6-month maintenance 15-18
   6,000-mile/12-month maintenance 18-19
Master cylinder 149-150
Misfiring 6-7

INDEX

N
Neutral switch and indicator 100-101

O
Oil and fitler 10, 14, 18, 43-44
Oil consumption 7
Oil pump 44
Oils and lubricants, recommended 12
Overheating 7

P
Painting 156
Piston seizure 7
Pistons, pins, and rings 36-37
Power loss 7

R
Rectifier 92-93
Regulator 93

S
Safety hints 2-3
Serial number location 3
Service hints 2
Shock absorbers, rear 138-139
Spark plugs 20-22
Specifications
    450 158
    CB500T 159
Spokes 115
Sprocket, rear 138
Starter
    clutch 96-97
    motor 94-96
    solenoid 97-98
Starting difficulties 6
Steering 116-118
Suspension, front (see Forks, front)
Suspension, rear
    shock absorbers 138-139
    swinging arm 139-143
Swinging arm, rear 139-143

T
Tachometer drive seal 33
Tail/stoplights 99-100
Throttle cable 15
Throttle linkage 83
Tightening torques 12-13
Timing 22-25
Tires 14
Transmission
    description 58-59
    disassembly, inspection, and assembly
      (4-speed)
    disassembly, inspection, and assembly
      (5-speed) 64-71
    gearshift (4-speed) 62-64
    gearshift (5-speed) 71-72
    specifications (4-speed) 64
    specifications (5-speed) 69
    troubleshooting 7
Troubleshooting
    operating difficulties 6-8
    operating requirements 5-6
    starting difficulties 6
    troubleshooting guide 8-9
Tune-up
    breaker points 22
    carburetor 25
    description 19-20
    ignition advance 25
    ignition timing 22-25
    spark plugs 20-22
    specifications 20
    valves 20

V
Valves
    clearance adjustment 20
    timing 33-34
    valve and guides removal 40-43

W
Wheel, front (disc brake) 112-116
Wheel, front (drum brake) 110-112
Wheel, general 15-16, 115-116
Wheel, rear 133-137
Wiring diagrams 107-109, 163-169
Wiring harness 104-106

WIRING DIAGRAMS

WIRING DIAGRAMS

CB450 (4 SPEED)

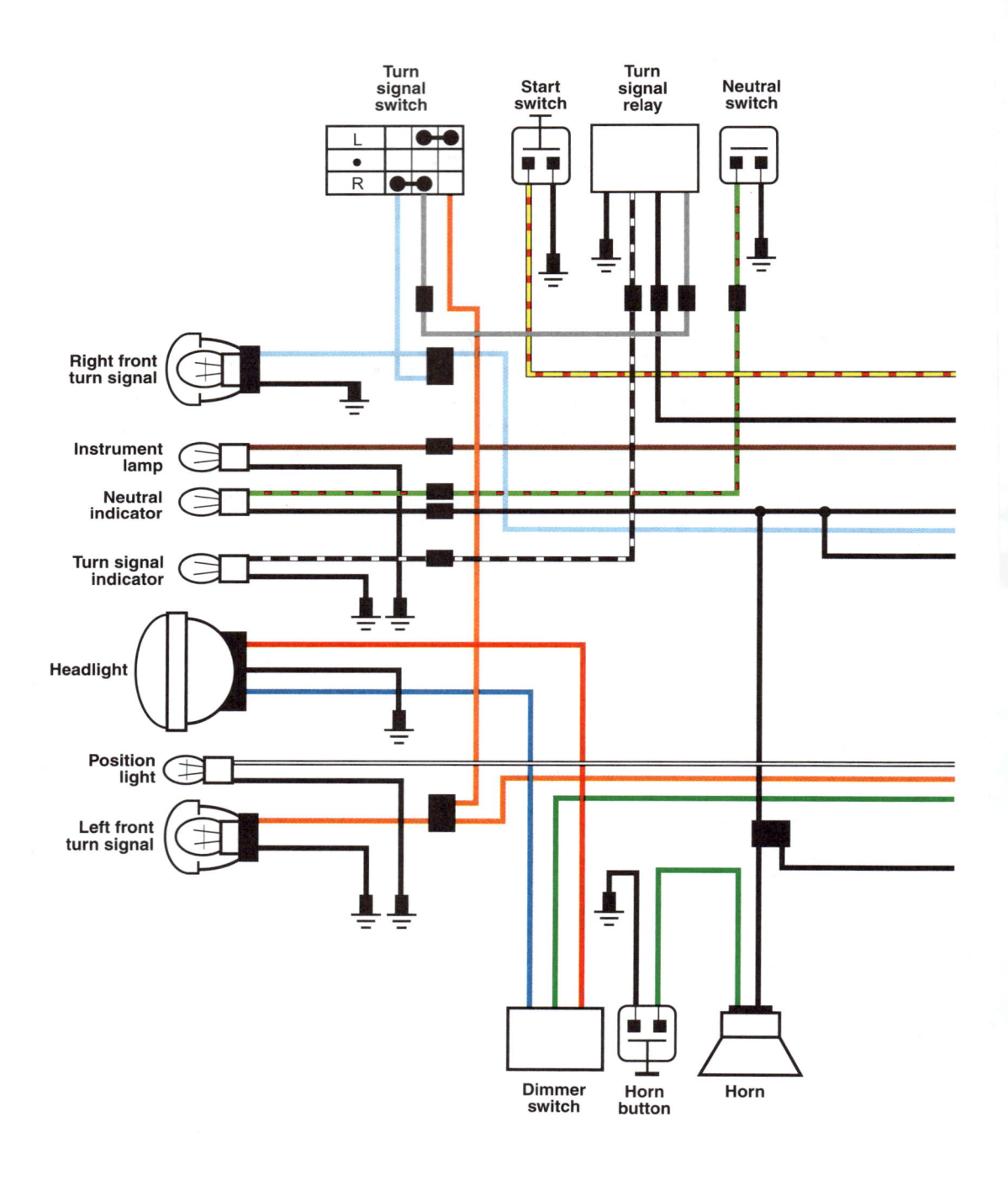

WIRING DIAGRAMS

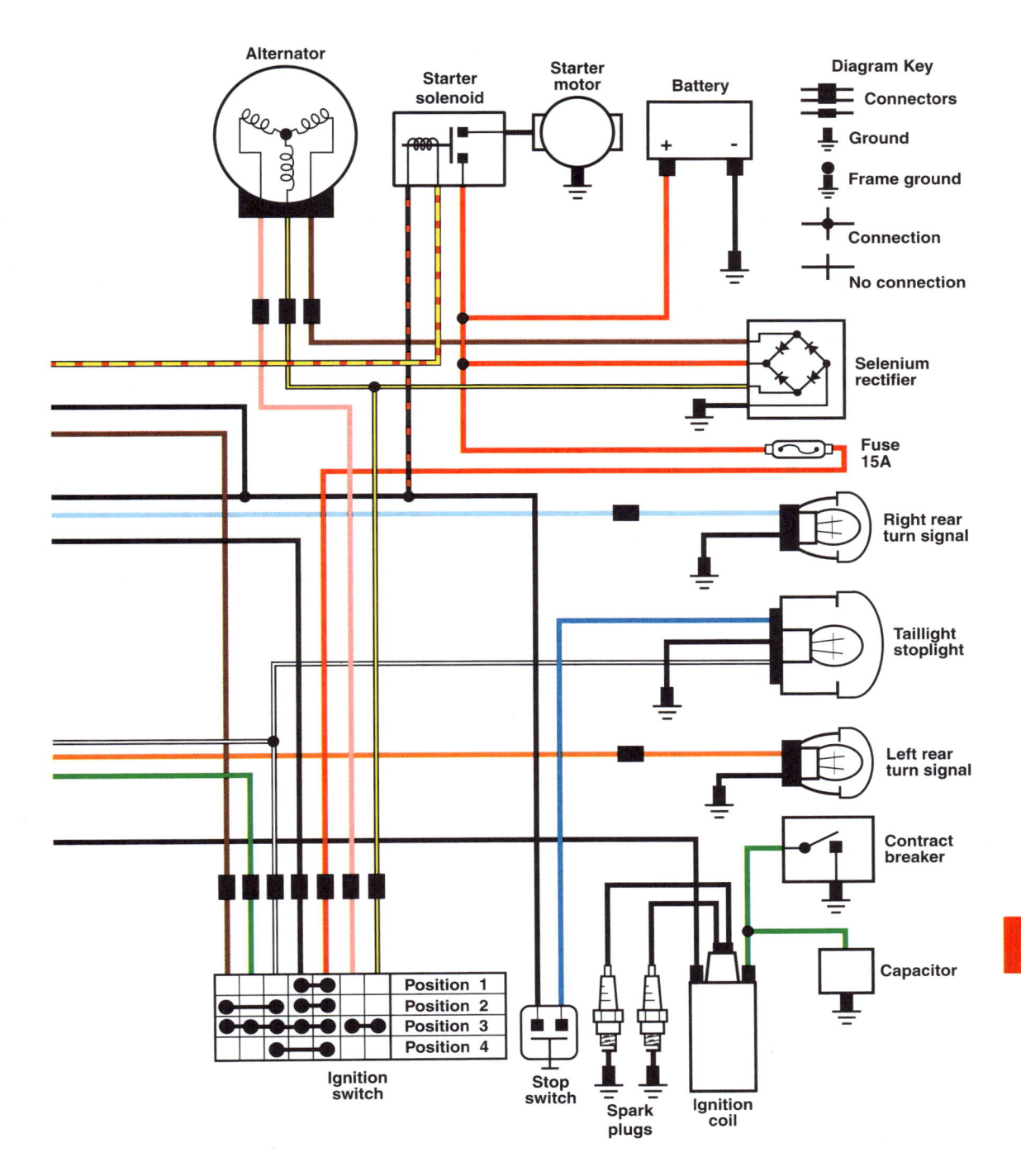

14

CB/CL450 (5-SPEED) AND CB500 (U.S.)

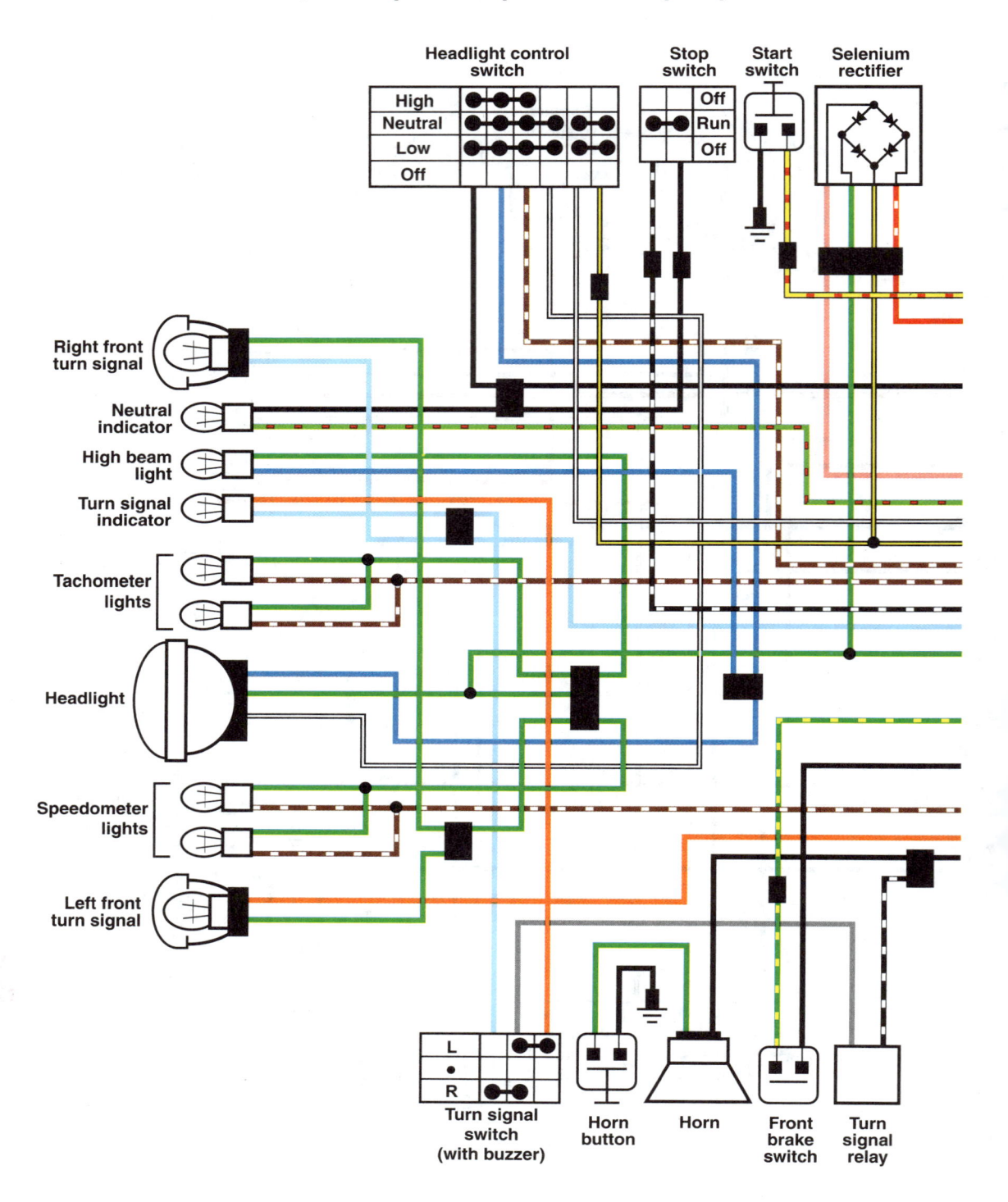

WIRING DIAGRAMS

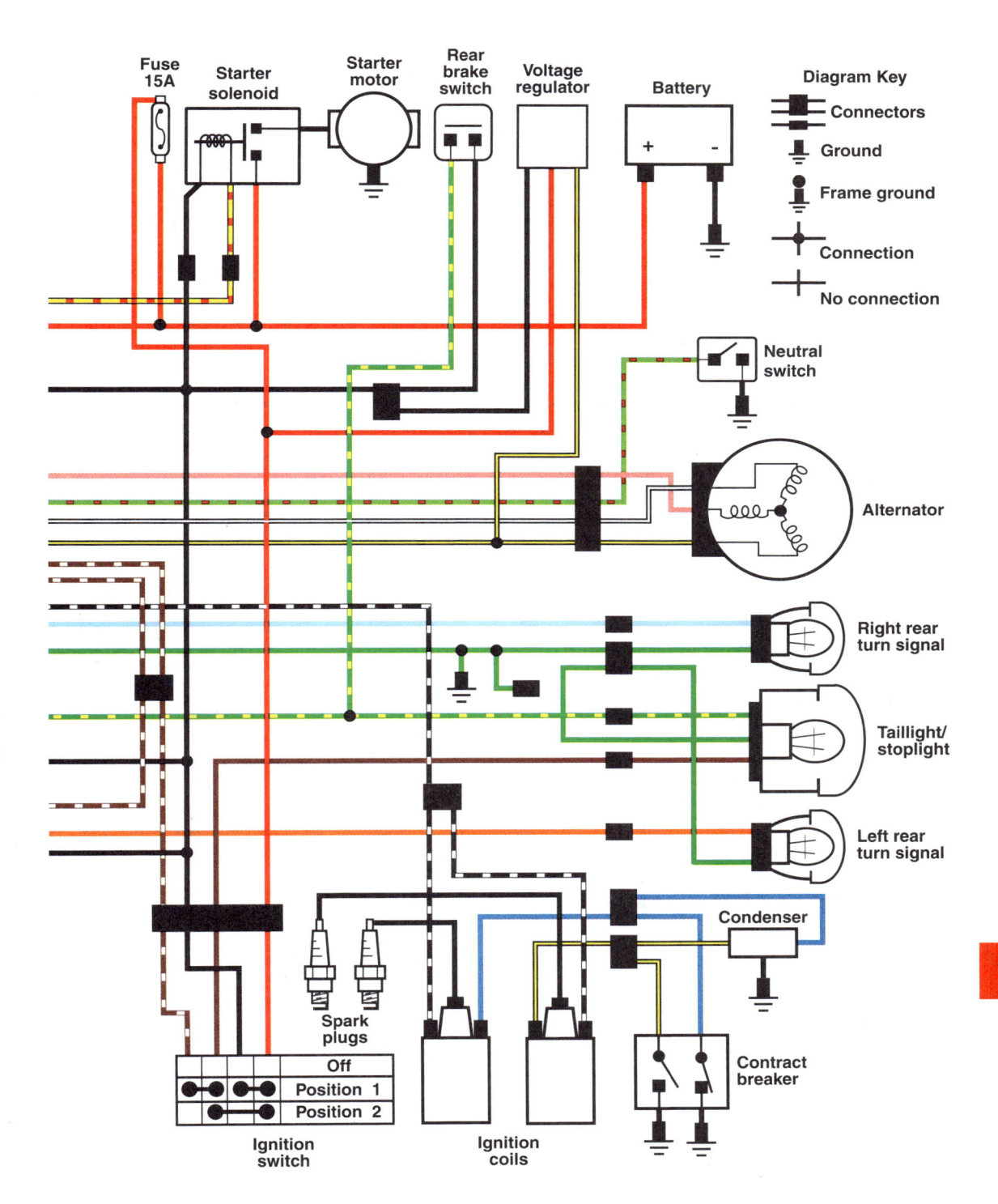

WIRING DIAGRAMS

CB/CL450 (5-SPEED) AND CB500 (U.K.)

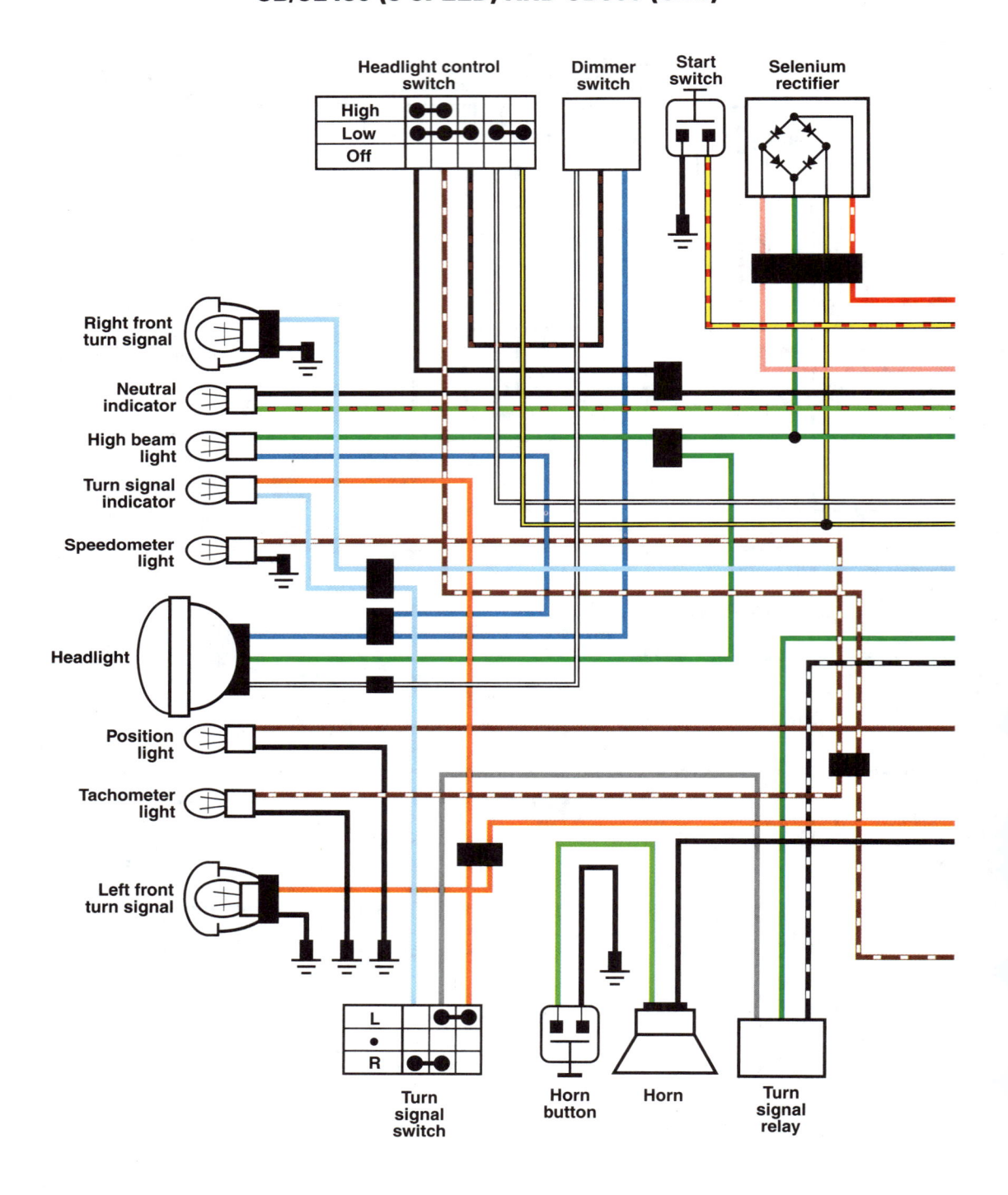

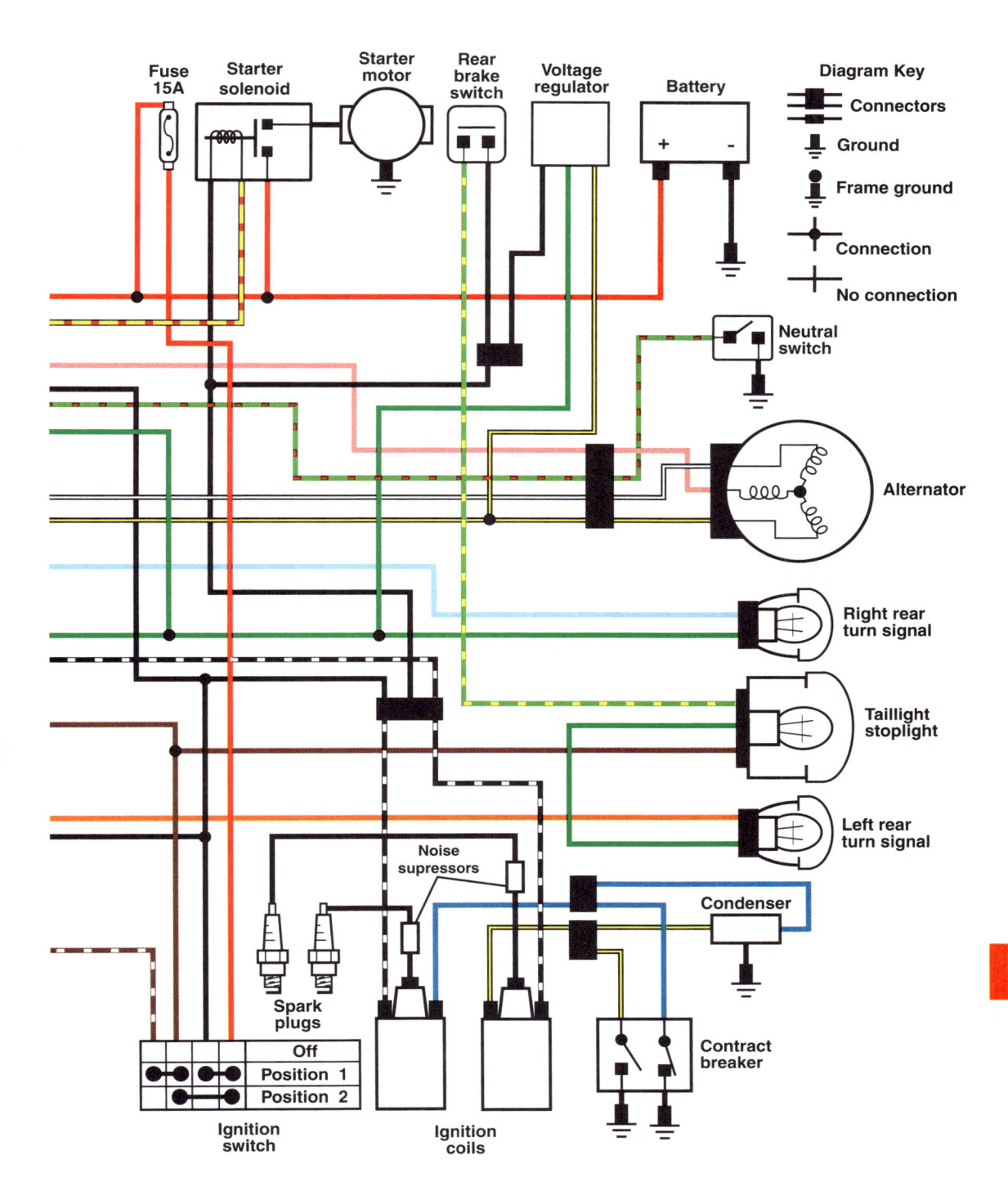

WIRING DIAGRAMS

169

14

NOTES

NOTES

NOTES

MAINTENANCE LOG

Date	Miles	Type of Service

Check out *clymer.com* for our full line of powersport repair manuals.

BMW

M308	500 & 600cc Twins, 55-69
M309	F650, 1994-2000
M500-3	BMW K-Series, 85-97
M501	K1200RS, GT & LT, 98-05
M502-3	BMW R50/5-R100GS PD, 70-96
M503-3	R850, R1100, R1150 and R1200C, 93-05

HARLEY-DAVIDSON

M419	Sportsters, 59-85
M429-5	XL/XLH Sportster, 86-03
M427-1	XL Sportster, 04-06
M418	Panheads, 48-65
M420	Shovelheads, 66-84
M421-3	FLS/FXS Evolution, 84-99
M423-2	FLS/FXS Twin Cam, 00-05
M422-3	FLH/FLT/FXR Evolution, 84-98
M430-4	FLH/FLT Twin Cam, 99-05
M424-2	FXD Evolution, 91-98
M425-3	FXD Twin Cam, 99-05
M426	VRSC Series, 02-07

HONDA

ATVs

M316	Odyssey FL250, 77-84
M311	ATC, TRX & Fourtrax 70-125, 70-87
M433	Fourtrax 90, 93-00
M326	ATC185 & 200, 80-86
M347	ATC200X & Fourtrax 200SX, 86-88
M455	ATC250 & Fourtrax 200/250, 84-87
M342	ATC250R, 81-84
M348	TRX250R/Fourtrax 250R & ATC250R, 85-89
M456-3	TRX250X 87-92; TRX300EX 93-04
M215	TRX250EX, 01-05
M446-3	TRX250 Recon & Recon ES, 97-07
M346-3	TRX300/Fourtrax 300 & TRX300FW/Fourtrax 4x4, 88-00
M200-2	TRX350 Rancher, 00-06
M459-3	TRX400 Foreman 95-03
M454-2	TRX400EX 99-05
M205	TRX450 Foreman, 98-04
M210	TRX500 Rubicon, 01-04

Singles

M310-13	50-110cc OHC Singles, 65-99
M319-2	XR50R, CRF50F, XR70R & CRF70F, 97-05
M315	100-350cc OHC, 69-82
M317	125-250cc Elsinore, 73-80
M442	CR60-125R Pro-Link, 81-88
M431-2	CR80R, 89-95, CR125R, 89-91
M435	CR80R, 96-02
M457-2	CR125R & CR250R, 92-97
M464	CR125R, 1998-2002
M443	CR250R-500R Pro-Link, 81-87
M432-3	CR250R, 88-91 & CR500R, 88-01
M437	CR250R, 97-01
M352	CRF250R, CRF250X, CRF450R & CRF450X, 02-05
M312-13	XL/XR75-100, 75-03
M318-4	XL/XR/TLR 125-200, 79-03
M328-4	XL/XR250, 78-00; XL/XR350R 83-85; XR200R, 84-85; XR250L, 91-96
M320-2	XR400R, 96-04
M339-8	XL/XR 500-600, 79-90
M221	XR600R & XR650L, 91-07
M225	XR650R, 00-07

Twins

M321	125-200cc Twins, 65-78
M322	250-350cc Twins, 64-74
M323	250-360cc Twins, 74-77
M324-5	Twinstar, Rebel 250 & Nighthawk 250, 78-03
M334	400-450cc Twins, 78-87
M333	450 & 500cc Twins, 65-76
M335	CX & GL500/650, 78-83
M344	VT500, 83-88
M313	VT700 & 750, 83-87
M314-3	VT750 Shadow Chain Drive, 98-06
M440	VT1100C Shadow, 85-96
M460-4	VT1100 Series, 95-07
M230	VTX1800 Series, 02-08

Fours

M332	CB350-550, SOHC, 71-78
M345	CB550 & 650, 83-85
M336	CB650, 79-82
M341	CB750 SOHC, 69-78
M337	CB750 DOHC, 79-82
M436	CB750 Nighthawk, 91-93 & 95-99
M325	CB900, 1000 & 1100, 80-83
M439	600 Hurricane, 87-90
M441-2	CBR600F2 & F3, 91-98
M445-2	CBR600F4, 99-06
M220	CBR600RR, 03-06
M434-2	CBR900RR Fireblade, 93-99
M329	500cc V-Fours, 84-86
M438	VFR800 Interceptor, 98-00
M349	700-1000 Interceptor, 83-85
M458-2	VFR700F-750F, 86-97
M327	700-1100cc V-Fours, 82-88
M340	GL1000 & 1100, 75-83
M504	GL1200, 84-87
M508	ST1100/Pan European, 90-02

Sixes

M505	GL1500 Gold Wing, 88-92
M506-2	GL1500 Gold Wing, 93-00
M507-2	GL1800 Gold Wing, 01-05
M462-2	GL1500C Valkyrie, 97-03

KAWASAKI

ATVs

M465-2	Bayou KLF220 & KLF250, 88-03
M466-4	Bayou KLF300, 86-04
M467	Bayou KLF400, 93-99
M470	Lakota KEF300, 95-99
M385-2	Mojave KSF250, 87-04

Singles

M350-9	80-350cc Rotary Valve, 66-01
M444-2	KX60, 83-02, KX80 83-90
M448	KX80/85/100, 89-03
M351	KDX200, 83-88
M447-3	KX125 & KX250, 82-91 KX500, 83-04
M472-2	KX125, 92-00
M473-2	KX250, 92-00
M474-2	KLR650, 87-06

Twins

M355	KZ400, KZ/Z440, EN450 & EN500, 74-95
M360-3	EX500, GPZ500S, Ninja 500 R, 87-02
M356-5	Vulcan 700 & 750, 85-06
M354-3	Vulcan 800 & Vulcan 800 Classic, 95-05
M357-2	Vulcan 1500, 87-99
M471-3	Vulcan 1500 Series, 96-08

Fours

M449	KZ500/550 & ZX550, 79-85
M450	KZ, Z & ZX750, 80-85
M358	KZ650, 77-83
M359-3	Z & KZ 900-1000cc, 73-81
M451-3	KZ, ZX & ZN 1000 & 1100cc, 81-02
M452-3	ZX500 & Ninja ZX600, 85-97
M468-2	Ninja ZX-6, 90-04
M469	Ninja ZX-7, 91-98
M453-3	Ninja ZX900, ZX1000 & ZX1100, 84-01
M409	Concours, 86-04

POLARIS

ATVs

M496	3-, 4- and 6-Wheel Models w/250-425cc Engines, 85-95
M362	Magnum and Big Boss, 96-98
M363	Scrambler 500 4X4, 97-00
M365-3	Sportsman/Xplorer, 96-08

SUZUKI

ATVs

M381	ALT/LT 125 & 185, 83-87
M475	LT230 & LT250, 85-90
M380-2	LT250R Quad Racer, 85-92
M270	LT-Z400, 03-07
M343	LTF500F Quadrunner, 98-00
M483-2	King Quad/Quad Runner 250, 87-98

Singles

M371	RM50-400 Twin Shock, 75-81
M369	125-400cc 64-81
M379	RM125-500 Single Shock, 81-88
M476	DR250-350, 90-94
M477	DR-Z400, 00-06
M384-4	LS650 Savage/S40, 86-07
M386	RM80-250, 89-95
M400	RM125, 96-00
M401	RM250, 96-02

Twins

M372	GS400-450 Chain Drive, 77-87
M481-5	VS700-800 Intruder, 85-07
M260	Volusia/Boulevard C50, 01-06
M482-2	VS1400 Intruder, 87-03
M261	1500 Intruder/C90, 98-07
M484-3	GS500E Twins, 89-02
M361	SV650, 1999-2002

Triple

M368	GT380, GT550 & GT750, 72-77

Fours

M373	GS550, 77-86
M364	GS650, 81-83
M370	GS750, 77-82
M376	GS850-1100 Shaft Drive, 79-84
M378	GS1100 Chain Drive, 80-81
M383-3	Katana 600, 88-96
M378	GSX-R750-1100, 86-87
M331	GSX-R600, 97-00
M264	GSX-R600, 01-05
M478-2	GSX-R750, 88-92
	GSX750F Katana, 89-96
M485	GSX-R750, 96-99
M377	GSX-R1000, 01-04
M266	GSX-R1000, 05-06
M265	GSX1300R Hayabusa, 99-07
M338	Bandit 600, 95-00
M353	GSF1200 Bandit, 96-03

YAMAHA

ATVs

M499	YFM80 Badger, 85-88 & 92-01
M394	YTM200, 250 & YFM200, 83-86
M488-5	Blaster, 88-05
M489-2	Timberwolf, 89-00
M487-5	Warrior, 87-04
M486-6	Banshee, 87-06
M490-3	Moto-4 & Big Bear, 87-04
M493	Kodiak, 93-98
M280-2	Raptor 660R, 01-05
M285	Grizzly 660, 02-07

Singles

M492-2	PW50 & PW80, BW80 Big Wheel 80, 81-02
M410	80-175 Piston Port, 68-76
M415	250-400 Piston Port, 68-76
M412	DT & MX 100-400, 77-83
M414	IT125-490, 76-86
M393	YZ50-80 Monoshock, 78-90
M413	YZ100-490 Monoshock, 76-84
M390	YZ125-250, 85-87
M391	YZ125-250, 88-93 & WR250Z, 91-93
M497-2	YZ125, 94-01
M498	YZ250, 94-98 WR250Z, 94-97
M406	YZ250F & WR250F, 01-03
M491-2	YZ400F, YZ426F, WR400F WR426F, 98-02
M417	XT125-250, 80-84
M480-3	XT/TT 350, 85-00
M405	XT/TT 500, 76-81
M416	XT/TT 600, 83-89

Twins

M403	XS1, XS2, XS650 & TX650, 70-82
M395-10	XV535-1100 Virago, 81-03
M495-5	V-Star 650, 98-07
M281-3	V-Star 1100, 99-07
M282	Road Star, 99-05

Triple

M404	XS750 & XS850, 77-81

Fours

M387	XJ550, XJ600 & FJ600, 81-92
M494	XJ600 Seca II/Diversion, 92-98
M388	YX600 Radian & FZ600, 86-90
M396	FZR600, 89-93
M392	FZ700-750 & Fazer, 85-87
M411	XS1100, 78-81
M397	FJ1100 & 1200, 84-93
M375	V-Max, 85-03
M374	Royal Star, 96-03
M461	YZF-R6, 99-04
M398	YZF-R1, 98-03
M399	FZ1, 01-05

VINTAGE MOTORCYCLES

Clymer® Collection Series

M330	Vintage British Street Bikes, BSA, 500–650cc Unit Twins; Norton, 750 & 850cc Commandos; Triumph, 500-750cc Twins
M300	Vintage Dirt Bikes, V. 1 Bultaco, 125-370cc Singles; Montesa, 123-360cc Singles; Ossa, 125-250cc Singles
M305	Vintage Japanese Street Bikes, Honda, 250 & 305cc Twins; Kawasaki, 250-750cc Triples; Kawasaki, 900 & 1000cc Fours